Bible-Light
on Life's
Pathway

John A. Hash

Nashville / New York

Distributed to the book trade by
Thomas Nelson Publishers

Copyright © 1977 by John A. Hash

ISBN 0-8407-9502-5

"Thy word is a lamp
unto my feet,
and a light
unto my path."

Psalm 119:105

"No time, no time to study
To meditate and pray,
And yet much time for doing
In a fleshly, worldly way;
No time for things eternal,
But much for things of earth;
For things important set aside
For things of little worth.
Some things, tis true, are needful,
But first things come first;
And what displaces God's own Word
Of God is shall be cursed."

M.E.H.

TABLE OF CONTENTS

FOREWORD

Here is a new and fascinating way to discover inspiration and spiritual depth from the world's greatest book—the Bible—by reading only 15 minutes a day.

BIBLE-LIGHT ON LIFE'S PATHWAY will show you how this small fraction of time out of your daily routine can bring deeper meaning to your everyday life. Best of all, you will find yourself going through each page of the Bible with new interest, new direction, and new purpose.

There is a growing hunger among Christians today for spiritual discernment and a better understanding of God's Word. The God of this universe is not limited in ways He can communicate His will to His creation. Nevertheless, He has chosen to reveal His will through preaching, teaching, and personal Bible study.

The Holy Spirit uses preachers and teachers as channels to convict of sin; however, if we are to reach spiritual maturity, we must "desire the sincere milk of the word" in order to grow thereby (see I Peter 2:1).

We know that one cannot love the God of the Word without loving the Word of God! So it seems strange indeed that some Christians do not read *all* the Scriptures ". . . that the man of God may be perfect, throughly furnished unto all good works" (II Timothy 3:16,17). This simply means that through the Scriptures, God makes available the strength, wisdom, and insight to be well prepared to do His will.

God purposely demonstrated to Moses, Joshua, David, and Jeremiah and the prophets the criteria necessary for the true peace and blessing He has for each believer.

BIBLE-LIGHT ON LIFE'S PATHWAY was designed as a guide to explain difficult passages of Scripture and is the most complete and most comprehensive Bible reading guide available today.

As you begin your wonderful journey through God's Word, you will surely experience the daily fellowship that comes in a supernatural way to believers who are seeking fellowship with God.

D. L. Moody once said, "With my Bible closed, I prayed for faith, but faith did not seem to come. Then one day I opened my Bible and read, 'so then faith cometh by hearing, and hearing by the word of God' (Romans 10:17). Since I began reading my Bible, my faith has continued to grow."

None will be stronger in the faith than they are in His Word.

—Dr. Craig Lampe

GOD HATH SPOKEN!

Without the Bible, man's knowledge of sin is limited to what he learns through his own conscience and reasoning. He knows nothing of the 'exceeding sinfulness of sin' and how sin separates man from a holy God (see Romans 7:13). Furthermore, without the Bible, it would be impossible for him to know of God's love, His provision for salvation, or His desire for fellowship with man.

As you prayerfully read your Bible, keep in mind that it is the voice of God, your Creator, communicating with you.

"God, who at sundry times and in divers manners spake in time past unto the fathers by the prophets, hath in these last days spoken unto us by his Son . . ." (Hebrews 1:1-2).

ONE BIBLE—NO SUBSTITUTES

All the Bible—from Genesis to Revelation—is essential for man's complete spiritual well-being, "that the man of God may be perfect, throughly furnished . . ." (II Timothy 3:17).

God, in His infinite wisdom, arranged each of the 66 books of the Bible so man could have a special, supernatural revelation of who God is and what He has done and will do for mankind. Not one of these books can be omitted without impairing the whole.

Substitutes cannot satisfy.

There are numerous pamphlets that contain the advice, "When sickness comes, read such and such a chapter; when in doubt or in trouble, or in need of other spiritual advice, turn to this or that place in the Bible." It is not our prerogative to assume that certain books or chapters of the Bible are more important than others. Such help will leave artificial results. We dare not evaluate the various parts of the Bible as to what is important, for the consequences can obstruct His purpose in providing "all scripture . . ." (see II Timothy 3:16-17).

Furthermore, our discernment of His will is seriously hindered when we substitute reading good wholesome books *about* the Bible and Christian principles instead of day by day listening to the voice of God Almighty speaking in His own words as the indwelling Holy Spirit teaches us His Word.

So as you read the Bible continuously and consistently, remember that it is God who is speaking to you.

THE BIBLE IS UNIQUE

All other books are hopelessly out-classed when compared to the Bible because *millions* of believers have lived and died by its teachings. No such trust has ever been placed in any other book. On the other hand, nations and religions have tried to destroy the Bible. But in spite of all its opposition, millions of copies are distributed every year, and it remains the world's best seller.

The Bible is the incomparable Book among millions of books. But far more important, its life-giving wisdom actually imparts the very nature of the indwelling Christ to live as He lived; we "are changed into the same image" (II Corinthians 3:18).

Added to this, the Bible will transform the life of anyone who submits to its truths. And it will change you if you are serious about its message.

CENTRAL THEME

The Bible was written "that ye may believe that Jesus is the Christ, the Son of God; and that believing ye might have life through his name" (John 20:31). Christ is the central theme of all 66 books. This is clear from the statement of our risen Lord as He spoke to the two disciples who were on their way to the village of Emmaus, when "beginning at Moses and all the prophets, he expounded unto them in all the scriptures the things concerning himself" (Luke 24:27).

Seeing the progressive revelation of Christ unfold from Genesis to Revelation and the believer's relationship with Christ is the key to understanding the Scriptures.

Just before His ascension, Jesus further revealed to His disciples that He was indeed the central theme of the Old Testament when He said: "These are the words which I spake unto you, while I was yet with you, that all things must be fulfilled, which were written in the law of Moses, and in the prophets, and in the psalms, *concerning me.* Then opened he their understanding, that they might understand the scriptures" (Luke 24:44-45).

IS THE BIBLE TOO DIFFICULT TO UNDERSTAND?

The answer is an emphatic "NO!" Every Christian should read the Bible each day. It is our Lord's personal message to every child of God. Furthermore, it is the only source of strength for the inner life.

It is vitally important therefore that you accept His Word at face value, and earnestly, sincerely read all of it with an open heart and an open mind.

By saying that the Bible is too difficult to understand, we imply that God is to blame for our not knowing His will. Actually, the real reason Christians have difficulty in understanding the Bible is because they have never read it through. (See II Timothy 2:15).

12

There is no excuse for anyone misunderstanding God's Word if he will, like a child, accept the Bible for what it says and obey it. He must realize that God can and does express Himself clearly in human language.

The Bible is not a book that says one thing to one person and mean something else to another person. One cannot, as is commonly believed, get a dozen conflicting meanings from any one passage.

Although the Bible was written by about forty men over a period of one thousand five hundred years, the remarkable fact is that it has only one true meaning, and there is perfect harmony on every subject.

Any Christian who faithfully reads through the Bible with a hunger to know His will and walk in His ways has the Holy Spirit's promise that He will guide them "into all truth" (John 16:13).

HINTS FOR BETTER UNDERSTANDING THE BIBLE

First of all, recognize your inability to comprehend spiritual truth: "For the natural man receiveth not the things of the Spirit of God: for they are foolishness unto him: neither can he know them, because they are spiritually discerned" (I Corinthians 2:14).

As you read, pray that God will 'open your eyes of understanding, that you might understand the Scriptures' (Luke 24:45).

You can only become more accurate in "rightly dividing the word of truth" as you read the Bible in its entirety, comparing Scripture with Scripture (see II Timothy 2:15).

Beware of trying to twist His Word to your point of view, for you will find no peace of mind until you rest in the truth as God reveals it to you. He is waiting for receptive, hungry Christians who are willing to be submissive to His control.

Don't get so discouraged over difficult details that you miss the obvious points you do understand. It is the indwelling Holy Spirit who illuminates our understanding, and He will give us further insight if we are willing to walk in further light.

Many Christians limit the Holy Spirit's guidance and teaching because they do not read all of the Bible. How can the Holy Spirit guide them "into *all* truth" if they don't bother to read all of the truth? If we only read from certain portions of our Bible month after month, we limit what the Holy Spirit can reveal to us of God's will.

The Bible is its own best commentary, and only after you have read all of the Bible several times should you attempt to draw firm conclusions to difficult passages of Scripture. We should continue reading until other Scriptures explain the one in question.

HOW THE BIBLE SHOULD BE READ

God, in His infinite wisdom, has brought you face to face with the vital, eternal importance of reading His Word.

The one way that far excels all other ways of reading the Bible is to start with Genesis 1:1 and continue to read verse by verse, chapter by chapter, book by book until you have completed Revelation 22:21. This permits God to speak to you in the order He has chosen.

To fully understand any author's meaning, the reader must begin with page one of the book and carefully, consecutively read every page. This, of course, is how you should read the Bible if you expect to understand its message for your life.

Choose a definite time and place to read all the chapters for each day's Bible reading schedule at one time. Expect distractions, but be determined that nothing will keep you from reading through the Bible.

It's true that you can learn a little by studying certain subjects, such as love, grace, faith, or prophecy. But if that's the *best* plan, then why wasn't God smart enough to think of it?

Our full comprehension of any subject is dependent upon our knowledge of all Scripture. When you read the Bible the way God arranged it, you give the Lord an opportunity to speak to you the way *He* wants to instruct you.

WHY READ BIBLE-LIGHT ON LIFE'S PATHWAY?

The Christian's greatest need is to set aside time with the Lord each day. Although it may seem that adverse circumstances plague our lives, the actual cause of failure in Christian living is the lack of sufficient time spent with the Lord and His Word.

Unless you faithfully follow a systematic guide, you probably will not read your Bible very much. Few people do.

Bible-Light on Life's Pathway is a systematic plan that will guide the Christian in daily reading *God's OWN Plan* for his life. It will help the average Christian establish day by day stability in Bible reading. Bible-Pathway will create an awareness that every book is a progressive revelation of the Christian experience and that each book is essential to his spiritual need and is arranged in the exact order to meet those spiritual needs.

Read the Scriptures carefully and prayerfully, and you will be abundantly rewarded for your effort. Since the Bible is a spiritual book, you should pray from your heart: "Open thou mine eyes, that I may behold wondrous things out of thy law" (Psalm 119:18).

INTRODUCTION TO GENESIS

Genesis means "beginning," and it can be a new beginning of a deeper love for the Lord in your life as you begin reading through God's Word. It deals with values far beyond the realm of science to acquaint you with the eternal God.

God created you in His image that He might have fellowship with you. Are you in fellowship with Him, who made you for Himself? You have the privilege of beginning with Genesis and reading all the Bible—listening to all He has to say—in the way He prepared it for you.

The book of Genesis is to the Christian what the foundation is to a house. It is indispensable since it forms the basis for *all* revelation of the Bible.

Christ declared Genesis to be the infallible truth and vital to one's faith in Him by saying: "Had ye believed Moses, ye would have believed me: for he wrote of me" (John 5:46).

The book of Genesis covers a period of about 2,400 years (from Adam to the death of Joseph)—a far longer period than any other book in the Bible.

OUTLINE OF GENESIS

I. Early History of the World From Adam to the Flood—a Period of 1660 Years (Genesis 1-8)

II. History of Wickedness from the Flood to the Tower of Babel—a Period of 100 Years (Genesis 9-11)

III. History of the Patriarchs From the Call of Abram (12:1—about 325 years after Babel) to the Death of Jacob in Egypt (about 255 years) (Genesis 11-50)

Six (6) Prominent People Mentioned: Adam, Noah, Abraham, Isaac, Jacob, Joseph

Six (6) Major Events Took Place: Creation (1-2); the Fall (3-4); the Flood (5-9); Tower of Babel (10-11); Call of Abram (12-38); Descent into Egypt (39-50)

NOTE: These time periods are not given in the sense of setting an *accurate* historical reference, but rather to give the reader a general conception of events in relation to time intervals.

JANUARY 1: Read Genesis 1-3.

Genesis 1:2: "And the earth was *without form,* and *void;* and *darkness* was upon the face of the deep. And the Spirit of God moved upon the face of the waters."

Think about this: In the beginning, the earth was *"without form* and *void."* This is the spiritual condition of every unsaved person. His life is without form, for it has no eternal purpose, and it is void with wasted years.

There are two things that took place in creation which also take place when a sinner is saved. First, "the Spirit of God moved" (verse 2), and the Word was spoken, "And God *said,* Let there be light . . ." (verse 3). There is no realization or light of one's need until God speaks the Word; he is in darkness and unable to see the light of God's Word. The Holy Spirit and the Word of God together create that light, and man becomes a new creation in Christ.

Consider the following Scriptures: "Through faith we understand that the worlds were framed by the word of God" (Hebrews 11:3); and so also by faith, sinful man believes God and is "born again . . . by the word" (I Peter 1:23).

"For God, who commanded the light to shine out of darkness, hath shined in our hearts" (II Corinthians 4:6).

NOTE:
1:6 a **firmament** means the expanse of the sky surrounding the earth. **Patriarchs** is a name given in the New Testament to those who founded the Hebrew race and nation. (See Hebrews 7:4; Acts 2:29; 7:8-9.)

Genesis 1:1-2: See Acts 14:15; Heb. 11:3; Rev. 4:11; 10:6. **1:26-27:** See Matt. 19:4; Mark 10:6; Acts 17:26,28; I Cor. 11:7; Col. 3:10; James 3:9. **2:2:** See Heb. 4:4. **2:7:** See I Cor. 15:45-47; I Tim. 2:13. **2:21-22:** See I Cor. 11:8; I Tim. 2:13. **2:24:** See Matt. 19:5; Mark 10:7-8; Eph. 5:31. **3:1-5:** See II Cor. 11:3; I Tim. 2:14. **3:6-12:** See Rom. 5:12. **3:15:** See Luke 24:26-27; Rom. 16:20. **3:16:** See I Cor. 14:34.

JANUARY 2: Read Genesis 4-6.

Genesis 4:6: "And the Lord said unto Cain, Why art thou wroth? and why is thy countenance fallen?"

After Adam and Eve sinned, their fellowship with God was broken. They once loved to hear the voice of Jehovah, but now it caused them to fear, and they hid themselves from His presence. Their reaction was the same as the unsaved person's reaction today.

MEMORY VERSE FOR THE WEEK: II Peter 1:4

"Whereby are given unto us exceeding great and precious promises: that by these ye might be partakers of the divine nature, having escaped the corruption that is in the world through lust."

16

Adam and Eve's first son, Cain, represents the natural man who has gone "out from the presence of the Lord." He went to the land of Nod, where he "builded a city" (4:16,17).

This is typical of the man who has forsaken God. The Scriptures particularly point out the progress of the Cainites in building cities and creating inventions. As their "civilization" grew, "corruption" also increased, "and the earth was filled with violence" (6:11).

In contrast to Cain, Seth became the founder of the line of faith. (Compare Genesis 4:26 and Luke 3:38.)

Although "the wickedness of man was great in the earth" (6:5), we are told that Enoch, a descendant of Seth, "walked with God" *every day* of his *365* years. Regardless of environment, man is without excuse for being out of fellowship with God.

"By faith Enoch was translated that he should not see death; and was not found, because God had translated him: for before his translation he had this testimony, that he pleased God" (Hebrews 11:5).

NOTE:
4:5 **wroth** means exceedingly angry; 4:8 **slew** means killed; 4:22 **artificer** means craftsman; 6:14 **shalt pitch it** means cover it inside and out.

Genesis 4:3-5: See Matt. 23:35; Heb. 11:4. **4:8:** See Luke 11:51; I John 3:12; 4:8; Jude 11. **5:18:** See Jude 14. **5:24:** See Heb. 11:5. **6:5,13:** See Matt. 24:37-39; Luke 17:26; I Pet. 3:20. **6:15-22:** See Heb. 11:7.

> "And the Lord said unto Noah, Come thou and all thy house into the ark; for thee have I seen righteous before me in this generation." Genesis 7:1

JANUARY 3: Read Genesis 7-9.

Genesis 7:16-17: "And they that went in, went in male and female of all flesh, as God had commanded him: and the Lord shut him in. And the flood was forty days upon the earth; and the waters increased, and bare up the ark, and it was lifted up above the earth."

God had announced judgment upon sin when He said, "My spirit shall not always strive with man" (6:3). But Noah believed God and He did "according to all that God commanded him" (6:22). During the 120 years Noah was building the ark, the unbelieving world watched.

When the ark was completed, God said to Noah, "Come thou and all thy house into the ark" (7:1). He and his family entered into the ark and were saved. To reject the ark meant certain death. By trusting in God's promise concerning the ark, Noah was carried from the old world into the new. And in like manner, the Christian can say, "old things are passed away; behold, all things are become new" (II Corinthians 5:17).

MEMORY VERSE FOR THE WEEK: John 1:1-2
"In the beginning was the Word, and the Word was with God, and the Word was God. The same was in the beginning with God."

There was only one ark during Noah's time, and there is only one way to escape eternal destruction. Just as the ark meant salvation to Noah in the old world, Christ is the only salvation for the world today, "Neither is there salvation in any other" (Acts 4:12).

NOTE:
8:1 **assuaged** means lowered.

Genesis 7:1: See Luke 17:26; II Pet. 2:5.

JANUARY 4: Read Genesis 10-12.
Genesis 12:4,7: "So Abraham departed, as the Lord had spoken unto him . . . and there builded he an altar unto the Lord, who appeared unto him."

Abraham is mentioned more than 70 times in the New Testament. His life provides a pattern for those who desire to walk by faith, for "they which are of faith, the same are the children of Abraham" (Galatians 3:7).

Abraham immediately obeyed God's Word and gave up all that was precious to him—country, home, and friends. "By faith Abraham, when he was called to go out into a place which he should after receive for an inheritance, obeyed; and he went out, not knowing whither he went" (Hebrews 11:8). He endured many years of severe testings but he believed there was something more important in life than material gain, and he took God at His word.

It is one thing to intellectually know the Bible reveals God's will, but it is quite another to prayerfully read it daily with a heartfelt desire to please Him.

"That the blessing of Abraham might come on the Gentiles through Jesus Christ; that we might receive the promise of the Spirit through faith" (Galatians 3:14).

NOTE:
Genesis 10:1-7: See Acts 7:5. **11:31:** See Acts 7:4. **12:1:** See Acts 7:3; Heb. 11:8. **12:3:** See Acts 3:25; Gal. 3:8; Luke 1:73. **12:4:** See Acts 7:4. **12:5:** See Acts 7:4; Heb. 11:9. **12:7:** See Luke 24:26,27,32; Acts 7:5; Gal. 3:16.

MEMORY VERSE FOR THE WEEK: John 1:1-2
"In the beginning was the Word, and the Word was with God, and the Word was God. The same was in the beginning with God."

JANUARY 5: Read Genesis 13-15.

Genesis 13:11-12: "Then Lot chose him all the plain of Jordan; and Lot journeyed east: and they separated themselves the one from the other . . . and Lot dwelled in the cities of the plain, and pitched his tent toward Sodom."

Lot was occupied with the things which are seen—earthly possessions. His self-centered desire for wealth resulted in a loss of fellowship with godly Abraham.

Lot may have considered himself a shrewd man who couldn't afford to lose an opportunity for material gain, and even though he knew "the men of Sodom were wicked and sinners before the Lord exceedingly" (verse 13), he still "pitched his tent toward Sodom" and finally lived there.

Lot is an example of the worldly minded, professing Christian. He did not pray or consult the Lord about decisions. When he departed from Abraham, he became more and more influenced by the world. His desire was to have *all* the fertile valley, and nothing less would satisfy him.

Lot didn't possess the same spirit as that of Abraham, who was more concerned over their peace with one another than he was over material wealth. This is why Jesus said, "Remember Lot's wife. Whosoever shall seek to save his life shall lose it; and whosoever shall lose his life shall preserve it" (Luke 17:32-33).

NOTE:
Genesis 13:15: See Acts 7:5. **14:19:** See Heb. 7:1-10. **15:5:** See Rom. 4:18. **15:6:** See Rom. 4:3; Gal. 3:6; James 2:23. **15:7:** See Acts 7:2. **15:13,16:** See Acts 7:6.

JANUARY 6: Read Genesis 16-18.

Genesis 18:1,14: "And the Lord appeared unto him in the plains of Mamre: and he sat in the tent door in the heat of the day . . . Is any thing too hard for the Lord? At the time appointed I will return unto thee, according to the time of life, and Sarah shall have a son."

This wonderful appearance of the Lord's presence came as a result of Abraham's willing obedience to God's command regarding circumcision.

"The secret of the Lord is with them that fear him; and he will shew them his covenant" (Psalm 25:14). God reveals Himself and the knowledge of His ways to those who faithfully obey Him. "If any man will do his will, he shall know of the doctrine" (John 7:17).

MEMORY VERSE FOR THE WEEK: John 1:1-2

"In the beginning was the Word, and the Word was with God, and the Word was God. The same was in the beginning with God."

19

Sarah's laugh was one of unbelief in the promise of God, but the Lord sees that smile of distrust, the sneer of ridicule, or the look of contempt upon any of His promises. God's promises often seem absurd and ridiculous to human reasoning; but when all *human* hope is gone, we must remain assured that He is able to fulfill His Word. ". . . Is any thing too hard for the Lord?" Never! "For with God nothing shall be impossible" (Luke 1:37).

NOTE:
17:1 **be thou perfect** means be wholeheartedly sincere.

Genesis 16:15: See Gal. 4:23,25. **17:1:** See Matt. 5:48. **17:5:** See Rom. 4:17. **17:19:** See Luke 1:55. **18:2:** See Rom. 9:9; Heb. 13:2. **18:11-14:** See Heb. 11:14.

> Abraham went and took the ram, and offered him up for a burnt offering in the stead of his son."
> Genesis 22:13

JANUARY 7: Read Genesis 19-21.
Genesis 21:10: "Wherefore she said unto Abraham, Cast out this bondwoman and her son: for the son of this bondwoman shall not be heir with my son, even with Isaac."

Abraham's two sons—one born of a bondwoman and the other born of a free woman—represent two vastly different natures.

Ishmael represents the Law and the natural man's efforts to satisfy God by doing good works. Isaac represents the new nature made possible through the sacrifice of God's only Son.

Isaac's birth was supernatural—"the child of promise." As a special gift from God he represents those who are "partakers of the divine nature" (II Peter 1:4). But Ishmael's birth was natural, like that of any other child, and represents those who are "by nature the children of wrath" (Ephesians 2:3).

Ishmael was born a slave and remained a slave. Although he gained much material wealth, he received no spiritual inheritance from Father Abraham.

Isaac, on the other hand, was "freeborn" and no earthly power could rob him of that liberty. It was his birthright.

"Now we, brethren, as Isaac was, are the children of promise" (Galatians 4:28).

NOTE:
Genesis 19:13,24,26: See Mark 6:11; Luke 17:29,32; II Pet. 2:6. **19:16:** See Luke 17:29. **19:21:** See Luke 17:32. **21:3,4:** See Acts 7:8. **21:10:** See Gal. 4:30. **21:12:** See Rom. 9:7; Heb. 11:18.

MEMORY VERSE FOR THE WEEK: John 1:1-2
"In the beginning was the Word, and the Word was with God, and the Word was God. The same was in the beginning with God."

JANUARY 8: Read Genesis 22-24.

Genesis 24:2-3: "And Abraham said unto his eldest servant of his house, that ruled over all that he had, Put, I pray thee, thy hand under my thigh: and I will make thee swear by the Lord, the God of heaven, and the God of the earth, that thou shalt not take a wife unto my son of the daughters of the Canaanites, among whom I dwell."

Abraham did not permit Isaac to marry a Canaanite. He was concerned that his son have a wife worthy of the high calling of God. Therefore, he commanded his servant, Eleazar, to make the long journey to Mesopotamia to choose a bride for Isaac from Abraham's own people.

When Eleazar met Rebekah at the well, he told her of Abraham's love for his son, Isaac. When Rebekah heard the message which the servant brought, she was attracted to Isaac, although she had never seen him. She, like Eleazar, placed her confidence in God's guidance.

This is a beautiful picture of God's great love for Christ and His Church.

The heavenly Father, like Abraham, has sent the Holy Spirit to represent the beloved Son. As the servant represented the son to Rebekah, so the Holy Spirit represents Christ to all who make up the Bride of Christ.

Just as the servant took Rebekah on the long journey to Isaac's home, so the Holy Spirit guides the believer. (Compare 16:13-15.)

We do not know how long the journey will take, but we wait expectantly for that great day when He says, "Come hither, I will shew thee the bride, the Lamb's wife" (Revelation 21:9).

NOTE:
Genesis 22:1,2,17: See Heb. 6:14; 11:17-19. **22:18:** See Acts 3:25. **23:4:** See Heb. 11:13. **23:9:** See Acts 7:16.

"And Isaac's servants digged in the valley, and found there a well of springing water (Living Water)."   Genesis 26:19

JANUARY 9: Read Genesis 25-27.
Genesis 25:22-23: "She went to enquire of the Lord. And the Lord said unto her, Two nations are in thy womb, and two manner of people . . . the elder shall serve the younger."

Rebekah gave birth to twins in answer to Isaac's prayer that God bless them with children. Before they were born, an unusual incident occurred which caused her to "enquire of the Lord." In reply, God foretold that "the elder shall serve the younger." This revealed that Jacob, "the younger," would be the family head through whom the promise to Abraham would be fulfilled and in whom the Savior was to come.

MEMORY VERSE FOR THE WEEK: John 1:3
"All things were made by him; and without him was not any thing made that was made."

We are told that Esau, "the elder," was a "profane person." But he forfeited spiritual privileges for physical satisfactions (Hebrews 12:16).

When Isaac made plans to bestow the Abrahamic Covenant blessing upon his *favorite* son Esau, he not only disregarded the fact that Esau sold his birthright to Jacob, but he also ignored God's prophecy to Rebekah that "the elder shall serve the younger."

Isaac was not only blind physically, but his spiritual perception had also grown dim. It is not said that "he enquired of the Lord" before the most important event; instead, he prepared a banquet for the occasion such as *he* loved (see 27:4). God overruled his spiritual blindness by allowing Rebekah to overhear his well-laid plans with Esau.

Thank God, our destiny is in the hands of God. Try as they may, the Christian's future cannot be manipulated by stubborn and spiritually blind people.

"So then it is not of him that willeth, nor him that runneth, but of God that sheweth mercy" (Romans 9:16).

NOTE:
25:29 **sod pottage** means made lentil stew; 27:31 **savory meat** means tasty food.

Genesis 25:23: See Rom. 9:12. **25:26:** See Acts 7:8. **25:34:** See Heb. 12:17. **27:29:** See Heb. 11:20.

JANUARY 10: Read Genesis 28-30.
Genesis 28:1-2: "And Isaac called Jacob, and blessed him, and charged him, and said unto him, Thou shalt not take a wife of the daughters of Canaan. Arise, go to Padanaram, to the house of Bethuel thy mother's father; and take thee a wife from thence of the daughters of Laban thy mother's brother."

When Isaac discovered that he had bestowed the Abrahamic Covenant blessing upon Jacob rather than upon his favorite son Esau, he trembled with a startling sense of the intervention of the Almighty God (27:33).

After this, Isaac willingly acknowledged Jacob's real destiny, saying, "God Almighty bless thee, . . . and give thee the blessing of Abraham" (28:3,4).

Then Jacob, who should have received a double portion of all the family wealth, left home with nothing but his father's blessing (see 32:10). It appears that Esau occupied the position of heir in his father's house and retained that control. He soon received his interitance—the family wealth—but Jacob had something far more priceless. He possessed God's promise, "I am with thee" (28:15). Furthermore, his inheritance not only included the promised *land,* but it included the promised *Messiah,* who "shall reign over the house of Jacob forever" (Luke 1:33).

MEMORY VERSE FOR THE WEEK: John 1:3
"All things were made by him; and without him was not any thing made that was made."

What difference does it make if a Christian is penniless? He shall soon possess the priceless treasures of "an inheritance incorruptible, and undefiled, and that fadeth not away, reserved in heaven for you, who are kept by the power of God through faith unto salvation ready to be revealed in the last time" (1 Peter 1:4-5).

"And Esau ran to meet him, and embraced him, and fell on his neck, and kissed him: and they wept." Genesis 33:4

JANUARY 11: Read Genesis 31-33.

Genesis 31:3 "And the Lord said unto Jacob, Return unto the land of thy fathers, and to thy kindred; and I will be with thee."

Jacob had just escaped from the hatred of Laban and his sons and was returning home when he was told that his brother Esau "cometh to meet thee, and four hundred men with him. Jacob was greatly afraid and distressed" (32:6-7).

Twenty years earlier, Esau had said, "The days of mourning for my father are at hand; then will I slay my brother Jacob" (27:41). Therefore, Jacob faced certain death unless God intervened and caused Esau to change his mind.

This was the turning point in Jacob's life. He was forced to recognize his utter helplessness. He had to rely on the power and mercy of God for deliverance. He came to a new realization of the true source of his strength.

We can be assured that God permits every trial in order to increase our faith in His power to provide and protect.

"Therefore I take pleasure in infirmities, in reproaches, in necessities, in persecutions, in distresses for Christ's sake: for when I am weak, then am I strong" (II Corinthians 12:10).

NOTE:
31:34 **camel's furniture** means camel's saddle; 32:10 **two bands** means two companies; 32:15 **kine** means cows.

Genesis 33:19: See Acts 7:16.

JANUARY 12: Read Genesis 34-36.

Genesis 35:1-2: "And God said unto Jacob, Arise, go up to Bethel, and dwell there: and make there an altar unto God, that appeared unto thee when thou fleddest from the face of Esau thy brother. Then Jacob said unto his household, and to all that were with him, Put away the strange gods that are among you, and be clean, and change your garments."

If Jacob had gone to Bethel as God had directed instead of going just part of the way, he may have avoided the disgrace and ruin of his daughter. But God allowed the humiliation of His servant Jacob in order to awaken him to the necessity of leaving the ungodly, corrupt influence of Shechem and to bring him to a full realization of God's purpose for his life.

MEMORY VERSE FOR THE WEEK: John 1:3
"All things were made by him; and without him was not any thing made that was made."

God told him to return to Bethel, but he did not go all the way. On his way to Bethel, he bought some land in the fertile valley of Succoth, built a house, and enjoyed financial prosperity for ten years.

It was when Jacob renewed his obedience, saying, "Let us arise, and go up to Bethel," that he had a deeper revelation of God as being God Almighty (verses 3 and 11).

The same God who spoke to Jacob speaks to us today. Our knowledge of God and our ability to understand His ways increase as we continue to prayerfully read His Word. There is no other reliable source of knowing His will than reading His Word. When you decide to fully obey Him and begin reading all His Word, He will give you deeper insight of His plan for your life.

"All scripture is given . . . that the man of God may be . . . throughly furnished unto *all* good works" (II Timothy 3:16,17).

"Now Israel loved Joseph more than all his children, because he was the son of his old age: and he made him a coat of many colours."
Genesis 37:3

JANUARY 13: Read Genesis 37-39.

Genesis 37:33-35: "And he knew it, and said, It is my son's coat; an evil beast hath devoured him; Joseph is without doubt rent in pieces. And Jacob rent his clothes . . . and *refused to be comforted;* and he said, For I will go down into the grave unto my son mourning. Thus his father wept for him."

Jacob was more aware of his *miserable* circumstances than he was in the faith he should have in God's promise, "I will bless thee."

Jacob's conclusions were wrong! The fact is, He did *not* "go down into his grave mourning." To the contrary, the circumstances which took place in his old age brought much honor and satisfaction to him.

Many of us tend to live like Jacob. We expect the worst about our situations, and in self-pity, assume "all these things are against me" (42:36). Yet, many of the things we consider tragedies are actually blessings when we eventually see God's purposes. Remember, *"all things* work together for good" (Romans 8:28).

When we face an overwhelming experience, we should remember what God said to the Apostle Paul, "My grace is sufficient for thee," to which Paul replied, "Therefore I take pleasure in infirmities, in reproaches, in necessities, in persecutions, in distresses for Christ's sake: for when I am weak, then am I strong" (II Corinthians 12:9-10).

NOTE:
Genesis 37:4,11,28: See Acts 7:9. **39:2,21:** See Acts 7:9.

MEMORY VERSE FOR THE WEEK: John 1:3
"All things were made by him; and without him was not any thing made that was made."

JANUARY 14: Read Genesis 40-42.

Genesis 41:16: "And Joseph answered Pharaoh, saying, It is not in me: *God shall give* Pharaoh an answer of peace."

Joseph confidently told Pharaoh that *God ruled* over the affairs of earth, although from all outward appearances, the events which took place in Joseph's life would seem to contradict that fact.

Two years earlier, two of Pharaoh's officers were in prison and depressed over their dreams. Even in that situation, Joseph pointed out how *God ruled* by asking, "Do not interpretations belong to God?" He then told them about his own circumstances, but he did not blame his brothers for his situation. He simply stated that he had been "stolen out of the land of the Hebrews" and that he had "done nothing" for which he should have been put into the dungeon (40:15).

In every crisis, Joseph acknowledged that God was with him, although for years it seemed that his enemies triumphed over him.

God's ways are not man's ways. Behind what often *appears* to be failure on God's part in taking care of our needs is the wisdom of a loving Father who is able to overrule all things to accomplish His will.

"O, the depth of the riches both of the wisdom and knowledge of God! How unsearchable are his judgments, and his ways past finding out!" (Romans 11:33).

NOTE:
42:34 **shall traffic** means do business.

Genesis 41:37-40: See Acts 7:10. **41:54:** See Acts 7:11. **42:2:** See Acts 7:12. **42:13:** See Acts 7:8.

"Moreover he kissed all his brethren, and wept upon them: and after that his brethren talked with him." Genesis 45:15

JANUARY 15: Read Genesis 43-45.

Genesis 43:6: "And Israel [Jacob] said, Wherefore dealt ye so ill with me, as to tell the man whether ye had yet a brother?"

All of Jacob's earthly hopes seemed lost when he was forced to let Benjamin go to Egypt with his brothers. Human reasoning caused Jacob to ask his son Judah, "Wherefore dealt ye so ill with me?" He really had not "dealt ill" with him; this was part of God's wonderful plan to provide for His people. Jacob again failed to see that if God promised to be with him, no evil could possibly triumph over him.

Jacob did not possess great faith, as did his grandfather, Abraham, who was willing to give up his *only* son Isaac when God asked him to make the sacrifice.

MEMORY VERSE FOR THE WEEK: John 1:3

"All things were made by him; and without him was not any thing made that was made."

When Jacob said "all these things are against me," he had lost faith in God's promise, "I will surely do thee good." His lack of faith caused him to talk like an unbeliever, and gloom and depression filled his life. He began to recall his great misery and suffering in losing Joseph, and now he feared the possibility of losing Benjamin. In reality, "all these things" were not against him, as he soon discovered.

All our mental anguish arises from a lack of confidence in the promises of God. Christians need the confidence of Job, who could say, even after his great loss, ". . . The Lord gave, and the Lord hath taken away; blessed be the name of the Lord. In all this Job sinned not, nor charged God foolishly" (Job 1:21-22).

NOTE:
Genesis 45:1: See Acts 7:13. **45:9:** See Acts 7:14-15.

JANUARY 16: Read Genesis 46-48.
Genesis 48:15-16: "And he blessed Joseph, and said, God, before whom my fathers Abraham and Isaac did walk, the God which fed me all my life long unto this day. The angel which redeemed me from all evil, bless the lads; and let my name be named on them, and the name of my fathers Abraham and Isaac; and let them grow into a multitude in the midst of the earth."

As "the time drew nigh that Israel [Jacob] must die" (47:29), he bestowed his prophetic blessing upon Joseph's two sons, Manasseh and Ephraim. It was as binding as a last will and testament. Though several hundred years passed before the nation reached Canaan, all of God's blessings, as well as the curse that remained upon Reuben and his tribe, were fulfilled.

Manasseh and Ephraim were selected to receive the inheritance that would have gone to Reuben, the oldest son. Although Reuben possessed great natural abilities, in addition to having the dignity and inheritance rights of the firstborn, he forfeited all his rights of inheritance because of his sinful living. (Note I Chronicles 5:1; Genesis 49:5-7.)

If Christians could realize what those in eternity now know, they would drop *all* interest in this world's allurements and listen breathlessly as they prayerfully read all that God has written. But there are rival voices sounding everywhere, demanding attention and filling our ears with such a multitude of sounds that we often neglect the Voice from the throne. God's voice, heard through His Word, is too often ignored.

"Take therefore the talent from him, and give unto him which hath ten talents" (Matthew 25:28).

NOTE:
Genesis 46:5-6: See Acts 7:14-15. **47:9:** See Heb. 11:13. **48:11-15:** See Heb. 11:21.

MEMORY VERSE FOR THE WEEK: John 1:4
"In him was life; and the life was the light of men."

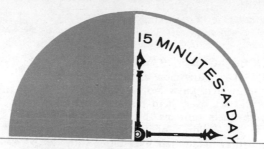

INTRODUCTION TO EXODUS

After Joseph's death, the prestige that he and the Israelites held in Egypt gradually ceased to exist. (Note Genesis 50:6-9.)

When Jacob entered Egypt, his family consisted of 70 people. When they were delivered from slavery, there were about 600,000 men, besides women and children (12:37), an estimated total of 3 million people. This meant that they probably made up half the population of Egypt. Because of this, Pharaoh tried to prevent any further increase in their population (Exodus 1:8-14).

Some believe that Jacob's descendants were in Egypt 430 years, and others believe the 430 years date back from the time Abraham entered Canaan to the time of Moses' exodus from Egypt, which would mean that the Israelites were in Egypt 215 years. (Compare Exodus 12:40; Acts 7:6; and Galatians 3:17.)

Exodus closes with the erection of the Tabernacle, which was completed in the second year of the exodus.

The overthrow and complete destruction of the Egyptian power in the Red Sea reveals not only how God is able to deliver His people from the *guilt* of sin, but also to deliver them from the *power* of sin. These two great events picture two great truths concerning the death of Christ, which are also fully revealed in the book of Romans.

OUTLINE OF EXODUS

I. Nation of Israel—Helpless and Enslaved (Exodus 1-11)

II. Passover Instituted and Deliverance from Egypt (Exodus 12-13)

III. Journey from the Red Sea to Mt. Sinai, and "the Lord went before them" (13:21; 14:31—about two months). They arrived at Mt. Sinai "in the third month" (19:1).

IV. Ten Commandments Given and the Nation Set Apart as "a kingdom of priests, and an holy nation" (Exodus 19-24)

V. Tabernacle—They remained at Mt. Sinai for about 10 months and completed construction on the Tabernacle "in the first month in the second year" (40:17; compare Numbers 10:11) (Exodus 25-40)

Four (4) Prominent People Mentioned: Moses, Aaron, Miriam, Joshua

Four (4) Major Events Took Place: Passover celebrated, crossing the Red Sea, the Ten Commandments given, and the Tabernacle completed

JANUARY 17: Read Genesis 49 thru Exodus 1.

Exodus 1:8,11,13-14: "Now there arose up a new king over Egypt, which knew not Joseph . . . Therefore they did set over them taskmasters to afflict them with their burdens . . . And the Egyptians made the children of Israel to serve with rigour: and they made their lives bitter with hard bondage . . ."

After Joseph and his brothers died, there was a gradual change in the status of their descendants from a favored status to one of slavery.

The place where they once enjoyed satisfaction soon became the scene of their affliction. But their slavery and suffering were allowed to prepare them for the exodus (escape) out of Egypt and to enhance their love for the Promised Land. It caused them to pray earnestly for deliverance, and thereby God was able to reveal His great mercy in bringing about their freedom. Through this experience, they learned that they had a King above all kings. Even so, all true spiritual growth and progress are characterized by suffering and sorrow.

"Though he were a Son, yet learned he obedience by the things which he suffered; and being made perfect he became the author of eternal salvation unto all them that obey him" (Hebrews 5:8-9).

NOTE:
1:13 **rigour** means severe slavery.

Genesis 49:10: See Rev. 5:5. **49:33:** See Acts 7:15. **50:25:** See Heb. 11:22. **Exodus 1:7:** See Acts 7:17. **1:8:** See Acts 7:18. **1:10:** See Acts 7:19.

JANUARY 18: Read Exodus 2-4.

Exodus 2:3: "And when she could not longer hide him, she took for him an ark of bulrushes, and daubed it with slime and with pitch, and put the child therein; and she laid it in the flags by the river's brink."

After Moses' mother had tried every conceivable way to protect her baby from Pharaoh's wrath, she made an ark (basket) and committed the baby to the care of a loving God.

We cannot measure the power of faith, but this is an example of how a mother's faith saved the child who was to become the great lawgiver. This act of faith prevented the powers of Satan and the laws of Pharaoh from obstructing God's purpose.

MEMORY VERSE FOR THE WEEK: John 1:4
"In him was life; and the life was the light of men."

28

We can have the utmost confidence that, having done all we know to do, we can trust the future of our loved ones to the care of God.

"Faithful is he that calleth you, who also will do it" (I Thessalonians 5:24).

NOTE:
Exodus 2:2: See Heb. 11:23; Acts 7:20. 2:3-10: See Acts 7:21. 2:11: See Heb. 11:25. 2:12,13: See Acts 7:24-29. 2:14-15: See Acts 7:24-29; Heb. 11:27. 3:2: See Acts 7:30. 3:5: See Acts 7:33-34. 3:6: See Matt. 22:32; Mk. 12:26; Acts 7:32. 3:7-10: See Acts 7:33-34. 3:15-18: See Acts 7:35.

"And Moses went up unto God, and the Lord called unto him out of the mountain." Exodus 19:3

JANUARY 19: Read Exodus 5-7.

Exodus 5:6,9,14: "And Pharaoh commanded . . . Let there more work be laid upon the men . . . and the officers of the children of Israel . . . were beaten, and demanded, Wherefore have ye not fulfilled your task?"

Instead of freeing Israel from slavery, it seemed that Moses and Aaron had *increased* the pain and suffering of the Israelites.

Moses and Aaron not only experienced ridicule and resistance from Pharaoh, but they were criticized by those whom they attempted to free from slavery.

There are times when our service seems to please no one but God, but Christians must expect this. (Note I Timothy 4:16.)

After the seeming *failure* of a first attempt (if you choose to call it failure), we must continue to seek the Lord in prayer as Moses did. God *always* gives further insight to those who ask, seek, and knock. So keep in mind what God said to Moses after his bitter experience, *"Now* shalt thou see what I will do to Pharaoh . . ." 6:11).

The "Pharaohs" of this world will not willingly yield to the request of a "Moses," who boldly makes known the Word of God.

"Grace be to you and peace from God the Father, and from our Lord Jesus Christ, who gave Himself for our sins, that he might deliver us from this present evil world, according to the will of God and our Father" (Galatians 1:3-4).

NOTE:
7:22 **enchantments** means magic, tricks.

Exodus 7:11: See II Tim. 3:8. **7:12:** See Heb. 11:7.

MEMORY VERSE FOR THE WEEK: John 1:4
"In him was life; and the life was the light of men."

JANUARY 20: Read Exodus 8-10.

Exodus 8:28: "And Pharaoh said, I will let you go, that ye may sacrifice to the Lord your God in the wilderness; only ye shall not go very far away: entreat for me."

Egypt was the most powerful kingdom on earth, and its idols and gods were considered equally powerful. Consequently, when Moses requested that the Israelites be permitted to worship the one true God, it was an insult to Pharaoh, who believed in the gods of Egypt.

Pharaoh did not refuse Moses' request to let the people worship God, but he disagreed with the way they should worship. By studying Pharaoh's three compromises, we will see the pitfalls and the reasons so many have succumbed to spiritual defeat.

(Pharaoh's *first compromise*, 8:26; *second compromise*, 8:28; *third compromise*, 10:11,24.)

These three compromises reveal Satan's attempt to keep Christians ensnared in the world (Egypt). Pharaoh represents Satan and the worldly influences that hinder many from fully surrendering to doing the Lord's will. Satan seeks to deceive us into the false belief that it is enough just to worship God. Yet, our worship is unacceptable to God unless it is consistent with His Word.

"In burnt offerings and sacrifices for sin thou hast had no pleasure. Then said I, Lo, I come (in the volume of the book it is written of me,) to do thy will, O God" (Hebrews 10:6-7).

NOTE:
Exodus 9:16: See Rom. 9:17.

> "And ye shall observe the feast of unleavened bread; for in this selfsame day have I brought your armies out of the land of Egypt."
> Exodus 12:17

JANUARY 21: Read Exodus 11-13.

Exodus 12:23: "For the Lord will pass through to smite the Egyptians; and when he seeth the blood upon the lintel, and on the two side posts, the Lord will pass over the door, and will not suffer the destroyer to come in unto your houses to smite you."

It was not enough for the Israelites to kill the Passover Lamb, but its blood had to be sprinkled upon the upper doorposts of the house to save the life of the eldest son within.

Christ, the Lamb of God, is the Christian's Passover Lamb (John 1:29 and I Peter 1:19). Just as the blood on the doorposts satisfied God, so "the blood of Jesus Christ his Son cleanseth us from all sin" (I John 1:9). It was not

MEMORY VERSE FOR THE WEEK: John 1:4
"In him was life; and the life was the light of men."

necessary for the Israelites to understand *why* the blood satisfied God; neither is it necessary for Christians to understand *all* the meaning of the blood of Christ; but we must believe what the Bible says about it.

After the lamb was slain, the believers were to eat *all of the lamb*—none of it was to be left. This lamb provided the strength the Israelites needed to leave Egypt. Likewise, we also receive our strength for each day by eating of the Bread of Life—God's Word. *All the Word* must be read in order to gain *all the strength* that the Lord has provided.

"Moreover he said unto me, Son of man, *all my words* that I shall speak unto thee receive in thine heart, and hear with thine ears" (Ezekiel 3:10).

NOTE:
Exodus 12:21-29: See Heb. 11:28. **12:41:** See Acts 7:36; 13:17; Jude 5. **12:46:** See John 19:36. **13:2-12:** See Luke 2:2. **13:21:** See I Cor. 10:1.

JANUARY 22: Read Exodus 14-16.
Exodus 14:10,14: "And when Pharaoh drew nigh, the children of Israel lifted up their eyes, and, behold, the Egyptians marched after them; and they were sore afraid: and the children of Israel cried out unto the Lord . . . The Lord shall fight for you, and ye shall hold your peace."

The Israelites had gone only a short distance in their march for freedom when they saw Pharaoh with his mighty army and chariots rushing toward them. They were helpless: and in fear, they cried out to the Lord and murmured against Moses. Although Moses did not know how the Lord would deliver them, he declared, "The Lord shall fight for you."

Israel, in passing through the Red Sea and reaching the other side, represents the believer being buried with Christ, then rising to walk in newness of life (see Romans 6:5). Even though our enemies may seem very much alive, we can look upon them as dead, as were the Egyptians in the Red Sea. They have been buried by the atoning sacrifice on the cross.

God often withholds His *presence* in order to reveal His *power*. He may permit overwhelming difficulties in our lives in order to manifest His glory and to increase our faith and trust in Him. Fears vanish in the presence of faith. "For whatsoever is born of God overcometh the world: and this is the victory that overcometh the world, even our faith" (I John 5:4).

NOTE:
15:25 **proved them** means put them to the test; 16:18 **did mete it** means measured it; 16:23 **seethe** means bake and boil; 16:36 **ephah** means basket 3/5 bushel.

Exodus 14:21: See Acts 7:36. **14:22:** See I Cor. 10:1. **15:23:** See Acts 7:36. **16:3-35:** See I Cor. 10:3. **16:15:** See John 6:31. **16:18:** See II Cor. 8:15. **16:33-34:** See Heb. 9:4.

MEMORY VERSE FOR THE WEEK: John 1:4
"In him was life; and the life was the light of men."

"And they took their journey from Succoth, and encamped in Etham, in the edge of the wilderness." Exodus 13:20

JANUARY 23: Read Exodus 17-19.

Exodus 17:6,8,15-16: ". . . thou shalt smite the rock, and there shall come water out of it, that the people may drink . . . Then came Amalek, and fought with Israel . . . And Moses built an altar, and called the name of it Jehovahnissi: for he said, because the Lord hath sworn that the Lord will have war with Amalek from generation to generation."

The Israelites' hunger had been satisfied by the manna. Jesus said that He was the "true bread from heaven . . . and giveth life unto the world" (John 6:32-33). Their thirst was satisfied with water from the rock when Moses followed God's directions.

Soon after the water had been given in such wonderful abundance, the Israelites fought their first battle against the Amalekites. Amalek represents the inward conflicts as revealed in Galatians 5:17, "The flesh lusteth against the Spirit, and the Spirit against the flesh."

The attack came when the Israelites questioned the *presence of God*, asking, "Is the Lord among us, or not?" (Exodus 17:7). Even so, when our fleshly nature becomes attracted to the things of this world, we no longer feel the presence of the Lord, and all kinds of evil thoughts attack us.

"Thanks be to God, which giveth us the victory through our Lord Jesus Christ" (I Corinthians 15:57).

NOTE:
Exodus 17:6: See I Cor. 10:4. **18:3:** See Acts 7:29.

JANUARY 24: Read Exodus 20-22.

Exodus 20:1,3: "And God spake all these words . . . Thou shalt have no other gods before me."

The Ten Commandments expose man's sinful nature, reveal God's righteousness, and forever remove all possibility of our being saved through our own efforts. These commandments—not society or man's ethics—are the basis for acceptable conduct. (Compare Romans 7:7.)

The Law was never intended as a means of salvation, for it was given to a nation who had *already* experienced deliverance from death through the Passover. Instead, the Law was a revelation of the true nature of God and was to become an expression of the new nature of the believer, "written with the Spirit of the living God; not in tables of stone, but in fleshly tables of the heart" (II Corinthians 3:3).

Christians do not keep the Law in order to receive eternal life any more than the Israelites were delivered from Egypt by demonstrating their ability to keep the Ten Commandments. To the contrary, "the Law was our school-

MEMORY VERSE FOR THE WEEK: John 1:5
"And the light shineth in darkness; and the darkness comprehended it not."

master to bring us unto Christ, that we might be justified by faith" (Galatians 3:24).

NOTE:
21:14 **with guile** means with trickery; 22:25 **usury** means interest on money loaned; 22:30 **his dam** means his mother.

Exodus 20:12-14: See Matt. 15:4,21,27; 19:18-19; Mark 7:10; 10:9; Luke 18:20; Rom. 13:9; Eph. 6:2-3. **20:15-17:** See Luke 18:20; Rom. 13:9. **21:17:** See Matt. 15:4; Mark 7:10. **21:24:** See Matt. 5:38. **22:28:** See Acts 23:5.

"The ark of the testimony, and the staves thereof, and the mercy seat."　Exodus 39:35

JANUARY 25: Read Exodus 23-25.
Exodus 25:21-22: "And thou shalt put the mercy seat above upon the ark; and in the ark thou shalt put the testimony that I shall give thee. And there I will meet with thee, and *I will commune with thee* from above the mercy seat."

The "mercy seat" was the solid gold lid to the ark of the covenant, where the Ten Commandments were kept. The holy Law revealed how all the world was guilty before God and deserved death. (See Romans 3:19.) This golden lid was a symbol of the purity and holiness of God.

Therefore, our holy God in His mercy commanded that the blood of an innocent lamb be sprinkled on this mercy seat for the atonement of sins, representing forgiveness, cleansing, redemption, and satisfaction. This beautifully expresses how the salvation of God's people depends on One who, through the sacrifice of His own blood, entered into the presence of God to make atonement for our sins.

Only on that basis, God could say, *"I will commune with thee."* The full revelation of the mercy of God was fulfilled in Christ. "Blessed be the Lord God of Israel; for he hath visited and redeemed his people . . . to perform the mercy promised to our fathers" (Luke 2:68,72).
NOTE:
Exodus 24:8: See Heb. 9:19-20. **25:16:** See Heb. 9:4. **25:40:** See Acts 7:44; Heb. 8:5.

"And he made the laver of brass, and the foot of it of brass, of the lookingglasses of the women assembling, which assembled at the door of the tabernacle of the congregation."　Exodus 38:8

JANUARY 26: Read Exodus 26-28.
Exodus 26:30: "And thou shalt rear up the tabernacle according to the fashion thereof which was shewed thee in the mount."

The Tabernacle was a rectangular structure about 45 feet long and 15 feet wide. It was protected by an enclosure that was approximately 150 feet long by 75 feet wide. (A cubit was approximately 18 inches.) The enclosure consisted of 60 posts that were 7½ feet high and equally

MEMORY VERSE FOR THE WEEK: John 1:5
"And the light shineth in darkness; and the darkness comprehended it not."

---

spaced around the 450 feet. The posts supported the continuous curtain around the Tabernacle and prevented anyone outside from seeing what took place within.

This wall separated the unbeliever from the worshiper and was symbolic of the righteousness of God that forever bars the sinner from His presence. But God in His mercy provided a gate for sinful man to approach Him (27:16). Christ is that gate.

Although an unsaved person may go to church, hear sermons, sing hymns, and read the Bible, only a true Christian can experience fellowship with God. Our Savior said, "I am the door: by me if any man enter in, he shall be saved" (John 10:9).

NOTE:
26:17 **tenons** means clamps; 27:6 **staves** means poles; 27:10 **fillets** means supports; 28:4 **mitre** means turban; 28:8 **curious girdle** means artistic ribbon; 28:11 **ouches** means settings; 28:17 **carbuncle** means crystal; 28:19 **ligure** means amber, jacinth.

Exodus 26:30: See Acts 7:44.

"And the golden altar, and the anointing oil, and the sweet incense, and the hanging for the tabernacle door." Exodus 39:38

JANUARY 27: Read Exodus 29-31.
Exodus 29:42-43: "This shall be a continual burnt offering throughout your generations at the door of the tabernacle. And there I will meet with the children of Israel, and the tabernacle shall be sanctified *by my glory.*"

Jehovah God filled the Tabernacle with His *glory* (cloud) as a visible sign of His presence. This cloud afterward withdrew to the most holy place to dwell above the outspread wings of the cherubim over the ark of the covenant. As long as the Israelites were traveling toward Canaan, the presence of Jehovah was manifested by that cloud.

The expression "temple of God" is used to describe the Christian believer and refers to the most holy place where God had promised to speak to His people. As Israel could see the cloud, so should the Christian recognize God's leading as He clearly points the way through His Word.

"In whom all the building fitly framed together groweth unto an holy temple in the Lord: in whom ye also are builded together for an habitation of God through the Spirit" (Ephesians 2:21-22).

NOTE:
29:22 **caul** means fat; 29:24 **wave them** means present them; 30:25 **apothecary** means perfumer.

Exodus 29:28: See Heb. 10:11. **30:10:** See Heb. 9:7.

MEMORY VERSE FOR THE WEEK: John 1:5
"And the light shineth in darkness; and the darkness comprehended it not."

JANUARY 28: Read Exodus 32-34.

Exodus 32:5,6: "And when Aaron saw it, he built an altar before it; and Aaron made proclamation, and said, To morrow is a feast to the Lord. And they rose up early on the morrow, and offered burnt offerings, and brought peace offerings; and the people sat down to eat and to drink, and rose up to play."

Aaron's "feast to the Lord" and "peace offerings" were totally unacceptable; and instead of bringing peace, they brought God's immediate judgment. The people had sacrificed their personal wealth to make the golden calf. However, sacrifice is never a substitute for obedience. (See I Samuel 15:22.)

God has given instructions for worship, and nothing should be added, altered, or deleted.

Many self-willed worshipers today are "doing their own thing." And many people believe that as long as they are sincere, they can worship in whatever way they choose. But Israel was taught a far different theology.

"Who serve unto the example and shadow of heavenly things, as Moses was admonished of God when he was about to make the tabernacle: for, See, saith he, that thou make all things according to the pattern shewed to thee in the mount" (Hebrews 8:5).

NOTE:
32:12 **mischief** means evil; 32:20 **strawed it** means scattered it.

Exodus 32:1: See Acts 7:40. **32:6:** See I Cor. 10:7. **32:19:** See Acts 7:41; Rom. 9:15. **34:33:** See II Cor. 3:13.

"The altar of burnt offering, with his brasen grate, his staves, and all his vessels, the laver and his foot."
Exodus 35:16

JANUARY 29: Read Exodus 35-37.

Exodus 35:16: "The altar of burnt offering, with his brasen grate, his staves, and all his vessels, the laver and his foot."

The fire on the brazen altar, known as the Altar of burnt offering, was never permitted to go out (Leviticus 6:13). This is to teach us that anytime, day or night, "He [Christ] ever liveth to make intercession" for the Christian. (See Hebrews 7:25.)

ALTAR OF
BURNT OFFERING

The precious gold which was so freely used elsewhere was not used on the altar. It was overlaid with brass—a symbol of God's judgment.

Christ gave Himself on the cross as an offering for our sins—"the Lamb of God, which taketh away the sin of the world" (John 1:29).

MEMORY VERSE FOR THE WEEK: John 1:5

"And the light shineth in darkness; and the darkness comprehended it not."

Between the altar and the Holy Place was the laver of brass (38:8), containing water for the cleansing of the hands and the feet of those who entered the Holy Place.

The laver was made from the brass mirrors which were offered by the women (Exodus 38:8). This represents our need for examining ourselves in the mirror of God's Word and separating ourselves from evil if we are to proceed into the presence of the Lord. (See I Corinthians 11:28-32.) We must be willing to surrender all that satisfies our vanity in order to obtain cleansing from Him.

". . . Christ also loved the church, and gave himself for it; that he might sanctify and cleanse it with the washing of water by the word" (Ephesians 5:25-26).

NOTE:
35:32 **curious** means artistic; 36:22 **tenons** means pegs.

"The pure candlestick, with the lamps thereof, even with the lamps to be set in order, and all the vessels thereof, and the oil for light." Exodus 39:37

JANUARY 30: Read Exodus 38-39.
Exodus 39:36,37,41: "The table, and all the vessels thereof, and the shewbread, the pure candlestick, with the lamps thereof, even with the lamps to be set in order, and all the vessels thereof, and the oil for light, . . . the cloths of service to do service in the holy place, and the holy garments for Aaron the priest, and his sons' garments, to minister in the priest's office."

After the priest had washed his hands and feet at the laver, he proceeded toward the Tabernacle and entered the only door to the Holy Place.

On the left was the seven-branched golden candlestick that provided the only source of light in the Holy Place. The golden candlestick represents Christ, who is the Light of the World and who bestows light to make Himself known through His Word. (Compare Revelation 1:12 and John 8:12.)

On the right was the table of shewbread with its twelve loaves sprinkled with incense. They were eaten by the priests only in the holy place. None could be removed and eaten elsewhere. Its name "shewbread" suggests more than bodily nourishment. It indicates seeing God—gaining spiritual insight from God that is not obtainable in any other way. Something beyond our ability to explain enlightens, empowers, and then transforms the life of one who prayerfully continues to eat the Bread of Life.

MEMORY VERSE FOR THE WEEK: Philippians 4:4
"Rejoice in the Lord alway: and again I say, Rejoice."

"Now we have received, not the spirit of the world, but the spirit which is of God; that we might know the things that are freely given to us of God" (I Corinthians 2:12).

NOTE:
38:4 **compass** means ledge; 38:11 **fillets of silver** means hooks and rods; 38:17 **chapiters of silver** means tops of silver; 39:23 **habergeon** means linen corcelet.

> "And thou shalt make a veil of blue, and purple, and scarlet, and fine twined linen of cunning work: with cherubims shall it be made."
> Exodus 26:31

JANUARY 31: Read Exodus 40.

Exodus 40:5,34: "And thou shalt set the altar of gold for the incense before the ark of the testimony, and put the hanging of the door to the tabernacle . . . Then a cloud covered the tent of the congregation, and the glory of the Lord filled the tabernacle."

Immediately in front of the one entrance to the holy of holies stood the golden altar where the priest offered incense each morning and evening. Its fragrant smoke rising up before the holy of holies was a symbol of intercessory prayer and of Christ giving Himself wholly unto His disciples. The altar reveals that all our prayers have been made acceptable to God through Him.

"For Christ is not entered into the holy places made with hands, which are the figures of the true; but into heaven itself, now to appear in the presence of God for us" (Hebrews 9:24).

In the holy of holies was the ark of the covenant, which contained the Law, written on two tables of stone which God gave to Moses. Even the priests, though very devout, were unfit to enter the holy of holies. Once a year, on the day of Atonement, the high priest, in his official robes, entered into the holy of holies to sprinkle the blood of the slain lamb on the golden mercy seat.

The veil of the Temple that barred entrance into the holy of holies was torn from top to bottom by the hand of God when Christ was crucified, thus giving us access to the presence of God through prayer.

"Having therefore, brethren, boldness to enter into the holiest by the blood of Jesus, . . . Let us draw near . . ." (Hebrews 10:19,22).

NOTE:
40:8 **the hanging** means the veil, or screen.

BIBLICAL REFERENCE INDEX

PRAYERS IN GENESIS AND EXODUS

Abraham—for a son .... Genesis 15:1-6

Abraham—for Ishmael .... Genesis 17:17-21

Abraham—for Sodom .... Genesis 18:20-32

Abraham—for Abimelech .... Genesis 20:17

Abraham's servant Eleazar—a wife for Isaac .... Genesis 24:12-14

Isaac—for children .... Genesis 25:21, 24-26

Jacob—all night .... Genesis 32:9,11,24-30

Israel—for deliverance .... Exodus 2:23-25

Moses—for Pharaoh .... Exodus 8:12

Moses—for water .... Exodus 15:24,25

Moses—for Israel .... Exodus 32:31-34

PROPHETIC REFERENCES TO CHRIST

PROPHETIC SCRIPTURES	SUBJECT	FULFILLED
Genesis 3:15	Seed of a woman	Galatians 4:4
Genesis 4:4-7	Christ's atoning death	Hebrews 11:4
Genesis 12:3; 18:18	Seed of Abraham	Matthew 1:1; Acts 3:25-26; Galatians 3:16
Genesis 14:18-20	High Priest-Melchizedek	Hebrews 5:5-10; 7:1-4
Genesis 17:19; 21:22; 22:18; 26:4	Seed of Isaac	Luke 3:34; Romans 9:7; Hebrews 11:18
Genesis 49:10	From the tribe of Judah	Luke 3:33
Exodus 12:7	The Lamb without blemish	I Peter 1:19; John 6:53,54

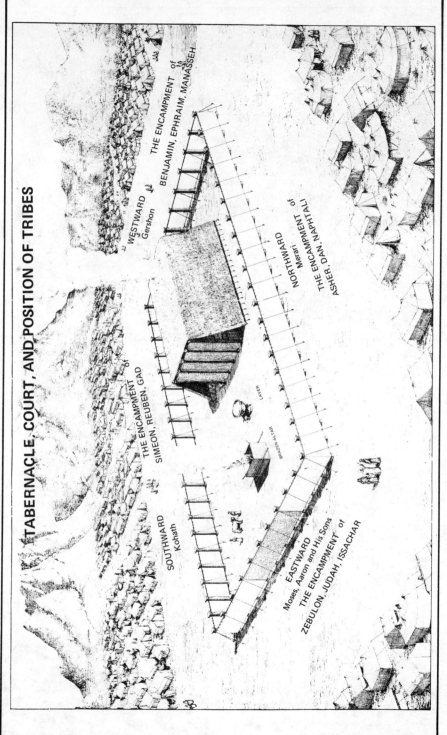

TABERNACLE, COURT, AND POSITION OF TRIBES

WESTWARD
Gershon

THE ENCAMPMENT of
BENJAMIN, EPHRAIM, MANASSEH

NORTHWARD of
Merari

THE ENCAMPMENT of
ASHER, DAN, NAPHTALI

THE ENCAMPMENT of
SIMEON, REUBEN, GAD

SOUTHWARD
Kohath

LAVER

BRAZEN ALTAR

EASTWARD
Moses, Aaron and His Sons
THE ENCAMPMENT of
ZEBULON, JUDAH, ISSACHAR

THE TABERNACLE IN THE WILDERNESS

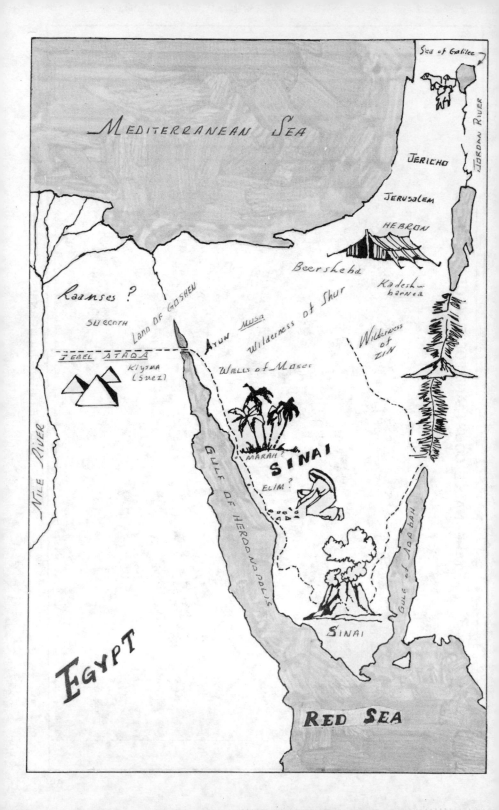

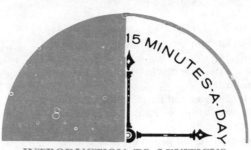

INTRODUCTION TO LEVITICUS

The book of Leviticus covers one month at Mt. Sinai.

The word Leviticus means "pertaining to Levites." It is a continuation of Exodus.

Leviticus contains the laws that would show Israel how to live as a holy nation in fellowship with God.

The central theme of this book is "Be ye holy." The word "holy" appears more than 87 times to impress upon Israel that they were not to defile the camp "in the midst whereof I dwell" (Numbers 5:3).

God desired to dwell with His people—not on a lonely mountaintop Sinai, but in the midst of the congregation. To do this, Israel had to be taught how a sinful man could properly approach a holy God.

The purpose of the "sanitary and dietary laws" was to make them realize the need to be consecrated people—separated from their uncleanness—to retain the presence of God (15:31).

The Levite tribe received special status in Israel as God's representatives in administering all the functions pertaining to the laws and commandments God gave Moses.

OUTLINE TO LEVITICUS

FEBRUARY 1: Read Leviticus 1-3.

Leviticus 1:3: "If his offering be a burnt sacrifice of the herd, let him offer a male without blemish: he shall offer it of his own voluntary will at the door of the tabernacle of the congregation before the Lord."

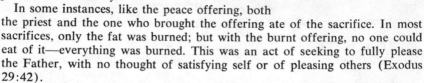

The burnt offering was unlike all other sacrifices in that it was entirely burned and was presented voluntarily.

In some instances, like the peace offering, both the priest and the one who brought the offering ate of the sacrifice. In most sacrifices, only the fat was burned; but with the burnt offering, no one could eat of it—everything was burned. This was an act of seeking to fully please the Father, with no thought of satisfying self or of pleasing others (Exodus 29:42).

The burnt offering was often a valuable ox that normally plowed in a field or pulled a huge cart. To offer less than his best, his offering would not qualify as a "burnt offering." As the sacrifice was reduced to ashes, a sweet savor ascended to God and satisfied Him.

Just as a transformation took place from the time the ox was plowing the field to the time it was reduced to ashes, so every Christian who presents himself a "living sacrifice" will be transformed by the indwelling Holy Spirit.

As Christ takes control of our life, pride, self-sufficiency, and self-interest will be reduced to ashes. The Christian then becomes a sweet savor—a satisfaction to God.

"I beseech you therefore, brethren, by the mercies of God, that ye present your bodies a living sacrifice, holy, acceptable unto God, which is your reasonable service. And be not conformed to this world: but be ye transformed by the renewing of your mind, that ye may prove what is that good, and acceptable and perfect will of God" (Romans 12:1-2).

NOTE:
1:6 **flay** means skin; 1:9 **sweet savor** means pleasing; 2:1 **meat offering** means mixture of fine flour, oil, and frankincense; 2:3 **a thing most holy** means used only for God; 2:4 **anointed** means to apply oil to a person or thing dedicated to God; 2:9 **memorial thereof** means a portion thereof; 2:12 **oblation** means offering; 3:3 **inwards** means internal organs; 3:4 **flanks, caul** means loins, appendage of; 3:9 **hard by** means near, 3:15 **caul** means lobe of the liver.

Leviticus **1:10, 13:** See Matt. 8:4, Mark 1:44, Luke 5:14, Rom. 12:1, II Cor. 2:15, Eph. 5:2,27, Phil. 4:18, I Pet. 1:19. **2:11, 13:** See Matt. 16:12, Mark 8:15; 9:49, Luke 12:1, I Cor. 5:8, Gal. 5:9, Col. 4:6.

MEMORY VERSE FOR THE WEEK: Philippians 4:4
"Rejoice in the Lord alway: and again I say, Rejoice."

FEBRUARY 2: Read Leviticus 4-6.

Leviticus 4:2,3: ". . . . If a soul shall sin through ignorance against any of the commandments of the Lord . . . let him bring for his sin . . . a young bullock without blemish unto the Lord for a sin offering."

The sin offering was mandatory and had to be offered before any other sacrifice could be made. Recognizing himself as a sinner, the worshiper first presented a sacrifice for his sins. Then he was qualified to worship and was allowed to voluntarily present the burnt offering, the meat offering, and the peace offering.

The sin offering typifies the faith of a sinner who is trusting in the fact that his sins have been borne by another.

These animal sacrifices were no longer required after Christ, "the Lamb of God," became our sin offering when He died on the cross. No one will ever be saved by offering other "sacrifices," such as keeping the Golden Rule, doing the best he can, or by joining a good church.

As the sin offering was mandatory, so was Christ's death on the cross. Before we can accept Christ as our Savior, we must recognize that we are sinners.

"But in those sacrifices there is a remembrance again made of sins every year. For it is not possible that the blood of bulls and of goats should take away sins. Wherefore when he cometh into the world, he saith, Sacrifice and offering thou wouldest not, but a body hast thou prepared me: In burnt offerings and sacrifices for sin thou hast had no pleasure . . . by the which will we are sanctified through the offering of the body of Jesus Christ once for all" (Hebrews 10:3-6,10).

NOTE:
4:13 **the thing be hid from the eyes of the assembly** means no one realizes the wrong that was done; 4:20 **atonement** means to reconcile; 5:1 **unclean** means unfit, defiled; 5:4 **swear** means make a vow; 5:11 **tenth part of an ephah** means 15 cups; 5:17 **wist it not** means knew it not; 5:18 **estimation** means valuation; 6:5 **appertaineth** means belongs; 6:11 **without the camp** means outside the camp; 6:22 **wholly burnt** means entirely given to the Lord; 6:28 **sodden** means boil or bake.

Leviticus 4:31: See Heb. 5:3; 7:27,28; 9:7. **6:4:** See Luke 19:8.

"I pray God your whole spirit and soul and body be preserved blameless unto the coming of our Lord Jesus Christ."
I Thessalonians 5:23

FEBRUARY 3: Read Leviticus 7-8.

Leviticus 8:22-23: "And he brought the other ram, the ram of consecration: and Aaron and his sons laid their hands upon the head of the ram. And he slew it; and Moses took of the blood of it, and put it upon the tip of Aaron's right ear, and upon the thumb of his right hand, and upon the great toe of his right foot."

God chose Aaron to be the high priest. This was the most prominent position in Israel's wor-

---

MEMORY VERSE FOR THE WEEK: Philippians 4:4
"Rejoice in the Lord alway: and again I say, Rejoice."

---

ship. To prepare him for this service, God commanded Moses to wash Aaron with water (verse 6). In addition, God commanded that the blood of the sacrificed ram be put upon the tip of Aaron's right ear, upon the thumb of his right hand, and upon the great toe of his right foot.

This signified that his entire body was set apart for service to God—the ear was prepared to hear; the hand was prepared to work, and the foot was prepared to walk in the way and in the will of God.

As a member of Christ's Church, the Christian is to be "holy and without blemish," for Christ "gave himself for it; that he might sanctify and cleanse it with the washing of water by the word" (see Ephesians 5:25-27).

We should prayerfully weigh each decision and conduct their daily walk in ways which honor the Lord.

"Let us draw near with a true heart in full assurance of faith, having our hearts sprinkled from an evil conscience, and our bodies washed with pure water" (Hebrews 10:22).

NOTE:
7:1 **trespass** means guilt or sin; 7:21 **shall touch** means has anything to do with; 8:3 **unto the door of** means in the front of; 8:8 **Urim, Thummin** means unknown objects worn by the high priest; 8:13 **bonnets** means headpieces; 8:22 **consecration** means an act of dedication; 8:35 **the charge of the Lord** means the regulations.

Leviticus 8:14,19: See Heb. 9:12-23; 10:11; 12:24; 13:11; I Pet. 1:2.

FEBRUARY 4: Read Leviticus 9-10.

Leviticus 10:1-2: "And Nadab and Abihu . . . offered *strange fire* before the Lord, which he commanded them not. And there went out fire from the Lord, and devoured them, and they died before the Lord."

What a fearful story—Nadab and Abihu were struck dead while working for the Lord! The "strange fire" is left unexplained because the act was not as important as the principle that was violated. These two sons of Aaron were serving at the altar, but they failed to recognize the supreme importance of God's authority in the way they were to worship. They robbed God of the honor due Him and focused attention upon themselves.

The uninformed observer would not discern the difference between acceptably serving God and offering *strange fire,* but acceptable worship must be according to Divine command. We do not actually offer "strange fire" in our worship services today, but it is possible for Christians to neglect the study of God's Word, resulting in numerous things being substituted for true worship.

"For the wrath of God is revealed from heaven against all ungodliness and unrighteousness of men, who hold the truth in unrighteousness . . . Because that, when they knew God, they glorified him not as God, neither were thankful; but became vain in their imagination, and their foolish heart was darkened. Professing themselves to be wise, they became fools . . . who changed the truth of God into a lie, and worshipped and served the creature more than the Creator, who is blessed for ever. Amen" (Romans 1:21,22,25).

MEMORY VERSE FOR THE WEEK: Philippians 4:4
"Rejoice in the Lord alway: and again I say, Rejoice."

NOTE:
10:3 **glorified** means reverential honor; 10:10 **unholy** means unacceptable; 10:13 **thy due** means your share; 10:19 **befallen** means happened to.

Leviticus 9:23: See Luke 1:9,10. **10:9:** See Luke 1:15; I Tim. 3:3.

"The ten commandments . . . written with the finger of God . . . were the work of God, and the writing was the writing of God." Exodus 34:28; 32:16

FEBRUARY 5: Read Leviticus 11-13.

Leviticus 11:47: "To make a difference between the unclean and the clean, and between the beast that may be eaten and the beast that may not be eaten."

Rigid commandments were given concerning which animals could be eaten and which ones could not be eaten. These laws clearly separated the Israelites from all other nations and were intended to teach the holiness of God.

Only the food that was considered clean according to Divine command was to be eaten. The animals that were acceptable for food were those that chewed their cud and had a divided hoof.

These two features represent two characteristics of the Christian life: (1) God's people must be separated from worldliness as a "purchased possession, unto the praise of his glory" (Ephesians 1:14). (2) In order for a Christian to remain clean, he should continue to meditate upon God's Word (like "chewing the cud"). We must daily read and feed upon His Word, for Jesus said, "Now ye are clean through the word which I have spoken unto you" (John 15:3).

Peter's vision on the housetop of Joppa clearly confirms that we Christians today are not regulated by these ceremonial laws (Acts 10). But they do teach us the necessity of a clean mind and heart if we are to live in harmony with God. "As obedient children, not fashioning yourselves according to the former lusts in your ignorance: But as he which hath called you is holy, so be ye holy in all manner of conversation" (I Peter 1:14-15).

NOTE:
11:10 **abomination** means unfit to use; 11:35 **ranges for pots** means hearth; 11:36 **fountain** means spring; 13:2 **rising** means swelling; 13:3 **plague in the skin of the flesh** means infection; 13:31 **plague of the scall** means skin diseases; 13:39 **freckled spot** means possibly eczema; 13:48 **warp, or woff** means woven or knitted; 13:51 **fretting** means spreading; 13:56 **rend** means tear.

Leviticus 11: See Acts 10:12,14,15; 15:29; Rom. 14:14,17; I Cor. 8:8; I Thes. 4:7; Heb. 9:10; I Pet. 1:15, 16. **Chapter 12:** See Matt. 9:20; Mark 5:25; 8:4-8; Luke 1:59; 2:21,22,24; John 7:22,23; Heb. 10:22. **13:49:** See Mark 1:44; Luke 5:14.

MEMORY VERSE FOR THE WEEK: Philippians 4:4
"Rejoice in the Lord alway: and again I say, Rejoice."

FEBRUARY 6: Read Leviticus 14-15.

Leviticus 14:2-3,5: "This shall be the law of the leper in the day of his cleansing . . . And the priest shall go forth out of the camp; . . . and the priest shall command that one of the birds be killed in an earthen vessel over running water."

The disease of leprosy made a man unfit for society, separated him from the place of worship, and even forced him to leave his home and loved ones. "He shall dwell alone; without the camp . . ." (13:46). He was an outcast and had to confess himself as unclean to anyone who approached him. He defiled everything and everyone he touched.

The leper is a picture of an unsaved person. Just as the leper was banned from the place of worship and the assembly of Israel, so the unsaved sinner is shut out from Jehovah's presence because of his defilement. He is unfit for fellowship with God.

The leper was helpless to pronounce himself cleansed. The priest had to first "go forth out of the camp" and make the sacrifice for the leper's cleansing (14:3). The restoration of the leper represents the precious forgiveness of our Savior, who cleanses us "from all unrighteousness" (I John 1:9).

Throughout the entire ceremony, the leper did nothing until the blood was sprinkled (verse 7). It is only after a sinner confesses his sin and is cleansed by the blood that he is brought into fellowship with God as a redeemed worshiper.

"And, behold, there came a leper and worshipped him, saying, Lord, if thou wilt, thou canst make me clean. And Jesus put forth his hand, and touched him, saying, I will; be thou clean. And immediately his leprosy was cleansed" (Matthew 8:2-3).

NOTE:
14:10 **three tenth deals** means 2.8 gallons; 14:10 **log** means pint; 15:21 **one tenth deal** means 15 pints; 14:32 **whose hand is not able** means who cannot afford; 14:37 **hollow strakes** means a depression; 14:37 **lower than the wall** means deeper than the surface; 15:2 **issue out of his flesh** means sore; 15:18 **an issue** means a running sore.
Leviticus 14:1-7: See Matt. 8:2,4; Mark 1:40,44; Luke 5:12; 17:12,14.

". . . we also joy in God through our Lord Jesus Christ, by whom we have now received the atonement . . . For if we have been planted together in the likeness of his death, we shall be also in the likeness of his resurrection."
Romans 5:11; 6:5

FEBRUARY 7: Leviticus 16-18.

Leviticus 16:30-31: "For on that day [of atonement] shall the priest make an atonement for you, to cleanse you, that ye may be clean from all your sins before the Lord. Ye shall . . . afflict your souls, by a statute for ever."

The day of Atonement was the most important day in the year. "That day" is referred to as a sabbath of sabbaths. The sacrifices offered on the annual day of Atonement cleansed Israel from all

MEMORY VERSE FOR THE WEEK: Philippians 4:5
"Let your moderation be known unto all men. The Lord is at hand."

their sins and failures so that Jehovah in His holiness might dwell in their midst.

On *that day*, Aaron, the high priest, received two goats for the sin offering, at the door of the Tabernacle. The first goat was sacrificed as a sin offering. Aaron then entered the holy of holies with the blood of this sacrifice and sprinkled it upon the mercy seat.

When Aaron's work was completed within the holiest of holies, he put his hands on the second goat (known as the scapegoat, verse 26) and confessed all the sins of the children of Israel. "And the goat shall bear upon him all their iniquities unto a land not inhabited; and he shall let go the goat in the wilderness" (16:22).

The scapegoat was forced to leave the camp—out of sight, forgotten, never to be seen again.

These two goats represent the two-fold purpose of our Lord's death on the cross. The first goat was slain, typifying that our peace with God was restored by the blood of Christ. The second goat represents the precious mercy of God in forever removing from His sight the sins of His people. God's promise forever stands, "I will remember their sin no more" (Jeremiah 31:34). We dare not condemn ourselves over sins already confessed and forsaken when God has forgiven and forgotten them. But we can only expect God to forgive and forget our sins to the extent that we forgive others. (See Matthew 6:14-15; 18:21-35).

"If we confess our sins, he is faithful and just to forgive us our sins, and to cleanse us from all unrighteousness' (I John 1:9).

NOTE:
16:4 **mitre** means turban; 16:19 **hallow it** means dedicated only for God; 16:31 **afflict your souls** means by fasting with penitence and humiliation; 17:4 **cut off** means destroyed; 18:3 **ordinances** means laws.

Leviticus 16:15,21,30: See John 1:29; Eph. 5:26; Heb. 6:19; 9:3,7, 12-14,25,28; 10:1,2,19; 13:11; I John 2:2. **17:11:** See Matt. 26:28; Mark 14:24; Rom. 3:25; 5:9; Eph. 1:7; Col. 1:14,20; Heb. 9:22; 13:12; I Pet. 1:2; I John 1:7. **18:5:** See Luke 10:28; Rom. 10:5. **18:20:** See Matt. 5:27; 14:14; Rom. 2:22; I Cor. 6:9; Heb. 13:4.

FEBRUARY 8: Read Leviticus 19-21.

Leviticus 20:6,7: "And the soul that turneth after such as have familiar spirits, and after wizards . . . I will even set my face against that soul, and will cut him off from among his people. Sanctify yourselves therefore, and be ye holy: for I am the Lord your God."

The death penalty was mandatory for many crimes. Among those mentioned that are becoming acceptable in our society today included worshiping false gods, association with familiar spirits (spirit mediums), and sexual perversions (homosexuality and other sex deviations).

Millions of Americans have rejected Christ and His Word; consequently, they are confused. They have turned to astrology, palm readers, fortune-tellers, and spirit mediums to find answers to their questions about life,

MEMORY VERSE FOR THE WEEK: Philippians 4:5
"Let your moderation be known unto all men. The Lord is at hand."

thereby rejecting Christ and the guidance of the Holy Spirit. These counterfeit guides have caused millions of unstable persons to be deceived.

Christ foretold that the immorality which existed in Sodom during Lot's lifetime will become acceptable in society just preceding the second coming of Christ (Luke 17:26-32).

It can be very dangerous to participate in these sins. It would be equally serious to find fault with God because He imposed the death sentence for committing them.

"Unto the pure all things are pure: but unto them that are defiled and unbelieving is nothing pure; but even their mind and conscience is defiled. They profess that they know God; but in works they deny him, being abominable, and disobedient, and unto every good work reprobate" (Titus 1:15-16).

NOTE:
19:4 **molten gods** means images; 19:5 **at your own will** means willingly; 19:16 **stand against the blood** means do anything to harm; 19:26 **enchantment** means magic, sorcery; 19:26 **observe times** means astrology; 19:27 **round the corners of your heads** means shave; 19:32 **the hoary head** means the aged; 19:35 **meteyard** means measures of length; 19:36 **just weight** means exact, legal; 20:2 **sojourn** means stay temporarily.

Leviticus 19:11-13,18: See Matt. 5:33,43; 19:19; 22:39; Mark 10:19; 12:31-33; Luke 5:3; Rom. 13:9; Gal. 5:14; I Thes. 4:6; Jas. 2:8; 5:4,12. **19:18:** See Matt. 5:43; 19:19; 22:39; Mark 12:31; Luke 10:37; Gal. 5:14; James 2:8. **20:9:** See Mark 7:10. **20:10:** See John 8:5.

> "And all the tithe of the land, whether of the seed of the land, or of the fruit of the tree, is the Lord's: it is holy unto the Lord."
> Leviticus 27:30

FEBRUARY 9: Read Leviticus 22-23.

Leviticus 23:1-2: "And the Lord spake unto Moses, saying, Speak unto the children of Israel . . . concerning the feasts of the Lord . . ."

The seven feasts of worship is a picture of the entire work of salvation.

The *Passover Feast* was first and pointed to the death of Christ for the sins of the world (23:5).

The *Feast of Unleavened Bread* was observed the day after the Passover (verses 6-8). This feast revealed the great truth that after his death, Christ became the "bread of life" (John 6:48). After we are saved we partake of His life through His Word.

The *Feast of Firstfruits* is symbolic of the resurrection of our Lord Jesus Christ (verses 9-14). At this feast, one sheaf (one handful of grain) from the first harvest was waved before Jehovah as an act of faith that God would give a great harvest. We also have faith that through Christ's resurrection we also shall be resurrected to join those who will be alive at His coming (I Thessalonians 4:15-17). "But now is Christ risen from the dead

---

MEMORY VERSE FOR THE WEEK: Philippians 4:5
"Let your moderation be known unto all men. The Lord is at hand."

48

and become the firstfruits of them that slept" (I Corinthians 15:20).

After seven sabbaths had passed, a new meat offering was brought, known as the *Feast of Weeks* (verses 15-22). This corresponds with the day of Pentecost that was exactly 50 days after the waving of the firstfruits (Acts 2). Then a long interval elapsed before the blowing of the trumpet (verses 23-25). The *Feast of the Trumpets* represents the time when this present age is about to close. It is God's call to the remnant of His people to regather in Jerusalem. The blowing of the trumpets on the first day of the seventh month preceded the great *Day of Atonement* (verses 26-32) and is the proclamation of that approaching day when the great High Priest, our Savior and Israel's King, comes the second time, in power and glory.

The final feast was the *Feast of Tabernacles* which was the feast of the in-gathering of the produce of the year (verses 33-44). It points to the coming glory of Christ's reign and the Christian's glorious inheritance in His kingdom.

"Therefore let us keep the feast, not with old leaven, neither with the leaven of malice and wickedness; but with the unleavened bread of sincerity and truth" (I Corinthians 5:8).

NOTE:
22:22 **a wen** means sores; 22:27 **dam** means a mother; 23:10 **sheaf** means handful; 23:13 **two tenth deals of fine flour** means 7.5 quarts; 23:13 **fourth part of a hin** means 3 pints; 23:39 **sabbath** means Saturday.

Leviticus 23:5,15,34: See Matt. 26:2,17; Mark 14:1,2,12; Luke 22:1; John 7:2; Acts 2:1; 20:16; Rom. 11:16; I Cor. 5:7,8; 15:20; 16:8; James 1:18; Rev. 14:4.

FEBRUARY 10: Read Leviticus 24-25.

Leviticus 24:4: "He shall order the lamps upon the pure candlestick before the Lord continually."

Aaron, the high priest, was responsible for keeping the light of the golden candlestick burning continually in the holy place, from evening to morning.

The light for the golden candlestick came from the sacred fire on the altar. It came directly from Jehovah and was not produced by either Moses or Aaron. Furthermore, there were no windows in the holy place to give light. The only light came from God's source of supply. This is also true in the life of the believer; he cannot receive light on spiritual things from any natural source. Unless the Holy Spirit reveals and sheds light upon God's Word, the Bible is a sealed book—even to the most educated person.

The light of His glorious Word continuously glows within and through the believer who prayerfully reads it each day. Although the candlestick was made with precious gold, it was not intended to draw attention to itself. Its only purpose was to hold the oil so the light could shine forth in the holy place. This is a picture of the Christian who has within him the Holy Spirit, who brings light and understanding of the living Christ through His Word.

"These things saith he that holdeth the seven stars in his right hand, who walketh in the midst of the seven golden candlesticks" (Revelation 2:1).

MEMORY VERSE FOR THE WEEK: Philippians 4:5
"Let your moderation be known unto all men. The Lord is at hand."

NOTE:

24:18 **beast for beast** means life for life; 25:44 **heathen** means Gentiles, a non-Israelite.

Leviticus 24:4: See Heb. 9:2. **24:7:** See Matt. 12:4; Mark 2:26; Luke 6:4. **24:16:** See Matt. 12:31; Mark 3:28; James 2:7.

> ". . . Except a corn of wheat fall into the ground and die, it abideth alone; but if it die, it bringeth forth much fruit."
> John 12:24

FEBRUARY 11: Read Leviticus 26-27.

Leviticus 26:3-4: "If ye walk in my statutes, and keep my commandments, and do them; then I will give you rain in due season, and the land shall yield her increase . . ."

Jehovah's great love to Israel was revealed when He said, "I will walk among you" (verse 12). He promised abundant prosperity, victory over every enemy, and peace in their land—"if ye . . . keep my commandments."

His presence would bring both personal and national peace. But it was also foretold that God would withdraw His blessings if they continued to be disobedient, and the end result would be, "Ye shall perish among the heathen, and the land of your enemies shall eat you up" (verse 38). Israel's history is proof of their rejection of His commands and persistent rebellion against His will.

If a man sows wheat, he does not reap barley. He reaps that which he sows. Sin and rebellion always produce destruction. (See Galatians 6-7.) Israel learned through bitter suffering that "the way of transgressors is hard" (Proverbs 13:5). This is an unalterable spiritual principle. It would be a perversion of God's love to imagine otherwise.

"And what agreement hath the temple of God with idols? for ye are the temple of the living God; as God hath said, I will dwell in them, and walk in them; and I will be their God, and they shall be my people. Wherefore come out from among them, and be ye separate . . . and I will receive you" (II Corinthians 6:16-17).

NOTE:

26:13 **bondmen** means slaves; 26:16 **consumption** means sickness; 26:16 **burning ague** means fever; 26:31 **will not smell the savor of your sweet odors** means will not accept your praise; 27:15 **redeem** means buy back; 27:26 firstling means first-born.

Leviticus 26:1: See Acts 7:43; I Cor. 10:14; I John 5:21. **26:12,41:** See Acts 7:51; Rom. 2:29; II Cor. 6:6; Col. 2:11.

MEMORY VERSE FOR THE WEEK: Philippians 4:5
    "Let your moderation be known unto all men. The Lord is at hand."

INTRODUCTION TO NUMBERS

There is just one-month interval in events between the last chapter of Exodus (40:17) and the first chapter of Numbers. The book of Numbers covers the 38 years of Israel's wanderings from the second month of the second year after the exodus from Egypt to the tenth month of the fortieth year.

The book of Numbers is the book of Israel's pilgrimage. It derived its name from the numberings of Israel.

In this book, the people of Israel are twice numbered—the first time at Mt. Sinai, when they started their journey; the second time at Moab, near the close of their 30 years of wandering (chapters 1 and 26; Deuteronomy 1:3).

After the first census was taken, the journey began, and Jehovah Himself led the way with the pillar of fire by night and the cloud by day. When they reached Kadesh-barnea, the Promised Land was within sight. But the report of unbelief by the ten spies destroyed the faith of the nation to claim the Promised Land, and they began 38 years of wandering.

Eventually, the old generation died and the new generation reassembled at Kadesh for a new numbering and a fresh start into the Promised Land.

The repeated complaints of Israel in the wilderness stand as a warning against all who find fault with the heavenly Father's arrangement of things. They could have entered the land of promise two years after leaving Egypt had it not been for the sin of unbelief. Think of the years lost— forever!

Unbelief bars access to God's promises, "So we see that they could not enter in because of unbelief" (see Hebrews 3:7-19).

Put your trust in the promises of God, as did Caleb who shouted, "Let us go up at once . . . for we are well able to overcome it" (Numbers 13:30).

OUTLINE OF NUMBERS

I. The Preparation for the Journey From Mt. Sinai
   to Kadesh-barnea near the Promised Land

First Numbering and Care of the Tabernacle	Numbers 1-14:32
Purity Regulations	Numbers 2- 4
The Offerings	Numbers 5- 6
The Passover	Numbers 7- 9
Leaving Mt. Sinai	Numbers 10
Spies' Evil Report	Numbers 13
II. The Wilderness Wanderings	Numbers 14:33-20
III. Kadesh to the Plains of Moab	Numbers 21-36
Brazen Serpent	Numbers 21
Numbering of the New Generation and Division of Canaan	Numbers 26
Levitical Cities	Numbers 34-35
Preservation of the Inheritance	Numbers 36

FEBRUARY 12: Read Numbers 1-2.

Numbers 1:3: "From twenty years old and upward, all that are able to go forth to war in Israel: thou and Aaron shall number them by their armies."

Nearly a year had elapsed from the time Israel left Egypt to the time God ordered Moses to organize an army and number "all that are able to go forth to war in Israel."

Only those who were true Israelites could be soldiers. "The mixed multitude" that left Egypt when the Israelites left were either Egyptians or those who were intermarried with Egyptians (Numbers 11:4). Because they were not true Israelites, they were not qualified to be soldiers.

God had promised to give the land of Canaan to the children of Israel, but not without many battles. Innumerable enemies had to be conquered before they could enter and possess the Promised Land.

This illustrates God's plan for His people today. There is a spiritual warfare, but many church members are like the *mixed multitude*—traveling with the true Christians but causing dissent and creating distrust in the promises of God.

The first qualification for spiritual service is the new birth—a true conversion whereby we become children of God, equipped by the Holy Spirit to victoriously claim His promises (see Ephesians 1:12-13).

"For they are not all Israel, which are of Israel: . . . That is, They which are the children of the flesh, these are not the children of God . . ." (Romans 9:6,8).

NOTE:
1:2 **Take ye the sum** means Take a census; 1:18 **pedigree** means ancestry; 2:2 **ensign** means banner; **far off about** means round about, on every side; 2:5 **pitch** means encamp; **set forth** means to begin journey; 2:31 **hindmost** means last.

Numbers 1:7: See Matt. 1:4; Luke 3:32,33. **2:13:** See Luke 2:23.

> "Thou shalt not avenge, nor bear any grudge against . . . the stranger that dwelleth with you . . . thou shalt love him as thyself." Leviticus 19:18,34

FEBRUARY 13: Read Numbers 3-4.

Numbers 3:12-13: ". . . the Levites shall be mine; because all the firstborn are mine; . . . both man and beast: mine shall they be: I am the Lord."

The Levites performed the sacred duties of the Tabernacle and were responsible for taking it down, transporting and erecting it.

Their service was to carry the Tabernacle and its furnishing through the wilderness. A careful study of the Old Testament suggests that the wilderness is symbolic of this

---

MEMORY VERSE FOR THE WEEK: Philippians 4:6
"Be careful for nothing; but in every thing by prayer and supplication with thanksgiving let your requests be made known unto God."

world through which we pass. And as Christians, it is our responsibility to manifest Christ on this journey. We must guard the holy things of our faith as faithfully as the Levites guarded the Tabernacle and its contents.

Many of God's people are unfit for service, out of fellowship with God, and have conformed to this present evil age. God has first claim on our life. Our priorities change when we recognize the lordship of Christ and realize that everything of eternal value must have its direction from Him.

Let us earnestly desire that our eyes be open to see the blessed privileges we have as Christians—called to be priests unto God.

"And hath made us kings and priests unto God and his Father; to him be glory and dominion for ever and ever" (Revelation 1:6).

NOTE:
3:3 **consecrated** means set aside for God; 3:12 **matrix** means womb; 3:31 **charge** means responsibility; 3:50 a **shekel** is a coin worth about a day's wages; 4:14 **flesh-hooks** means large forks, **basins** means bowls; 4:24 **burdens** means carriage; 4:48 **fourscore** means eighty.

FEBRUARY 14: Read Numbers 5-6.

Numbers 6:2,8: ". . . When either man or woman shall separate themselves to vow a vow of a Nazarite, to separate themselves unto the Lord . . . all the days of his separation he is holy unto the Lord."

The vow of the Nazarite meant that one separated himself unto Jehovah for a specific period of time—from a month to a lifetime. Among the lifetime Nazarites were Samuel, Samson, and John the Baptist.

The Nazarite separation involved three things: (1) his hair was to grow long; no razor was to come upon his head; (2) he could not touch or go near a dead body, not even the body of a dear loved one; (3) he could not drink wine or eat anything that came from the grapevine, such as grapes and raisins. These physical satisfactions were harmless in themselves, but the Nazarite willingly gave them up in order to be separated unto the Lord. The one who took the Nazarite vow was neither a legalist nor an extremist; he was simply a person who desired to go beyond the ordinary requirements of worship to give the Lord more of himself.

The performance of these three requirements was a *genuine* expression of the heart.

The Christian, like the Nazarite, should go beyond what he thinks is necessary to "just be a Christian" and should gladly give up all he holds dear to please the Father.

"Then said Jesus unto his disciples, If any man will come after me, let him deny himself, and take up his cross, and follow me" (Matthew 16:24).

NOTE:
5:2 **an issue** means a running sore; 5:3 **without** means outside, **defile** means contaminate; 5:7 **recompense** means make restitution, or pay back; 5:8 **kinsman** means a relative; 5:10 **hallowed** means sacred, for God alone; 5:13 **with the manner** means witnessed in the act; 5:31 **bear her iniquity** means have full responsibility; 6:2 **separate** means set aside in consecration; 6:4 **vine tree** means grapevine; 6:10 **turtles**

means young pigeons; 6:17 **meat** means meal made of fine flour, oil, and frankincense; 6:20 **wave them** means present them to God; 6:21 **vowed** means promised to God.

Numbers 6:1-12: See Luke 1:15; Acts 18:18; 21:23,24,26.

"Ye shall rejoice in all that ye put your hand unto."
Deuteronomy 12:7

FEBRUARY 15: Read Numbers 7.

Numbers 7:3: "And they brought their offerings before the Lord."

The princes (leaders) of the tribes were not to participate in the duties of the Tabernacle, but through their offerings, they were able to assist the Levites in their sacred responsibilities. Since they could not hold the position of preeminence, as did the Levites, they could have shown contempt or a jealous spirit and given little or nothing to them. Instead, the princes of the tribes brought large sacrifical gifts for the construction of the Tabernacle—they willingly brought huge offerings to help meet the needs of the Levites (Exodus 35:27-28).

Since the procedures for the offerings were exactly the same, it may seem monotonous to read all the details which were given for each offering. But the repetition of these offerings reveals the significance God places on *every* sacrifice given to support His ministry. Individual gifts and offerings may not seem important to man, but they are to God! He records every act of service —every cup of cold water given in His name.

As a Christian faithfully gives to the Lord's work, both his desire to give and his ability to give are increased. He experiences the joy of giving, and his faith increasingly grows as he accepts the truth of God's Word, "Give, and it shall be given you; good measure, pressed down, and shaken together, and running over, shall men give into your bosom. For with the same measure that ye mete withal it shall be measured to you again" (Luke 6:38).

NOTE:
7:14 a **shekel** is a coin worth about a day's wages; 7:19 **charger** means dish, platter; 7:21 **bullock** means young bull.

FEBRUARY 16: Read Numbers 8-9.

Numbers 9:1,5: ". . . In the first month of the second year after they were come out of the land of Egypt . . . they kept the passover . . . according to all that the Lord commanded Moses . . ."

The Passover Feast was a memorial of that great historic deliverance from the long slavery in Egypt (Exodus 12:41-42).

MEMORY VERSE FOR THE WEEK: Philippians 4:6
"Be careful for nothing; but in every thing by prayer and supplication with thanksgiving let your requests be made known unto God."

The first Passover was held in Egypt, where Israel's only hope of deliverance was the blood applied to the doorposts outside the house. Inside the house, the lamb was eaten by the undeserving Israelites who believed God's Word when He said, "When I see the blood, I will pass over you" (Exodus 12:13). Yes, the blood satisfied God and protected Israel from the death angel, while the eating of the Passover lamb satisfied and strengthened the family for their wilderness journey.

The second Passover was observed in the wilderness at Mt. Sinai as they faced the land of promise.

The third Passover feast was celebrated in the land of promise. This shows how essential the blood was in their redemption from start to finish.

The Passover is symbolic of the precious blood of Christ, the Lamb of God. (See Hebrews 9.) Every Christian looks back to the cross where Christ died to set him free from the power of sin. As we look forward to His soon coming, we have the assurance that His Word will sustain us through this wilderness journey.

"I am Alpha and Omega, the beginning and the end, the first and the last" (Revelation 22:13).

NOTE:
8:14 **mine** means for God's special purpose; 8:17 **sanctified** means set apart for God; 8:19 **plague** means epidemic affliction; 8:26 **their charge** means assignments or duties; 9:8 **still** means wait; 9:12 **ordinances** means rules and regulations; 9:13 **cut off** means severed, destroyed.

Numbers 9:12: See John 19:36.

"The people asked, and he brought quails, and satisfied them . . . but sent leanness into their soul." Psalms 105:40, 106:15

FEBRUARY 17: Read Numbers 10-11.

Numbers 11:4-6: "And the mixed multitude that was among them fell a lusting . . . and said, Who shall give us flesh to eat? We remember the fish, which we did eat in Egypt freely; . . . but now our soul is dried away: there is *nothing at all,* beside this manna, before our eyes."

The people of Israel could have reached the Promised Land in less than two years. They needed to endure the hardships for a little while and to praise God that they would soon possess the land which He had promised to them. But they refused to accept the wilderness trials and difficulties as God's plan to increase their faith and prepare them to fully possess the Promised Land. Instead, they repeatedly complained and hardened their hearts.

MEMORY VERSE FOR THE WEEK: Philippians 4:6
"Be careful for nothing; but in every thing by prayer and supplication with thanksgiving let your requests be made known unto God."

One of their complaints was their dissatisfaction with the manna. They complained that the manna was "nothing at all" compared to all the tasty food they enjoyed in Egypt.

Manna was to the Israelites what Christ and His Word are to the Christian. The food that God had provided for His people is often rejected for Egypt's dainties—the pleasures of the world which are daily perferred to the Word of God.

When they complained about the manna, God answered their prayer and gave them meat. It was His "permissive will" rather than His "perfect will." In Psalm 106:15 we see the results of their self-pleasure, "He gave them their request; but sent leanness into their soul."

Do we murmur or do we recognize that our present circumstances are "his good pleasure"? Is our supreme desire to please Him or to satisfy self? The believer's real satisfaction will be realized when we leave the choice to Him and truly pray, "Not my will, but thine, be done" (Luke 22:42).

NOTE:
11:16 **soul is dried away** means we are disappointed and discouraged; 11:10 **kindled** means intense; 11:12 **swarest** means solemnly promised; 11:20 **loathsome** means nauseating, disgusting; **despised** means regarded with contempt; 11:22 **suffice** means enough; 11:23 **waxed** means became; 11:32 **homers** means bushels.

Numbers 10:34: See I Cor. 10:1. **11:4,5:** See Acts 7:39; I Cor. 10:5,6,10; Jude 5.

FEBRUARY 18: Read Numbers 12-13.

Numbers 13:27,31: ". . . We came unto the land whither thou sentest us, and surely it floweth with milk and honey . . . We be not able to go up against the people; for they are stronger than we."

The twelve "heads of the children of Israel" were selected to "spy out the land" (verse 3), and the tribe of Reuben led the way. "So they went up and searched the land . . . and came unto Hebron" (13:21-22). It was at Hebron that Abraham had built an altar unto God. The spies had stood where Abraham stood when God promised him the land of Canaan. (See Genesis 13:18.) But neither of these thrilling events were included in their report. They could see only the high walls and the giants.

Although it was not God's "perfect" will, God knew their unbelief and "spake unto Moses, saying, Send thou men, that they might search out the land of Canaan" (13:1-2).

Moses spoke in faith when he said, "Behold, the Lord thy God hath set the land before thee. Go up and possess it. . . . Fear not, neither be discouraged." But the people refused and said, "We will send men before us, and they shall search us out the land, and bring us word again by what way we must go up . . ." (Deuteronomy 1:22). They wanted to see what lay ahead before they obeyed the Word of God. To depend upon our own logic and physical senses before we commit ourselves to the Lord's work is a denial of our faith in Him.

MEMORY VERSE FOR THE WEEK: Philippians 4:6
"Be careful for nothing; but in every thing by prayer and supplication with thanksgiving let your requests be made known unto God."

As Christians, we must recognize that spiritual victories are never obtained without a battle, and one must obey His Word in order to possess His promises.

"But without faith it is impossible to please him: for he that cometh to God must believe that he is, and that he is a rewarder of them that diligently seek him" (Hebrews 11:6).

NOTE:
12:8 **in dark speeches** means riddle in obscure language.

> "And they brought up an evil report of the land which they had searched . . . and said unto them, Would God that we had died in the land of Egypt!"
> Numbers 13:32; 14:2

FEBRUARY 19: Read Numbers 14-15.

Numbers 14:2,4: "And all the children of Israel murmured against Moses and against Aaron . . . Let us make a captain, and let us return into Egypt."

It seems incredible that the nation of Israel would ask, "Wherefore hath the Lord brought us unto this land, to fall by the sword . . . ?" (verse 3). How could they forget that God had miraculously delivered them from the death angel and from Egyptian slavery?

Little did they realize how their tenth complaint marked the transition of the nation from *pilgrims* being led to God to *wanderers* in the desert for the next 38 years. During this time, they made no further progress toward the Promised Land (verse 33).

When God pronounced judgment upon their unbelief, they confessed, "We have sinned," and they actually attempted to force their way into the Promised Land without God's direction (Numbers 14:44-45).

Many Christians today are just as determined as the Israelites were to guide their own lives. They are no longer pilgrims being led of God, but they are wanderers in the world.

"Having therefore these promises, dearly beloved, let us cleanse ourselves from all filthiness of the flesh and spirit, perfecting holiness in the fear of God" (II Corinthians 7:1).

NOTE:
14:11 **signs** means miracles; 14:27 **murmur** means complain; 14:32 **carcases** means bodies; 14:42 **smitten** means struck down, defeated; 15:2 **of your habitations** means your home where you live; 15:9 **three tenth deals** means 22.5 pints; 15:9 **half a hin** means 3 quarts; 15:22 **erred** means sinned; 15:30 **presumptuously** means openly, willfully; 15:34 **in ward** means in custody, jail; 15:39 **a whoring** means away from God, follow after desires of own heart and own eyes, play the harlot.

MEMORY VERSE FOR THE WEEK: Philippians 4:6
"Be careful for nothing; but in every thing by prayer and supplication with thanksgiving let your requests be made known unto God."

Number 14:11,22,23: See I Cor. 10:5; Heb. 3:8, 16-18. **14:23:** See Jude 5. **14:33:** See Acts 7:36; 13:18. **15:38:** See Matt. 23:5.

FEBRUARY 20: Read Numbers 16-18.

Numbers 16:2-3: "And they rose up before Moses . . . two hundred and fifty princes of the assembly, famous in the congregation, men of renown, and they gathered themselves together against Moses."

It appears that Korah was jealous over Moses' leadership; therefore, he became spokesman for the people and attempted to overthrow Moses so he could assume the leadership position for the nation. Two hundred and fifty "spiritual" leaders in Israel joined him in opposing Moses. But God viewed their opposition as a rebellion against Him and caused fire to come down from Heaven and destroy 250 people (16:35).

Korah and his followers may have been sincere in thinking that the majority should make the decision, but they failed to recognize God's authority in appointing Moses as the nation's leader.

It was not possible for Korah to have a right attitude toward God while maintaining a wrong attitude toward God's anointed leader. To the observer, it may have seemed like a mere personality conflict, but how different sin is from what it often appears to be!

Many ministers who are doing God's will today face criticism and opposition from those who do not recognize that God and His delegated leadership are inseparable (Numbers 16:5).

In the book of Jude, we read, "Woe unto them, for they have . . . perished in the gainsaying of Core*" (verse 11). This is a warning to us against the kind of politicking Korah did in his attempt to gain Moses' position.

The Bible warns us that opposition against God's Word and His authority is to be expected. "Mark them which cause divisions . . . and avoid them, for they that are such serve not our Lord Jesus Christ" (Romans 16:17-18).

*Core/Korah: *Core* is the New Testament Greek form of the Hebrew word *Korah* and refers to the cousin of Moses.

NOTE:
16:6 **censers** means firepans; 16:21 **consume** means to end, destroy; 16:30 **quick** means alive; 16:48 **stayed** means held back, ceased; 18:1 **bear the iniquity** means assume the guilt; 18:7 **a service of gift** means a freewill service; 18:17 **savor** means satisfying odor; 18:19 **a covenant** means an unbreakable agreement; **Gainsaying** means persuasiveness.

Numbers 16: See Jude 11. **16:5:** See II Tim. 2:19. **17:8:** See Heb. 9:4. **17:10:** See Heb. 9:4. **18:20-21:** See I Cor. 9:13; Heb. 7:5,8,9

MEMORY VERSE FOR THE WEEK: Philippians 4:7

"And the peace of God, which passeth all understanding, shall keep your hearts and minds through Christ Jesus."

FEBRUARY 21: Read Numbers 19-20.

Numbers 20:7-8,11: "And the Lord spake unto Moses, saying . . . *Speak ye unto the rock* . . . and it shall give forth his water . . . And Moses lifted up his hand, and with his rod *he smote the rock* twice: and the water came out abundantly."

In the first year of the nation's wanderings in the wilderness, God commanded Moses to smite the rock, and an abundance of water came forth (Exodus 17:1-6). The rock was a symbol of Christ, "They drank of the spiritual Rock that followed them: and that Rock was Christ" (I Corinthians 10:4). Just as there could be no water until the rock was smitten, there could be no indwelling of the Holy Spirit until Christ died. The water from the smitten rock is symbolic of the Holy Spirit, which was made available through Christ's death. The Lord announced this when He said, "If any man thirst, let him come unto me, and drink. (But this spake He of the Spirit, which they that believe on him should receive: for the Holy Ghost was not yet given; because that Jesus was not yet glorified.)'" (John 7:37,39).

The first smiting of the rock was a picture of God's judgment upon sin and a type of the death of Christ—once for all (Exodus 17). The spoken Word would have been sufficient thereafter, just as "whosoever shall call upon the name of the Lord shall be saved" (Romans 10:13). Striking the rock twice on this occasion, even though it was 40 years later, implied that the one sacrifice was not enough, thereby contradicting God's Word that says, "He died unto sin once" (Romans 6:10) and now He lives as a never-ending source to satisfy our every need.

"But whosoever drinketh of the water that I shall give him shall never thirst; but the water that I shall give him shall be in him a well of water springing up into everlasting life" (John 4:14).

NOTE:
19:2 **without spot** means no defect or flaw; 19:18 **hyssop** means an aromatic plant; 20:12 **sanctify me in the eyes** means hold me in reverential honor; 20:14 **travail** means painful trouble, adversity; 20:15 **vexed** means persecuted.

Numbers 19:1-3: See Heb. 13:11. **20:11:** See John 7:38; I Cor. 10:4.

FEBRUARY 22: Read Numbers 21-22.

Numbers 21:5: "And the people spake against God and against Moses, Wherefore have ye brought us up out of Egypt to die in the wilderness? for there is no bread, neither is there any water; and our soul loatheth this light bread."

MEMORY VERSE FOR THE WEEK: Philippians 4:7
"And the peace of God, which passeth all understanding, shall keep your hearts and minds through Christ Jesus."

The Israelites' discontent exposed their unbelief concerning God's provisions. They did not perceive God's purpose for bringing them out of Egypt.

Because of their complaints God's marvelous protection from the desert dangers was withdrawn, and thousands of people were bitten by poisonous snakes and died. Until this time, there is no record of anyone being bitten by a serpent. (Note Deuteronomy 8:15.)

After they realized their need for the Lord and His protection, God instructed Moses to make a "brazen serpent" and display it on a high pole. Although the dying Israelites may not have deserved to be healed, all who believed in the promise of God's Word and "beheld the serpent of brass" were healed (verse 9).

All mankind has been poisoned by "that old serpent, called the Devil" ((Revelation 12:9), and his painful bite perpetually torments his victims. "And sin, when it is finished, bringeth forth death" (James 1:15).

God sent His own Son "in the likeness of sinful flesh, and for sin, condemned sin in the flesh" (Romans 8:3; compare II Corinthians 5:21). Sin brought eternal death, but all who will believe God's Word and accept Christ as Savior will have eternal life.

"And as Moses lifted up the serpent in the wilderness, even so must the Son of man be lifted up: that whosoever believeth in him should not perish, but have eternal life" (John 3:14-15).

NOTE:
21:5 **loatheth** means detests; 22:3 **sore** means exceedingly; 22:4 **lick up** means consume, devour; 22:5 **over against me** means front, opposite; 22:6 **wot** means know; 22:7 **rewards of divination** means payment for his predictions; 22:11 **peradventure** means perhaps; 22:13 **leave** means permit; 22:22 **adversary** means enemy; 22:24 **thrust** means to press; 22:27 **staff** means long stick; 22:30 **wont** means customary; 22:41 **utmost part** means farthest extent.

Numbers 21:8-9: See Luke 24:26,27,32; John 3:14-15; I Cor. 10:9. **Numbers 22:** See Jude 11. **22:5:** See II Pet. 2:14-16; Jude 11; Rev. 2:14. **22:28-30:** See II Pet. 2:15.

"There shall come a Star out of Jacob." Numbers 24:17

FEBRUARY 23: Read Numbers 23-25.

Numbers 23:10: ". . . Let me die the death of the righteous, and let my last end be like his!"

The greatest prophetic revelation of Christ thus far in the Bible was given by the Gentile prophet Balaam. These prophecies were given when the Israelite nation moved near the borders of the Moabite kingdom. King Balak became very concerned for his own security. Knowing how the Israelites had overcome the mighty Egyptian empire, Balak attempted to hire Balaam to curse Israel. Balaam refused, saying,

"How can I curse, whom God hath not cursed? . . . Behold, I have received commandment to bless" (23:8,20).

King Balak offered huge rewards to Balaam several times if he would curse the Israelites. Balaam desired the recognition and rewards that King Balak offered, and they induced him to make several deviations from what he knew was God's will.

Balaam was one of many people who *know* the right Scriptures and "long to die the death of the righteous," but who are unwilling to live the life of the righteous. The Bible strongly warns us to beware of those "which have forsaken the right way, and are gone astray, following the way of Balaam" who run "greedily after . . . reward" (II Peter 2:15; Jude 11; also see Revelation 2:14).

NOTE:
23:22 **unicorn** means wild bull; 23:23 **enchantment** means magic spell; 25:3 **kindled** means aroused; 25:17 **vex** means provoke a war; 25:18 **wiles** means deceit.

Numbers 24:17: See Matt. 2:2; Rev. 22:16; Luke 1:78. **25:1-5:** See I Cor. 10:8.

FEBRUARY 24: Read Numbers 26-27.

Numbers 27:12,14-16: "And the Lord said unto Moses . . . Ye rebelled against my commandment . . . to sanctify me at the water before their eyes . . . And Moses spake unto the Lord, saying, Let the Lord, the God of the spirits of all flesh, set a man over the congregation."

In prayer, Moses had asked "to enter the good land that is beyond the Jordan," but the Lord informed the great lawgiver of Israel that he could not enter the Promised Land.

Moses' life was characterized by the often-repeated words, "And Moses did as the Lord commanded him" (27:22). Furthermore, it was said, "There arose not a prophet since in Israel like unto Moses, whom the Lord knew face to face" (Deuteronomy 34:10).

Only one recorded sin kept Moses from the Promised Land, but Moses represented the law that cannot allow one exception. "For whosoever shall keep the whole law, and yet offend in one point, he is guilty of all" (James 2:10).

Trying to live up to the law of God did not qualify anyone to enter the Promised Land—not even Moses. Yet, many people today believe that if they try to keep the Ten Commandments, God will be satisfied. But Christ said, "No man cometh unto the Father, but by me" (John 14:6). Although your external conduct may be as perfect as was Moses', without the Savior, you cannot be saved (See John 1:12).

"But before faith came, we were kept under the law, shut up unto the faith which shall afterwards be revealed. Wherefore the law was our schoolmaster to bring us unto Christ, that we might be justified by faith" (Galatians 3:23-24).

MEMORY VERSE FOR THE WEEK: Philippians 4:7
"And the peace of God, which passeth all understanding, shall keep your hearts and minds through Christ Jesus."

Numbers 28:9: See Matt. 12:5.

> "O Lord, open thou my lips; and my mouth shall shew forth thy praise. For thou desirest not sacrifice; else would I give it: . . . The sacrifices of God are a broken spirit: a broken and a contrite heart, O God, thou wilt not despise." Psalm 51:15-17

FEBRUARY 25: Read Numbers 28-29.

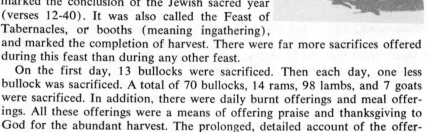

Numbers 29:12: "And on the fifteenth day of the seventh month ye shall have an holy convocation; ye shall do no servile work, and ye shall keep a feast unto the Lord seven days."

The Feast of the Ingathering was the last of the sacrifice festivals under the old covenant and marked the conclusion of the Jewish sacred year (verses 12-40). It was also called the Feast of Tabernacles, or booths (meaning ingathering), and marked the completion of harvest. There were far more sacrifices offered during this feast than during any other feast.

On the first day, 13 bullocks were sacrificed. Then each day, one less bullock was sacrificed. A total of 70 bullocks, 14 rams, 98 lambs, and 7 goats were sacrificed. In addition, there were daily burnt offerings and meal offerings. All these offerings were a means of offering praise and thanksgiving to God for the abundant harvest. The prolonged, detailed account of the offerings reveal how important—how vital—our praise is unto the Lord. Furthermore, acceptable praise is not primarily praising Him for what He gives us, but for who He is.

"That we should be to the praise of his glory . . . (Ephesians 1:12).

NOTE:
28:7 **hin** means 3 pints; 28:18 **servile** means laborious; 29:39 **set** means fixed schedule.

FEBRUARY 26: Read Numbers 30-31.

Numbers 31:7-8: "And they warred against the Midianites, as the Lord commanded Moses . . . Balaam also the son of Beor they slew with the sword."

Balaam failed in his efforts and his many sacrifices to keep Jehovah from blessing His people. But he did succeed in influencing the Midianites to invite the Israelites to participate in a religious ritual of Baal-peor. This resulted in the Israelite men committing fornication with the Midianite women. (See Numbers 25:1-3; 31:16).

MEMORY VERSE FOR THE WEEK: Philippians 4:7

"And the peace of God, which passeth all understanding, shall keep your hearts and minds through Christ Jesus."

Yes, it was the same Balaam who had said, "Let me die the death of the righteous" (23:10). However, the end result certainly was not what he had anticipated.

He was the prophet upon whom "the spirit of God came," the one who "saw the vision of the Almighty" (24:2,4). Yes, Balaam even prophesied the coming of Christ, saying, "I shall see him, but not now; I shall behold him, but *not nigh*. There shall come a Star out of Jacob, and a Scepter shall rise out of Israel, and shall smite the corners of Moab" (verse 17).

What a pathetic example of a double-minded man proclaiming God's prophetic message, yet instigating sinful acts among God's people for His own selfish gain!

"But I have a few things against thee, because thou hast there them that hold the doctrine of Balaam, who taught Balac to cast a stumblingblock before the children of Israel, to eat things sacrificed unto idols, and to commit fornication" (Revelation 2:14).

NOTE:
30:5 **disallow** means refuses to allow; 31:29 **for a heave offering** means to be presented as a sacrifice; 31:38 **beeves** means animals similar to oxen; 31:39 **tribute** means an assessment, taxes; 31:50 **tablets** means probably gold beads.

Numbers 30:2: See Matt. 5:33.

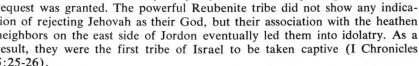

"And Caleb stilled the people before Moses, and said, Let us go up at once, and possess it; for we are well able to overcome it."
Numbers 13:30

FEBRUARY 27: Read Numbers 32-33.

Numbers 32:1,5: "Now the children of Reuben and the children of Gad had a very great multitude of cattle: and when they saw the land of Jazer . . . Wherefore, said they, if we have found grace in thy sight, let this land be given unto thy servants for a possession, and bring us not over Jordan."

When it was time for God's chosen people to cross the Jordan River and enter the Promised Land, the tribes of Reuben made the shameful request, "Bring us not over Jordon." What a contrast to the prayer of Moses, "O Lord God, . . . I pray thee, let me go over . . ." (Deuternomy 24:25).

The tribe of Reuben asked Moses' permission to settle just outside the Promised Land. Undoubtedly, they rejoiced and felt privileged when their request was granted. The powerful Reubenite tribe did not show any indication of rejecting Jehovah as their God, but their association with the heathen neighbors on the east side of Jordon eventually led them into idolatry. As a result, they were the first tribe of Israel to be taken captive (I Chronicles 5:25-26).

MEMORY VERSE FOR THE WEEK: Philippians 4:8

"Finally, brethren, whatsoever things are true, whatsoever things are honest, whatsoever things are just, whatsoever things are pure, whatsoever things are lovely, whatsoever things are of good report; if there be any virtue, and if there be any praise, think on these things."

Many Christians today are like the Reubenites. They are ignoring the Word of God and are inclined to be too concerned with worldly advantages.

"Wherefore I was grieved with that generation, and said, They do always err in their heart; and they have not known my ways" (Hebrews 3:10; also see Psalm 95:10). "Take heed, brethren, lest there be in any of you an evil heart of unbelief, in departing from the living God" (verse 12).

NOTE:
32:39 **dispossessed** means took possession; 33:52 **pictures** means carved idols.

FEBRUARY 28: Read Numbers 34-36.
Numbers 35:6: "And among the cities which ye shall give unto the Levites there shall be six cities for refuge, which ye shall appoint for the manslayer . . ."

God provided cities of refuge to protect those who had unintentionally committed murder until they could have a fair trial. If the manslayer could escape to one of these cities, he would be safe until the legal investigation had taken place.

If the crime was proven to be deliberate murder, the guilty person was handed over to the avenger. If the crime was justifiable or accidental homicide, he had to remain in the city of refuge until the death of the high priest. If he left the city before the death of the high priest, he could legally be put to death.

The laws of God demand the highest respect for human life. To spare the life of a guilty murderer would defile the nation, for "the murderer shall surely be put to death" (Numbers 35:16).

But Christ expects more from His followers than just keeping the old Law.

"Ye have heard that it was said by them of old time, Thou shalt not kill; and whosoever shall kill shall be in danger of the judgment: But I say unto you, That whosoever is angry with his brother without a cause shall be in danger of the judgment: and whosoever shall say to his brother, Raca [a term of contempt, such as "you empty-headed idiot"], shall be in danger of the council: but whosoever shall say, Thou fool, shall be in danger of hell fire" (Matthew 5:21-22).

NOTE:
35:11 **unawares** means unintentional; 35:18 **hand weapon of wood** means club; 36:11 **father's brother's sons** means cousins.

Numbers 35:30: See Matt. 18:16; II Cor. 13:1; Heb. 10:28.

MEMORY VERSE FOR THE WEEK: Philippians 4:8
"Finally, brethren, whatsoever things are true, whatsoever things are honest, whatsoever things are just, whatsoever things are pure, whatsoever things are lovely, whatsoever things are of good report; if there be any virtue, and if there be any praise, think on these things."

BIBLICAL REFERENCE INDEX

PRAYERS IN NUMBERS

Moses—at the starting and stopping of the ark .... Numbers 10:35,36
Moses—for more leadership .... Numbers 11:11-15
Moses—for Miriam .... Numbers 12:11-14
Moses—for Israel .... Numbers 14:13-19
Moses—for a successor .... Numbers 27:15-19

PROPHETIC REFERENCES TO CHRIST IN NUMBERS

Numbers 24:17	**PROMISED SEED OF JACOB**	Matthew 1:2

MESSIANIC TYPES

Numbers 24:19	The Messiah King	Revelation 19:16
Numbers 20:7-11	The Smitten Rock	I Corinthians 10:4
Numbers 21:6-9	The Brazen Serpent	John 3:14
Numbers 35	The City of Refuge	Hebrews 6:18

FIVE ANNUAL FEASTS

FEASTS	DATE			LEVITICUS
Feast of the Passover and Unleavened Bread	April 14-21 (7 days)	Nisan	Beginning of the religious year commemorating the Exodus and the establishment of Israel as a nation by God's redeeming power	23:5
Feast of Pentecost (also called Feast of Weeks, Feast of Harvest or First Fruits)	June 6 (1 day)	Sivan	Commemorating the First Fruits of Harvest and later the giving of the law. Observed 50 days after the Passover. (also see Ex. 26:16, 34:22; Num. 28:26; Deut. 16:9-10)	23:15
Feast of Trumpets	October 1-2 (2 days)	Tishri	Beginning of the civil year corresponding to our New Year's Day	23:23-25
Day of Atonement	October 10	Tishri	A day of remembrance when the high priest made confession of all the sins of the past year and made atonement in the Most Holy Place	Ch. 16 and 23:27-32
Feast of Tabernacles (Also called Feast of Ingathering, or Booths)	October 15-22 (8 days)	Tishri		
			Commemorating the life in the wilderness; thanksgiving for harvest; and marked the end of the religious year	23:34-43 also see Deut. 16:13

65

OFFERING	THE SACRIFICE	SIGNIFICANCE	REFERENCE
Burnt Offerings	Bullocks, Rams, Goats, Doves, Pigeons—were wholly consumed on the altar. It was offered every day, each morning and night.	signified complete self-dedication and entire consecration to Jehovah	Lev. 1
Meat (meal) offerings	Fine Flour, Unleaven Bread, Cakes, Wafers, Grain always with salt—a handful was burned on the altar, the rest was for the priests who ate it in a holy place. Always followed the morning and evening burnt offerings.	signified thanksgiving	Lev. 2:1-16 6:14-18
Peace offerings	Oxen, Sheep, Goats—the fat was burned: the rest was eaten by priests; by the sacrificer and his friends. There were three kinds of peace offerings; praise offering, votive offering, and free will offering. A meat and drink offering always accompanied this sacrifice.	signified fellowship between God and the worshiper.	Lev. 3
Sin offerings	Bullocks, Goats, Lambs—the whole animal was burned outside the camp. Sin offering was made for the whole congregation in all the feast days, especially on the Day of Atonement.	signified cleansing from the sin and reconciliation between God the worshiper.	Lev. 4
Trespass offerings	Always a lamb, with one exception (Lev. 14:12). The ritual was the same as in the sin offering except the blood was not sprinkled, but was poured over the surface of the altar. Where wrong has been done to another, restitution was made, including an additional 20% of its value.	signified reconciliation for wrongs committed against God's Law	Lev. 5:14—6:7

NOTE: Besides the offerings mentioned, there were drink offerings, wave offerings, heave offerings, and other offerings.

DATE	CHRONOLOGY OF THE	TEN MURMURINGS	REFERENCE
1st month	Egyptians pursued the Israelites	1st murmuring	Exodus 14:9-12
	Departure from Egypt		Exodus 12:37-38
	Cross the Red Sea		Exodus 14:15-30
	Bitter water of Marah	2nd murmuring	Exodus 15:22-24
	Elim		Exodus 16:1-3
	Wilderness of Sin		Exodus 16
2nd month	Food depleted: quails and manna	3rd murmuring	Exodus 16:1-22
	Greed and gluttony in gathering manna	4th murmuring	Exodus 16:20
	Gathering manna on the sabbath	5th murmuring	Exodus 16:26-28
	No water at Rephidim:	6th murmuring	
	water from rock		Exodus 17:1-6
	Battle with Amalek		Exodus 17:8-16
	Jethro		Exodus 18:1-27
3rd month	At Mt. Sinai: Ten Commandments		Exodus 20:1-17; 34:28
	Book of Laws		Exodus 21 & 24
	Moses 40 days in Mt.		Exodus 24:18; 34:28
	Moses' face shone		Exodus 34:29-35
	Golden calf worship	7th murmuring	Exodus 32:1-6
2nd year	Tabernacle built; Census		Exodus 25 thru 40
	Set forward from Mt. Sinai		Numbers 9:15
	after about one year		Numbers 10:11-12
	Complain concerning the way		Numbers 11:1-3
	Taberah: Fire, Quails, Plague		Numbers 11:4-6
	At Hazeroth:		
	Sedition of Miriam & Aaron		Numbers 12:1-16
	At Kadesh-barnea: Spies sent	10th murmuring	Numbers 13:33; 14:2
	People defeated; more laws		Numbers 14:45; 15:31
	Korah; 14,700 die		Numbers 16:1-50
	Aaron's Rod		Numbers 17:8

Until now they had been pilgrims. From this point on, they were wanderers. (See Numbers 14:32 through chapter 22.)

40th year	At Mt. Hor: Aaron's death		Numbers 20:28
	Israel defeats Canaanites		Numbers 21:1-3
	South from Mt. Hor: Serpents		Numbers 21:4-9
	East and North around Edom		Numbers 21:4
	North along East Border of Moab		Numbers 21:10-13
	Conquer Amorites and Bashan		Numbers 21:21-35
	Camp on the Plains of Moab		Numbers 22:1
	Balaam; Sin of Peor		Numbers 22 & 25
	24,000 Slain; Census		Numbers 25 & 26
	Destruction of Midianites		Numbers 31:1-18
	2½ Tribes Settle East of Jordan		Numbers 32
	Moses' Farewell; His death		Deut. 33 & 34
41st year	Crossed the Jordan		Joshua 3:16-17
	Keep Passover		Joshua 5:10-11
	Manna Ceases		Joshua 5:12

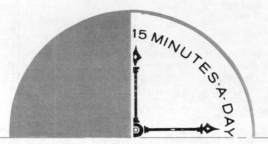

INTRODUCTION TO DEUTERONOMY

Deuteronomy is the fifth and final book of Moses. In 1:2-3 we learn that it was just an eleven-day journey from Horeb (Mt. Sinai, where the law was given) to Kadesh-barnea, near the southern border of the Promised Land.

For forty years their parents had wandered in the wilderness. They learned that God kept His promises—both in the times of blessing when they obeyed Him and in the times of judgment when they sinned against Him and disobeyed His law.

Deuteronomy was quoted by Jesus and the apostles more than any other book of the Old Testament. There are more than eighty references from this book in the New Testament. The key word in Deuteronomy is "obedience." When Jesus was tempted by the devil in the wilderness, every Scripture He quoted was from Deuteronomy (see Matthew 4:1-10).

"Deuteronomy" means *second law*. *It is* actually a review of the original Law to the second generation. The covenant which was first established at Sinai was renewed on the plains of Moab as the children of Israel prepared to enter the Promised Land.

The renewal of the covenant was more meaningful than merely a repetition of the law. Moses began "to declare this law" (1:5). ("Declare" means *to dig in* or *to go deep*.) It was important that this generation know the full truth and all its implications.

The most important lesson we should learn from the book of Deuteronomy is that if we are to cease our aimless existence, claim His promises, and see answers to our prayers, then we must recognize the importance of His Word.

OUTLINE OF DEUTERONOMY

I. History Reviewed	Deuteronomy 1 - 4
II. The Covenant and the Law	Deuteronomy 5 - 28
III. Moses' Final Preparation and Joshua Commissioned	Deuteronomy 29 - 34

"Behold, I have set the land before you: go in and possess the land which the Lord sware unto your fathers . . ."

Deuteronomy 1:8

MARCH 1: Read Deuteronomy 1-2.

Deuteronomy 2:24: "Rise ye up, take your journey, and pass over the river Arnon: behold, I have given into thine hand Sihon the Amorite, king of Heshbon, and his land: begin to possess it, and contend with him in battle."

For 40 years the children of Israel had wandered in the wilderness. Here on the plains of Moab near the border of the Promised Land, Moses renewed the covenant with the new generation of Israelites. He reminded them of their parents' disobedience to God and warned the new generation of the necessity to "Hearken, O Israel, unto the statutes" (4:1).

Passing around the borders of Edom, they encountered the Moabites and Ammonites (descendants of Abraham's nephew Lot—Genesis 19:37-38). The Israelites were forbidden to take anything belonging to either of these countries.

They were instructed to peacefully pass the Edomites (descendants of Esau), for God had given Mount Seir to Esau as his inheritance (Genesis 32:3; 36:1; Joshua 24:4).

The Israelites were to possess only the land the Lord gave them, and they were not to covet what He had not given them.

Some Christians don't accept God's authority and wisdom to bestow His gifts as pleases Him. We should never be dissatisfied with our own God-given gifts, nor be jealous or envious of another person's abilities or talents. What happy contentment there would be among God's people if we left the choice to Him.

"But godliness with contentment is great gain" (I Timothy 6:6).

NOTE:

1:12 **bear you cumbrance** means endure your problems; 1:17 **cause** means problem or dispute; 1:42 **smitten** means defeated; 2:9 **Distress not** means Do not fight with.

Deut. 1:16, 17: See John 7:24.

MARCH 2: Read Deuteronomy 3:4.

Deuteronomy 4:11: "And ye came near and stood under the mountain; and the mountain burned with fire unto the midst of heaven, with darkness, clouds, and thick darkness." (See also 5:22.)

MEMORY VERSE FOR THE WEEK: Philippians 4:8

"Finally, brethren, whatsoever things are true, whatsoever things are honest, whatsoever things are just, whatsoever things are pure, whatsoever things are lovely, whatsoever things are of good report; if there be any virtue, and if there be any praise, think on these things."

In reminding Israel of God's gracious care, Moses said, "These forty years the Lord thy God hath been with thee; thou hast lacked nothing" (2:7). Then he appealed to them, "Now therefore hearken, O Israel" (4:1)— seriously consider your responsibility as His chosen nation.

This same principle applies to Christians who, having accepted God's grace, walk worthy of their calling by being obedient to His Word.

We do not see a visible mountain burning, as was Sinai, nor do we audibly hear God's voice, as did the Israelites (4:12). Far better, through the shed blood of Christ we can approach the Living God in prayer and enjoy the fulfillment of our faith in Him. As we daily read our Bibles, the Holy Spirit will illuminate our understanding and direct our lives. We should listen to Him. (See Hebrews 12:18-24.)

"See that ye refuse not him that speaketh, For if they escaped not who refused him that spake on earth, much more shall not we escape, if we turn away from him that speaketh from heaven" (Hebrews 12:25).

NOTE:
3:18 **charge** means command; 4:12 **similitude** means form; 4:34 **God assayed** means undertaken; 4:42 **the slayer** means anyone who had killed a man; 4:42 **unawares** means unintentionally.

Deut. 4:2: See Matt. 5:18, I Pet. 2:9. **4:7:** See Jas. 4:8. **4:11:** See Heb. 12:18-21. **4:24:** See Heb. 12:29. **4:29-31:** See Heb. 11:6. **4:35:** See Mark 12:31-33.

> "And Moses called all Israel, and said unto them, Hear, O Israel, the statutes and judgments . . . that ye may learn them, and keep, and do them."
> Deuteronomy 5:1

MARCH 3: Read Deuteronomy 5-7.

Deuteronomy 6:4-6: "Hear, O Israel: the Lord our God is one Lord: And thou shalt love the Lord thy God with *all thine heart,* and with *all thy soul,* and with *all thy might.* And these words, which I command thee this day, shall be in thine heart."

The Israelites had to *believe* with all their hearts that Moses had spoken the word of God. To believe with "all thine heart" means that we must adhere to, rely on and trust in Him. This commandment was repeated many times and reemphasized by Jesus as the great commandment. (Note Deuteronomy 10:12; 11:1, 13, 22; Matthew 22:37.)

But Jesus revealed that our love for God must also include "all thy mind" (Mark 12:30; Luke 10:27). Not only our emotions must be ignored, but our intellect and understanding as well. To serve God, we must know His Word in order to discern His will. Then we can say with Christ as He spoke to the Samaritan woman, "We know what we worship" (John 4:22).

MEMORY VERSE FOR THE WEEK: Philippians 4:8
"Finally, brethren, whatsoever things are true, whatsoever things are honest, whatsoever things are just, whatsoever things are pure, whatsoever things are lovely, whatsoever things are of good report; if there be any virtue, and if there be any praise, think on these things."

Love for God also involves our physical being. We must not have an attitude of halfheartedness, but one of pleasing Him "with all thy might."

We can love God only to the extent we genuinely love our neighbor—"as thy self" (Luke 10:27). It is easy to assume that we love mankind, but the true test comes in expressing that love to those with whom we daily come in contact—"thy neighbor." We can "fake it" before others, but God sees our heart.

"If a man say, I love God, and hateth his brother, he is a liar: for he that loveth not his brother whom he hath seen, how can he love God whom he hath not seen?" (I John 4:20).

NOTE:
6:22 **sore** means grievous; 7:13 **fruit of thy womb** means your children; **kine** means cattle.

Deut. 5:3: See Heb. 8:9. **5:5** See Gal. 3:19. **5:7-21:** See Matt. 19:18, 19, Rom. 7:7. **5:11:** See Matt. 26:11. **5:22:** See Heb. 12:18-21. **5:31:** See Gal. 3:19. **6:4:** See Matt. 22:37, Mark 12:29-33. **6:5:** See Matt. 22:37. **6:6:** See Luke 10:27. **6:13:** See Luke 4:8. **6:16:** See Luke 4:12. **7:1:** See Acts 13:19. **7:8:** See Luke 1:54-55.

MARCH 4: Read Deuteronomy 8-10.

Deuteronomy 8:3: "And he humbled thee, and suffered thee to hunger, and fed thee with manna, which thou knewest not, neither did thy fathers know; that he might make thee know that man doth not live by bread only, but by every word that proceedeth out of the mouth of the Lord doth man live."

The desert wanderings were to teach the Israelites to lose confidence in self and to cause them to daily depend on His Word and realize that man does not live by bread alone but by the Word of the Lord.

Our Lord quoted from Deuteronomy 8:3 when He, too, was in the wilderness being tempted by Satan. His victory over Satan is an example of the power of God's Word to overcome the enemy. In each of His three testings, Christ overcame Satan by quoting the Word.

The Bible is the Bread of Life—our spiritual nourishment; and as we read it, His power and life become a part of us.

By the time most textbooks are ten years old, they are out of date. One of the most remarkable facts of modern times is that the Bible, although it is hundreds of years old, is still the world's "best seller."

God has preserved His written Word through many centuries and through it, He speaks to our generation today. The Christian who desires to please His Master will let the Scripture be his daily food and meditation.

"But he answered and said, It is written, Man shall not live by bread alone, but by every word that proceedeth out of the mouth of God" (Matthew 4:4).

MEMORY VERSE FOR THE WEEK: Philippians 4:8
"Finally, brethren, whatsoever things are true, whatsoever things are honest, whatsoever things are just, whatsoever things are pure, whatsoever things are lovely, whatsoever things are of good report; if there be any virtue, and if there be any praise, think on these things.

> "Observe and hear all these words which I command thee, that it may go well with thee, and with thy children after thee for ever . . ."
>
> Deuteronomy 12:28

MARCH 5: Read Deuteronomy 11-13.

Deuteronomy 11:13: ". . . to love the Lord your God, and to serve him with all your heart and with all your soul . . ."

Only by *loving* the Lord with all their heart was Israel able to *serve* Him with all their heart. It was then that He could bless their land (11:14-15).

Obedience to His Word would bring the Israelites into a land of prosperity. However, if in their prosperity they forgot God and served false gods, then He would withhold His blessings. Therefore, He told them to obey His Word, to hide it in their hearts, to bind it on their hands, to keep it in their minds, to write it on the door posts and upon the gates, and to teach it to their children (see 11:18-20).

The Christian who continues to neglect reading the Bible will not remain loyal to Christ.

Just remember, you will forfeit many blessings if you do not spend time each day with the Lord in reading His Word.

"And he answering said, Thou shalt love the Lord thy God with all thy heart, and with all thy soul, and with all thy strength, and with all thy mind; and thy neighbour as thyself" (Luke 10:27).

NOTE:
13:5 **thrust** means draw you away.

Deut. 11:14: See James 5:7. **12:32:** See Rev. 22:18-19. **13:14:** See II Cor. 6:15.

MARCH 6: Read Deuteronomy 14-16.

Deuteronomy 15:10, 11: ". . . thine heart shall not be grieved when thou givest unto him: because that for this thing the Lord thy God shall bless thee . . . Thou shalt open thine hand wide unto thy brother, to thy poor, and to thy needy, in thy land."

The Israelites were instructed to observe a "year of release" every seven years, whereby any indebtedness was to be cleared from all records. God promised to bless this peculiar covenant arrangement, saying, "for this thing the Lord thy God shall bless thee" (compare Leviticus 25:20-21).

MEMORY VERSE FOR THE WEEK: I Peter 1:13

"Wherefore gird up the loins of your mind, be sober, and hope to the end for the grace that is to be brought unto you at the revelation of Jesus Christ."

God has always identified Himself with the poor, the needy, and the helpless. The sufferings of distressed people touch His heart. When one gives to the poor, he lends to the Lord, who repays a hundredfold. (See Proverbs 19:17.)

At the "resurrection of the just" (Luke 14:14), those who manifest God's compassion for the needs of others will receive the joy and satisfaction of hearing the King say to them, "Come, ye blessed of my Father, inherit the kingdom prepared for you from the foundation of the world: for I was an hungred, and ye gave me meat: I was thirsty, and ye gave drink: I was a stranger, and ye took me in: naked, and ye clothed me . . ." (Matthew 25:34-36).

NOTE:
14:7 **cloven** means split in two; 14:21 **seethe** means boil; 15:1 **release** means cancellation of debts; 16:16 **empty** means without an offering to give; 16:19 **a gift** means a bribe.

Deut. 15:11: See Matt. 26:11, John 12:8. **16:9, 10:** See Acts 2:1, I Cor. 16:8. **16:17:** See I Cor. 16:1, 2. **16:19:** See James 2:1 **16:20:** See I Tim. 6:11.

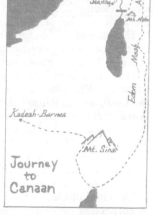

MARCH 7: Read Deuteronomy 17-20.

Deuteronomy 20:1, 4: "When thou goest out to battle against thine enemies, and seest horses, and chariots, and a people more than thou, be not afraid of them: . . . for the Lord your God is he that goeth with you, to fight for you against your enemies, to save you."

God directed Israel to completely destroy the people who were living in Canaan. No peace alliances were to be made with them, and none of the inhabitants were to be spared to share the Promised Land with Israel. This drastic dealing with the Canaanites was not done as revenge upon enemies, but it was God's judgment for their wickedness and rebellion (compare Genesis 15:16).

Although Israel was faced with these enemies who were far superior in number and ability to fight, they had no reason to fear. God had promised that He would fight for them, and their past experiences provided proof that God keeps His Word.

It was "God that brought thee up out of the land of Egypt," and to the believing Israelite, this was not only proof, but it was a promise that what He had done in the past, He would continue to do in the future.

MEMORY VERSE FOR THE WEEK: I Peter 1:13
"Wherefore gird up the loins of your mind, be sober, and hope to the end for the grace that is to be brought unto you at the revelation of Jesus Christ."

The Christian has an even greater promise that should give him added confidence and hope. "Being confident of this very thing, that he which hath begun a good work in you will perform it until the day of Jesus Christ" (Philippians 1:6).

MARCH 8: Read Deuteronomy 21-23.

Deuteronomy 22:9: "Thou shalt not sow thy vineyard with divers seeds: lest the fruit . . . be defiled."

The laws of this chapter were established by a loving Creator to protect His people from being corrupted by the surrounding nations and thus their ability to fulfill God's purpose be destroyed.

The same principle is true in the New Testament where Christians are warned, "Wherefore come out from among them, and be ye separate, saith the Lord, and touch not the unclean thing" (II Corinthians 6:17). Again, the Word declares, "Be ye not unequally yoked together with unbelievers" (II Corinthians 6:14). The Lord also asked, "How can two walk together except they be agreed?" (Amos 3:3).

A single-hearted love for God is the secret to victorious Christian living because "no man can serve two masters" (Matthew 6:24). There is room for only one lord in our life, and we must decide who this lord will be.

The child of God is not *of* the world but is *in* the world as a witness against its corrupting influences. He must live as one who represents the "light of the world." (Note John 1:4-5 and Matthew 5:14-16.)

"Be not ye therefore partakers with them. For ye were sometimes darkness, but now are ye light in the Lord: walk as children of light" (Ephesians 5:7-8).

MEMORY VERSE FOR THE WEEK: I Peter 1:13

"Wherefore gird up the loins of your mind, be sober, and hope to the end for the grace that is to be brought unto you at the revelation of Jesus Christ."

"Thou shalt not plow with an ox
and an ass together."
Deuteronomy 22:10

MARCH 9: Read Deuteronomy 24-27.

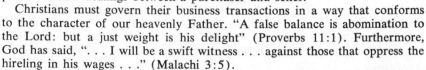

Deuteronomy 25:14-16: "Thou shalt not have in thine house divers measures . . . but thou shalt have a perfect and just weight . . . that thy days may be lengthened . . . and all that do unrighteously are an abomination unto the Lord thy God."

The Israelites were taught that all business transactions should reflect the integrity and justice of God. therefore, laws were established to prevent unfair dealings between a purchaser and seller.

Christians must govern their business transactions in a way that conforms to the character of our heavenly Father. "A false balance is abomination to the Lord: but a just weight is his delight" (Proverbs 11:1). Furthermore, God has said, ". . . I will be a swift witness . . . against those that oppress the hireling in his wages . . ." (Malachi 3:5).

These laws remind us of the necessity of conscientiously considering the rights and benefits of others in our business dealings. The Christian should always uphold God's high standard of honesty.

Taking advantage of those who are less knowledgeable than we are, or misrepresenting the facts are abhorred by the Lord. Refusing to pay what one owes another is dishonest, and we are admonished, "Owe no man any thing but to love one another" (Romans 13:8). On the other hand, we should forgive those who cannot pay us what they owe. (See March 6th: "year of release.")

Christians experience much joy in practicing the golden rule of doing to others as we would have others do to us (see Matthew 7:12). The Christian should live by the principle, let "no man go beyond and defraud his brother in any matter" (I Thessalonians 4:6).

NOTE:
24:10 **to fetch his pledge** means some security; 24:12 **not sleep with his pledge** means not keep it overnight; 26:17 **avouched** means openly declared; 27:17 **removeth his neighbor's landmark** means schemes to get his property.

Deut. 24:1: See Matt. 5:31, 19:7, Mark 10:4. **24:3:** See Rom. 2:29. **24:14:** See James 5:4. **25:2, 3:** See Matt. 10:17, Luke 12:48, II Cor. 11:24. **25:4:** See I Cor. 9:9, I Tim. 5:18. **25:5:** See Matt. 22:24, Mark 12:19, Luke 20:28. **26:19:** See I Pet. 2:9. **27:26:** See Gal. 3:10.

MARCH 10: Read Deuteronomy 28.

Deuteronomy 28:9, 15: "The Lord shall establish thee an holy people unto himself . . . if thou shalt keep the commandments of the Lord thy God, and walk in his ways . . . if thou wilt not . . . all these curses shall come upon thee, and overtake thee."

MEMORY VERSE FOR THE WEEK: I Peter 1:13
"Wherefore gird up the loins of your mind, be sober, and hope to the end for the grace that is to be brought unto you at the revelation of Jesus Christ."

Moses' final appeal to the Israelite nation was to make them understand that their enjoyment of Canaan depended upon their being submissive to God. Then he solemnly warned them of the consequences of sin: "Because thou servedst not the Lord, . . . therefore shalt thou serve thine enemies . . ." (Deuteronomy 28:47-48).

Many Christians are like the Old Testament nation of Israel—they have never realized the relationship that obedience to God has to their enjoying life.

"He that hath my commandments, and keepeth them, he it is that loveth me: and he that loveth me shall be loved of my Father, and I will love him, and will manifest myself to him" (John 14:21).

A seed will sprout in low-quality soil, but it will not grow into a healthy and useful plant unless the soil in which it grows has the necessary nutrients. The same thing is true spiritually. We can "sprout" [that is, be saved with very little scriptural knowledge], but just as plants need good soil to produce, we need spiritual nourishment. The person who lives a victorious Christian life sets aside time every day for reading the Bible and praying. This fellowship with God is vital for daily nourishment.

"If ye know these things, happy are ye if ye do them" (John 13:17).

NOTE:
28:27 **botch** means boil; **emerods** means tumors; 28:28 **madness** means mental disorder; **astonishment** means panic.

Deut. 28:9: See I Pet. 2:9.

"And Moses called unto Joshua, and said unto him in the sight of all Israel, Be strong and of a good courage: for thou must go with this people unto the land . . ." Deuteronomy 31:7

MARCH 11: Read Deuteronomy 29-31.

Deuteronomy 30:11-14: "For this commandment . . . is not hidden from thee, neither is it far off. It is not in heaven, that thou shouldest say, Who shall go up for us to heaven . . . but the word is very nigh unto thee, in thy mouth, and in thy heart, that thou mayest do it."

These words were spoken by Moses in his final message to the Israelites as he urged them to see God's commandments as more than just the Law written on stone or words to be obeyed. He referred to the Law as their life— "I have set before you life and death . . . therefore choose life . . . for *he* is thy life" (verses 19-20). These words reveal that the Word of God actually personified the presence of the living God Himself.

MEMORY VERSE FOR THE WEEK: I Peter 1:13
"Wherefore gird up the loins of your mind, be sober, and hope to the end for the grace that is to be brought unto you at the revelation of Jesus Christ."

Furthermore, he said, "But the word is very nigh unto thee, in thy mouth, and in thy heart, that thou mayest do it" (verse 14). In Romans 10:6-8, we find that this was speaking of Christ. Moses foretold of the time when Israel would see Christ as their Messiah. This Scripture goes beyond their lifetime to the time when the Messiah—who is the Living Word, the Way, the Truth, and the Life—would be in their midst.

"Who shall ascend into heaven? (that is, to bring Christ down from above:) Or, who shall descend into the deep? (that is, to bring up Christ again from the dead.) But what saith it? The word is nigh thee, even in thy mouth, and in thy heart: that is, the word of faith, which we preach" (Romans 10:6-8).

NOTE:
31:10 **solemnity** means set time.

Deut. 29:14: See Luke 1:55, Heb. 8:7, 8. **30:11-14:** See Rom. 10:6-8. **31:6-8:** See Heb. 13:5. **31:23:** See Gal. 3:13. **31:26:** See Rom. 3:19.

MARCH 12: Read Deuteronomy 32-34.

Deuteronomy 33:27: "The eternal God is thy refuge, and underneath are the everlasting arms . . ."

The wilderness journey through the Sinai desert was not an unfortunate, geographical obstacle between Egypt and the Promised Land. It was God's way of preparing Israel for the Promised Land. As they recognized their own inabilities, they should have learned to trust in the eternal God as their "refuge," protected by His "everlasting arms."

Moses reminded the Israelites that it was Jehovah who led them from Egypt, preserved them in the wilderness, and could now defend them in the Promised Land—if they would obey His Word.

There is enough power in His *everlasting arms* to nourish the downcast, to forgive and lift up the most corrupt person, and to protect the weak. His *everlasting arms* are long enough to embrace eternity, so strong they never get weary, and they fulfill the needs of all who will come to Him.

The *everlasting arms* are the Christian's comfort in the midst of conflicts which threaten to destroy him.

> "What have I to dread, what have I to fear,
> Leaning on the everlasting arms?
> I have blessed peace with my Lord so near,
> Leaning on the everlasting arms."

> (from hymn by E. A. Hoffman and A. J. Showalter)

NOTE:
32:44 **Hoshea** means Joshua.

Deut. 32:5: See Matt. 17:17, Acts 2:40, Phil. 2:15. **32:21:** See Rom. 10:19. **32:35, 36:** See Rom. 12:19, Heb. 10:30. **32:43:** See Rom. 15:10. **34:5, 6:** See Jude 9.

MEMORY VERSE FOR THE WEEK: I Peter 1:13
"Wherefore gird up the loins of your mind, be sober, and hope to the end for the grace that is to be brought unto you at the revelation of Jesus Christ."

INTRODUCTION TO JOSHUA

The book of Joshua covers about 25 years. It continues the history of Israel's entering and possessing Canaan after wandering in the desert for 40 years.

More than 450 years had passed since the Lord made the covenant with Abraham to give Canaan, the Promised Land, to Abraham's descendants.

Joshua, of the tribe of Ephraim (Numbers 13:8), was born a slave in Egypt. During the wilderness journey, he was a servant of Moses (Numbers 11:28.) He was with Moses at Mt. Sinai when God gave the tables of stone (Exodus 24:13); he ministered in Moses' tabernacle prior to Israel's Tabernacle (Exodus 33:11), and he was chosen to be one of twelve people who spied out the Promised Land. He was almost stoned by the people when he tried to persuade them to take possession of Canaan. (See Numbers 14:6-10.)

About that time, Moses changed Joshua's name from Oshea (Numbers 13:16) to Joshua, the Hebrew form of Jesus, meaning "Jehovah is salvation."

There is no other person in the Old Testament who had a closer similarity to Christ than Joshua. He had worked with his people in the brick kilns of Egypt and, like our Savior, had shared in their afflictions (Hebrews 2:18).

It was at the Jordan River that God began to magnify Joshua (Joshua 3:7); centuries later, at the same river, the heavens opened and the voice of God declared, "This is my beloved Son, in whom I am well pleased (Matthew 3:17).

Moses, representing the law, had to die before Joshua could lead Israel into Canaan (Joshua 1:1-2). Even so for the believer, the law passed away and was fulfilled in Christ (Galatians 3:13).

Israel's entering and possessing Canaan illustrates the Christian's inward spiritual conflict, victory, and blessings in Christ, who enables us to conquer self and Satan and to enjoy His rest. (Compare Hebrews 4:3 and Ephesians 3:16-21.)

OUTLINE OF JOSHUA

I. Entering the Land	Joshua 1 - 5
II. Conquering the Land	Joshua 6 - 12
III. Assignment and Possession of Each Tribe's Territory	Joshua 13 - 21
IV. Conclusion of Joshua's Ministry	Joshua 22 - 24

MARCH 13: Read Joshua 1-3.

Joshua 1:8: "This book of the law shall not depart out of thy mouth; but thou shalt meditate therein day and night, that thou mayest observe to do according to all that is written therein: for then thou shalt make thy way prosperous, and then thou shalt have good success."

The key to Joshua's greatness was his faith in God's Word. Forty years earlier he and Caleb were the only two out of the twelve spies who believed they could conquer the Canaanites and take possession of the Promised Land. The report by the others showed they doubted God's Word that He would give them victory.

Therefore, the crossing of the Jordan River, led by Joshua, was a major step of faith in God's ability to fulfill His Word. The earlier generation refused to place their faith in God's promise.

Joshua's battles were outward, but our battles are primarily inward emotional conflicts. "We wrestle not against flesh and blood [that is, our conflicts are not actually with people], but against principalities, against powers . . ." (Ephesians 6:12). Just as Joshua was strengthened to do God's will by meditating upon God's Word day and night (Joshua 1:8), so our faith is also strengthened as we daily read the Bible.

The more we read His Word, the more we realize God's presence. The unfailing mark of true discipleship is reverence for the Word of God and humble submission to all its teaching.

Only once does God use the word "success" in the Bible and He directly relates it to reading His Word saying, "then thou shalt have good success." Therefore, it is of utmost importance that every Christian spend time reading His Word if he wants true success.

"But whoso looketh into the perfect law of liberty [the Bible], and continueth therein [reading the Bible daily and in its entirety], . . . this man shall be blessed in his deeds" (James 1:25).

NOTE:
1:11 **victuals** means food and provisions; 1:15 **toward the sunrising** means toward the east; 2:5 **wot not** means do not know; 2:20 **quit** means guiltless.

Joshua 1:5: See Heb. 13:5. **2:1-5:** See Heb. 11:31; James 2:25.

MEMORY VERSE FOR THE WEEK: I Peter 1:14

"As obedient children, not fashioning yourselves according to the former lusts in your ignorance."

Joshua 5:13-14: ". . . Behold, there stood a man over against him with his sword drawn in his hand: and Joshua went unto him and said unto him, Art thou for us, or for our adversaries? And he said, Nay, but as captain of the host of the Lord am I now come . . ."

The first drawn sword mentioned in the book of Joshua is in the hand of the Lord as He appeared to Joshua.

God fought for His people. He did not come to assist Joshua but to assume leadership. God does not stand in the midst of our conflicts, giving a little encouragement here and there, but He comes for one purpose—to be "Captain of the host of the Lord."

Some Christian leaders assume that since God used them in a special way, *they* are the captain of His army. These self-appointed captains soon lose power with God and start seeking preeminence among men. They want everything to circle around themselves and serve their interests. It is God's place to lead; it is man's place to submit to Him.

Not until we recognize Christ as the "Captain" will we know what it means to please Him—to have the sword drawn on our behalf.

". . . he put all in subjection under him, he left nothing that is not put under him . . . For it became him . . . in bringing many sons unto glory, to make the *captain of their salvation* perfect through sufferings" (Hebrews 2:8, 10).

NOTE:
4:9 **unto this day** means when this book was written; 5:11 **old corn** means ripe grain; **parched corn** means roasted grain; 6:1 **straitly shut up** means securely closed; 6:3 **compass** means march around; 6:9 **rearward** means rear guard; 6:23 **kindred** means families; 6:26 **adjured** means solemn oath.

Joshua 5:6: See Heb. 3:11. **6:12-20:** See Heb. 11:30. **6:22:** See Heb. 11:31; James 2:25.

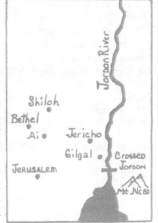

Joshua 7:11, 12: "Israel hath sinned, and they have also transgressed my covenant . . . therefore the children of Israel could not stand before their enemies, but turned their backs before their enemies. . . ."

Following the victory over Jericho, Joshua prepared to move into the hill country of central Palestine. A favorable report from *his* spies gave him even more confidence of victory than when

MEMORY VERSE FOR THE WEEK: I Peter 1:14
"As obedient children, not fashioning yourselves according to the former lusts in your ignorance."

they marched around Jericho. The Lord had not directed Joshua to send spies to Ai, nor did Joshua seek or receive instructions from the Lord to fight Ai. (See Joshua 7:2.) The most alarming aspect of this defeat was the fact that Joshua was unaware that the Lord was not with them to secure victory.

God withdrew His presence, protection, and power from Israel when Achan took a garment, some silver, and some gold from Jericho. Because of one man's disobedience, Israel lost God's presence and was defeated.

But the reason for defeat goes deeper than Achan's sin. God carefully exposed the fact that *"Israel* hath sinned, *they* [not just Achan] have transgressed . . ." (Joshua 7:11).

An important point that should be noted is that nine times in the first six chapters the Bible records how the Lord directed Joshua. (Note Joshua 1:1; 3:7; 4:1; 4:8; 4:10; 4:15; 5:2; 5:15; 6:2.) Then in Joshua 7:2-3, *Joshua and his committee* (not the Lord) unanimously decided what action was to be taken, which resulted in failure.

Often we make the same mistake as Joshua in that we sometimes take matters into our own hands rather than wait upon the Lord for *His* direction. Let us sincerely pray, "Shew me thy ways, O Lord; teach me thy paths" (Psalm 25:4).

NOTE:
7:5 **going down** means hillside; 7:6 **put dust upon their heads** means mourned; 7:11 **dissembled** means lied; 7:26 **Achor** means Troubling.

MARCH 16: Read Joshua 9-10.

Joshua 9:14-15: ". . . and asked not *counsel* at the mouth of the Lord. And Joshua made peace with them . . ."

The Gibeonites knew they would soon be destroyed unless, through lies and disguise, they could deceive Joshua into making a peaceful alliance.

The Gibeonites, with their pious talk, were *welcomed* by Joshua into the congregation of Israel. Had Joshua prayed and waited for God's answer, God would have exposed their deception. This is the second time Joshua made a decision without direction from God.

This experience reveals how impossible it is to discern God's will by human reasoning. By our having a knowledge of God's Word, the Holy Spirit can better expose the deceptions of Satan in our life.

Israel's enemies were visible—men, armies, and nations—but ours are spiritual—"rulers of the darkness of this world . ' ..' (Ephesians 6:12).

There are often unconquered strongholds within the mind, such as hate, jealously, greed, strife, and many forms of lust, that masquerade like the Gibeonites behind pious talk and persuasive prayers.

"These things I have spoken unto you, that in me ye might have peace. In the world ye shall have tribulation: but be of good cheer; I have overcome the world" (John 16:33).

MEMORY VERSE FOR THE WEEK: I Peter 1:14
"As obedient children, not fashioning yourselves according to the former lusts in your ignorance."

NOTE:
9:5 **clouted** means patched; 9:6 **league with us** means covenant treaty; 10:10 **discomfited** means caused them to panic; 10:40 **springs** means slopes.

MARCH 17: Read Joshua 11-13.

Joshua 11:5, 8a, 23a: "And when all these kings were met together, they came and pitched together at the waters of Merom, to fight against Israel . . . And the Lord delivered them into the hand of Israel, who smote them, and chased them unto great Zidon . . . So Joshua took the whole land, according to all that the Lord said unto Moses . . ."

In the battle of Beth-horon where the sun stood still, Joshua defeated the kings of the South.

As word of Israel's victories spread, the soldiers of the Canaanite cities of the North banded together against Israel, "even as the sand that is upon the seashore in multitude, with horses and chariots very many" (11:4). It was the largest army that the Israelites had faced, and this battle was the first time they had encountered horsemen and war chariots. Their victory over these kings of the North at Merom gave the Israelites control of the Promised Land.

This fierce battle did not come when they first entered Canaan, which indicates how God seeks to lead us one step at a time to accomplish His purposes. God's promises have been standing a long time! It is man's unwillingness to accept what is promised that causes the "wandering in the wilderness."

No matter how strong the enemy is, how cunningly his plans are laid, or how he may come upon us with a host to terrify, Christians can be "more than conquerors."

"For whatsoever is born of God overcometh the world: and this is the victory that overcometh the world, even our faith" (I John 5:4).

NOTE:
11:9 **houghed** means crippled; 13:1 **possessed** means conquered; 13:22 **soothsayer** means fortune-teller.

MEMORY VERSE FOR THE WEEK: I Peter 1:14
"As obedient children, not fashioning yourselves according to the former lusts in your ignorance."

MARCH 18: Read Joshua 14-16.

Joshua 14:1-3: ". . . the children of Israel inherited in the land of Canaan . . . as the Lord commanded by the hand of Moses, for the nine tribes, and for the half tribe. For Moses had given the inheritance of two tribes and an half tribe on the other side Jordan . . ."

The casual reader may fail to see God's guidance in the Israelites' taking possession of Canaan. The dividing of Canaan to the various tribes has a spiritual meaning. God is not merely filling up pages with unnecessary words. Why should the Holy Spirit record all these things if they have no meaning to our lives? God's Word says, "All scripture is given by inspiration of God, and is profitable . . ." (II Timothy 3:16).

The land of Canaan was to be divided among the twelve tribes as God directed; however, it appears He only directed in the site, and not the size. Just think! God's choice is interwoven with the willing efforts of His own people. The boundaries were determined by each tribe and their exercise of faith to possess the land allotted to them—"According to your faith be it unto you" (Matthew 9:29).

No life is ever left to chance, but God has a plan for everyone. He always gives His best to those who leave the choice to Him.

"Whatsoever thy hand findeth to do, do it with thy might" (Ecclesiastes 9:10).

NOTE:
14:7 **to espy** means to scout or spy; 14:9 **sware** means promised.

Within the Tabernacle at Shiloh was the Ark of the Covenant.

MARCH 19: Read Joshua 17-19.

Joshua 18:1: "And the whole congregation of the children of Israel assembled together at Shiloh, and set up the tabernacle of the congregation there. And the land was subdued before them."

The first mention of Shiloh was made centuries before Joshua was born. Jacob prophesied that the promised Messiah *would* come through the tribe of Judah, saying, "The sceptre shall not depart from Judah, nor a lawgiver from between his feet, until Shiloh come" (Genesis 49:10). The sceptre (a king's rod used as a symbol of royal authority) referred to the forthcoming reign of Christ. (See Numbers 24:17; Psalm 45:6; Hebrews 1:8.) This was one of the first prophetic revelations of Christ as King.

Shiloh was the place that God chose to set up the Tabernacle, thus making Shiloh the capital city of Canaan. The Tabernacle remained at Shiloh through the period of Joshua and the Judges until the time of Eli (I Samuel 4:3)—about 400 years later.

MEMORY VERSE FOR THE WEEK: I Peter 1:14
"As obedient children, not fashioning yourselves according to the former lusts in your ignorance."

Within the Tabernacle was the ark of the covenant, containing the commandments of God which represented the presence of the Lord, their King. When the presence of their King had been established at Shiloh, there was peace and security, "and the land was subdued before them" (18:1).

Whenever a decision had to be made, they assembled at Shiloh. It was at Shiloh that the Lord divided the land to each tribe. (See 18:8-10; 19:51; 21:2; 22:9, 12.) This emphasizes once again the importance of presenting every problem to God in prayer and then trusting Him. We should not be frustrated about anything if the God of Shiloh truly reigns in our lives.

"Now the Lord of peace himself give you peace always by all means" (II Thessalonians 3:16).

NOTE:
17:13 **to tribute** means forced labor; 17:18 **is a wood** means forest; 18:6 **describe the land** means diagram.

Joshua 18:1: See Acts 7:45.

MARCH 20: Read Joshua 20-21.

Joshua 21:43-45: "And the Lord gave unto Israel all the land which he sware to give unto his fathers [Abraham, Isaac, and Jacob] . . . according to all that he sware unto their fathers . . . there failed not ought of any good thing which the Lord had spoken unto the house of Israel; all came to pass."

Faith in God's Word led Abraham to the Promised Land, thus partially fulfilling God's covenant promise (see Hebrews 11:9). However, the real inheritance that God promised Abraham was more than a great Israelite nation in Canaan; it was a spiritual nation through Christ.

God's call to Abraham meant separating himself from all earthly ties and securities. The fulfillment of that promise was dependent upon Abraham's blind obedience, for "he went out, not knowing whither he went" (Hebrews 11:8). Abraham did more than just *believe* in God's ability to provide a country and a nation. By faith, he forsook everything in obedience to Divine command.

It is evident, then, that faith is more than having absolute confidence in the accuracy of historical biblical truths. It is believing the Lord will fulfill His promises, even though we do not see any outward evidence on which to base this faith.

Saving faith involves active, personal trust and commitment of oneself to the Lord Jesus Christ. We receive faith as we hear His Word (Romans 10:17). The *believer's faith* is accepting what our Lord has said, committing our everyday circumstances and problems to Him, and believing and trusting Him to work out the events in our lives.

"And being fully persuaded that, what he had promised, he was able to perform" (Romans 4:21).

NOTE:
20:3 **unwittingly** means unintentionally; 21:2 **suburbs** means pasture lands; 21:32 **refuse** means protection.

MEMORY VERSE FOR THE WEEK: I Peter 1:15
"But as he which hath called you is holy, so be ye holy in all manner of conversation."

MARCH 21: Read Joshua 22-24.

Joshua 22:9, 10: ". . . and the children of Reuben . . . Gad . . . and Manasseh . . . departed from the children of Israel *out of Shiloh* . . . and built there an altar by Jordan, a great altar to see . . ."

At the end of the united campaign to possess the Promised Land, Joshua released the tribes of Reuben, Gad, and Manasseh, and they "departed . . . out of Shiloh"—the place of God's presence—and returned to their homes where they had settled seven years earlier.

They had asked Moses for permission to settle in the territory "just outside the promised land" where the pasture for their herds was so plentiful.

This serious disregard for the Abrahamic Covenant revealed that the tribes of Reuben, Gad, and the half tribe of Manasseh were more concerned about increasing their possessions outside Canaan than they were in fulfilling God's purpose for them as a nation.

Upon reaching the Jordan River on their return home, a sense of uncertainty and insecurity caused them to make their second major mistake. They erected a "great altar" (22:10) as a *symbol of unity* between themselves and all the tribes within the Promised Land.

There was no direction from the Lord to build this second altar. Furthermore, the Hebrew word for "altar" has only one meaning—"place of sacrifice," and not "a symbol of unity," as they suggested. Some Christians are like those tribes—living outside the promises of God and missing the true meaning of the altar, which means sacrificing *their interest for God's will.* "If ye know these things, happy are ye if ye do them" (John 13:17).

NOTE:
22:10 **altar to see to** means look upon as one would a monument; 22:29 **meat offerings** means meal offerings; 23:1 **waxed old** means grew old; 23:8 **cleave** means remain faithful; 24:7 **covered them** means drowned.

Joshua 24:20: See Acts 7:42.

INTRODUCTION TO JUDGES

The book of Judges is a continuation of the history of God's covenant people from the days of Joshua to Samuel the prophet.

After Joshua died, "there arose another generation after them, which knew not the Lord . . . and served Baal and Ashtaroth" (see 2:10-13). This marked the turning point in the conquest of the Promised Land.

After Joshua's death, self-interest weakened national unity. Most of the tribes were unable to occupy their allotted territory (Judges 18); civil wars broke out (Judges 12:1-6; 20); and some, such as Simeon, ceased to exist as an independent tribe (Joshua 19:1-9).

There was no central government among the twelve tribes, nor did they have a leader such as Moses or Joshua. During this period of history, the Israelite nation did not take their covenant responsibilities seriously.

After the children of Israel were settled in prosperous Canaan, they did not fully obey God in completely destroying the inhabitants of the land. Instead, they made compromises, whenever possible, to avoid war, and they were soon participating in idol worship. Because of this, "the Lord delivered" them to invading nations who oppressed them. But each time the "children of Israel cried unto the Lord," He sent a deliverer, pointing out the spiritual lesson that when God's people pray, He brings deliverance; but when they continue to sin and refuse to repent, He withdraws His blessings and protection (2:6—3:6).

By the time of Samuel, the last of the Judges, the Israelites as a nation had almost been destroyed by the Philistines (I Samuel 4:7; 13:19-23).

The events of this book appear to have ended about a generation before Saul became king. The exact duration of the period of the Judges is uncertain, but Jephthah, who lived near the end of the period, spoke of it as 300 years (11:26).

OUTLINE OF JUDGES

MARCH 22: Read Judges 1-3.

Judges 1:19: "And the Lord was with Judah; and he drove out the inhabitants of the mountain; but could not drive out the inhabitants of the valley, because they had chariots of iron." (Also see 2:10-11.)

Following the death of Joshua, the tribe of Judah had been chosen to lead the war, but they did not have the faith of Caleb, who ". . . wholly followed the Lord God of Israel" (Joshua 14:14).

"The Lord said, *Judah* shall go up," but Judah said to *Simeon,* "Come up with me . . ." (Judges 1:2-3). Then it appears that Simeon took the leadership, for we read: "Judah went *with Simeon* . . ." (1:17). This revealed Judah's lack of faith in God alone, and he certainly did not trust the Lord later when they were confronted by an army with iron chariots.

Nowhere in all the history of Israel do we read of their being defeated by an army that had iron chariots. However, the tribe of Judah failed to believe God who said, "When thou goest out to battle against thine enemies, and seest horses and chariots, and people more than thou, be not afraid of them" (Deuteronomy 20:1).

Doubting God's ability to answer prayer and His willingness to keep His Word is a dishonor to Him. Our faith is weakened when we dishonor the Lord by trusting in something or someone other than God Himself.

"Let him ask in faith, nothing wavering. For he that wavereth is like a wave of the sea driven with the wind and tossed" (James 1:6).

NOTE:

1:23 **descry** means spy—as to search out; 1:30 **tributaries** means forced laborers; 2:5 **Bochim** means weepers.

Judges 2:16: See Acts 13:20.

"Barak pursued . . . and all the host of Sisera fell upon the edge of the sword." Judges 4:16

MARCH 23: Read Judges 3-5.

Judges 4:2, 14: "And the Lord sold them into the land of Jabin, king of Canaan . . . And Deborah said unto Barak, Up: for this is the day in which the Lord hath delievered Sisera into thine hand."

Because of their fear and lack of faith, the Lord delivered the Israelites into the hand of Jabin, king of Canaan, for 20 years. We do not find any record of Barak or any other man in Israel praying for the Lord's guidance or deliverance at this desperate time in their history.

Deborah's faith in God's Word gave her the courage to urge Barak to go to war against Sisera and the 900 chariots of iron. Through her spiritual leadership God brought peace to the land for forty years (5:31).

The name *Deborah* means "the Word." It is God's Word and intercessory prayer that delivers us from the oppressor. "He sent his word, and healed them, and delivered them from all their destructions" (Psalm 107:20).

The Lord is seeking Christians today who will intercede in prayer on behalf of His people. His Word tells us He is willing and waiting to release His people from the power of sin, but too many love this present evil age and are willing captives of Satan.

"And he saw that there was no man, and wondered that there was no intercessor: therefore his arm brought salvation unto him; and his righteousness, it sustained him" (Isaiah 59:16).

NOTE:

3:4 **prove** means test; 3:7 **groves** means idols; 3:16 **dagger** means sword; **gird** means fasten; 3:22 **haft** means hilt; 3:24 **covereth his feet** means is sleeping; 3:29 **all lusty** means able-bodied; 3:30 **fourscore years** means eighty; 4:3 **cried unto the Lord** means prayed; 4:15 **discomfited** means confused and terrified; 4:18 **mantle** means rug; 4:21 **nail of the tent** means tent pin; 5:2 **avenging** means bringing victory; 5:30 **sped** means pursued the enemy.

Judges 4:6: See Heb. 11:32, 35.

MARCH 24: Read Judges 6-7.

Judges 7:2: "And the Lord said unto Gideon, The people that are with thee are too many for me to give the Midianites into their hands, lest Israel vaunt themselves against me, saying, Mine own hand hath saved me."

There was peace in the land for forty years because of the faith and courage of the prophetess Deborah. Then once again, they did evil in the sight of the Lord and were "delivered . . . into the hand of Midian for seven years" (6:1). After they prayed, God appeared to Gideon.

Although Gideon risked his life, he destroyed the idolatrous image of Baal, erected an altar to Jehovah, and offered sacrifices.

At that time, Israel was confronted with a vast invading army of 135,000 Midianite soldiers. Only 30,000 men answered Gideon's call to go to battle, but 22,000 were dismissed because of their failure to be alert. Only 300 soldiers remained.

Far too many Christians today, like Gideon's original army, are unqualified to serve God and are glad to be excused from sacrifice and service. They are too occupied with earthly things and are waiting for a more convenient time. Like Gideon's three hundred, the number of men and women who have enough faith to accomplish the impossible for the glory of God is amazingly small because ". . . they loved not their lives unto the death" (Revelation 12:11).

NOTE:
6:24 **Jehovah-shalom** means The Lord is our peace.

Judges 6:11: See Heb. 11:32, 34.

MARCH 25: Read Judges 8-9.
Judges 8:1: "And the men of Ephraim said unto him, Why hast thou served us thus, that thou callest us not, when thou wentest to fight with the Midianites? And they did chide with him sharply."

Jehovah chose Gideon, a poor peasant from the small half tribe of Manasseh, to lead the Israelites in conquering the Midianites. The tribe of Ephraim was much larger in number, but because of their spirit of self-importance, God could not use them as part of the three hundred. Not until the battle was over and the Midianites were being pursued could God use them. After the victory was won, they complained to Gideon about the way he handled the whole affair.

MEMORY VERSE FOR THE WEEK: I Peter 1:15
"But as he which hath called you is holy, so be ye holy in all manner of conversation."

Gideon humbly conceded the place of honor to them by saying, "What have I done now in comparison of you?" (verse 2). He was willing to praise them for their superiority and concluded by reminding them that it was God who had delivered them from their enemies. Gideon was faithful to God in reminding these proud complainers that the glory for all victories belonged to God.

Their finding fault with Gideon was actually a complaint against God, who had called and guided Gideon in bringing defeat to the Midianites.

"Let nothing be done through strife or vainglory; but in lowliness of mind let each esteem others better than themselves" (Philippians 2:13).

NOTE:
8:1 **chide** means quarrel; 8:3 **abated** means cooled off; 9:14 **bramble** means thistle.

MARCH 26: Read Judges 10-11.

Judges 11:1: "Now Jephthah the Gileadite was a mighty man of valour, and he was the son of an harlot: and Gilead begat Jephthah."

The elders of the country of Gilead desperately sought a leader to fight against the Ammonites who had invaded their land. The only man who was qualified was Jephthah, son of a harlot. The same elders (leaders) who had once forced Jephthah to leave the country later sent for him, saying, "Come, and be our captain, that we may fight with the children of Ammon" (11:6).

Many people in Jephthah's circumstances of being rejected might have said, "If this is how they feel, let them fight their own battles." However, Romans 11:33 tells us that God's ways are past finding out! Who would have thought that this illegitimate son, exiled and living in Tob (now known as the Syrian region), would one day be the only man among the thousands of Israelites qualified to occupy the position of Judge in Israel?

We often do not understand the way God arranges circumstances, but He does. It is not necessary that we *feel* God in our circumstances, for even though we may not be conscious of His presence, *He is always there!*

Christians often tend to rate their influence and effectiveness by how well people accept them. God has not called us to be popular or successful, but He has called us to remain faithful. Great victory lies in accepting *all* things from the hand of the Lord.

"And base things of the world, and things which are despised, hath God chosen, yea, and things which are not, to bring to nought things that are: that no flesh should glory in his presence" (I Corinthians 1:28-29).

NOTE:
Judges 11:1 See Heb. 11:32. **13:24:** See Heb. 11:32.

MEMORY VERSE FOR THE WEEK: I Peter 1:15
"But as he which hath called you is holy, so be ye holy in all manner of conversation."

"O Lord God, . . . strengthen
me, I pray thee, only this once,
O God . . . and Samson took
hold of the two middle pillars
upon which the house stood . . ."
Judges 16:28-29

MARCH 27: Read Judges 12-14.

Judges 13:25: "And the Spirit of the Lord began to move him [Samson] at times . . ."

Although the Israelites had been slaves to the Philistines for about forty years, we do not find any record of their having prayed even once for deliverance.

Previously, whenever Israel departed from following the Lord, "the children of Israel cried [prayed] unto the Lord." But this time, there was no prayer or returning to the Lord.

Even though Israel had forsaken Jehovah, God extended His mercy to them. His Spirit began to move upon Samson, the man who would deliver them. But Samson fell far short of fulfilling his calling, as the Lord foretold, "He shall *begin* to deliver Israel out of the hand of the Philistines" (verse 5).

Samson's life was filled with failure because of his self-centered desires, as revealed when he said, "Get her for me; for she pleaseth me well" (see Judges 14:1-3).

Samson went "down"—geographically and spiritually—when "he went down to Timnath." While he was in enemy territory, he was not able to cope with the temptations he encountered there.

The three women in Samson's life are a type of worldly attractions, as sin often is. They represent the fair, pleasure-loving world which seeks to rob the true Christian of his power with God.

"See then that ye walk circumspectly, not as fools, but as wise, redeeming the time, because the days are evil" (Ephesians 5:15-16).

NOTE:
13:5 **Nazarite** means separated unto God (See Numbers 6:2 for Nazarite vow.); 13:6 **very terrible** means reverently feared; 13:18 **secret** means wonderful.

MARCH 28: Read Judges 15-17.

Judges 15:11: "Then three thousand men of Judah . . . said to Samson, knowest thou not that the Philistines are rulers over us? what is this that thou hast done unto us? . . ."

Samson had become an outlaw among the Philistines and an embarrassment to his own people. When he tried to hide in Judean territory, the tribe of Judah, fearing the Philistine's revenge, bound Samson and delivered him to the Philistines (15:13).

MEMORY VERSE FOR THE WEEK: I Peter 1:16
"Because it is written, Be ye holy; for I am holy."

The actions of the tribe of Judah were typical of the low spiritual concern of the nation of Israel. They chose to pacify the Philistines who ruled over them rather than unite with Samson, who was anointed of God, and claim God's promise to bring deliverance to the nation. (See Joshua 23:5.)

Samson's life was also typical of the spiritual condition of the nation who had lost the vision of the covenant promise to claim Canaan as God's possession. Not once in the twenty years of his leadership do we read of his building an altar or praying for guidance to fulfill his calling.

Satan effectively seeks to cut off the usefulness of every Christian as he did Samson. Our only safeguard is a daily dependence on the Lord. The person who is unfaithful in praying and meditating daily upon God's Word will, like Samson, be misdirected and eventually lose the purpose of God's call for his life.

"But I keep under my body, and bring it into subjection: lest that by any means, when I have preached to others, I myself should be a castaway" (I Corinthians 9:27).

NOTE:
15:4 **firebands** means torches of flax on fire; 16:11 **fast** means securely; 16:25 **make us sport** means entertain us; 16:26 **Suffer me** means Allow me; 17:4 **founder** means silversmith.

"And the children of Dan set up the graven image . . . until the day of the captivity of the land." Judges 18:30

MARCH 29: Read Judges 18-19.

Judges 18:1-6: ". . . the tribe of the Danites sought them an inheritance to dwell in; . . . when they came to mount Ephraim, to the house of Micah, they lodged there. When they were by the house of Micah, they knew the voice of the young man the Levite: . . . And they said unto him, Ask counsel, we pray thee, of God, that we may know whether our way which we go shall be prosperous. And the priest said unto them, Go in peace; before the Lord is your way wherein ye go."

The death of Samson marked the close of the long period of the Judges. What follows in the remaining chapters is not a continuation of Israel's history, but it is given to illustrate the moral and spiritual level within the Promised Land.

Although the tribe of Dan was powerful in number (more than 64,000 men), they did not succeed in driving the Amorites from their territory. In fact, the Amorites forced the Danites into the mountains. The faith by which Joshua, Caleb, and others achieved their victories was missing, and their failure in battle caused them to be dissatisfied with the territory God had allotted to them. As a result, their spiritual condition continued to decline. If they had remained in the territory God had given them, they would not have entered the house of Micah and become involved in idol worship.

MEMORY VERSE FOR THE WEEK: I Peter 1:16
"Because it is written, Be ye holy; for I am holy."

Multitudes are deceived into believing that it doesn't make any difference where or how you worship. They say, "Let your conscience be your guide." But God leaves nothing to human choice. The Apostle Paul, by inspiration of God, wrote, "But though we, or an angel from heaven, preach any other gospel unto you than that which we have preached unto you, let him be accursed" (Galatians 1:8).

NOTE:
18:15 **thitherward** means turned in that direction; 18:21 **carriage** means baggage; 19:11 **Jebus** means Jerusalem; 19:17 **wayfaring** means traveling; 19:19 **provender** means fodder.

MARCH 30: Read Judges 20-21.

Judges 21:25: "In those days there was no king in Israel: Every man did that which was right in his own eyes."

The book of Judges closes with an explanation for the moral decline and spiritual decay that prevailed in the nation of Israel.

After Israel forsook God as King, they were defeated by every nation God intended for them to conquer.

God should have been accepted as King over His people, but these heart-breaking words were recorded four different times in the book of Judges, "In those days there was no king in Israel, but every man did that which was right in his own eyes" (Judges 17:6; see also 18:1; 19:1; 21:25).

A person's conscience can be a true guide only when he is guided by God's Word and when his life is surrendered to Christ. Otherwise, when "every man does that which is right in his own eyes," we can only expect lawlessness, immorality, and the deceitful misleading of Satan to follow.

When God's Word is ignored, as in the tribe of Dan, man is without a true guide, and his self-willed spirit will eventually lead to some form of false worship.

"Holding faith, and a good conscience; which some having put away concerning faith have made shipwreck" (I Timothy 1:19).

NOTE:
20:5 **forced** means raped; 20:6 **lewdness** means wicked conduct; 20:10 **folly** means wicked conduct; 20:29 **set liers** means set an ambush; 20:34 **sore** means fierce; 20:45 **gleaned** means picked up; 21:6 **repented them** means had compassion on; 21:10 **valiantest** means bravest; 21:20 **lie in wait** means hide; 21:22 **Be favorable** means Be gracious.

MEMORY VERSE FOR THE WEEK: I Peter 1:16
"Because it is written, Be ye holy; for I am holy."

MARCH 31: Read Ruth 1-4.

Ruth 4:13, 17: "So Boaz took Ruth, and she was his wife: and when he went in unto her, the Lord gave her conception, and she bare a son . . . And the women her neighbours gave it a name, saying, There is a son born to Naomi; and they called his name Obed: he is the father of Jesse, the father of David."

The family of Elimelech, including Naomi and their two sons, left Bethlehem in search of a more prosperous country and moved to the heathen land of Moab.

During the next ten years, Elimelech and his two sons, both of whom had married Moabite women, died, leaving the three widows in desperate circumstances.

Heartbroken, bitter, and blaming God for her sorrows (1:13), Naomi decided to return to Bethlehem. Her reason for returning was not because of any repentance for leaving the Promised Land, but she had heard that Bethlehem was again prosperous.

When Naomi spoke to her daughters-in-law about her hopeless future and urged them to remain in Moab, she was not aware that Boaz, her kinsman in Bethlehem, had become wealthy. But no matter how bleak Naomi's future appeared, Ruth was willing to go with her, saying, "Thy people shall be my people, and thy God my God" (1:16). The loyalty and love of Ruth for Naomi was richly rewarded beyond what she could have gained had she remained in Moab to seek self-interest.

Little could Naomi realize how God used her to bring the Gentile Moabite Ruth to Boaz and unite the Gentiles in the ancestry of the Messiah!

The bitter experiences of Naomi and the destitute circumstances of Ruth should give assurance to every despondent, defeated Christian. Out of our most bitter experiences, God can perfect His will. We should find pleasure in His ways and trust in the God who can love even a Moabite (Amos 2:1-3).

"Come unto me, all ye that labour and are heavy laden, and I will give you rest" (Matthew 11:28).

NOTE:
2:1 **kinsman** means relative. The people of Israel were to preserve their family heritage from the time of Joshua to the birth of Christ; therefore, the law declared that if a man died, leaving a widow and no sons, a near relative (kinsman) must marry her, preserve the ancestry, and pay whatever was necessary to restore her late husband's inheritance. Naomi's case was even worse, for she was widowed, had no living sons, and she was too old to bear children. Aged Boaz accepted the responsibility of kinsman by marrying Ruth and purchasing the property of her first husband's father, a near relative (2:20-21; 4:13-14).

Ruth 4:18-22: See Matt. 1:3-6; Luke 3:32.

MEMORY VERSE FOR THE WEEK: I Peter 1:16
"Because it is written, Be ye holy; for I am holy."

PRAYERS IN DEUTERONOMY—JUDGES

Moses—to enter the Promised Land .... Deut. 3:24-25
Moses—forgiveness for the people's idolatry .... Deut. 9:26
Israel—making atonement for undiscovered murder .... Deut. 21:6-8
Israel—confession on presenting firstfruits .... Deut. 26:5-10
Israel—the prayer of the tithing years .... Deut. 26:13-15
Joshua—for help from Ai defeat .... Joshua 7:6-9
Gideon—at the time of God's calling .... Judges 6:13-15
Gideon—for proof of his calling .... Judges 6:36-40
Manoah—for guidance in training his child .... Judges 13:8-15
Samson—for water .... Judges 15:18-19
Samson—for strength .... Judges 16:29-30

PROPHETIC REFERENCES TO CHRIST IN DEUTERONOMY

Deuteronomy 18:15	**A PROPHET**	Acts 3:20, 22

THE RULE OF THE JUDGES

About 300 Years

JUDGE	TRIBE	PEACE	OPPRESSED BY		SCRIPTURE
1. Othniel	Judah	40	Mesopotamians	8 yrs.	3:8-11
2. Ehud	Benjamin	80	Moabites	18 yrs.	3:12-30
			Ammonites		
			Amalekites		
3. Shamgar	—	—	Philistines —		3:31
4. Deborah	Ephraim	40	Canaanite	20 yrs.	4—5
5. Gideon	Manasseh	40	Midianites	7 yrs.	6—8
			Amalekites		
6. Abimelech	Manasseh	3	—	—	9
(Usurper)					
7. Tola	Issachar	23	—	—	10:1, 2
8. Jair	Manasseh	22	—	—	10:3-5
9. Jephthah	Manasseh	6	Ammonites	18 yrs.	10:6—12:7
10. Ibzan	Judah	7	—	—	12:8-10
11. Elon	Zebulun	10	—	—	12:11-12
12. Abdon	Ephraim	8	—	—	12:13-15
13. **Samson**	Dan	20	Philistines	40 yrs.	13—16

NOTE: The oppressions and deliverances were not successive, but in part synchronous. They were local struggles; and it is probable that, while one part of the land was enjoying security under its judge, other tribes were suffering oppression by foreign countries.

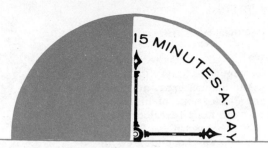

INTRODUCTION TO I AND II SAMUEL

The book of *I Samuel* is a continuation of the history of Israel from the book of *Judges*. It covers about 100 years. Preceding the time of Samuel, the twelve tribes were constantly at war with the surrounding nations and with each other. After Eli's death, Samuel became both a judge and a prophet, and he led the Israelites to a dependence on God, uniting them as a nation.

As Israel gained strength as a nation and Samuel grew old, the elders demanded, "make us a king to judge us like all the nations" (8:5). It was through the people's persistent demand for a king that Saul was chosen, and the result was failure.

Although Saul was privileged to live under the influence of one of the greatest prophets in history, he continually disobeyed the Lord's commandment, and eventually, "the spirit of the Lord departed from Saul" (16:14). Saul's forty-year reign is best expressed by his own words, "I have played the fool" (26:21).

The book of *II Samuel* is devoted to David's forty-year reign. *God* chose David, a man 'after God's own heart' (I Samuel 13:14). The key to his success throughout his life was his recognition of God's administrative authority over all the affairs in life. This was evident in David's challenge to Goliath, "I come to thee in the name of the Lord of hosts" (I Samuel 17:45). It can also be seen in his attitude toward Saul when he said, "I will not touch God's anointed." Throughout his forty-year reign, this beloved king maintained this attitude as stated near the close of his reign, saying, "For I have kept the ways of the Lord . . . For *all* his judgments were before me: and as for his statutes, I did not depart from them" (II Samuel 22:22-23).

OUTLINE OF I AND II SAMUEL

APRIL 1: Read I Samuel 1-3.

I Samuel 3:1,19,21: ". . . And the word of the Lord was precious in those days; there was no open vision . . . And Samuel grew, and the Lord was with him, and did let none of his *words* fall to the ground. . . . the Lord revealed himself to Samuel in Shiloh by the *word* of the Lord."

Samuel and the two sons of Eli grew up together in Shiloh, performing their duties in the Tabernacle. Hophni and Phinehas were indifferent . to God's Word, but Samuel grew in favor with the Lord, because he "let none of *his words* fall to the ground." This means that Samuel considered all of God's Word important. During that time, Eli's vision "began to wax dim," spiritually as well as physically (2:26; compare 3:2).

The Tabernacle and the ark of the covenant, which represented God's Word and His presence among them, had been at Shiloh since Joshua placed it there about 450 years earlier. But general indifference to God's will prevailed. Consequently, "the word of the Lord was precious"—meaning, it was seldom referred to in those days. It is said, "There was no *open vision,*" meaning, God's Word was not clearly understood.

The reason the Word of the Lord was not clearly understood is the same reason it is not clearly understood today. We cannot understand God's Word and will if we never read the Bible. We cannot keep His commandments if we do not know what they are. In the hectic pace of 20th-century America, countless thousands of *words* fill our minds every day from newspapers, magazines, books, television and radio. Consequently, there is a serious neglect of setting aside time to read the only written *Word* from God to mankind.

"Let the word of Christ dwell in your richly in all wisdom . . ." (Colossians 3:16).

NOTE:
1:4 **offered** means went to worship God; 1:5 **worthy** means double; 1:10 **sore** means much; 1:15 **poured out my soul** means prayed earnestly; 1:24 **ephah** means 1.1 bushels; 2:1 **horn** means strength; 2:3 **weighed** means judged; 2:12 **sons of Belial** means wicked men; 2:13 **in seething** means boiling; 2:15 **sodden** means boiled; 2:16 **presently** means first; 2:29 **kick ye** means are you dissatisfied; 2:31 **cut off thine arm** means reduce your strength; 2:33 **consume** means blind; 3:19 **did let none of his words fall to the ground** means was obedient to all of God's Word.

I Samuel 1:20: See Heb. 11:32. **3:20:** See Acts 13:20.

MEMORY VERSE FOR THE WEEK: I Peter 1:16
    "Because it is written, Be ye holy; for I am holy."

ARK TAKEN AND RETURNED

I Samuel 4:3: ". . . Wherefore hath the Lord smitten us today before the Philistines? Let us fetch the ark of the covenant of the Lord out of Shiloh unto us, that, when it cometh among us, it may save us out of the hand of our enemies."

The Israelites had declared war against the Philistines without having direction from God. Consequently, they were defeated.

After their defeat, they remembered that the presence of the ark of the covenant had always meant victory. Therefore, they brought it from Shiloh to the battlefield. They assumed that by having the ark in their possession, God would protect them from their enemies. But the defeat was even greater, and 30,000 Israelites died in battle.

They had taken the ark to the battlefield, but they had not repented of their sins or sought the Lord. If God had permitted Israel to win the war while they disregarded His will, it would have been a greater national calamity than being defeated by the Philistines. God used Israel's defeats to transfer His authority from Eli the priest to Samuel, who led the people to inward repentance.

Just as the ark in itself could not save Israel, neither can sacrifice or mere formality in worship take the place of inward obedience. This is why many Christians are suffering defeat; they are more concerned with outward things being right than they are in allowing God to control their lives.

". . . as God hath said, I will dwell in them, and walk in them; and I will be their God, and they shall be my people" (II Corinthians 6:16).

NOTE:
4:12 **with earth upon his head** means a sign of grief; 4:13 **his heart trembled** means he was much concerned; 5:9 **emerods** means tumors; 6:2 **diviners** means fortune-tellers; 6:7 **kine** means cows; 6:8 **coffer** means box; 6:14 **clave** means split.

I Samuel 4:9: See I Cor. 16:13. **7:8,15:** See Acts 13:20.

APRIL 3: Read I Samuel 8-11.

I Samuel 10:19: "And ye have this day rejected your God, who himself saved you out of all your adversities and tribulations; and ye have said unto him, Nay, but set a king over us . . ."

Samuel and the judges who ruled the nation of Israel desired to please God—their invisible King. These judges were chosen by God and received direction from Him. However, Israel openly rejected God as King and persistently asked to have a king such as other nations.

Samuel's Ministry
(See I Sam. 7:13-17)

MEMORY VERSE FOR THE WEEK: James 1:22
"But be ye doers of the word, and not hearers only, deceiving your own selves."

The Lord knew what was best for the Israelites, but the nation insisted, "Nay, but we will have a king over us . . . to go out before us, and fight our battles" (8:19-20). This decision represented rebellion against God.

Samuel called a national assembly at Mizpeh and again warned the people of their serious mistake in demanding a king. Saul *looked* like a king and the people were satisfied with his external appearance, but he was a symbol of the spiritual weakness of the nation.

Desiring to be like the majority has caused many to ignore the Bible and seek counsel from others. God leaves the choice to us to accept or reject His leadership.

God "gave unto them judges about the space of four hundred and fifty years, until Samuel the prophet. And afterward they desired a king" (Acts 13:20-21).

NOTE:
8:3 **lucre** means money; 8:12 **ear** means plow; 9:26 **spring** means dawn.

I Samuel 8:5: See Acts 13:21. **10:21:** See Acts 13:21.

APRIL 4: Read I Samuel 12 thru 14:23.

I Samuel 12:24; 13:9,13: "Only fear the Lord, and serve him in truth with all your heart . . . And Saul said, bring hither a burnt offering to me, and peace offerings . . . And Samuel said to Saul, Thou hast done foolishly: thou hast not kept the commandment of the Lord thy God . . ."

Saul had been commanded to abstain from offering sacrifices for battle until Samuel returned. His failure to wait until Samuel arrived revealed his lack of submission and faith in God's Word.

Saul seemed more concerned about being successful in the eyes of the people than in obeying God's Word. Some might excuse this as a weakness on the part of Israel's first king, but it revealed his proud heart.

Saul attempted to justify himself in making the peace offering because war was imminent, and many of his soldiers were deserting. He attempted to bring success to the nation by violating *one* spiritual principle (waiting on God) and performing *another* (offering sacrifices). But the faith that God honors comes as a result of surrendering one's life to doing God's will.

Obedience is being willing to give up one's own will to submit to God's commands. This is the principle that makes a sacrifice acceptable.

"Then said I, Lo, I come (in the volume of the book it is written of me,) to do thy will, O God" (Hebrews 10:17).

NOTE:
13:20 **share** means sickle; **coulter** means tool; **mattock** means hoe.

I Samuel 13:14: See Acts 13:22.

MEMORY VERSE FOR THE WEEK: James 1:22
"But be ye doers of the word, and not hearers only, deceiving your own selves."

APRIL 5: Read I Samuel 14:24 thru 16.

I Samuel 15:1,3,9: "Samuel also said unto Saul . . . hearken thou unto the voice of the words of the Lord . . . Now go and smite Amalek, and utterly destroy all . . . But Saul and the people spared Agag, and the best of the sheep and of the oxen . . . and would not utterly destroy them . . ."

After defeating the Amalekites, Saul proudly announced, "I have performed the commandment of the Lord" (verse 13). However, God's command to "utterly destroy all" was not obeyed. Pride held a firm grip upon his heart when he admitted that he "feared" the loss of his popularity if he insisted that the people "utterly destroy all," so he "obeyed their voice" (15:24). Once again, Saul used his own discretion and diplomacy to win the goodwill of the people.

This is the second time that we read of Saul sacrificing to the Lord when it was a means of exalting himself.

There is nothing so self-deceiving and so destroying to our relationship with God as obeying *only* what we want to obey. Doing *almost* all of what God commands is the same as being completely disobedient. Pride and self-will inevitably divert the Christian's attention away from the principle of obedience.

"Therefore to him that knoweth to do good, and doeth it not, to him it is sin" (James 4:17).

NOTE:
14:24 **adjured** means solemnly commanded; 15:32 **delicately** means trembling.

I Samuel 15:22: See Mark 12:33.

APRIL 6: Read I Samuel 17-18.

I Samuel 18:7,9,14: ". . . Saul hath slain his thousands, and David his ten thousands . . . And Saul eyed David from that day and forward . . . David behaved himself wisely in all his ways; and the Lord was with him."

David became a hero with the people after his victory over Goliath, the Philistine. His popularity was too much for the pride-filled King Saul. It became evident to Saul that another man was gradually gaining the influence and honor which was once exclusively his own, and he became obsessed with a jealous spirit.

MEMORY VERSE FOR THE WEEK: James 1:22
"But be ye doers of the word, and not hearers only, deceiving your own selves."

Saul faced a spiritual crisis as his jealous spirit took control. He eventually ruled Israel with this thought, "How will this affect me? What can I get out of it?"

There are people like Saul who are anxious to serve God if it brings recognition to themselves.

Success often leads to a sense of self-sufficiency. Many people start speaking of "my accomplishment" and do not give God the glory for their accomplishments. The self-seekers are left on their own like Saul—destitute in the hour of crisis.

"Pride goeth before destruction, and an haughty spirit before a fall" (Proverbs 16:18).

NOTE:
17:4 **six cubits and a span** means 9 feet, 9 inches; 17:6 **greaves of brass** means bronze shin-armor; 17:40 **a scrip** means his wallet; 17:53 **spoiled their tents** means looted their camp; 17:56 **stripling** means youth; 18:9 **eyed** means viewed with suspicion and malice.

I Samuel 17:45: See Heb. 11:32-34.

APRIL 7: Read I Samuel 19-21.

I Samuel 21:10: "And David arose, and fled that day for fear of Saul, and went to Achish the king of Gath."

Although David had been anointed as king, the possibilities of his reigning looked very doubtful, and he feared that Saul would eventually capture and execute him. Therefore, he fled to the city of Gath, a powerful Philistine enemy of Israel.

Apparently he had hoped to live inconspicuously among the Philistines, but suspicious soldiers arrested him and brought him before the Philistine king, Achish. When his true identity was discovered, David, in desperation, pretended to be insane and was released. Miserably discouraged, he hid in the caves of Adullam.

It was in this cave that he turned to God and prayed, "Refuge failed me, no man cared for my soul. I cried unto thee, O Lord: I said, Thou art my refuge and my portion in the land of the living. Attend unto my cry; for I am brought very low: deliver me from my persecutors; for they are stronger than I. Bring my soul out of prison, that I may praise thy name" (Psalm 142:4-7).

In the caves and dark hours, David realized that he was not in Saul's hands, but in the Lord's. This is often the way God works when He is seeking to strengthen our faith in Him.

MEMORY VERSE FOR THE WEEK: James 1:22
"But be ye doers of the word, and not hearers only, deceiving your own selves."

Most of our fears and frustrations result from not knowing God's Word and consequently failing to commit our lives and circumstances to Him.

In mercy, God brought David to the place where he could say, "It is good that a man should both hope and quietly wait for the salvation of the Lord" (Lamentations 3:26).

NOTE:
20:5 **at meat** means at dinner; 20:17 **swear** means promise; 20:26 **not clean** means ceremonially unfit; 20:33 **javelin** means spear; 21:4 **hallowed bread** means bread set aside for worship use.

I Samuel 21:6: See Matt. 12:3-4; Mark 2:26; Luke 6:4.

APRIL 8: Read I Samuel 22-24.

I Samuel 23:8: "And Saul called all the people together to war . . . to beseige David and his men."

Saul made a great mistake when he said, "God hath delivered him [David] into mine hand" (I Samuel 23:7). It shows how man can be deceived in his interpretation of providential events when he is not in subjection to God.

Such a misinterpretation of circumstances is more than poor judgment; it is the result of "the god of this world [who] hath blinded the minds of them which believe not" (II Corinthians 4:4).

When David knew that Saul planned to kill him, he did not know which way to turn. The friends he had once trusted turned against him. The way seemed to be more uncertain each day, but he continued to pray for guidance (I Samuel 23:10-12). Our all-wise heavenly Father often allows us to experience times of deep distress in order to develop a greater faith in Him.

At times, our circumstances seem to make us think that God does not care; but, like David, we can be confident in the unchanging, eternal Word of God. He *does* care, and He stands ready to answer our call for help when we are in submission to Him.

"And whatsoever we ask, we receive of him, because we keep his commandments, and do those things that are pleasing in his sight" (I John 3:22).

NOTE:
22:4 **hold** means security; 22:17 **footmen** means the runners; 23:16 **strengthened his hand** means encouraged; 24:3 **cover his feet** means sleep; 24:7 **stayed** means restrained.

MEMORY VERSE FOR THE WEEK: James 1:22
"But be ye doers of the word, and not hearers only, deceiving your own selves."

101

APRIL 9: Read I Samuel 25-27.

I Samuel 26:8-9: "Then said Abishai to David, God hath delivered thine enemy into thine hand this day: now therefore let me smite him, I pray thee, with the spear . . . And David said to Abishai, Destroy him not: for who can stretch forth his hand against the Lord's anointed, and be guiltless?"

David had an opportunity to remove the only person blocking his reign over Israel (23:15-18).

Never were David's men more wrong than when they quoted a prophecy to justify killing Saul (24:4). Saul was still the Lord's anointed king—the man whom God had appointed to rule over His people Israel. David realized he must honor the "powers ordained of God" until the Lord Himself removed Saul from the throne.

On another occasion, Abishai insisted, "God hath delivered thine enemy into thine hand this day: now therefore let me smite him" (26:8). On both occasions, David's reaction proved his submission to God's authority when he refused to kill Saul and seize the throne. He had been anointed king of Israel long ago, but he would not mar this sacred responsibility.

Through many days of humbly seeking the Lord, God had prepared David to receive the kingdom in a spirit of grateful dependence upon Him. His prayer revealed his submission to God when he said, "My times are in thy hand. . . ." (Psalm 31:15).

NOTE:
25:3 **churlish** means cruel; 25:21 **requited** means repaid; 25:28 **a sure house** means an established family; 25:29 **bound in a bundle of life** means protected to live; 26:11 **bolster** means pillow; 27:10 **road** means raid; 27:11 **so will be his manner** means this was his policy.

APRIL 10: Read I Samuel 28-31.

I Samuel 28:5-6: "And when Saul saw the host of the Philistines, he was afraid, and his heart greatly trembled. And when Saul enquired of the Lord, the Lord answered him not. . . ."

Israel's kingdom seemed doomed as the Philistines declared war. David, the champion over the Philistines, was gone, and Samuel, the godly prophet, was dead. King Saul was panic stricken, and in fear, he hastily turned to God in prayer. It was his final opportunity to seek the Lord, who alone controls the destiny of all battles. But God did not answer Saul, and true to his impatient nature, Saul sought advice from a God-forbidden source—the witch of Endor.

MEMORY VERSE OF THE WEEK: James 1:23
"For if any be a hearer of the word, and not a doer, he is like unto a man beholding his natural face in a glass."

Often when prayers seem to go unanswered, we assume the request was not according to God's will. Perhaps God was withholding His blessing because our lives were not in harmony with the biblical requirements for effective prayer.

"If I regard iniquity in my heart, the Lord will not hear me" (Psalm 66:18).

NOTE:
28:7 **hath a familiar spirit** means is a fortune-teller; 28:14 **mantle** means robe; 29:3 **fell unto me** means came over on my side.

"Then came all the tribes of Israel to David . . . and spake . . . and the Lord said to thee, Thou shalt feed my people Israel, and thou shalt be a captain over Israel." II Samuel 5:1,2

APRIL 11: Read II Samuel 1-2.

II Samuel 2:1: "And it came to pass after this, that David enquired of the Lord, saying, Shall I go up into any of the cities of Judah? And the Lord said unto him, Go up. And David said, whither shall I go up? And he said, Unto Hebron."

The first thing David did after Saul's death was to pray for the Lord's will in assuming leadership. Years earlier, Samuel had anointed him to be king over all the tribes of Israel, but David knew he could not take anything for granted. Therefore, he prayed for guidance, and God directed him to Hebron.

David had to wait seven years after Saul's death before he could assume leadership over all the tribes. If David had not prayed for guidance, he would not have accepted his delay. However, he acknowledged complete dependence upon God, who had chosen him as king.

The wise Christian will pray and seek direction from the Lord. One of the greatest dangers confronting Christians in our fast-moving society is the temptation to rush through life, hoping God will bless our hurried efforts. But the Lord is not in a hurry, and He often waits until all human hope is gone before He accomplishes His purpose, as in the case of God giving Abraham a son, Isaac.

"Trust in the Lord with all thine heart; and lean not unto thine own understanding. In all thy ways acknowledge him, and he shall direct thy paths" (Proverbs 3:5-6).

NOTE:
1:2 **rent** means torn; 1:18 **use** means song; 2:6 **requite** means repay; 2:14 **play before us** means stage a contest; 2:32 **sepulcher** means grave.

MEMORY VERSE OF THE WEEK: James 1:23
"For if any be a hearer of the word, and not a doer, he is like unto a man beholding his natural face in a glass."

II Samuel 5:3: "So all the elders of Israel came to the king to Hebron; and king David made a league with them in Hebron before the Lord; and they anointed David king over Israel."

After David had reigned over Judah for seven years, the elders of all the tribes anointed David as king. They did not ask David to be their king, but they reminded him that the Lord had said, "Thou shalt feed my people Israel, and thou shalt be a captain over Israel" (II Samuel 5:2).

The Old Testament prophets often referred to the shepherd as a symbol of the love and care God expects from His leaders. The true "undershepherd" of the Lord does not seek honor from men or the honor of being served, but he gives himself for the flock, as did our Messiah-Shepherd-King.

In each new difficulty, God was preparing David to be His faithful servant —a man after God's own heart—to be a true shepherd over His people.

"Thou therefore endure hardness, as a good soldier of Jesus Christ. No man that warreth entangleth himself with the affairs of this life; that he may please him who hath chosen him to be a soldier" (II Timothy 2:3-4).

NOTE:
3:1 **waxed** means grew; 3:12 **league** means covenant; 3:31 **bier** means coffin; 5:8 **getteth up to the gutter** means manages to enter the city.

"Uzzah put forth his hand to the ark of God, and took hold of it; . . . And the anger of the Lord was kindled . . . and God smote him there for his error."
II Samuel 6:6-7

APRIL 13: Read II Samuel 6-9.

II Samuel 6:2: "And David arose, and went with all the people that were with him . . . to bring up from thence the ark of God, whose name is called by the name of the Lord of hosts that dwelleth between the cherubims."

David conquered Jerusalem and established a united kingdom. It was his desire that Jerusalem not only would be the center of his government, but that it would also be the center of worship.

During the forty years Saul reigned, there is no mention of the ark of the covenant (the symbol of the Lord's presence) being of the midst of Israel.

David recognized from the first that a successful reign as king of God's chosen nation was dependent upon his obedience to the invisible King of Kings. Therefore, he planned to bring the ark of the covenant to Jerusalem.

David's wife, Michal, expressed the same indifference for the ark as did her father, Saul. She criticized David as he led the procession, saying he "uncovered himself in the eyes of the handmaids." This simply meant that on this

"For if any be a hearer of the word, and not a doer, he is like unto a man beholding his natural face in a glass."

occasion, David did not wear the impressive royal robes of a king. Instead, he wore the simple white linen ephod garment (II Samuel 6:14) as the head of the kingdom of priests—a holy nation. (See I Samuel 22:18; Exodus 19:6.)

David's greatness can be attributed to his humble spirit as expressed in his answer to Michal. He would gladly "be more vile" (be willing to take an even lower position) if it would bring honor to the true King of Israel (6:22).

"For whosoever exalteth himself shall be abased; and he that humbleth himself shall be exalted" (Luke 4:11).

NOTE:
6:8 **made a breach** means broken forth; 7:8 **sheepcote** means pasture; 7:23 **terrible** means wonderful; 8:13 **being** means slaying.

II Samuel 7:12: See Acts 13:22,23. **7:14:** See II Cor. 6:18, Heb. 1:5.

APRIL 14: Read II Samuel 10-12.

II Samuel 11:1-2: ". . . at the time when kings go forth to battle . . . David tarried still at Jerusalem. And it came to pass in an eveningtide, that David arose from off his bed, and walked upon the roof of the king's house: and from the roof he saw a woman washing herself . . ."

David was a man of exceptional character—"a man after God's own heart." But David fell for a married woman. On inquiring, he learned that she was the wife of one of his soldiers who was away in battle. Instead of turning from the lust that was in his heart, he dishonored the God-ordained family relationship of Uriah and Bathsheba and stole his neighbor's wife. In an attempt to cover up one evil, David committed many other sins.

Sin seldom ends with one act alone, but one sin usually leads to another.

Perhaps Bathsheba could have prevented this wickedness if she had resisted and said, as did Tamar, "Nay, my brother, do not force me; for no such thing ought to be done in Israel" (II Samuel 13:12).

From the moment David first lusted after this woman until their marriage, there was not one adverse circumstance to interfere with his plan—except that "it displeased the Lord." This is the treacherous thing about sin.

God forgave David's sin, but the prophet Nathan foretold the bitter consequences of suffering, incest, murder, rebellion, and civil war that would continue throughout David's lifetime. (See II Samuel 12:10-12.)

"Then when lust hath conceived, it bringeth forth sin: and sin, when it is finished, bringeth forth death" (James 1:15; see also II Samuel 12:14).

NOTE:
12:30 **talent** equals about 100 lbs.

II Samuel 12:24: See Matt. 1:6.

MEMORY VERSE OF THE WEEK: James 1:23
"For if any be a hearer of the word, and not a doer, he is like unto a man beholding his natural face in a glass."

APRIL 15: Read II Samuel 13-14.

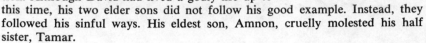

II Samuel 13:37: "But Absalom fled . . . And David mourned for his son every day."

After the great sin that David committed became public knowledge, it appears that David was filled with remorse. He was no longer seen in public, but his palace became his hiding place.

Sin always produces side effects with consequences far beyond all possible human calculation. Although David had lived a godly life up to this time, his two elder sons did not follow his good example. Instead, they followed his sinful ways. His eldest son, Amnon, cruelly molested his half sister, Tamar.

David did not punish his son as the law required, and Absalom, motivated by a selfish ambition to become king, welcomed the opportunity to carry out "justice." Eventually, he murdered his half brother, Amnon, who was heir to the throne. The crimes of his two sons must have caused David to recall memories of the two similar sins he had committed.

The consequences of sin is no respecter of persons, whether king of peasant, Christian or unsaved. It can produce immeasurable, unending suffering and sorrow.

"But exhort one another daily, while it is called To day; lest any of you be hardened through the deceitfulness of sin" (Hebrews 3:13).

NOTE:
13:3 **subtil man** means crafty; 13:25 **chargeable** means a burden; 14:2 **feign** means pretend; 14:4 **did obeisance** means showed respect; 14:7 **quench my coal which is left** means destroy the last of my family; 14:26 **polled his head** means cut his hair.

APRIL 16: Read II Samuel 15-16.
II Samuel 15:13-14: "And there came a messenger to David, saying, The hearts of the men of Israel are after Absalom. And David said unto all his servants that were with him at Jerusalem, Arise and let us flee; for we shall not else escape from Absalom: make speed to depart lest he . . . smite the city with the edge of the sword."

One of the most pitiful passages in the Bible is of King David having to escape from his son, Absalom. Heartbroken, the aged king is described as barefooted, his head covered, running across the rough hills leading to the Mount of Olives.

Shimei, one of Saul's relatives, followed David as he fled from Jerusalem, cursing him and throwing stones at him. He accused David of being responsible for Saul's death and "all the blood of the house of Saul." This accusation was not true, and Abishai asked David for permission to kill Shimei. David refused, saying "Let him curse, because the Lord hath said unto him, Curse David" (II Samuel 16:10).

MEMORY VERSE OF THE WEEK: James 1:23
"For if any be a hearer of the word, and not a doer, he is like unto a man beholding his natural face in a glass."

David felt he had lost the throne because of his sin and therefore deserved the humiliation and insults by Saul's relative.

Too often we retaliate, fight back, or seek revenge, and do not see the hand of God in our sufferings. But once we see this truth and yield to Him, we discover His perfect will. The highest privilege we Christians have is yielding our will to *His ways*. May God teach us the precious privilege of accepting and loving His ways!

"For as the heavens are higher than the earth, so are my ways higher than your ways, and my thoughts than your thoughts" (Isaiah 55:9).

NOTE:
15:27 **seer** means prophet; 15:28 **certify** means assure.

Absolom's Rebellion

Mahanaim
Woods of Ephraim
Jerusalem

APRIL 17: Read II Samuel 17-18.

II Samuel 18:9,15 ". . . And Absalom rode upon a mule, and the mule went under the thick boughs of a great oak, and his head caught hold of the oak, and he was taken up between heaven and the earth; . . . and ten young men that bare Joab's armour compassed about and smote Absalom, and slew him."

The majority of Israel's leaders and great numbers of discontented people joined Absalom in an attempt to overthrow King David. Absalom was declared king and entered the capital without resistance. He took control without losing one man. Up to this point all his plans had been successful. Absalom was determined to pursue and execute David (17:2-4). However, in the battle that ensued, Absalom suffered heavy losses, "a great slaughter that day of twenty thousand men" (18:7).

When the time of Absalom's judgment arrived, he didn't have a friend to help him escape. There were many who had once stayed by him; but now, with his head caught in the limbs of the oak tree, everyone rushed past him, intent on saving their own lives.

Absalom's rebellion against David is typical of the men who "take counsel . . . against the Lord, and against his anointed . . . " (Psalm 2:2). They seem to prosper for a while, but after God's purpose has been fulfilled, they are destroyed. ". . . for God resisteth the proud, and giveth grace to the humble" (I Peter 5:5).

NOTE:
17:8 **chafed** means angered; **whelps** means cubs; 17:17 **wench** means maidservant; 17:28 **pulse** means peas and beans; 18:3 **succor** means assist.

II Samuel 17:23: See Matt. 27:5.

MEMORY VERSE FOR THE WEEK: James 1:24
"For he beholdeth himself, and goeth his way, and straightway forgetteth what manner of man he was."

II Samuel 19:2: "And the victory that day was turned into mourning unto all the people: for the people heard say that day how the king was grieved for his son."

David's deep grief over the death of his traitorous son, Absalom, made him incapable of assuming his responsibility to the nation.

Joab was angry with David and rebuked him for the weakness and selfishness he displayed by his overwhelming sorrow. David was disregarding the loyalty of his faithful followers who had won the war, and a sense of shame pervaded the nation rather than rejoicing over the victory. A crisis faced the nation; and if Joab had not awakened David to see his God-appointed responsibility to the nation, the consequences could have been disastrous.

This is a problem we all face sooner or later when a loved one is taken. It brings us face-to-face with feelings that are too deep and intense for words, and it seems that a part of our own life was taken.

The healing touch for hearts that are breaking comes from the heart of Him who died of a broken heart. He is touched "with the feeling of our infirmities . . ." (Hebrews 4:15). We must realize how important it is to yield to His tender command, "Let not your heart be troubled . . ." (John 14:1). He is with you now; His presence is very real to comfort and to heal. He "will never leave thee, nor forsake thee" (Hebrews 13:5).

NOTE:
19:3 **by stealth** means secretly; 19:27 **an angel** means messenger; 20:18 **wont to speak** means used to say.

> "If, when evil cometh upon us . . . or famine, we cry unto thee in our affliction, then thou wilt hear and help."
> II Chronicles 20:9

II Samuel 21:1: "Then there was a famine in the days of David three years . . ."

After three years of famine, David prayed, asking God to reveal the reason for the famine. God told him it was because Saul had broken the covenant Joshua had made with the Gibeonites more than 400 years earlier (Joshua 9:16-27).

This incident in the life of David shows how sacred God considers a vow, even though it was made to an unbelieving Canaanite nation.

God has clearly stated, "When thou shalt vow a vow unto the Lord thy God, thou shalt not slack to pay it: for the Lord thy God will surely require it of thee . . ." (Deuteronomy 23:21; also, see Numbers 30:2).

The three years of famine that resulted from a broken vow reveals the seriousness of keeping one's word.

Can people depend upon what you say, or are your vows meaningless? Do you say only what others want to hear? Far too many Christians have good

MEMORY VERSE FOR THE WEEK: James 1:24
"For he beholdeth himself, and goeth his way, and straightway forgetteth what manner of man he was."

intentions, but they are often unreliable because they allow circumstances to sway their convictions.

"That which is gone out of thy lips thou shalt keep and perform . . ." (Deuteronomy 23:23).

NOTE:
II Samuel 22:3: See Luke 1:69. **22:50:** See Rom. 15:9.

APRIL 20: Read II Samuel 23-24.

II Samuel 24:24: "And the king said unto Araunah, Nay, but I will surely buy it of thee at a price: neither will I offer burnt offerings unto the Lord my God of that which doth cost me nothing. So David bought the threshingfloor and the oxen for fifty shekels of silver."

In chapter 23 the achievements of David's mighty men were made known. David's heart swelled with pride and Satan tempted him into taking a census of all soldiers throughout the nation. (See 24:1; also see I Chronicles 21:1-7.) Immediately after this we read, "He [God] moved David" which, in Hebrew, means, "He allowed him to be moved"—He permitted David to have his way.

God had not authorized this numbering of the tribes of Israel, and seventy thousand men died as a result of David's sin. David confessed to God, "I have sinned greatly" (II Samuel 24:10). He then attempted to buy the threshingfloor of Araunah to build an altar unto the Lord. Araunah wanted to give both the plot of ground and the sacrifice to David, but David refused them. He would not offer something to the Lord that had not cost him anything.

How contrary to the popular get-something-for-nothing philosophy which dominates many people in our society today! But what God wants is not *yours,* but *you.* Self, service, and then your sacrifice—that is the Divine order. A gift to the church means nothing to Him if we withhold ourselves.

"And that he died for all, that they which live should not henceforth live unto themselves, but unto him which died for them, and rose again" (II Corinthians 5:15).

NOTE:
23:30 **brooks** means valleys; 24:10 **heart smote** means conscience bothered.

MEMORY VERSE FOR THE WEEK: James 1:24
"For he beholdeth himself, and goeth his way, and straightway forgetteth what manner of man he was."

INTRODUCTION TO I KINGS

The book of *I Kings* is a continuation of Israel's history from the book of *II Samuel*. It covers the forty-year reign of Solomon, under whom Israel had her most glorious era of peace and prosperity.

Solomon had the privilege of building the most magnificent Temple ever to be constructed for the purpose of worshiping God. When he was at the height of his fame, God appeared to him the second time with a word of warning, "Walk before me, as David thy father walked" (9:4).

Although Solomon inherited a powerful united kingdom which was growing in wealth and world preeminence, he brought about its division and ultimate destruction as pronounced by the Lord, "thou hast not kept my covenant and my statutes, which I have commanded thee, I will surely rend the kingdom from thee" (11:11). Ten tribes (referred to as Israel —the Northern Kingdom) immediately rejected Solomon's son, Rehoboam, and appointed Jeroboam as king. He is referred to throughout history as the king "who made Israel to sin" (I Kings 22:52; II Kings 10:29).

This book records the history of the divided kingdom for another 80 years, giving parallel accounts of the first seven kings of Israel (the Northern Kingdom) and the first four kings of Judah (the Southern Kingdom). The book of *I Kings* shows how the rise and the decline of the Hebrew kingdom was in direct relation to the people's obedience or rejection of God's will.

OUTLINE OF I KINGS

I. David's Last Days and Crowning of Solomon   I Kings   1 to 2:11
II. Solomon's Glorious Reign and Failure   I Kings 2:12 to 11
III. The Divided Kingdom   I Kings   12-16
IV. The Prophet Elijah and King Ahab   I Kings   17-22

APRIL 21: Read I Kings 1 thru 2:25.

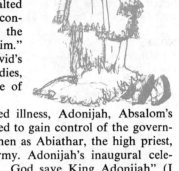

I Kings 1:1,5,7: "Now king David was old and stricken in years . . . Then Adonijah . . . exalted himself, saying, I will be king . . . and he conferred with Joab . . . and with Abiathar the priest: and they following Adonijah helped him."

Following Nathan's prophecy against David's great sin, David's life was filled with tragedies, heartbreaks, and disappointments to the time of his death.

Taking advantage of his father's prolonged illness, Adonijah, Absalom's brother and David's oldest living son, attempted to gain control of the government. He gained support of such prominent men as Abiathar, the high priest, and Joab, commander-in-chief of David's army. Adonijah's inaugural celebration was climaxed by a great shout, ". . . God save King Adonijah" (I Kings 1:25). It appears that he had succeeded. However, the events that followed reveal that God, not man, overrules the affairs of earth and controls our lives.

Many people never experience the blessedness of His keeping power because they refuse to commit themselves into His care. They have never said, "Lord, I surrender my will to do thy will. I give myself to You and commit to You the keeping of my life." You can be sure He will fulfill His promises in you just as His Word promises: "Wherefore let them that suffer according to the will of God commit the keeping of their souls to him in well doing, as unto a faithful Creator" (I Peter 4:19).

NOTE:
1:40 **pipes** means flutes; 2:6 **hoar** means gray.

APRIL 22: Read I Kings 2:26 thru 4.

I Kings 3:1: "And Solomon made affinity with Pharaoh king of Egypt, and took Pharaoh's daughter and brought her into the city of David, until he had made an end of building his own house, and the house of the Lord, and the wall of Jerusalem round about."

Solomon's marriage to the Egyptian princess was politically motivated to prevent war with Egypt and to increase his fame among other nations. It was the first association between the two nations since the time the Israelites had been slaves in Egypt 480 years earlier (see 6:1).

MEMORY VERSE FOR THE WEEK: James 1:24
"For he beholdeth himself, and goeth his way, and straightway forgetteth what manner of man he was."

111

Just think! Moses, the great deliverer, brought the Israelites out of Egypt (representing worldliness) to worship Jehovah. But Solomon brought the Egyptian princess into the city of God and opened the way for idol worship in Israel.

Solomon had begun his reign by sacrificing a thousand burnt offerings. He "loved the Lord, walking in the statutes of David his father" (3:3), but Pharoah's daughter caused Solomon to turn "away his heart after other gods" (11:4).

Worldly associations, compromise, and powerlessness are inseparably linked. Christians must recognize that ". . . friendship of the world is enmity with God . . ." (James 4:4).

NOTE:
3:1 **affinity** means alliance, 4:28 **dromedaries** means camels trained for fast riding; **charge** means responsibility.

APRIL 23: Read I Kings 5-7.

I Kings 6:1,38: "And it came to pass in the four hundred and eightieth year after the children of Israel were come out of the land of Egypt, in the fourth year of Solomon's reign over Israel . . . he began to build the house of the Lord . . . and in the eleventh year . . . was the house finished . . ."

No other building in all the world compared with Solomon's Temple. The most costly materials and treasures were lavished upon it. But the world only observed the external beauty of the Temple; its true glory was inside. The Shekinah glory—the presence of God—dwelled within the holy of holies. The world could only hear about this glory, but they could never experience it.

This is also true of the Christian, who is the temple of God. His glory dwells within each believer. The miracle of the new birth and the indwelling Holy Spirit is what makes the difference between the Christian and the unsaved, who cannot share in His glory.

God's presence is experienced by those who honor Him. Just think! the God of Heaven dwells within the heart of every Christian, "In whom ye also are builded together for an habitation of God through the Spirit" (Ephesians 2:22).

NOTE:
5:4 **occurrent** means activity; 5:13 **levy** means forced labor; 6:5 **oracle** means chapel; 7:9 **coping** means top; 7:14 **cunning** means skilled; 7:26 **handbreadth** means 3 inches; **two thousand baths** means 17,000 gallons; 7:33 **axletrees** means axles; **naves** means hubs; **folloes** means rims; 7:34 **undersetters** means supports; 7:50 **censers** means fire pans.

I Kings 6:1: See Acts 7:47.

MEMORY VERSE FOR THE WEEK: James 1:24
"For he beholdeth himself, and goeth his way, and straightway forgetteth what manner of man he was."

APRIL 24: Read I Kings 8.

I Kings 8:11: "So that the priests could not stand to minister because of the cloud: for the glory of the Lord had filled the house of the Lord."

After Solomon dedicated the Temple, *he stood* before the altar of the Lord and *began* to pray, but when he *finished* praying, he was *on his knees*. (Compare 8:22 and 8:54.) The realization of the presence of God humbled wise Solomon as he acknowledged his unworthiness to stand before the most holy God. But Jehovah's presence was even more fully manifested following Solomon's prayer.

First, the glory of the Lord came down in a cloud; then, "fire came down from heaven, and consumed the burnt offering and the sacrifices; and the glory of the Lord filled the house" (II Chronicles 7:1).

All the Israelites saw the fire and "the *glory of the Lord* . . . they bowed themselves . . . and worshipped, and praised the Lord, saying, For he is good; for his mercy endureth for ever" (II Chronicles 7:3).

From the beginning of time, it was God's plan to dwell among man and show forth His glory. Through man's sin, this plan seemingly failed. But God first carried out His plan through His chosen people, the Israelites. He dwelt in the midst of His people—first in the Tabernacle, and then in the Temple. And now He dwells within the heart of all Christians.

". . . ye are the temple of the living God; as God hath said, I will dwell in them, and walk in them; and I will be their God, and they shall be my people" (II Corinthians 6:16).

NOTE:
8:64 **hallow** means set aside for holy use.

I Kings 8:46: See I John 1:8.

APRIL 25: Read I Kings 9-11.

I Kings 11:6 "And Solomon did evil in the sight of the Lord, and went not fully after the Lord, as did David his father."

God gave Solomon special privileges that far exceeded those of all the other kings. Although the Lord appeared to Solomon three times (see I Kings 3:5; 9:2; 11:9-11), he did not appear to David even once. God gave Solomon the privilege of building the Temple, but denied David that privilege. He gave Solomon superior wisdom that brought him recognition throughout the world.

The Divided Kingdom

But as Solomon forsook God's commandments, his splendor began to decline and God raised up adversaries against him. First, Hadad the Edomite organized resistance to Solomon; then, Rezon of Syria became a troublemaker.

MEMORY VERSE FOR THE WEEK: James 1:25
"But whoso looketh into the perfect law of liberty, and continueth therein, he being not a forgetful hearer, but a doer of the work, this man shall be blessed in his deed."

But Solomon's greatest threat was the discontent of the Ephraimites. Jeroboam, who at one time was highly honored in Solomon's administration, became a spokesman for the tribe of Ephraim and instigated the division of Solomon's kingdom soon after his death (11:26).

Solomon turned from God. There was no repentance from Solomon—no tears like those his father David shed after each failure—and Solomon's kingdom crumbled because of his sin.

What happened to Solomon can happen to anyone who allows pleasure, riches, or lust to crowd out devotion to God.

"Good understanding giveth favour: but the way of transgressors is hard" (Proverbs 13:15).

NOTE:
9:21 **levy** means tax; 9:22 **bondmen** means slaves; 10:2 **train** means company of followers; 10:21 **nothing accounted** means not considered important; 10:24 **sought** means consulted; 11:10 **commanded** means warned; 11:27 **repaired** means closed; 11:28 **charge** means forced labor; 11:31 **rend** means tear.

APRIL 26: Read I Kings 12-13.

I Kings 13:26: "And when the prophet that brought him back from the way heard thereof, he said, It is the man of God, who was disobedient unto the word of the Lord: therefore the Lord hath delivered him unto the lion, which hath torn him, and slain him, according to the word of the Lord, which he spake unto him."

Jeroboam successfully led a revolt against the united kingdom and gained the support of the ten northern tribes. The tribe of Judah, as well as the tribe of Benjamin and most of the Levites, remained faithful to the Davidic dynasty and worshiped in Jerusalem.

Jeroboam feared that if the people went to Jerusalem to worship, they might desire to unite the kingdom; therefore, he established two golden altars, one in Dan and the other in Bethel.

Three tragedies are presented in this chapter. First, King Jeroboam was more concerned about his control over a nation than he was about God's control over him. Second, although the old prophet knew the will of God, he lied. He influenced the young prophet not to complete what God had called him to do. The third tragedy was the young prophet's untimely, tragic death. He had God's message and the courage to preach it, and he refused all the king's bribes. But the young prophet made a mistake when he accepted the warm reception of the aged, backslidden prophet.

Much religion today is as shallow and superficial as the "First Church of Jeroboam." But the most difficult deception to discern is not the liberalist who denies the Word, but the fundamentally-sound prophet-leader who has left his first love and is no longer as concerned about the guidance of the Holy Spirit as he is in seeking his own interests.

MEMORY VERSE FOR THE WEEK: James 1:25
"But whoso looketh into the perfect law of liberty, and continueth therein, he being not a forgetful hearer, but a doer of the work, this man shall be blessed in his deed."

"Nevertheless I have somewhat against thee, because thou has left thy first love" (Revelation 2:4).

NOTE:
12:32 **high places** means pagan shrines; 13:6 **Entreat** means Pray to; 11:32 **cried** means preached.

> ". . . Every kingdom divided against itself is brought to desolation; and every city or house divided against itself shall not stand." Matthew 12:25

APRIL 27: Read I Kings 14-15.

I Kings 14:25-27: ". . . Shishak king of Egypt came up against Jerusalem: and he took away the treasures of the house of the Lord, . . . he took away all the shields of gold which Solomon had made. And King Rehoboam made in their stead brazen shields . . ."

Jeroboam, the wicked king of the Northern Kingdom, went from bad to worse. Rehoboam, king of Judah, was almost as evil. They both built shrines to false gods.

God was Jerusalem's strength, but He withdrew His presence and protection when idolatry became acceptable in Jerusalem. Therefore, the kingdom of Judah was powerless against her enemies.

Shishak, king of Egypt, invaded Jerusalem and carried away its immense wealth, including the golden shields—the symbol of Jehovah's protection. For the first time since the days of the exodus, the kingdom of Judah was threatened with Egyptian bondage.

Rehoboam, not wanting to be embarrassed by the absence of the golden shields, substituted shields made of brass and continued his ceremonies as though nothing had happened. They had substituted the gold of pure worship for the brass of idolatry. Unless one looked closely, he could not tell the difference.

The deadness and discord that exists in some churches today may be well hidden by all the activities going on, but a careful observer will notice the emptiness of that ministry.

"Having a form of godliness, but denying the power thereof: from such turn away" (II Timothy 3:5).

NOTE:
14:3 **cracknels** means cakes; **cruse** means jar; 14:15 **groves** means pagan shrines; 15:17 **suffer** means allow.

APRIL 28: Read I Kings 16-18.

I Kings 16:30-31: "And Ahab the son of Omri did evil in the sight of the Lord above all that were before him. And it came to pass, as if it had been a light thing for him to walk in the sins of Jeroboam the son of Nebat, that he took to wife Jezebel the daughter of Ethbaal king of the Zidonians, and went and served Baal, and worshipped him."

MEMORY VERSE FOR THE WEEK: James 1:25

"But whoso looketh into the perfect law of liberty, and continueth therein, he being not a forgetful hearer, but a doer of the work, this man shall be blessed in his deed."

Ahab, king of Samaria, was one of the most powerful kings ever to rule the Northern Kingdom, "But there was none like unto Ahab, which did sell himself to work wickedness in the sight of the Lord, whom Jezebel his wife stirred up" (I Kings 21:25). Jezebel had an intense zeal for Baal worship; therefore, all who worshiped Jehovah were fiercely persecuted (I Kings 18:5; compare 19:14).

Elijah must have felt that his efforts to restore true worship of Jehovah were in vain and his influence worthless. The Lord who once said, "I have commanded the *ravens* to feed thee" afterwards said, "I have commanded a widow woman . . . to sustain thee" (I Kings 17:4-9). God had not revealed to him that the wicked queen, Jezebel, would seek to destroy him. But God's grace is always sufficient when the hour of need arises.

God often allows the Christian to face unusual and difficult situations in order to remind us of our absolute dependence upon Him.

Through difficulties, we discover whether our confidence is in the Lord or in circumstances. ". . . The effectual fervent prayer of a righteous man availeth much. Elias [Elijah] was a man subject to like passions as we are, and he prayed earnestly that it might not rain: and it rained not . . ." (James 5:16-17).

NOTE:
16:13 **vanities** means sinful ways; 17:9 **sustain** means feed; 17:16 **wasted not** means was not used up.

I Kings 16:31-33: See Rev. 2:20. **17:1:** See James 5:17. **17:9:** See Luke 4:26. **17:23:** See Heb. 11:35.

Journeys of Elijah

APRIL 29: Read I Kings 19-20.

I Kings 19:1: "And Ahab told Jezebel all that Elijah had done, and withal how he had slain all the prophets [of Baal] with the sword."

Because of Ahab's wickedness, God withheld the rain. After three years of drought, God told Elijah to go again to Ahab. Elijah challenged the king to assemble all the prophets of Baal at Mt. Carmel to prove who was really the living God. Elijah proved that the God of Israel was still alive.

Elijah probably expected the miracle on Mt. Carmel and the execution of the Baal priests to turn the nation from idols and bring national repentance,

---

MEMORY VERSE FOR THE WEEK: James 1:25
"But whoso looketh into the perfect law of liberty, and continueth therein, he being not a forgetful hearer, but a doer of the work, this man shall be blessed in his deed."

---

but he was bitterly disappointed. When Ahab told Jezebel that Elijah had killed the prophets of Baal, she vowed she would kill him. Elijah fled to Beersheba, discouraged and wanting to die. He felt he had failed, and in his hour of deepest disappointment, he cried out to God, "It is enough; now, O Lord, take away my life" (I Kings 19:4).

"Elias [Elijah] was a man of *like passions* as we are . . . ," and at this time, he was altogether occupied with his own problems and did not turn to God for renewed strength. However, God neither rebuked Elijah for his fears nor answered his prayer for death, nor did He permit Jezebel to kill him. Instead, God gave him rest and food (see 19:5-8).

"Come unto me, all ye that labour and are heavy laden, and I will give you rest" (Matthew 11:28).

NOTE:
19:6 **head** means pillow; 19:13 **wrapped** means covered; 19:4 **jealous** means zealous; 19:21 **instruments** means yokes; 20:11 **harness** means armor; 20:24 **rooms** means positions; 20:43 **heavy and displeasing** means downhearted.

I Kings 19:10,14: See Rom. 11:13. **19:18:** See Rom. 11:4.

APRIL 30: Read I Kings 21-22.

I Kings 22:8: "And the king of Israel said unto Jehoshaphat, There is yet one man, Micaiah the son of Imlah, by whom we may enquire of the Lord: but I hate him; for he doth not prophesy good concerning me, but evil . . ."

Benhadad, king of Syria, had attacked the Northern Kingdom two different times, but could not defeat them. He then promised Ahab, king of the Northern Kingdom, favorable trade with Damascus. But after three years of peace, Ahab persuaded Jehoshaphat, king of Judah, to join him in capturing Ramoth-Gilead from the Syrians.

Ahab consulted his four hundred prophets, and they unanimously agreed with what Ahab wanted to hear, "Go up; for the Lord shall deliver it into the hand of the king" (22:6). However, Jehoshaphat had no confidence in Ahab's prophets and insisted on consulting one other prophet.

Reluctantly, Ahab sent a messenger to bring Micaiah, a prophet of the Lord, from prison. The messenger tried to persuade Micaiah to give the same optimistic advice as the others, but he refused, saying, ". . . what the Lord saith unto me, that will I speak" (22:14).

MEMORY VERSE FOR THE WEEK: James 1:25
"But whoso looketh into the perfect law of liberty, and continueth therein, he being not a forgetful hearer, but a doer of the work, this man shall be blessed in his deed."

He told them they would not only lose the battle, but also that King Ahab would be slain. Because he told the truth, he was dragged back to prison and fed with "the bread of affliction" (22:27).

Unlike Micaiah, far too many of God's people do not experience the presence and power of God upon their lives because they are persuaded by men or circumstances to modify the truth.

If need be, we can sacrifice all we possess, but we dare not sacrifice the truth. "And ye shall know the truth, and the truth shall make you free" (John 8:32).

NOTE:
21:5 **bread** means food; 21:25 **stirred up** means inspired; 22:10 **void** means an open; 22:16 **adjure** means command; 22:35 **stayed** means propped.

BIBLICAL REFERENCE INDEX

PRAYERS IN I & II SAMUEL AND I KINGS

PSALMS THAT ARE RELATED TO EVENTS IN DAVID'S LIFE

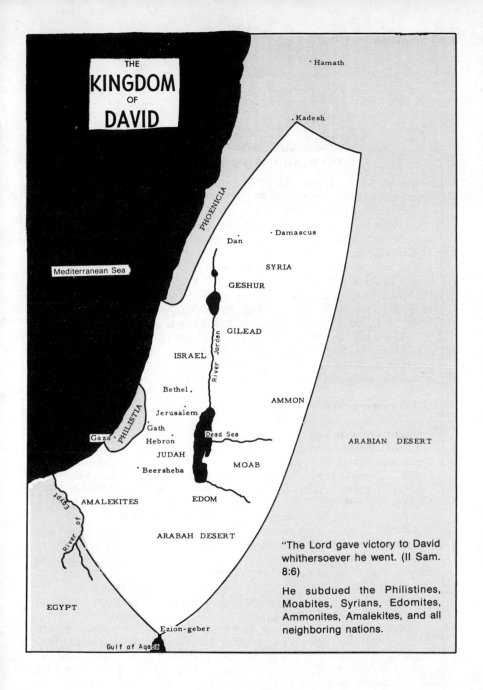

THE
KINGDOM
OF
DAVID

· Hamath

. Kadesh

PHOENICIA

Mediterranean Sea

Dan · Damascus

SYRIA

GESHUR

GILEAD

River Jordan

ISRAEL

Bethel .

Jerusalem ·

Gath ·

Gaza · PHILISTIA

Hebron

Dead Sea

AMMON

ARABIAN DESERT

JUDAH

· Beersheba

MOAB

River of Egypt

AMALEKITES

EDOM

ARABAH DESERT

EGYPT

Ezion-geber

Gulf of Aqaba

"The Lord gave victory to David
whithersoever he went. (II Sam.
8:6)

He subdued the Philistines,
Moabites, Syrians, Edomites,
Ammonites, Amalekites, and all
neighboring nations.

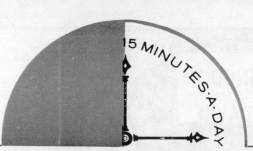
INTRODUCTION TO II KINGS

Except for Saul and David, all the kings of Judah and Israel are recorded in the two books of Kings.

The book of *I Kings* (chapters 1-11) contains the record of Solomon's great reign of peace. But the glory soon passed away because of his sins, and the nation became a divided kingdom immediately after his death (I Kings 12 thru II Kings 18).

The book of *II Kings* is a continuation of the history of the two kingdoms. Rehoboam, Solomon's son, was the first king to reign over Judah, the Southern Kingdom. The tribes of Judah, Benjamin, and Levi remained faithful to the God-appointed Temple worship in Jerusalem and to the house of David, through whom the Messiah was promised.

The remaining ten tribes, led by Jeroboam of Ephraim, seceded and established the Northern Kingdom, called Israel. Jeroboam immediately established golden calf worship centers at Dan and Bethel, as well as a new order of priests in order to sever all loyalty to the Temple at Jerusalem.

The prophets were prominent throughout the history of the kings. They were Jehovah's gracious appeal to Israel to return to Him. They exposed the nation's corruption and foretold God's judgment.

In the opening chapters, the prophet Elijah and Elisha are prominent. Amos and Hosea prophesied to the Northern Kingdom (also Ahijah). Isaiah, Jeremiah, Jonah, Joel, Obadiah, Micah, Nahum, Habakkuk, and Zephaniah were prophets in Judah. (Other prophets who did not write books were Azariah, Eliezer, Iddo, Jahaziel, Jehu, Shemaiah). Ezekiel prophesied among the captives while Daniel was in Babylon.

About 250 years after the division of the united kingdom, Israel was defeated by the Assyrian king, who deported most of the Israelites to various parts of his empire. He then populated the land of Israel with people from other nations. Their intermarriage of these people with the remaining Israelites became the ancestors of the Samaritans.

Judah, the small Southern Kingdom, continued as a nation for about 125 years after Israel's defeat.

During the last few years of Judah's history, Assyria was conquered by the Medes and the Babylonians; Egypt declined in power, and Babylon began to grow in world power. It took Nebuchadnezzar twenty years to destroy Jerusalem. (Compare II Kings 24:14-16; 25:3-12; II Chronicles 36:3-8; Jeremiah 52:28-30; Daniel 1:3.) Judah was defeated by the Babylonians, who destroyed both Solomon's Temple and Jerusalem. The remaining population was deported to Babylon. Cyrus, king of Persia, eventually conquered Babylon, and the Jewish exiles were given the privilege of returning to Jerusalem. (See Ezra 1:1-4.)

MAY 1: Read II Kings 1-3.

II Kings 2:6, 11: "And Elijah said unto him, Tarry, I pray thee, here; for the Lord hath sent me to Jordan. And he said, As the Lord liveth, and as thy soul liveth, I will not leave thee. And they two went on . . . And it came to pass . . . there appeared a chariot of fire, . . . and Elijah went up by a whirlwind into heaven."

All the prophets at Bethel knew that the Lord would take away Elijah the prophet (see 2:3), but when God was choosing the man who would take Elijah's place, He by-passed the sons of the prophets, the theological students. Instead, He chose a farm boy (I Kings 19:19-21) who was known only as a servant (see II Kings 3:11).

Elisha was more concerned about assisting Elijah and being a servant of God than he was in fulfilling any worldly interest. He had already bid farewell to his family, the world, and the approval "of the school of the prophets," and was willing to surrender everything in order to obtain God's best.

Underscore in your Bible the statements in chapter two that reveal the close fellowship Elisha had with Elijah. "So they went down" (verse 2); "so they came to Jericho" (verse 4); "and they two went on" (verse 6); "and they two stood by Jordan" (verse 7); "they two went over on dry ground" (verse 8). Because of Elisha's persistence in remaining faithful to Elijah, God

---

MEMORY VERSE FOR THE WEEK: II Chronicles 7:14

"If my people, which are called by my name, shall humble themselves, and pray, and seek my face, and turn from their wicked ways; then will I hear from heaven, and will forgive their sin, and will heal their land."

121

gave him the privilege of becoming his successor. The honor that came to Elisha has been missed by many today.

Why not call your pastor today and ask him how you can help him? Develop a loyalty to your minister and spiritual counselor. Establish a close fellowship with him. Be willing to be just a servant—an errand boy—a prayer partner. Recognize the spiritual principle of subjection to God's authority as subjection to God Himself.

"Remember them which have the rule over you, who have spoken unto you the word of God: whose faith follow . . . Obey them . . .and submit yourselves . . ." (Hebrews 13:7,17).

NOTE:
3:11 **which poured water on the hands** means personal servant.
II Kings 1:10-12: *See Luke 9:54.*

MAY 2: Read II Kings 4-5.

II Kings 5:7: "And it came to pass, when the king of Israel [Jehoram] had read the letter, that he rent his clothes, and said, Am I God, to kill and to make alive, that this man doth send unto me to recover a man of his leprosy? Wherefore consider, I pray you, and see how he seeketh a quarrel against me."

When Jehoram read the letter that the king of Syria wrote concerning the leper Naaman, King Jehoram jumped to the wrong conclusion and accused Naaman, the powerful captain of the Assyrian army, of seeking to declare war. Even after Naaman was miraculously healed, King Jehoram refused to worship God, as did his brother, Ahaziah, and his father, Ahab, before him.

Like Jehoram, far too many Christians fail to realize that the providential arrangements of *God*—not *men*—have placed us exactly where we are at this very moment. Therefore, we should look for God's message rather than blame the messenger He uses.

We may not be responsible for the circumstances in which we find ourselves, but we are responsible for the way these events affect us. It is not necessary in all instances for us to understand the reason for our circumstances, but we should submissively yield to God and seek His will. Let us always remember that God is seeking to use our circumstances to transform us into the image of His Son.

"That the trial of your faith, being much more precious than of gold that perisheth, though it be tried with fire, might be found unto praise and honour and glory at the appearing of Jesus Christ" (1 Peter 1:7).

NOTE:
4:6 **oil stayed** means oil ceased; 4:27 **vexed** means distressed; 4:38 **seethe** means boil; 4:43 **servitor** means servant; 5:10 **clean** means healed; 5:24 **tower** means a mound (i.e., a fortress); **bestowed** means hid.
II Kings 4:23: *See Heb. 11:35.* **5:14:** *See Luke 4:27.*

MEMORY VERSE FOR THE WEEK: II Chronicles 7:14

"If my people, which are called by my name, shall humble themselves, and pray, and seek my face, and turn from their wicked ways; then will I hear from heaven, and will forgive their sin, and will heal their land."

MAY 3: Read II Kings 6-8.

II Kings 8:13: "And Hazael said, But what! is thy servant a dog, that he should do this great thing? And Elisha answered, *The Lord* hath shewed me that thou shalt be king over Syria."

Benhadad, the king of Syria, was sick; and Hazael, his trusted advisor, outwardly displayed deep concern. Actually, he was deceptively waiting for an opportunity to assassinate the king. He "took a thick cloth, and dipped it in water, and spread it on his [Benhadad's] face, so that he died; and Hazael reigned in his stead" (II Kings 8:15).

Hazael had seemed horrified with Elisha's look of accusation—that he would heartlessly assassinate his royal master. He declared, "Is thy servant a dog, that he should do this great thing?"

Circumstances often present new temptations which we have never encountered before. Some have allowed jealousy and coveting another's good fortune to blind their conscience, causing them to use deceitful methods to attain their desires.

Had Joseph's brothers been told that one day they would consider murdering their brother, they undoubtedly also would have answered, "Is thy servant a dog, that he should do this great thing?" Joseph's brothers would never have sold him into slavery had they not first allowed jealousy and covetousness to blind their consciences.

"Is thy servant a dog?" No, thy servant is not a dog, he is a man—a sinner by nature. Unless we yield to the indwelling Christ, we will yield readily to the passions which war against the soul.

"This wisdom descendeth not from above, but is earthly, sensual, devilish. For where envying and strife is, there is confusion and every evil work" (James 3:15-16).

NOTE:
7:1 **measure** means fourth bushel; 7:5 **uttermost part** mean border; 8:11 **settled his countenance** means fixed his gaze.

MAY 4: Read II Kings 9-10.

II Kings 9:6-8: "... Thus saith the Lord God of Israel, I have anointed thee king over the people of the Lord, even over Israel. And thou shalt smite the house of Ahab thy master, that I may avenge the blood of my servants the prophets ... For the whole house of Ahab shall perish."

After Ahab's death, his son Ahaziah reigned over Israel for two years,

---

MEMORY VERSE FOR THE WEEK: II Chronicles 7:14
"If my people, which are called by my name, shall humble themselves, and pray, and seek my face, and turn from their wicked ways; then will I hear from heaven, and will forgive their sin, and will heal their land."

---

followed by the 12-year reign of Ahaziah's brother, Jehoram. All three of these kings of the Northern Kingdom had so zealously promoted idolatry in Israel that it spread into Judah and seriously weakened the true worship of Jehovah in Jerusalem.

During this serious spiritual decline, the Lord was preparing Jehu, the powerful captain commander of the Northern Kingdom armies. God had told Elijah, "Jehu, the son of Nimshi halt thou anoint to be king over Israel . . ." (I Kings 19:16). Perhaps as many as 20 years passed before God told Elisha to send a young prophet to anoint Jehu as Israel's king and the executioner of Jehoram and all the descendants of Ahab. What appeared to be a coincidence when Jehu met Jehoram (Joram) in the field of Naboth was actually the fulfillment of God's Word against Ahab as foretold in that very place by Elijah. (See I Kings 21:19-23).

The violent and untimely death of Jezebel, King Ahab, and King Jehoram confirms the transient worthlessness of earthly power. Once again God verifies the inflexible, infallibility of His Word.

"The word of our God shall stand for ever" (Isaiah 40:8).

NOTE:
9:22 **treachery** means treason; 9:30 **tired her head** means dressed her hair; 10:3 **Look even out the best and meetest** means Select the best and most fit; 10:27 **draught house** means dung shed.

"And they set them up images . . ."
(II Kings 17:10)

MAY 5: Read II Kings 11-13.

II Kings 11:1: "And when Athaliah the mother of Ahaziah [Judah's king] saw that her son was dead, she arose and destroyed all the seed royal."

Just nine years following the great and godly reign of Jehoshaphat, Athaliah gained control of the Southern Kingdom and ruled as queen in the City of David. Her evil six-year reign was the result of a compromise made by Jehoshaphat.

Little could Jehoshaphat realize that the "unequal yoke" of his son Jehoram's marriage to Athaliah, the daughter of wicked Jezebel, would one day destroy all the influence of godliness that he had spent his life building.

The eventual downfall of the nation is easily traced to their association with unbelievers. Beginning with Solomon, we see how his heathen wives turned his heart from the Lord (see I Kings 11:4).

Nothing is so deceptive and destructive to a Christian's usefulness and lasting effectiveness as close association and partnership with those who oppose

---

MEMORY VERSE FOR THE WEEK: II Chronicles 7:14
"If my people, which are called by my name, shall humble themselves, and pray, and seek my face, and turn from their wicked ways; then will I hear from heaven, and will forgive their sin, and will heal their land."

---

the Lord. Many Christians today have discovered, like Peter, that when you "warm yourself at the enemies' fire," it is impossible to take a firm, undeviating stand for Christ against a world that crucified Him.

"Be ye not unequally yoked together with unbelievers: for what fellowship hath righteousness with unrighteousness? and what communion hath light with darkness?" (II Corinthians 6:14).

NOTE:
11:7 **two parts** means two divisions; 11:8 **compass** means surround; 11:16 **way** means gate; 12:5 **breaches** means broken places; 12:11 **laid it out** means paid it out; 13:6 **grove** means shrine to Asherah.

MAY 6: Read II Kings 14-15.

II Kings 14:25: "He restored the coast of Israel from the entering of Hamath unto the sea of the plain, according to the word of the Lord God of Israel, which he spake by the hand of his servant Jonah, the son of Amittai, the prophet, which was of Gathhepher."

King Jeroboam II (son of Jehoash) was very successful in all his battles and brought great prosperity to the nation, but this recognition did not lead him to worship God. Instead, "he did that which was evil in the sight of the Lord . . ." He practiced all the sins of Jeroboam I. (See II Kings 14:24.) Furthermore, Jeroboam II ignored God's prophets (Amos, Hosea, Joel, and Jonah) who prophesied during his reign. Therefore, God commanded Amos to go to Bethel to prophesy the destruction of this king and his kingdom. (See Amos 7:9.)

The Israelites seemed to believe that because they prospered, God approved of their worshiping idols. More and more, they placed their confidence in the supremacy of Baal worship.

The times when we are receiving the most material blessings are often the times when we experience greater tests of our loyalty and humility before God. It is in times of prosperity that we are usually less concerned about prayerfully seeking the Lord's guidance and will for our lives.

Many, like Jeroboam, boast of their material success, even though it was achieved at the cost of spiritual neglect. How tragic that some parents have left their children much material wealth but have failed to emphasize the real spiritual wealth of the Word of God!

"What is a man profited, if he shall gain the whole world, and lose his own soul?" (Matthew 16:26).

NOTE:
14:7 **Selah** means the rock city of Petra; 14:12 **put to the worse** means defeated; 15:4 **Save** means Except; 15:5 **a several house** means an isolated house; 15:20 **exacted** means took; 15:25 **in his room** means in his stead, place.

MEMORY VERSE FOR THE WEEK: II Chronicles 7:14
"If my people, which are called by my name, shall humble themselves, and pray, and seek my face, and turn from their wicked ways; then will I hear from heaven, and will forgive their sin, and will heal their land."

MAY 7: Read II Kings 16-17.

". . . Hoshea the king of As-syria . . . carried Israel away into Assyria . . ." (II Kings 17:6)

II Kings 17:6: "In the ninth year of Hoshea the king of Assyria took Samaria, and carried Israel away into Assyria. . . ."

Hoshea, who "did that which was evil in the sight of the Lord," was the last king to reign over the ten tribes, the Northern Kingdom.

The ten tribes who were delivered from Egyptian bondage and kept from slavery for over 700 years were now conquered by the Assyrians and deported from the Promised Land to be slaves. (See I Chronicles 5:25-26.) Hoshea made a last desperate effort to strengthen the Northern Kingdom against Assyria by making a secret alliance with the king of Egypt.

During the reign of King Hoshea, the prophet Hosea pleaded with the nation, "O Israel, return unto the Lord thy God; for thou hast fallen by thine iniquity" (Hosea 14:1). However, the nation disregarded this warning. There is no record that King Hoshea every prayed or turned to God for help. In fact, not one of the 19 kings of Israel in more than 250 years' history was recorded as being a true worshiper of Jehovah (with the possible exception of Jehu).

How different could have been the outcome of the nation if King Hoshea had made a covenant with the King of all kingdoms and had humbled himself and prayed, as the Lord ordered when He appeared to Solomon. (See II Chronicles 7:12-15.)

"Through thee will we push down our enemies: through thy name will we tread them under that rise up against us" (Psalm 44:5).

NOTE:
16:11 **against** means before; 16:13 **meat offering** means meal offering; 17:11 **heathen** means nations.

II Kings 17:16: *See Acts 7:42.*

MAY 8: Read II Kings 18-20.

II Kings 18:1,5,7: ". . . Hezekiah . . . trusted in the Lord God of Israel; so that after him was none like him among all the kings of Judah, nor any that were before him . . . And the Lord was with him . . ."

The Northern Kingdom had already been conquered by the Assyrians, and most of the people had been deported as slaves. Sennacherib, the Assyrian king, was determined then to conquer Judah, the Southern Kingdom; therefore, he surrounded Jerusalem with his seemingly invincible army. The chances for escape looked impossible, and to all human appearance, there was no hope. But King Hezekiah bypassed all his advisors and went

---

MEMORY VERSE FOR THE WEEK: I Peter 1:22

"Seeing ye have purified your souls in obeying the truth through the Spirit unto unfeigned love of the brethren, see that ye love one another with a pure heart fervently:"

---

immediately to the Temple and prayed. He then sent messengers to the prophet, Isaiah.

After that prayer meeting, the entire Assyrian army of 185,000 men were destroyed by the angel of God. Furthermore, when Sennacherib returned to his palace in Nineveh, he was assassinated by two of his own sons (II Kings 19:37; Isaiah 37:38).

We should never be fearful about our future but we do need to pray and commit our need to Him. No matter how hopeless everything may appear, just remember that when Hezekiah prayed, ". . . the Lord was with him," and He will be with you.

"Again I say unto you, That if two of you shall agree on earth as touching any thing that they shall ask, it shall be done for them of my Father which is in heaven" (Matthew 18:19).

NOTE:
19:7 **blast** means spirit of bad fortune; 20:3 **sore** means bitterly.

MAY 9: Read II Kings 21 thru 23:20.

". . . I have found the book of the law in the house of the Lord . . ."

II Kings 22:8

II Kings 22:8,11: "Hilkiah the high priest . . . said . . . I have found the book of the law in the house of the Lord . . . And it came to pass, when the king had heard the words of the book of the law, that he rent his clothes."

When Josiah heard the Word of the Lord read, he tore his clothes (displaying grief over the nation's turning from God), destroyed the altars of Baal, and "burnt the bones of the [false] priests upon their altars." By doing this, he fulfilled the prophecy foretold 300 years earlier by the man of God from Judah (I Kings 13:2; compare II Chronicles 34:5).

Josiah was a godly king. "Like unto him was there no king before him, that turned to the Lord with *all* his heart, and with *all* his soul, and with *all* his might, according to *all* the law of Moses; neither after him arose there any like him" (II Kings 23:25).

Prayerfully consider the key to Josiah's greatness as revealed through Huldah, "As touching *the words which thou hast heard*; because *thine heart was tender* . . . when thou heardest what I spake against this place . . . *I also have heard thee,* saith the Lord" (II Kings 22:18-19).

In order to have a lasting revival, there must be a renewed interest in prayer and reading and hearing the Word of God. "Seek ye out of *the book of the Lord,* and read . . ." (Isaiah 34:16).

NOTE:
22:4 **sum the silver** means count the money; 23:17 **title** means monument.

MEMORY VERSE FOR THE WEEK: I Peter 1:22

"Seeing ye have purified your souls in obeying the truth through the Spirit unto unfeigned love of the brethren, see that ye love one another with a pure heart fervently:"

II Kings 25:21: "And the king of Babylon smote them . . . So Judah was carried away out of their land."

Nebuchadnezzar, the great king of Babylon, defeated the Egyptians, captured Syria and Palestine, and then attacked Jerusalem.

Zedekiah, the last king of Judah, tried to escape when Nebuchadnezzar besieged Jerusalem, but he was captured and forced to witness the slaughter of his sons. Then they put out his eyes and carried him in chains to Babylon. This agonizing ordeal was the fulfillment of two prophecies: (1) Jeremiah had foretold that Zedekiah, king of Jerusalem, would be led to Babylon; (2) Ezekiel had said, "yet shall he not see it" (Jeremiah 32:5; 34:3; Ezekiel 12:13).

Jerusalem was invincible as long as they acknowledged and worshiped Jehovah, but that great city became powerless when she forsook the Word of God.

Today, similar events are being re-enacted before our eyes. The "Zedekiahs" and false prophets are leading our nation further into sin and farther away from God. But the "Jeremiahs" of our day are telling the world that God's Word should have absolute authority over our lives.

"Thou hast known the holy scriptures, which are able to make thee wise unto salvation through faith which is in Christ Jesus" (II Timothy 3:15).

NOTE:
25:12 **husbandmen** means farmers; 25:27 **lift up the head** means show favor to, release.

II Kings 24:15: *See Acts 7:43.*

INTRODUCTION TO I AND II CHRONICLES

The largest genealogical tables of names in the Bible is found in the first nine chapters of *I Chronicles*. They are devoted to the divinely chosen families through whom the Lord carried out His purpose. Beginning with Adam, they coincide with the genealogy of Christ as recorded in the Gospels of Matthew and Luke. Many names are omitted, but those that were related to the prophetic fulfillment of the promised Savior are recorded.

The book of *II Chronicles* records the history of the Southern Kingdom of Judah from the reign of Solomon to the return of the exiles from Babylon. It contains forty duplications of history already recorded in II Samuel, I Kings and II Kings, but with supplements that emphasize the nation's covenant relationship to God. Therefore, hardly anything is mentioned about the apostate Northern Kingdom.

The book of II Chronicles closes with the decree of Cyrus, king of Persia, permitting the Jews to return from captivity to rebuild the Temple (36:22-23).

Throughout these books, God is revealing that, apart from Himself, human history can only lead to failure.

MAY 11: Read I Chronicles 1-2.

I Chronicles 1:1,4: Adam, Seth, Enosh . . . Noah, Shem, Ham, and Japheth."

Beginning wtih the creation of Adam by God's own hand, the Bible gives us a carefully documented genealogy that eventually leads to our Savior. Not everyone's name appears in these genealogies, but the main line of ancestry is there. In fact the first verse of the genealogy in I Chronicles, Adam and then Seth is mentioned. No mention is made of Cain or Abel. Cain became a murderer who forfeited his opportunity to be in the ancestry of Christ; Abel's name is missing because he had no descendants. Shem was selected from the family of Noah; Isaac was selected from the family of Abraham; Jacob was chosen, but Esau was rejected.

Today Jehovah is calling to Himself a second "chosen generation, a royal priesthood" (I Peter 2:9), united not by a genealogy that dates back to Adam but through Christ, the second Adam.

Just think! The name of cach person who has accepted Christ as his Savior is recorded in God's infallible, indestructible book—the Lamb's Book of Life. The most important question in your life is, Has your name been written in the Lamb's Book of Life? If it has, you may "Rejoice, because your names are written in heaven" (Luke 10:20).

MAY 12: Read I Chronicles 3-5.

I Chronicles 4:9-10: "And Jabez was *more honorable* than his brethren . . . and Jabez called on the God of Israel, saying, Oh that thou *wouldest bless me indeed,* and enlarge my coast, and that thine hand might be with me, and that thou wouldest keep me from evil . . . and God granted him that which he requested."

We know very little about Jabez except that he prayed for something besides worldly fame. He was "more honorable than his brethren, . . . and God granted him that which he requested."

Jabez found the joy that comes as one gives himself to God for His pleasure alone, seeking to be led in the path of God's choice. Accomplishments

---

MEMORY VERSE FOR THE WEEK: I Peter 1:22

"Seeing ye have purified your souls in obeying the truth through the Spirit unto unfeigned love of the brethren, see that ye love one another with a pure heart fervently:"

---

that bring eternal results are those that God initiates. Therefore, when we are faithfully serving Christ, we shall neither murmur about anything nor be proud of our accomplishments. Furthermore, we should never be jealous of the advantages which other people have. If our supreme desire is to gain His blessing, there is no need to fear that we are being cheated. Our main goal in life should be to do the best we can each day with what we have (Philippians 4:11). The only important thing is what we are *in the eyes of God*. Anything God wants us to do, He will help us do if we are willing to yield to His will for our lives.

"God . . . is a rewarder of them that diligently seek him" (Hebrews 11:6).

MAY 13: Read I Chronicles 6-7.

". . . Cain rose up against Abel his brother and slew him"
Genesis 4:8

I Chronicles 7:40: ". . . And the number throughout the genealogy . . . was twenty and six thousand men."

The name of every individual, as well as the family and tribe to which they belonged, was carefully registered. There is a striking difference in the character of the men who are mentioned in these chapters. Some were devoted to their God-given responsibilities, while other profaned their holy calling.

Aaron was a devoted priest, but his sons were hypocrites. Samuel was a godly judge, but his sons were evil. For years, Abiathar was a high priest, but he later became a traitor to King David (I Kings 1:7; 2:26-35). What a strange mixture of devout saints and sinful, undisciplined men! What a contrast between heaven-born beginnings and forfeited opportunities.

The long, uninteresting list of names shows us that God does not look on mankind as a crowd of human beings which populate a world. In fact, He is so concerned over each individual that even the hairs on our head were numbered by Him (Matthew 10:30). He knows each of us by name, and our name is either written in the Lamb's Book of Life or the great white throne judgment awaits those whose names are not recorded. "And I saw the dead, small and great, stand before God; and the books were opened: and another book was opened, which is the book of life: and the dead were judged out of those things which were written in the books, according to their works" (Revelation 20:12).

NOTE:
6:32 **waited on** means performed service in; 6:66 **the residue** means some; 6:74 **suburbs** means pasture lands; 7:24 **nether** means lower.

MEMORY VERSE FOR THE WEEK: I Peter 1:22

"Seeing ye have purified your souls in obeying the truth through the Spirit unto unfeigned love of the brethren, see that ye love one another with a pure heart fervently:"

MAY 14: Read I Chronicles 8-10.

I Chronicles 10:13: "So Saul died for his transgression which he committed against the Lord, even against the word of the Lord, which he kept not, and also for asking counsel of one that had a familiar spirit, to enquire of it."

God had commanded Saul to "utterly destroy all" of the Amalekites, and their possessions, but they spared King Agag and took home the choicest animals. His partial "obedience" was self-deceiving, for he proudly announced to Samuel, "Blessed be thou of the Lord: I have performed the command-ment of the Lord" (I Samuel 15:13). His obedience was only as complete as it pleased himself and the people.

The night before his final battle with the Philistines on Mt. Gilboa, Saul hastily prayed, but he did not wait for God to answer. He rushed through the night to the village of Endor to seek counsel from a spiritualist medium concerning the outcome of the battle. This exposed Saul's disloyalty as God's representative to enforce His Word that said, "There shall not be found among you any one . . . that useth divination, or an observer of times, or an en-chanter, or a witch, or a charmer, or a consulter with familiar spirits, or a wizard, or a necromancer. For all that do these things are an abomination unto the Lord . . ." (Deuteronomy 18:10-12).

Saul is not the only person who has missed God's best for their lives and created serious problems by patronizing palm readers, fortune tellers, spiri-tualists, and other deceptive evil advisors rather than turning to God.

"These things have I written unto you concerning them that seduce you" (I John 2:26).

NOTE:
8:33 **Eshbaal** means Ishbosheth; 9:23 **wards** means guards; 9:28 **out by tale** means take them out by count.

MAY 15: Read I Chronicles 11-13.

". . . The Lord saveth not with sword and spear: for the battle is the Lord's . . ."
(I Samuel 17:47)

I Chronicles 12:18: "Then the spirit came upon Amasai, who was chief of the captains, and he said, Thine are we, David, and on thy side, thou son of Jesse: peace, peace be unto thee, and peace be to thine helpers; for thy God helpeth thee. Then David received them and made them cap-tains of the band."

The ten tribes of the Northern Kingdom were very slow to recognize God's authority and ac-cept David, whom God had anointed years earlier to be their king.

Once we recognize God's order of authority as revealed in His Word, we will no longer be satisfied with serving the Lord with an independent, self-willed spirit.

Without exception, obedience to God's Word must have priority in each decision. We are all prone to ignore the truth when it clashes with our personal interests, but God's Word must always be our only rule of life, even if it contradicts our experience and baffles our understanding. God's rule of authority permeates each page of the Bible and includes: (1) the church being in subjection to Christ, (2) citizens being in subjection to the laws of the land, (3) wives being in subjection to their husbands, (4) children being in subjection to their parents, and (5) Christians being in subjection to those who have the rule over them. (See Romans 13:1; Ephesians 5:24; 6:1.)

"Obey them that have the rule over you, submit yourselves: for they watch for your souls, as they that must give account, that they may do it with joy, and not with grief: for that is unprofitable for you" (Hebrews 13:17).

NOTE:
11:16 **hold** means fortress; 12:1 **close** means concealed; 12:8 **separated themselves** means came to support; 12:17 **knit** means joined; 12:19 **fall to** means desert us and return to Saul.

MAY 16: Read I Chronicles 14-16.

I Chronicles 14:17: "And the fame of David went out into all the lands; and the Lord brought the fear of him upon all nations."

After David conquered the formidable Jebusites, who had never been conquered, even in the days of Joshua, he established his capital in Jerusalem.

The Philistines feared his growing power, so they "spread themselves in the valley" near Bethlehem and prepared to attack Jerusalem. David immediately "inquired of God." He would not take his men into battle until he knew the will of God. It was a great victory, but the defeated Philistines renewed their force with a second attack. But notice! Although the first battle was very successful, David did not assume to know God's will concerning the second attack. He "inquired again of God" (verse 14). This time God directed in an altogether different way. Again David did as God commanded him, and he gained another great victory.

The often-recorded phrase "David inquired of the Lord" was the key to his greatness. (See I Samuel 23:2,4; 30:8; II Samuel 2:1; 5:19,23; 21:1; I Chronicles 14:10,14.)

Once we are awakened to the importance of prayer, Satan uses well-planned strategies to disrupt our prayers by such seemingly innocent things as an unexpected knock at the door, the children causing a disturbance, or by calling to remembrance something important we forgot to do.

We are privileged to pray always "with all prayer and supplication in the Spirit, and watching thereunto with all perseverance and supplication for all saints" (Ephesians 6:18).

NOTE:
14:13 **spread themselves abroad** means made a hostile invasion.

MEMORY VERSE FOR THE WEEK: 1 Peter 1:23

"Being born again, not of corruptible seed, but of incorruptible, by the word of God, which liveth and abideth for ever."

MAY 17: Read I Chronicles 17-20.

"Thus saith the Lord, Thou shalt not build me an house . . ."
I Chronicles 17:4

II Chronicles 17:1: "David said to Nathan the prophet, Lo, I dwell in an house of cedars, but the ark of the covenant of the Lord remaineth under curtains."

David lived in a beautiful, luxurious palace made of cedars, and he felt ashamed that the tabernacle of God where he worshiped was only an old tent. The gods of heathen nations had beautiful temples; why should Jehovah have less?

When David expressed to the prophet Nathan his desire to build a house for God, Nathan probably assumed that God would be pleased. Without inquiring of the Lord, he gave David his approval. But his answer was his own personal opinion. God spoke to Nathan, saying, "Tell David . . . Thou shalt not build me an house" (verse 4).

Although David was greatly disappointed, he expressed humility in his reply, "Who am I . . . that thou hast brought me hitherto?" (verse 16). And in adoration of the infinite greatness of the incomparable God, David acknowledged, "O Lord, there is none like thee . . ." (verse 20).

The choice of what is pleasing to God must always be left to Him. All who please the Lord adore and worship His ways and have learned to confess, "O Lord, I know that the way of man is not in himself; it is not in man that walketh to direct his steps" (Jeremiah 10:23).

NOTE:
17:1 **under curtains** means in the tent tabernacle; 18:4 **houghed** means crippled; 19:4 **hard by** means near; 19:6 **odious** means detestable.
I Chron. 17:14. *See Luke 1:33.*

MAY 18: Read I Chronicles 21-23.

I Chronicles 22:19: "Now set your heart and your soul to seek the Lord your God; arise therefore, and build ye the sanctuary of the Lord God."

When God refused David the privilege of building the Temple, He was not condemning David for his wars, for these had to be fought if the enemies within the Promised Land were to be conquered.

David carefully laid the plans for building the Temple, but his son Solomon built it. God appoints different men for different tasks, and the character of the men chosen to do the work was just as important as gathering the money and materials for the construction of the Temple. David appealed for willing workers who possessed the spirit of giving glory and honor to God—which is what the Temple represented. What value would the Temple be to God if it did not represent the adoration and dedication of those who built it?

MEMORY VERSE FOR THE WEEK: I Peter 1:23

"Being born again, not of corruptible seed, but of incorruptible, by the word of God, which liveth and abideth for ever."

This requirement for singlehearted devotion to God would disqualify many of our volunteers today who would reply, "If you can't find anyone else, I'll do it"; or, "If you can match my gift, then you can count on mine"; or, "I'll do my share and no more."

Oh, how much more intense our love should be as "living stones" in building His "spiritual house" (I Peter 2:4-5), that we might bring glory and honor to His name.

"I have laid the foundation, another buildeth thereon. But let every man take heed how he buildeth thereupon" (I Corinthians 3:10).

NOTE:
22:3 **without weight** means beyond calculation; 23:11 **one reckoning** means one group.

"So David went and brought up the ark of God from the house of Obededom . . ."
II Samuel 6:10

MAY 19: Read I Chronicles 24-26.

I Chronicles 26:4,5: "Moreover the sons of Obededom . . . for God blessed him."

Once again we are confronted with a great number of unfamiliar names that appear to be meaningless. But no person goes unnoticed before God. Among all these names, we discover the name "Obededom," a man whom God especially blessed.

ARK

When Uzzah was struck dead for touching the ark, David refused to proceed toward Jerusalem and left the ark with Obededom, where it remained for 3 months (II Samuel 6:1-11; I Chronicles 13:13).

God remembered and greatly blessed Obededom for faithfully welcoming the ark that contained His Word. Without the indwelling Word, the ark was worthless.

When Obededom received the ark, he not only received God's Word, but the very presence of God dwelled within his home.

Determine *now* to give more time to allowing God to speak to you through daily reading His Word. Oh, let us recognize that Christ in all His fullness is waiting to bless all who welcome His Word! Let us prayerfully desire that our whole being be taken up with His presence.

"He taught me also, and said unto me, Let thine heart retain my words: keep my commandments, and live . . . for they are life unto those that find them . . ." (Proverbs 4:4,22).

NOTE:
24:2 **executed** means performed.
I Chron. 24:20: *See Matt. 23:35.*

MEMORY VERSE FOR THE WEEK: I Peter 1:23

"Being born again, not of corruptible seed, but of incorruptible, by the word of God, which liveth and abideth for ever."

I Chronicles 29:10: "Wherefore David blessed the Lord before all the congregation: and David said, Blessed be thou, Lord God of Israel our father, for ever and ever."

David's last message to his kingdom was one of the greatest outbursts of praise found in the Old Testament. David adored the Lord and proclaimed His unspeakable grandeur, "Thine, O Lord, is the greatness, and the power, and the glory, and the victory, and the majesty" (I Chronicles 29:11).

Remember, too, that David had grown old and was fully aware that his reign was finished; but the nearer he came to the world of everlasting praise, the more he spoke the language of that world.

We are told of "much people in heaven saying, "Alleluia! Salvation, and glory, and honour, and power, unto the Lord our God" (Revelation 19:1).

Praise is the natural, spontaneous expression of one who has a deep sense of unworthiness and adores the Father for who He is and for what He does.

Under every circumstance we should praise Him, for we have the assurance that our lives are fashioned "according to the good pleasure of His will." To grumble about our circumstances is to question "the exceeding greatness of his power to usward who believe" (Ephesians 1:19).

"By him therefore let us offer the sacrifice of praise to God *continually,* that is, the fruit of our lips giving thanks to his name" (Hebrews 13:15).

NOTE:
27:2 **course** means division; 28:4 **liked** means chose; 28:7 **constant** means faithful; 28:14 **instruments** means vessels, articles; 29:1 **tender** means inexperienced; 29:3 **proper good** means personal treasure.
I Chron. 29:15: *See Heb. 11:13.*

MAY 21: Read II Chronicles 1-3.

II Chronicles 1:12: "Wisdom and knowledge is granted unto thee; and I will give thee riches, and wealth, and honour, such as none of the kings have had that have been before thee, neither shall there any after thee have the like."

"Give me now wisdom and knowledge . . ."
II Chronicles 1:10

Solomon's kingdom was unequaled in wealth and splendor. It seems strange that someone could receive such wealth and wisdom from God and still not live in obedience to God's Word. The wisest man on earth "did evil in the sight of the Lord and . . . turned from the Lord God of Israel" (I Kings 11:6,11).

Possessions give a false sense of security and self-sufficiency which often robs us of the true values of life. The Scriptures teach that "the wisdom of this world is foolishness with God" (I Corinthians 3:19).

We are living in days of unusual pressure, and the principle that must guide

MEMORY VERSE FOR THE WEEK: I Peter 1:23

"Being born again, not of corruptible seed, but of incorruptible, by the word of God, which liveth and abideth for ever."

us is this: that "they that buy, as though they possessed not; and they that use this world, as not abusing it . . ." (I Corinthians 7:29-32).

There is a satanic power at work today, seeking to entangle us in the affairs of this world. (See Ephesians 2:2.) Therefore, it is vital that every Christian be aware of the spirit of this world because "the Spirit speaketh expressly, that in the latter times some shall depart from the faith, giving heed to seducing spirits, and doctrines of devils" (I Timothy 4:1).

NOTE:
2:2 **told out** means counted out; **hew** means cut; 2:7 **cunning** means skillful; 2:14 **find out every device** means execute any design.
II Chron. 3:14: *See Matt. 27:51.*

MAY 22: Read II Chronicles 4-6.

II Chronicles 5:13: "It came even to pass, as the trumpeters and singers were as one, to make one sound to be heard in praising and thanking the Lord . . . then the house was filled with a cloud, even the house of the Lord."

In the dedication of the Temple, the trumpeters and singers were expressing the unity of the nation in giving praise to God. They were experiencing the meaning of King David's psalm, "Whoso offereth praise glorifieth me" (Psalm 50:23). How much more should we, His redeemed people who are enjoying the precious promises of Christ, be of one mind in praising Him!

There is a great lack among some of God's people today of day by day expressing praise to God. Are we too occupied with expecting recognition and praise from others that we fail to praise Him? The less we are occupied with self, the more spontaneous will be our daily praise to Him.

He is the incomparable One, and the great purpose of redemption is to "shew forth the praises of him who hath called you out of darkness into his marvellous light" (1 Peter 2:9).

NOTE:
4:4 **sea** means large basin; 4:5 **three thousand baths** means 255,000 gallons; 4:22 **censers** means firepans; 6:28 **dearth** means famine.
II Chron. 6:18: *See Acts 7:47.*

MAY 23: Read II Chronicles 7-9.

II Chronicles 7:14: "If my people, which are called by my name, shall humble themselves, and pray, and seek my face, and turn from their wicked ways; then will I hear from heaven, and will forgive their sin, and will heal their land."

When God appeared to Solomon this second time, He said, "But if ye shall at all turn from following me, ye or your children . . . and serve other gods, and worship them, then will I cut off Israel out of the land" (see I Kings 9:6-9).

". . . I will surely rend the kingdom from thee . . ."
I Kings 11:11

MEMORY VERSE FOR THE WEEK: I Peter 1:24

"For all flesh is as grass, and all the glory of man as the flower of grass. The grass withereth, and the flower thereof falleth away:"

He did not say, as He did the first time, "Ask what shall I give thee." But this time God revealed to Solomon that His promised blessings were dependent on Israel's faithfulness and obedience, "But if ye turn away, and forsake . . . my commandments . . . Then will I pluck them up . . ." (II Chronicles 7:19-20). Then, in mercy, God assured King Solomon that if in the future, when the nation was being punished by drought, locust, or pestilence, if they would humble themselves and seek His face, turning from their wicked ways, He would forgive them and heal their land.

God withholds His blessing until His people first humble themselves, pray, seek His face, and turn from their evil ways. "If I regard iniquity in my heart, the Lord will not hear me" (Psalm 66:18).

NOTE:
8:5 **nether** means lower; 8:16 **perfected** means completed; 9:1 **prove** means test; 9:14 **chapmen** means traders; 9:18 **stays** means arm rests.
II Chron. 9:1: *See Matt. 12:52; Luke 11:31.*

MAY 24: Read II Chronicles 10-13.

II Chronicles 10:19: "And Israel rebelled against the house of David unto this day.

Solomon's ambitious desire for worldly glory, his taste for foreign luxuries, and his many wives eventually corrupted his heart, and "Solomon did evil in the sight of the Lord" (I Kings 11:6). Solomon's reign, which began so gloriously with God, showed no evidence in later years that he prayed, offered sacrifices, or worshiped God.

Then God appeared for the third and final time to Solomon, saying, ". . . I will surely rend the kingdom from thee, and will give it to thy servant" (I Kings 11:11).

Solomon's sins prepared the way for the kingdom's division and decline in power. How empty it all sounds to read of Solomon's "great wisdom and fame" when we know how he prepared the nation for division and eventual destruction!

Solomon's life was one of self-indulgence, but the Christian should not live for selfish gratifications. Good athletes subject themselves to strict training and rigid discipline. They are willing to give up certain pleasures in anticipation of the rewards of their accomplishments. Surely a Christian should not feel cheated for any self-denial that might help someone find eternal life!

"And every man that striveth for the mastery is temperate in all things. Now they do it to obtain a corruptible crown; but we an incorruptible" (I Corinthians 9:25).

NOTE:
11:15 **devils** means he-goats.

MEMORY VERSE FOR THE WEEK: I Peter 1:24

"For all flesh is as grass, and all the glory of man as the flower of grass. The grass withereth, and the flower thereof falleth away."

"Asa brought out silver and gold out of the treasures of house of the Lord"
II Chronicles 16:2

II Chronicles 15:2: "And he went out to meet Asa, and said unto him, Hear ye me, Asa, and all Judah and Benjamin; The Lord is with you, while ye be with him; and if ye seek him, he will be found of you; but if ye forsake him, he will forsake you."

When Asa, king of Judah, heard how the Lord would be with him as long as he would seek the Lord, he was overjoyed. In fact, he led the nation in a great revival.

Then his faith was tested by the largest army recorded in Scripture—an army of a million soldiers led by Zerah, the Ethiopian king who had declared war on his kingdom. Asa had only 580,000 men. The odds were almost two-to-one against them, but Asa prayed: "Lord, it is nothing with thee to help, whether with many, or with them that hath no power: help us, O Lord our God; for we rest on thee, and in thy name we go against this multitude" (14:11).

The victory was so remarkable ". . . that there was no more war unto the five and thirtieth year of the reign of Asa" (15:19).

As the years passed and Asa's wealth and power increased, he lost sight of his daily dependence on God. When he was threatened by the invading army of Baasha, king of the ten tribes, Asa made an unholy alliance with Benhadad, king of Syria, and used the treasures from the Temple to pay Benhadad to fight the battle for him. Therefore, Asa could no longer say to God, "We rest on Thee."

The temptation to rely on our clever manipulations are as real today as they were for Asa. Without daily fellowship with Him, the danger of losing our first love is real.

"Nevertheless, I have somewhat against thee, because thou hast left thy first love" (Revelation 2:4).

NOTE:
15:16 **mother** means grandmother; **stamped it** means crushed it; 16:14 **sepulchers** means tombs; 17:12 **castles** means strongholds.

MAY 26: Read II Chronicles 18-20.

II Chronicles 20:12: "O our God, wilt thou not judge them? for we have no might against this great company that cometh against us; neither know we what to do: but our eyes are upon thee."

Surrounded by the vast combined armies of Moab, Ammon, and Mt. Seir, Jehoshaphat called for a nationwide prayer meeting and proclaimed a fast throughout Judah.

MEMORY VERSE FOR THE WEEK: I Peter 1:24

"For all flesh is as grass, and all the glory of man as the flower of grass. The grass withereth, and the flower thereof falleth away."

The king stood in the midst of a great congregation in Jerusalem and began to pray. He confessed, "We have no might against this great company that cometh against us; neither know we what to do; but our eyes are upon thee." God responded to their prayer by saying, "Ye shall not need to fight in this battle." The Lord confused the enemy and they miraculously destroyed each other. None escaped.

Even before the battle was won, *Jehoshaphat began praising the Lord for victory.* He appointed singers to go before the army and sing, *"Praise the Lord; for his mercy endureth for ever"* (verse 21).

If God brings us into circumstances that reveal an area in our lives where we have been relying on ourselves, we should immediately thank Him for our helpless situation and begin praising Him for the privilege of depending upon His wisdom and strength. Yes, God wants us to know that no one can treat us unfairly unless He permits it *for our good.* So we can thank Him for every unkind word—every thoughtless deed that comes our way. The most helpless Christian can simply look up and "praise the Lord."

"In every thing give thanks: for this is the will of God in Christ Jesus concerning you" (I Thessalonians 5:18).

NOTE:
18:1 **joined affinity** means made a peace agreement; 18:15 **adjure** means warn, command; 18:33 **harness** means armor.
II Chron. 20:7: *See James 2:23.*

The Divided Kingdom

MAY 27: Read II Chronicles 21-24.

II Chronicles 21:4-6: ". . . Jehoram . . . had the daughter of Ahab to wife: and he wrought that which was evil in the eyes of the Lord."

Jehoram, Jehoshaphat's oldest son, married the daughter of Ahab and Jezebel. As is usually the case, the influence of his ungodly wife had a greater influence on Jehoram than the godly influence of his father. This unfaithful king, Jehoram, led the nation to worship Baal and to participate in heathen abominations, "as did the house of Ahab" (verse 6).

How often Christian parents have seen their children depart from God and go in the ways of the world after they marry one who will oppose their Christian faith.

Can a young couple stand side by side and take their wedding vows before God to be perfectly united with each other except on the one most important thing in life? Can they have all interests in common except their worship and still live together in harmony? Can they talk about everyone else with complete freedom except the most precious Person of all—the Lord Jesus Christ? While one is treasuring up "wrath against the day of wrath," can the other be preparing for the "inheritance incorruptible"? (Romans 2:5; I Peter 1:4).

"Wherefore come out from among them, and be ye separate, saith the Lord . . ." (II Corinthians 6:17).

NOTE:
21:19 **of sore diseases** means in severe agony; **no burning for him** means no public mourning; 22:9 **keep still** means maintain rule; 22:10 **seed royal** means royal family, children of the king; 23:14 **Have her forth of the ranges** means Bring her out into the open; 24:22 **father** means foster father.
II Chron. 24:20,21: *See Matt. 23:35.*

MAY 28: Read II Chronicles 25-27.

II Chronicles 26:5,16: ". . . as long as he [Uzziah] sought the Lord, God made him to prosper . . . but when he was strong, his heart was lifted up to his destruction."

Uzziah did more to restore lost territory and strengthen the prestige of Judah than any king since the divided kingdom. But with his great military success and popularity, he lost sight of the fact that he was only a servant of God. He assumed the position of a priest when he offered incense on the altar, but only a Levite was permitted to approach the altar of incense. (See Leviticus 8.)

Uzziah "sought the Lord." This is followed by a little word we often find in the Scripture—*"but* . . . when he was strong, his heart was lifted up . . ." His zeal for worship turned out to be an over-estimation of his own importance and a love for self-exaltation. God suddenly inflicted King Uzziah with leprosy, and he was an outcast from society until his death (verse 21).

No one ever becomes so spiritual or important in the service of God that he is exempt from judgment for being disobedient to the Word of God. Allow God to be all that He is—Lord of all—"For thine is the kingdom, and the power, and the glory, for ever. Amen" (Matthew 6:13).

NOTE:
26:10 **husbandry** means agriculture farming.

MEMORY VERSE FOR THE WEEK: I Peter 1:24

"For all flesh is as grass, and all the glory of man as the flower of grass. The grass withereth, and the flower thereof falleth away."

II Chronicles 29:10: "Now it is in mine heart to make a covenant with the Lord Go ' of Israel, that his fierce wrath may turn away from us."

"For even Christ our passover is sacrificed for us:"
(I Corinthians 5:7)

In the first month of Hezekiah's reign, he began the greatest religious reforms in Judah's history.

Unlike his wicked father Ahaz, Hezekiah "did that which was good and right and true before the Lord his God." He immediately restored worship in the Temple and effectively removed idolatry.

He then proclaimed a national passover that exceeded all passover observances since the time of Solomon. He sent special letters to the Northern Kingdom of Israel, including Ephraim and Manassah, inviting them to unite in keeping this Passover. Hezekiah neither feared the reaction of King Hoshea of Israel nor the Assyrian kingdom that dominated them.

Many scoffed but others from the Northern Kingdom participated in that great Passover Feast. This is the only record in 250 years of all the ten tribes returning to Jerusalem to worship God.

The importance we place on Christ—our Passover Lamb (I Corinthians 5:7)—determines what we do with our time and effort. Christ makes our position clear: "as my Father hath sent me, even so send I you" (John 20:21) —into homes, factories, offices, and to other nations to witness of the Gospel of Christ, which is ". . . the power of God unto salvation to everyone that believeth . . ." (Romans 1:16).

NOTE:
29:24 **reconciliation** means atonement, sin offering; 29:34 **flay** means skin; 30:22 **comfortably** means encouragingly.

MAY 30: Read II Chronicles 31-33.

II Chronicles 32:31: "Howbeit in the business of the ambassadors of the princes of Babylon, who sent unto him to enquire of the wonder that was done in the land, God left him, *to try him, that he might know all that was in his heart.*"

Babylonian ambassadors came to visit Hezekiah after his miraculous recovery from illness. Hezekiah was so flattered by the Babylonian ambassador, who supposedly came to congratulate him on his recovery, that "his heart was lifted up," and he proudly made a great display of all his wealth.

Hezekiah could have told the heathen ambassadors of all the miraculous things God had done for him—how 185,000 Syrian soldiers who threatened Jerusalem had been destroyed; how he had been miraculously healed when he expected to die; and how all his possessions came as a result of the protec-

---

MEMORY VERSE FOR THE WEEK: I Peter 1:25
"But the word of the Lord endureth for ever. And this is the word which by the gospel is preached unto you."

---

tion, provision, and power of God. God tested him, "that he might know all that was in his heart." Sad to say, he attached much importance to his material wealth. Hezekiah forever forfeited the opportunity to tell the ambassadors of his *true treasures*.

When we talk with unbelievers, do we talk about the weather, clothes, sports, politics, or social affairs most of the time, or do we prayerfully look for an opportunity to talk about our eternal treasures?

"Let us pray as did the early Christians: ". . . grant unto thy servants, that with all boldness they [we] may speak thy word" (Acts 4:29).

NOTE:
31:14 **oblations** refer to meal offerings; **libations** refer to drink offerings; 31:16 **courses** means assigned tasks, divisions; 32:17 **rail on** means belittle, denounce; 32:27 **pleasant jewels** means costly and attractive vessels.

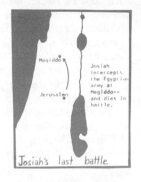

Josiah's last battle

MAY 31: Read II Chronicles 34-36.

II Chronicles 35:21-24: ". . .forbear thee from meddling with God, who is with me, that he destroy thee not. Nevertheless Josiah would not turn his face. . . And the archer shot at king Josiah . . . and he died. . ."

The highest tribute ever given to a king was given to Josiah, king of Judah: "like unto him was there no king before him, that turned to the Lord with all his heart. . ." (II Kings 23:25).

During the reign of Josiah, Pharaoh-nechoh of Egypt wanted to pass through Palestine with his armies to join the Assyrians in a war against Nebuchadnezzar, king of Babylon. The Egyptian king urged Josiah not to interfere, saying "forbear thee from meddling with God, who is with me, that he destroy thee not."

However, on this occasion, Josiah neither sought counsel from the Lord nor asked for advice from the godly prophet Jeremiah. Instead, he attempted to keep the Egyptian king from passing through his country and was fatally wounded. Just three months after his death, the kingdom of Judah lost its political independence and all of his spiritual reformation vanished.

Had someone failed to pray for the godly, 39-year-old king? Oh, how vital it is to pray for those in authority and for those who are effectively being used of God. Pause right now to pray for your pastor, for other men (and ministries) of God, and for our nation's leaders, that God will protect them and guide their every action.

MEMORY VERSE FOR THE WEEK: I Peter 1:25

"But the word of the Lord endureth for ever. And this is the word which by the gospel is preached unto you."

"I exhort therefore, that, first of all, supplications, prayers, intercessions, and giving of thanks, be made for all men; for kings, and for all that are in authority. . ." (I Timothy 2:1-2).

NOTE:

35:8 **small cattle** means sheep; 35:13 **sod they in pots** means cooked in pots; 36:3 **put him down** means deposed him; **condemned** means taxed; 36:15 **betimes** means early.

BIBLICAL REFERENCE INDEX

PRAYERS IN II KINGS AND II CHRONICLES

MEMORY VERSE FOR THE WEEK: I Peter 1:25

"But the word of the Lord endureth for ever. And this is the word which by the gospel is preached unto you."

This chart provides an approximate correlation of the kings, as well as the prophets that lived during their reign.

(S) or (N) denote to what kingdom, Northern or Southern, the prophet primarily spoke.

DIVIDED KINGDOM

I Kings II Kings	II Chron.	Southern Kingdom Judah-2 tribes	Years of Reign	Northern Kingdom Israel-10 tribes	Years of Reign	Prophets
I Kings						
13-14	10-12	Rehoboam	17	Jeroboam I	22	Ahijah (N)
15	13	Abijah (Abijam)	3			Shemaiah (S)
15	14-16	Asa	41	Nadab	2	
16				Baasha	24	
16				Elah	2	
16				Zimri	7 days	
16				Omri	12	
16-22	17-20	Jehoshaphat	25	Ahab	22	Elijah (N), Micaiah (N)
II Kings						
1-8	21	Joram (Jehoram)	8	Ahaziah	2	Elisha (N)
8	21-22	Ahaziah (Jehoahaz)	1	Jehoram (Joram)	12	
9-11	22	Queen Athaliah	6	Jehu	28	
12-13	24	Joah (Jehoash)	40	Jehoahaz	17	Jehoiada (S)—High priest
13-14	25	Amaziah	29	Jehoash (Joash)	16	Joel (S), Jonah (N & Nineveh)
15	26	Azariah (Uzziah)	52	Jeroboam II	41	Amos 1:1 (N)
15				Zechariah	6 mo.	Hosea (N)
15				Shallum	1 mo.	
15	27	Jotham	16	Menahem	10	
15				Pekahiah	2	Isaiah (S)
15-16	28	Ahaz	16	Pekah	20	
17				Hoshea	9	

FALL OF SAMARIA   END OF NORTHERN KINGDOM
(Approx. 250 yrs. since divided kingdom) 722 B.C.

18-20	29-32	Hezekiah	29			Micah (S)
21	33	Manasseh	55			Nahum (S)
21	33	Amon	2			Zephaniah (S)
22-23	34-35	Josiah	31			Jeremiah (S)
23	36	Jehoahaz (Also Johaz, Shallum)	3 mo.			Habakkuk (S)
23	36	Jehoiakim (also Eliakim)	11			
24	36	Jehoiachin (Also Jeconiah & Coniah)	3 mo.			
24-25	36	Zedekiah	11			
25		Gedaliah		Destruction of Jerusalem		

> Ezekiel, Obadiah, Daniel prophesied during the Captivity. Haggai, Zechariah, Malachi prophesied during the Restoration.

LAST DEPORTATION OF JEWS TO BABYLON—END OF SOUTHERN KINGDOM
(Approx. 375 yrs. since divided kingdom) 586 B.C.

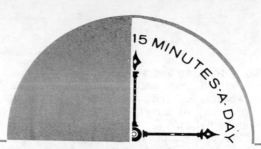

INTRODUCTION TO EZRA

The last two verses of II Chronicles are the same as the first two verses of Ezra to emphasize "that the word of the Lord by the mouth of Jeremiah" *was* fulfilled. (See II Chronicles 36:22 and Ezra 1:1.)

Long before the kingdom of Judah was defeated by King Nebuchadnezzar of Babylon, Jeremiah had foretold: "This whole land shall be a desolation, and . . . shall serve the king of Babylon seventy years . . . For thus said the Lord, . . I will visit you, and perform my good word toward you in causing you to return to this place" (Jeremiah 25:11; 29:10).

Later, Daniel foretold Babylon's downfall, saying, "Thy kingdom is divided, and given to the Medes and Persians" (See Daniel 5:25-31).

Darius, the Mede, divided the kingdom into 120 providences, and Daniel was appointed as one of the presidents and presided over them. (See Daniel 5:28; 6:1-3.)

When King Cyrus arrived at the palace, we can assume that Daniel related the prophecy of Isaiah, who 200 years earlier wrote: "That saith of Cyrus, He is my shepherd, and shall perform all my pleasure: even saying to Jerusalem, Thou shalt be built; and to the temple, Thy foundation shall be laid" (see also Isaiah 44:28; 45:1, 13).

Zerubbabel, with about 50,000 people, returned to Jerusalem. (See Ezra 2:64-65.) In the seventh month of the first year of their return, they built an altar and kept the Feast of Tabernacles. In the second month of the following year, the foundation of the Temple was laid. Fierce Samaritan opposition resulted in a command by Artaxerxes to cease the work. (See Ezra 4:23-24.)

Fourteen years later, Haggai and Zechariah began preaching God's Word. A revival took place; and with the permission of King Darius, they "began to build the house of God" (5:1-2), which was completed within four years.

Nothing is recorded for the next 57 years (between chapters 6 and 7.) Then Ezra took a small expedition from the Persian capital (Babylon) to Jerusalem to teach the Law (chapters 7-8).

OUTLINE OF EZRA

JUNE 1: Read Ezra 1-2.

Ezra 1:3: "Who is there among you of all his people? his God be with him, and let him go up to Jerusalem, which is in Judah, and build the house of the Lord God of Israel, (he is the God,) which is in Jerusalem."

Cyrus, king of Persia, urged the Jews to return to Jerusalem to rebuild the Temple, but only a few recognized the importance of God's covenant relationship to their nation and were willing to make the sacrifice to return with Zerubbabel. Of all the millions of Jews, only about 50,000 returned. Most of the nation remained in Babylon.

Did love for an easier life with fewer hardships overrule their faith and love for their God? Perhaps they feared the risk of robbery and death on the four-month journey. Perhaps they dreaded the economic and material losses which awaited them in Jerusalem. Maybe they simply didn't believe they were capable of accomplishing the task of building a Temple. Or was it just lack of interest or concern?

As we daily read His Word, we realize that to follow Christ, we must be willing to forsake all—"father, and mother, and wife, and children, and brethren, and sisters, yea, and even his own life also, [or else] he cannot be my disciple" (Luke 14:26). Furthermore, God's work—even the details of our daily life—can only be accomplished in God's strength.

In our Christian work, we are often so conscious of our human abilities that each of us is in danger of losing the one thing most needful in our work— God working in us, "to be strengthened with might by his Spirit . . ." (Ephesians 3:16).

NOTE:
2:40 **Hodavian** means Judah; 2:42 **porters** means gate and doorkeepers; **Babylon** is the same as Chaldea (Daniel 5:30)

JUNE 2: Read Ezra 3-5.

Ezra 3:11-12: ". . . And all the people shouted with a great shout, when they praised the Lord, because the foundation of the house of the Lord was laid. But many of the priests . . . who were ancient men, that had seen the first house . . . wept with a loud voice."

When Zerubbabel and the returning Jews left the pleasures and prosperity of Persia for the hardships in Jerusalem, they could have assumed that the first thing to do was build their own homes, but instead, they "builded the altar of the God of Israel, to offer burnt offerings thereon, as it is written in the law of Moses . . ."(3:2). The burnt offering sacrifices were not a mere religious ritual, for these Jews had sacrificed everything in Persia to restore fellowship with God in Jerusalem.

MEMORY VERSE FOR THE WEEK: I Peter 1:25

"But the word of the Lord endureth for ever. And this is the word which by the gospel is preached unto you."

Christians must first make a definite break from the world and "have no fellowship with the unfruitful work of darkness." This is only the beginning of Jesus' call to "take up thy cross daily and follow me."

For the returned Jew, it was only the beginning of a slow, day-by-day, difficult task of laying the foundation of the Temple, which brought fierce opposition.

Laying the foundation of the Temple is symbolic of spiritual growth in the Christian life. The Christian's spiritual foundation is God's Word. As we experience true spiritual growth, there will be fierce opposition, quite often from *self-interest* that must be resisted.

"Wherefore laying aside all malice, and all guile, and hypocrisies, and all evil speakings, as newborn babes, desire the sincere milk of the word, that ye may grow thereby; if so be ye have tasted that the Lord is gracious" (I Peter 2:1-3).

NOTE:
4:1 **adversaries** means enemies.

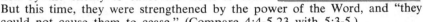

JUNE 3: Read Ezra 6-7.

Ezra 6:15: "And this house was finished on the third day of the month of Adar. . . ."

The building of the Temple had been at a standstill for 14 years, but once God's Word and authority was recognized, they "began to build the house of God" (5:2). What caused this revival? The circumstances had not changed; there was the same intense opposition and determination by the enemy to cause the work to cease. But this time, they were strengthened by the power of the Word, and "they could not cause them to cease." (Compare 4:4-5,23 with 5:3-5.)

The key to their overcoming opposition and gaining power to complete the Temple is clearly stated: "And they prospered through the prophesying of Haggai the prophet and Zechariah . . ." (6:14). God's work can only be sustained and strengthened through God's Word, which is the foundation of our Christian life—one power that Satan *cannot* overcome. God's Word is the source of strength by which the child of God cannot be defeated.

Many of God's people go year after year, making little or no spiritual progress, mainly because they have neglected and consequently disobeyed the Word of God!

The Book of Ezra reveals the importance God places on obedience to His Word in order to accomplish His purposes. We are prone to be careless in listening to God's Word and more or less live much of our life in the spirit that prevailed during the days of the people in the book of Judges when everyone did "that which was right in his own eyes" (see Judges 17:6; 21:25).

MEMORY VERSE FOR THE WEEK: I Peter 1:25

"But the word of the Lord endureth for ever. And this is the word which by the gospel is preached unto you."

The more we are concerned over obedience, the greater hunger we will have to read His Word in order to do His will. ". . . If ye continue in my word, then are ye my disciples indeed" (John 8:31).

NOTE:
6:1 **treasures** means documents; 6:4 **house** means royal treasury; 7:6 **ready scribe** means thoroughly knowledgeable of the Scriptures.

JUNE 4: Read Ezra 8-9.

Ezra 9:6,10: ". . . I am ashamed . . . we have forsaken thy commandments."

Ezra, the priest, not only prepared *his* heart to seek the law of God, but he wanted all of God's people to know God's will. His purpose for going to Jerusalem was "to teach in Israel statutes and judgments" (7:10).

Four months after leaving Babylon, Ezra and his 1800 followers completed the 800-mile journey and arrived in the Holy City. He was heartbroken over the low moral and spiritual condition that prevailed.

Fifty-seven years had passed since Haggai and Zechariah, through their prophetic ministry, had inspired the nation "to seek the Lord God of Israel" (6:21), but there had been no prophets to teach God's commandments to the new generation.

Although God's people did not have the complete Old Testament Scripture at that time, when Ezra read and taught what Scripture they did have, it resulted in a great, sweeping revival (see 10:12).

The foundation of our Christian faith is found in the Old Testament. Our Lord's words to His disciples confirm the necessity of knowing the Old Testament when, "beginning at Moses and all the prophets, he expounded unto them *all the scriptures* and the things concerning himself." Surely they had a good knowledge of the Old Testament Scriptures, but they needed a further revelation of Christ. So the Lord "opened . . . their understanding that they might understand the scriptures" (Luke 24:27,44-45).

Today the Holy Spirit indwells every believer, and we should pray that He will guide us "into all truth" (John 16:13).

JUNE 5: Read Ezra 10.

THE PEOPLE CONFESS THEIR SINS

Ezra 10:10-11: "And Ezra the priest stood up, and said unto them, Ye have transgressed, and have taken strange wives . . . Now therefore . . . separate yourselves from the people of the land, and from the strange wives."

When Ezra arrived in Jerusalem, he discovered that the priests, Levites, and rulers had intermarried with their idolatrous neighbors—the very thing that had caused their captivity and destruction (see Deuteronomy 7:3-4).

MEMORY VERSE FOR THE WEEK: Psalm 1:1,2

"Blessed is the man that walketh not in the counsel of the ungodly, nor standeth in the way of sinners, nor sitteth in the seat of the scornful. But his delight is in the law of the Lord; and in his law doth he meditate day and night."

Ezra recognized his nation's spiritual and moral needs because he knew God's Word. He urged an immediate separation from their foreign wives ". . . until the fierce wrath of our God for this matter be turned from us" (10:14).

Naturally, this involved much heartbreak and many tears. Everyone involved was hurt very deeply, but there could be no return to God without a complete and final separation. This may seem severe, but Ezra knew that the great sin of marrying the heathen could only lead to another period of captivity and once again hinder God's promise to Abraham and David concerning the coming Messiah. (Note Deuteronomy 7:1-9.)

There are those who are more precious to us than life itself, but for Christ and His cause, we should, if necessary, be willing to forsake them and every other earthly personal pleasure. This is the cross of self-denial to all the satisfactions that life has to offer. Our Lord does not intend for us to accept the name "Christian" lightly or thoughtlessly. He said, "If any man will come after me, let him deny himself, and take up his cross daily, and follow me" (Luke 9:23).

NOTE:
10:18 **strange** means non-Jewish, foreign women.

INTRODUCTION TO NEHEMIAH

About 12 years after Ezra went to Jerusalem, Nehemiah's brother, Hanani, brought him a report of the spiritual and physical poverty that prevailed in Jerusalem. Added to this, the city walls and the gates of the city remained in ruins, just as they had been about 140 years earlier after Nebuchadnezzar invaded and burned the city (II Kings 25:10). This left the inhabitants open to attacks and plundering by vicious bandits.

Nehemiah was heartbroken over the report, and he began to fast. Nehemiah was a man of prayer, courage, and perseverance. He evidently felt a strong need for prayer. (See 1:4; 2:4; 4:4-9; 6:9-14.) He prayed over a period of four months before he made his request to the king. (See Ezra 1:1, 2:1, four months involved.) Not only did the king give him a leave of absence, but he also appointed Nehemiah governor of Jerusalem, which position he held for at least 12 years (5:14).

He organized working shifts; and in spite of all the opposition, the walls were completed in just 52 days (6:15).

As Daniel the prophet had prophesied years earlier, the walls were rebuilt and the work finished in troublous times (Daniel 9:25).

After the walls were completed, Ezra "opened the book" and read the Scriptures from early morning until midday for 7 days. It is important to realize it was the people who wanted the Word to be read. This resulted in prayer, confession, fasting, and a renewed covenant with God.

MEMORY VERSE FOR THE WEEK: Psalm 1:1,2
"Blessed is the man that walketh not in the counsel of the ungodly, nor standeth in the way of sinners, nor sitteth in the seat of the scornful. But his delight is in the law of the Lord; and in his law doth he meditate day and night."

JUNE 6: Read Nehemiah 1-3.

Nehemiah 2:18: "Then I told them of the hand of my God which was good upon me; as also the king's lords that he had spoken unto me. And they said, Let us rise up and build. So they strengthened their hands for this good work."

It was an answer to prayer and fasting that the king of Persia overruled a former decree "that this city [Jerusalem] be not builded." Up to this time the Medes and Persians had never reversed a decree. (Compare Ezra 4:21 to Daniel 6:8.) The Persian king not only reversed the decree, but he appointed Nehemiah governor over Jerusalem and commissioned him to build the walls (Nehemiah 2:6-8).

Nehemiah soon faced opposition similar to the opposition Zerubbabel faced 100 years earlier. In addition, we find that many of the leaders would not help, ". . . their nobles put not their necks to the work of their Lord" (3:5).

Nehemiah was surely disappointed at the opposition from these administrative leaders of the nation who should have helped him organize the work, but Nehemiah knew that his God could give him the wisdom and strength necessary to get the job done.

It is human nature to react against the humiliation and injustice by those who refuse to cooperate; under such circumstances, we want to assert our own rights. It is sometimes more difficult to discern the will of God when we seem to stand alone, but we receive spiritual strength through suffering wrong done to us only when we accept it in the spirit in which Christ suffered. Don't be upset with the person who wronged you, but recognize that God allowed this trouble so that we would glorify Him through it— whether it be some great wrong that is done or the little offenses that confront us each day. Remember these words, "For consider him that endured . . . lest ye be wearied and faint in your minds" (Hebrews 12:3).

NOTE:
Chisleu was the same as our December; **Nisan** was the same as our April.

MEMORY VERSE FOR THE WEEK: Psalm 1:1,2

"Blessed is the man that walketh not in the counsel of the ungodly, nor standeth in the way of sinners, nor sitteth in the seat of the scornful. But his delight is in the law of the Lord; and in his law doth he meditate day and night."

JUNE 7: Read Nehemiah 4-6.

Nehemiah 4:20: ". . . our God shall fight for us."

Sanballat had done all he could through ridicule, trickery, and flattery. He finally resorted to openly accusing the Jews of rebelling against Persia. He made every effort to distract Nehemiah, asking often for an opportunity to discuss the situation. But his intentions were only to do evil, and Nehemiah replied: ". . . I am doing a great work, so that I cannot come down: why should the work cease, whilst I leave it, and come down to you?" (6:3).

For more than a hundred years it had seemed impossible to restore the walls, but in just 52 days, Nehemiah and his few organized workers rebuilt them. This seems incredible compared to the highly skilled laborers David used in building the first walls. This again reinforces our faith that "With men this is impossible; but with God all things are possible" (Matthew 19:26).

Nehemiah did not depend on *human* strategy, power, or ability. His eyes were upon the Lord as he said, "The God of heaven, he will prosper us . . ." (2:20). "So the wall was finished . . ." (Nehemiah 6:15).

True obedience comes as a result of continual fellowship with God. The fellowship that Christ had with the Father was so complete and real that Christ lived in full dependence upon the Father, saying, ". . . The Son can do nothing of himself . . ." (John 5:19). This is what Nehemiah was acknowledging when he said, "Our God shall fight for us."

Isn't that what the Apostle Paul said of us, "It is God which worketh in you both to will and to do of his good pleasure" (Philippians 2:13)?

JUNE 8: Read Nehemiah 7-8.

Nehemiah 8:1,8: "And all the people gathered themselves together as one man . . . and they spake unto Ezra the scribe to bring the book of the law of Moses, which the Lord had commanded to Israel . . . So they read in the book in the law of God distinctly, and gave the sense, and caused them to understand the reading."

Thirteen years after Ezra's first expedition to Jerusalem, he returned to the Holy City (Ezra 8-9). After the walls were completed under Nehemiah's supervision, he may well have sent for Ezra to bring about a spiritual reformation.

MEMORY VERSE FOR THE WEEK: Psalm 1:1,2

"Blessed is the man that walketh not in the counsel of the ungodly, nor standeth in the way of sinners, nor sitteth in the seat of the scornful. But his delight is in the law of the Lord; and in his law doth he meditate day and night."

Thousands of people assembled at sunrise in Jerusalem to hear Ezra read from the book of the law, explaining the Scriptures day after day. Even though they had only a small portion of the Bible that we possess today, it brought a marvelous revival, as is always the case when God's people seek Him and turn from their wicked ways. (Compare II Chronicles 7:14 to Ezra 8:21.)

We have the message of all the prophets, the four Gospels of Christ, the Book of Acts, the further revelation of God's will for us through the Epistles, and finally, a description of the eternal destiny of man as revealed in the Book of Revelation.

A true revival begins with His Word—just as it did in the days of Ezra and Nehemiah. One of the greatest needs today is for Christians to become seriously concerned in reading the Bible as the voice of God speaking personally to them—then respond in believing submission.

"But whoso looketh into the perfect law of liberty, and continueth therein, he being not a forgetful hearer, but a doer of the work, this man shall be blessed in his deed" (James 1:25).

JUNE 9: Read Nehemiah 9-10.

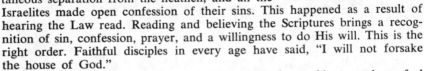

Nehemiah 10:32,35,36,39: "Also we made ordinances for us, to charge ourselves yearly with the third part of a shekel for the service of the house of our God; . . . and to bring the first-fruits of our ground . . . of our cattle . . . and *we will not forsake* the house of our God."

Following the greatest feast of the tabernacles held since the days of Joshua, there was a spontaneous separation from the heathen, and all the Israelites made open confession of their sins. This happened as a result of hearing the Law read. Reading and believing the Scriptures brings a recognition of sin, confession, prayer, and a willingness to do His will. This is the right order. Faithful disciples in every age have said, "I will not forsake the house of God."

Those who come believing hear a voice which the world cannot hear; feel a presence the unbeliever does not feel; enjoy a blessing that only the saved can enjoy; and receive an inner strength and peace which the world cannot comprehend. Christians love the places where His Word is preached. By not assembling with other Christians, we fail to meet our Christian responsibility.

"Not forsaking the assembling of ourselves together, as the manner of some is; but exhorting one another: and so much the more, as ye see the day approaching" (Hebrews 10:25).

NOTE:
10:37 **chambers of the house** means storerooms.

MEMORY VERSE FOR THE WEEK: Psalm 1:1,2

"Blessed is the man that walketh not in the counsel of the ungodly, nor standeth in the way of sinners, nor sitteth in the seat of the scornful. But his delight is in the law of the Lord; and in his law doth he meditate day and night."

JUNE 10: Read Nehemiah 11-12.

Nehemiah 12:27,43: "And at the dedication of the wall of Jerusalem . . . they offered great sacrifices, and rejoiced . . ."

The building of the wall of Jerusalem was accomplished through sacrificial work, mingled with fear and trembling, by ordinary people. Even though they were not skilled in building walls, they did the best they could. If Nehemiah had waited for "qualified" workers, the walls would never have been built (see 3:5).

Just as the Lord called His people out of Babylon with a plea to forsake personal gain and rebuild Jerusalem that He might be worshiped, so our Lord and Savior has called us to "seek . . . first the kingdom of God and his righteousness . . ." (Matthew 6:33). Yet, the majority of Christians· lack the wholehearted devotion of the workers who completed the walls. Far too many are not "seeking first" His kingdom's interest.

We as Christians are set apart to tell the world about God's love; yet, there are millions who have never been told the Good News and are still lost. To many, the Great Commission has become a doctrine rather than a call to serve Him.

"Go ye therefore, and teach all nations, baptizing them in the name of the Father, and of the Son, and of the Holy Ghost: Teaching them to observe all things whatsoever I have commanded you: and, lo, I am with you always, even unto the end of the world. Amen" (Matthew 28:19-20).

NOTE:
12:44 **that waited** means served faithfully

"And he had prepared for him a great chamber, where aforetime they laid . . . the tithes of the corn, the new wine, and the oil, which was commanded to be given to the Levites"
Nehemiah 13:5

JUNE 11: Read Nehemiah 13.

Nehemiah 13:11: "Then contended I with the rulers, and said, Why is the house of God forsaken? And I gathered them together, and set them in their place."

Before Nehemiah left Jerusalem and returned to Persia, he restored worship in the Temple and assigned the priests and Levites to their responsible positions. However, when Nehemiah returned to Jerusalem (possibly 15 years later), many God-dishonoring practices were being permitted.

He found that many of the Levites had taken part-time jobs in the fields in order to earn their living because many of the people no longer were giving their tithes and offerings to support these God-ordained Levites. (See 12:27-30,47. Compare 10:35-39 with I Corinthians 9:8-14.)

MEMORY VERSE FOR THE WEEK: Psalm 1:1,2

"Blessed is the man that walketh not in the counsel of the ungodly, nor standeth in the way of sinners, nor sitteth in the seat of the scornful. But his delight is the law of the Lord; and in his law doth he meditate day and night."

What should be the attitude of the Church toward their minister regarding money matters? This was illustrated by the apostle Paul when he was talking to the Corinthians: "For it is written in the law of Moses, Thou shalt not muzzle the mouth of the ox that treadeth out the corn. Doth God take care for oxen? . . . If we have sown unto you spiritual things, is it a great thing if we shall reap your carnal things?" (I Corinthians 9:9,11).

Jesus said, "He that receiveth you receiveth me . . ." (Matthew 10:40). Our ministers represent Christ. For a congregation to withhold adequate wages in order to give more to missions or for an expansion program distorts the high calling of the ministry.

The Scriptures clearly reveal the manner in which we should provide for the man who has been called of God for full-time service: "Even so hath the Lord ordained that they which preach the gospel should live of the gospel" (I Corinthians 9:14).

JUNE 12: Read Esther 1-3.

Esther 3:13: "And the letters were sent by posts into all the king's provinces, to destroy, to kill, and to cause to perish, all Jews, both young and old, little children and women, in one day, even upon the thirteenth day of the twelfth month, which is the month Adar, and to take the spoil of them for a prey."

When the Persians defeated King Nebuchadnezzar and the Babylonian empire, all the Jews were urged to return to Jerusalem. They had lived in Babylon for 50 years, so most of them had never seen Jerusalem because they were descendants of those who had been taken to Babylon as captives. Since they were now free from Babylonian slavery, most of them preferred to remain in the friendly, prosperous atmosphere of the Persian kingdom rather than leave Babylon and return to Jerusalem, as God had said they should.

Perhaps another 50 years had passed before Haman's decree to destroy all the Jews.

It is no surprise then that in the book of Esther there is no direct mention of God, of prayer, or of the Scriptures. When we refuse to obey God's Word, our prayers and Bible reading become merely ritual, and God seems far removed from our daily experiences.

". . . Come out of her, my people, that ye be not partakers of her sins, . . . Standing afar off for the fear of her torment, saying, Alas, alas that great city Babylon . . . for in one hour is thy judgment come" (Revelation 18:4,10).

NOTE:
3:15 **posts** means special messengers.

MEMORY VERSE FOR THE WEEK: Psalm 1:3
"And he shall be like a tree planted by the rivers of water, that bringeth forth his fruit in his season; his leaf also shall not wither; and whatsoever he doth shall prosper."

JUNE 13: Read Esther 4-7.

Esther 4:16: ". . . so will I go in unto the king, which is not according to the law: and if I perish, I perish."

Queen Esther was willing to relinquish all—even lose her life—for what she knew was the will of God for her people. With the words, "If I perish, I perish," she stood in the inner court of the king's palace, waiting for the word that would mean life or death from the monarch who ruled the world.

The former queen, Vashti, had been dismissed, so the risk was real. To make Esther's situation even more serious, she had not been called to see the king for thirty days. If the king had lost interest in Esther, how could she hope to influence him for the condemned Jewish race?

A further temptation presented itself when the king not only accepted her, but he offered her "half of the kingdom" (5:3,6; 7:2). She could have clutched her prize, considering it far too precious to risk losing by mentioning her request to the king.

The world's attitude is to firmly clutch our rights and possessions. We run the risk of losing God's best for our lives, our children, and our spouse by reacting to the fear of losing them. But the way to gain the most for our lives, our children, or our mate is to commit them to God. By clutching anything too tightly, we can squeeze the life out of it. Both love and life are choked, strangled, and smothered to death by clinging selfishness and jealousy.

Jesus said, "For whosoever will save his life shall lose it; but whosoever shall lose his life for my sake and the gospel's, the same shall save it" (Mark 8:25).

JUNE 14: Read Esther 8-10.

Esther 9:24,26: "Because Haman . . . the enemy of all the Jews, had devised against the Jews to destroy them, and had cast Pur, that is, the lot, to consume them, and to destroy them . . . Wherefore they called these days Purim after the name of Pur."

Haman appeared to be invincible, and his decree to execute all the Jews seemed to be final. The law had been established, and the decree had been approved by the Persian king; and under the law of the Medes and Persians, a decree could not be altered.

Haman's astrologers "had cast Pur" (meaning "had cast lots") to determine the most favorable time for the execution of all Jews. Haman's "lucky day" fell on the 13th of the last month. The divine principle which Haman did not realize was, "The lot is cast into the lap; but the whole disposing thereof is of the Lord" (Proverbs 16:33).

MEMORY VERSE FOR THE WEEK: Psalm 1:3

"And he shall be like a tree planted by the rivers of water, that bringeth forth his fruit in his season; his leaf also shall not wither; and whatsoever he doeth shall prosper."

The determined day of execution, known as Purim, was turned from death to deliverance, and the Jews have celebrated it each year throughout all generations.

The feast of Purim is a testimony to the fact that what appears to be "chance" and "good luck" is really the work of the Almighty Controller of world affairs.

How tragic that, in later years when Christ, their Messiah, came, bringing them a far greater deliverance, they failed to recognize Him.

The judgment of death has passed upon all men, for all have sinned. Through the acceptance of Christ as our Savior, we receive deliverance from sin and death and have been granted eternal life.

"For God so loved the world, that he gave his only begotten Son . . . that the world through him might be saved" (John 3:16-17).

NOTE:
9:19 **portions** means gifts.

INTRODUCTION TO JOB

What an honor God bestowed upon Job when He said, "there is none like him in the earth" (Job 1:8)! Job was "perfect and upright." Even after his fierce trials, God still assures us that Job hath "spoken the thing that is right" (1:1,8; 2:3; 42:7).

Satan tortured Job by every conceivable means, but nothing could destroy his faith in God. His trials and suffering actually brought him into a closer relationship with God.

The tendency of human nature is to agree with Job's critics. In the book of Job we find the reasonings of God, Satan, Job, his wife, Elihu, and Job's three friends. As you read each chapter, be careful to distinguish between the wisdom of Job, whom God highly complimented, and the well-intended, but inaccurate and misleading, arguments of Job's friends whom God said "darkeneth counsel."

By *earthly* wisdom man cannot know God or His will. This is even more reason why we need to encourage Christians to read the Word of God. Only His Word is fully reliable, and God will reveal His will to every "Job" who will patiently wait upon Him.

Through reading of Job's experiences, we learn that it is not important for us to know *why* we suffer, but we must recognize *who* controls our suffering.

The book of Job clearly reveals that "the natural man receiveth not the things of the Spirit of God: for they are foolishness with him: neither can he know them, because they are spiritually discerned" (I Corinthians 2:14).

OUTLINE OF JOB

I. Job's Sudden Affliction (Chapter 1)
II. Satan's Part in the Affliction (Chapter 2)
III. Job's Speech and His Friends' Replies (Chapters 3-42)

JUNE 15: Read Job 1-4.

Job 2:1: "Again there was a day when the sons of God came to present themselves before the Lord, and Satan came also among them to present himself before the Lord."

We are startled to find Satan "in the presence of the Lord" (2:1-7). He was there to slander and accuse "a perfect and an upright man, one that feareth God, and escheweth evil" (1:1,8; 2:3).

"There was a man in the land of Uz, whose name was Job, and that man was perfect and upright..." Job 1:1

Satan is exposed as "the accuser of our brethren . . ." (Revelation 12:10) who often uses "friends" to talk down, belittle, and accuse other Christians. By speaking against other believers, we are acting as Satan's mouthpiece to make ineffective the life of Christ in other Christians.

Who can understand the heartache and sorrow of Job—the servant of the Lord who was stripped of family, possessions, and health (see 1:8)? This suffering was not a misfortune or a "bad piece of luck." It was far from being punishment from God, as Job's friends supposed. All of Job's sufferings were the attacks of Satan, but the result was to bring him into a closer relationship with God.

Spiritual victories do not "just happen"—they are dependent upon the indwelling power of God's Word and upon much prayer. All efforts to live a victorious Christian life are doomed to failure in our warfare "against spiritual wickedness" without the "whole armour of God . . . which is the word of God: praying always" (see Ephesians 6:10-18).

NOTE:
1:1 **eschewed** means shunned; 1:9 **nought** means nothing; 1:20 **rent** means tore; **mantle** means robe; 3:24 **roarings** means groanings.
Job 1:21: *See 1 Tim. 6:7.*

JUNE 16: Read Job 5-8.

Job 6:2-4: "Oh, that my grief were throughly weighed . . . For now it would be heavier than the sand of the sea; therefore my words are swallowed up. For the arrows of the Almighty are within me, the poison whereof drinketh up my spirit: the terrors of God do set themselves in array against me."

After one full week of silent contemplation about Job's suffering, Eliphaz, the eldest of his friends, was first to speak. What he had learned by observation led him to conclude that all suffering was the result of sin. Therefore, he said to Job, "I have seen, they that plow iniquity, and sow wickedness, reap the same" (4:8), implying that Job should confess his sins.

Added to Job's physical suffering, financial loss, his children's death, and his wife's hypocrisy, his friends had misjudged his integrity.

MEMORY VERSE FOR THE WEEK: Psalm 1:3

"And he shall be like a tree planted by the rivers of water, that bringeth forth his fruit in his season; his leaf also shall not wither; and whatsoever he doeth shall prosper."

Job was no hypocrite, as his "comforters" had alleged; and for reasons which Job did not understand, God was not coming to his defense. Even worse, it seemed that he had been struck down by "the arrows of the Almighty." He said, "Therefore my words are swallowed up"—meaning, "I just can't explain it! I don't understand it."

"Pity thyself" is one of Satan's most popular doctrines, for he delights in embittering the believer, thus causing him to question God's wisdom. We suffer for Christ's sake not only when we encounter the hatred of the world, as did Christ, but also when we endure the ordinary afflictions of life in which the Man of Sorrows shared.

"Unto you it is given in the behalf of Christ, not only to believe on him, but also to suffer for his sake" (Philippians 1:29).

NOTE:
7:21 **sleep in the dust** means be dead in the grave.
Job 5:13: *See I Cor. 3:19.* **5:16:** *See Rom. 3:19.* **7:17:** *See Heb. 2:6-8.*

JUNE 17: Read Job 9-12.

"Though he slay me, yet will I trust in him: but I will maintain mine own ways before him"
Job 13:15

Job 9:1,11-12: "Then Job answered and said, . . . Lo, he goeth by me, and I see him not; he passeth on also, but I perceive him not. Behold, he taketh away, who can hinder him? who will say unto him, What doest thou?"

Bildad, Job's second friend to speak, was noticeably less sympathetic than was Eliphaz. He critically attacked Job, saying, "How long shall the words of thy mouth be like a strong wind?" (8:2).

Bildad agreed with Eliphaz that Job's suffering was caused by his sins. But Bildad did not base his conclusions on observation of just one lifetime, but on traditions established over many years, saying, "For inquire, I pray thee, of the *former age*, and prepare thyself to the search of *their fathers*: (For we are but of yesterday, and know nothing, because our days upon earth are a shadow:)" (8:8-9).

Job confessed that God's dealings with him were beyond his ability to comprehend. When Job said, "Lo, he goeth by me," he was expressing assurance of God's presence, even though there was no evidence to substantiate his faith.

MEMORY VERSE FOR THE WEEK: Psalm 1:3

"And he shall be like a tree planted by the rivers of water, that bringeth forth his fruit in his season; his leaf also shall not wither; and whatsoever he doeth shall prosper."

God may never reveal a *reason* for our trials. To try to seek God's will for us may be proper, but to *question* God's actions—"What doest Thou?"—is as ignorant as it is sinful. The child of faith need not know *why* he is in the dark; he only needs to know who controls the darkness (compare 1:21-22).

Our Lord did not exaggerate in the least when He said, "Are not two sparrows sold for a farthing? and one of them shall not fall on the ground without your Father . . . *Fear ye not* therefore, ye are of more value than many sparrows" (Matthew 10:29,31).

NOTE:
11:6 **exacteth** means demands.

JUNE 18: Read Job 13-16.
Job 13:15,23: "Though he slay me, yet will I trust in him: but I will maintain mine own ways before him . . . How many are mine iniquities and sins? make me to know my transgression and my sin."

Zophar, a highly opinionated man, was convinced (by mere outward circumstances) that Job was guilty of great sin, since tragedy had struck in every area of Job's life. His conclusions led him to say, "Should thy *lies* make men hold their peace? . . . *Know* therefore that God exacteth of thee less than *thine iniquity* deserveth" (11:3,6).

Satan instigated the criticisms by Job's wife and his "devoted" friends in order to substantiate his satanic accusation that even Job would curse God if he were put to the test of death—that he would give up everything, even his faith in God, in order to save his own life. But each accusation only deepened Job's faith and love for God until he could say, "Though he slay me, yet will I trust in him." This was the turning point in Job's testing.

To be conformed to Christ's death, we must be willing to give up everything dear—even life itself, if necessary—for the privilege of pleasing Him. "For I reckon that the sufferings of this present time are not worthy to be compared with the glory which shall be revealed in us" (Romans 8:18).

NOTE:
15:4 **restrainest prayer** means hinders prayer; 15:25 **strengtheneth** means conducts proudly.

Job 14:2: *See Jas. 1:10.*

MEMORY VERSE FOR THE WEEK: Psalm 1:3

"And he shall be like a tree planted by the rivers of water, that bringeth forth his fruit in his season; his leaf also shall not wither; and whatsoever he doeth shall prosper."

JUNE 19: Read Job 17-20.

Job 19:25: "For I know that my redeemer liveth, and that he shall stand at the latter days upon the earth."

Bildad's second speech was the most critical of all, saying that Job's sufferings exposed him as a sinful hypocrite who was trapped by his own evils (18:8). He concluded by saying of Job, "Surely such are the dwellings of the wicked, and this is the place of him that knoweth not God" (18:21).

These scathing accusations from Job's friends must have been a bitter blow. But each day's suffering and continuous harrassment drove him closer to his Lord. Job could see beyond his suffering as he looked triumphantly into the future. Each trial deepened his faith in the eternal truth, "I know that my redeemer liveth." This magnificent revelation was uttered by Job when he had no one who cared; and by all outward observation, it appeared that God did not exist. However, he could bear the intense suffering and unjust reproaches because he was living in the expectation of the glorious appearing of his Redeemer.

"Wherein I suffer trouble, as an evil doer, even unto bonds; but the word of God is not bound. Therefore I endure all things for the elect's sakes, that they may also obtain the salvation which is in Christ Jesus with eternal glory" (II Timothy 2:9-10).

NOTE:

17:1 **breath** means spirit; 19:14 **familiar** means intimate; 19:17 **strange** means repulsive; 19:19 **inward** means close.

JUNE 20: Read Job 21-24.

Job 23:11-12: "My foot hath held his steps, his way have I kept, and not declined. Neither have I gone back from the commandment of his lips; I have esteemed the *words of his mouth* more than my necessary food."

Eliphaz reasoned that wicked men are miserable. So, since Job was very miserable, he must be a very wicked man. His final attempt to convince Job that he was a hypocrite was a stunning blow, saying, "Acquaint now thyself with him, and be at peace; thereby good shall come unto thee" (22:21). Job admitted: "I go forward, but he is not there; and backward, but I cannot perceive him: On the left hand . . . I cannot behold him . . . on the right hand . . . I cannot see him" (Job 23:8-9). In fact, regardless of which way Job turned, God was nowhere to be found. However, his faith did not rest on tangible evidence of *feeling* God's presence, but God's Word became more precious to Job than "necessary food."

MEMORY VERSE FOR THE WEEK: Psalm 1:4,5

"The ungodly are not so: but are like the chaff which the wind driveth away. Therefore the ungodly shall not stand in the judgment, nor sinners in the congregation of the righteous."

It is as if Job had said, "In the midst of my confusion and suffering, *when all else failed,* I discovered the source of true strength to be the *words of His mouth.* So great was my hunger for Him that I seized His words as a starving man." The secret to Job's faithfulness was the nourishment and strength he obtained from God's Word.

Spiritual defeat inevitably faces the Christian who lives year after year, never reading through the only written revelation of God's Word.

"Unless thy law had been my delights, I should then have perished in mine affliction" (Psalm 119:92).

NOTE:
21:2 **consolations** means comfort; 21:3 **suffer** means allow; 21:8 **seed** means children; 21:10 **gendereth** means breeds.

Job 22:29: *See Jas. 4:6; I Pet. 5:5.*

JUNE 21: Read Job 25-29.

". . . keep my commandments, and live. Get wisdom, get understanding . . . from the words of my mouth"

Proverbs 4:4-5

Job 28:12,28: "But where shall wisdom be found? and where is the place of understanding? . . . And unto man he said, Behold, the fear of the Lord, that is wisdom; and to depart from evil is understanding."

Bildad's final comments insinuated that Job was an "unclean worm" who could not "be justified with God" (see 25:1-6). But God revealed Job's true nature, saying he was "perfect [blameless] and upright, and one that feared God, and eschewed [shunned] evil" (1:1). In the midst of all the false insinuations, Job looked beyond the criticisms to the Source of all wisdom.

Job was never as concerned about knowing the answer to his problems as he was about having a right relationship with God, as he proved by saying, "Behold, the fear of the Lord, that is wisdom." The Psalmist confirmed Job's conviction and added, ". . . a good understanding have all they that do his commandments . . ." (Psalm 111:10).

How true it is that man, through mere human intellect, cannot comprehend the wisdom or the ways of God!

Those who leave Christ—the Living Word—out of their lives will never discover true wisdom and understanding, and they miss the greatest discovery of life. They overlook Christ, who is Truth. To reject Him is to remain in ignorance and spiritual darkness.

"Howbeit we speak wisdom among them that are perfect: yet not the wisdom of this world, not the princes of this world, that come to nought: But we speak the wisdom of God in a mystery, even the hidden wisdom, which God ordained before the world unto our glory" (I Corinthians 2:6-7).

NOTE:
27:22 **would fain flee** means flees in haste; 28:1 **a vein** means a mine.

MEMORY VERSE FOR THE WEEK: Psalm 1:4,5

"The ungodly are not so: but are like the chaff which the wind driveth away. Therefore the ungodly shall not stand in the judgment, nor sinners in the congregation of the righteous."

JUNE 22: Read Job 30-33.

Job 30:10; 31:6: "Thy abhor me, they flee far from me, and spare not to spit in my face . . . Let me be weighed in an even balance that God may know mine integrity."

The Jews, as well as other Eastern people, seldom spit except as an expression of insult and great contempt (Deuteronomy 25:9). The shame was so great that if a father spit upon his daughter, she was not allowed to have fellowship with her people and was required to stay outside the camp for a full week (Numbers 12:14).

Job probably was still sitting among the ashes, covered from head to foot with painful boils—a lonely sufferer who had been unjustly criticized by his wife and his friends. As the people walked by him, they spit on him. Job confessed his bitter humiliation by saying, "They abhor me . . . and . . . spit in my face."

Christians are often falsely accused, criticized, and condemned as hypocrites. The best Christian often receives the worst indignation from a self-righteous, thoughtless crowd—too often from others who profess to be Christians.

Christ Himself was shamefully slandered and abused on many occasions. He, too, was spit upon; therefore, we need not be surprised when others show contempt toward us. "Remember the word that I said unto you, The servant is not greater than his lord, If they have persecuted me, they will also persecute you; if they have kept my saying, they will keep yours also" (John 15:20).

NOTE:
30:3 **solitary** means dry and barren ground; 31:40 **cockle** means weeds; 33:13 **strive** means contend

"Blessed are the merciful: for they shall obtain mercy"
Matthew 5:7

JUNE 23: Read Job 34-37.

Job 34:36-37; 35:16: "My desire is that Job may be *tried unto the end* . . . For he addeth rebellion unto his sin . . . Therefore doth Job open his mouth in vain; he multiplieth words without knowledge."

The youngest man, Elihu, did not speak until the three friends had ended their complaints, criticism, and condemnation of Job.

He agreed that the *experience* of Eliphaz, the *traditional views* given by Bildad, and the *good judgment* of Zophar were all in vain.

MEMORY VERSE FOR THE WEEK: Psalm 1:4,5

"The ungodly are not so: but are like the chaff which the wind driveth away. Therefore the ungodly shall not stand in the judgment, nor sinners in the congregation of the righteous."

When he overheard Job's prayer, "Oh that one would hear me" (31:35), he wrongly assumed that God was not hearing Job. Therefore, Elihu believed that he alone could act as God's priest to intercede on Job's behalf. "Behold, I am according to thy wish in God's stead" (33:6).

We are often prone to criticize and condemn another's actions when we simply don't know what God is doing or how God is working in the heart of someone with whom we do not agree. But judging another is a serious sin. It robs us of the "joy of the Lord" and instills a "root of bitterness" (Hebrews 12:15). They that judge shall receive the "greater condemnation" (James 3:1).

"Who art thou that judgest another man's servant? to his own master he standeth or falleth. Yea, he shall be holden up: for God is able to make him stand" (Romans 14:4).

NOTE:
37:10 **straitened** means frozen over.
Job 34:19: *See Acts 10:34.* **34:19:** *See Acts 10:24.*

JUNE 24: Read Job 38-40.

Job 38:1-2: "Then the Lord answered Job out of the whirlwind, and said, Who is this that darkeneth counsel by words without knowledge?"

Elihu, the self-confident, self-appointed intercessor for Job (the words *my, me,* or *I* are mentioned 19 times in just 8 verses of chapter 33), was interrupted by the wrath of the Almighty as He said, "Who is this that darkeneth counsel by words without knowledge?" (38:2). (The verb *darkeneth* means "make hazy, obscure, confuse.") The advice from all the "know-it-alls" came to an end.

Even though a counselor may have an earned degree and credentials that appear to qualify him, unless the counsel is in harmony with God's Word, it is "darkened counsel."

Thousands of books, magazines, and advisors today are "darkening counsel"—deceiving the confused.

Every Christian has the precious privilege of turning to God's Word—the one source in all the world that brings light upon "darkened counsel."

"The entrance of thy words giveth light; it giveth understanding unto the simple" (Psalm 119:130).

NOTE:
39:10 **unicorn** means wild ox.
Job 39:30: *See Matt. 24:28.*

MEMORY VERSE FOR THE WEEK: Psalm 1:4,5

"The ungodly are not so: but are like the chaff which the wind driveth away. Therefore the ungodly shall not stand in the judgment, nor sinners in the congregation of the righteous."

JUNE 25: Read Job 41-42.

Job 42:12: "So the Lord blessed the latter end of Job more than his beginning . . ."

From all outward appearance, it seemed that Job's four friends were enjoying God's favor and that God was displeased only with Job.

Job's friends fully expected God's approval on their efforts to convince Job how wrong he was. Eliphaz must have been astounded to hear the voice from heaven say, "My wrath is kindled against thee, and against thy two friends: for ye have not spoken of me the thing that is right, as my servant Job hath" (Job 42:7). On the other hand, Job must have been equally surprised to hear that God was pleased with him, for immediately preceding the voice from heaven, Job had said, "I abhor myself, and repent in dust and ashes" (42:6).

God is often most pleased with us when we are least pleased with ourselves. Human reasoning has never been able to explain the great mystery of human suffering. If God did not see an absolute necessity for suffering, it would not exist. The one who knows *Him* does not need to know *why* things happen.

God's ways are often very different from man's expectations. "For my thoughts are not your thoughts, neither are your ways my ways, saith the Lord" (Isaiah 55:8).

NOTE:
41:17 **sundered** means separated; 42:6 **abhor** means despise.
Job 41:11: *See Rom. 11:35.*

JUNE 26: Read Psalms 1-9.

Psalm 8:3-4: "When I consider thy heavens, the work of thy fingers, the moon and the stars, which thou hast ordained; What is man, that thou art mindful of him? and the son of man, that thou visitest him?"

The Psalmist was overwhelmed with the beauty and immensity of the heavens compared to his own unimportance. He was amazed that God should be so mindful of such an insignificant creature as man.

Yes, compared to the greatness of God, man is as weak and helpless as a baby. A baby must be fed and is totally dependent on others. What does a baby know compared to a mature adult? Compared to the wisdom of God, man, with his vast accumulation of knowledge, is no more intelligent than a baby.

MEMORY VERSE FOR THE WEEK: Psalm 1:6

"For the Lord knoweth the way of the righteous: but the way of the ungodly shall perish."

The weakest Christian is empowered by the mighty God of creation. What a thrilling thought! We are made in His image in order to magnify Him. The Lord has chosen to manifest Himself only through man—in all his weakness—to give forth His perfect Word.

The Lord says, "Except ye be converted, and become as little children, ye shall not enter into the kingdom of heaven" (Matthew 18:3).

NOTE:
2:2 **Anointed** means Christ.

Psalm 2:1-2: *See Acts 4:25-26.* **2:7:** *See Heb. 1:5; 5:5; Acts 13:33.* **5:9:** *See Rom. 3:13.* **6:8:** *See Matt. 7:23; 25:41; Luke 13:27.* **8.2:** *See Matt. 21:16.* **8:4-6.** *See Heb. 2:6-8; 1 Cor. 15:27.*

". . . God hath given to us eternal life, and this life is in his son"

1 John 5:11

JUNE 27: Read Psalms 10-17.

Psalm 16: 10, 11: "For thou wilt not leave my soul in hell; neither wilt thou suffer thine Holy One to see corruption. Thou wilt shew me the *path of life:* in thy presence is fulness of joy; at thy right hand there are pleasures for evermore."

David's thoughts went beyond his immediate surroundings and caused him to consider the day of his death. He spoke in confidence, "Thou wilt not leave my soul in hell." He looked beyond the grave with assurance, saying, "In thy presence is fulness of joy . . . pleasures for evermore." He spoke with a settled calm that was based on the promise of living in the presence of God eternally.

As we read the book of Acts, we find that these remarkable words are referring to the death and resurrection of Christ. Who would have known that Christ was referred to in Psalm 16 had it not been revealed by the Holy Spirit hundreds of years later? (See Acts 2:25, 31; 13:35.)

So much of the revelation of the Lord is missed when we don't read all the Scriptures! David could see a "path of life," but we see the cross of Christ as the *path of life* into the presence of God, where "there are pleasures for evermore." In the eyes of the world, the cross may look like a path to death, but in reality, one who goes to be with the Lord passes from death into life, where there is "fulness of joy . . . and pleasures for evermore." For us, the path of life is clear, for Jesus said, "Where I am, there ye may be also" (John 14:3).

NOTE:
11:3 **foundations** means truth.

Psalm 10:7: *See Rom. 3:14.* **14:1-3:** *See Rom. 3:10-12.* **16:8-11:** *See Acts 2:25-28; 13:35; John 20:9.*

MEMORY VERSE FOR THE WEEK: Psalm 1:6

"For the Lord knoweth the way of the righteous: but the way of the ungodly shall perish."

JUNE 28: Read Psalms 18-22.

Psalm 19:7,8,10: "The law of the Lord is perfect, converting the soul . . . the statutes of the Lord are right, *rejoicing the heart . . . sweeter also than honey . . ."*

God's Word is *"sweeter . . . than honey."* Not only are we to *learn* from the Word of God, but we are also to eat and enjoy it. God's Word is *food to nourish* the believer, and then it becomes a "joy and rejoicing in the heart." (Compare Psalm 119:103.)

Jeremiah said, "Thy words were found, and I did *eat* them; and thy word was unto me the joy and rejoicing of mine heart (Jeremiah 15:16).

When a baby is born, his immediate need is to drink milk. Without nourishment, the baby will fail to grow. Our immediate need is to recognize the purpose of reading the Bible: "As newborn babes, desire the sincere milk of the word, *that ye may grow* thereby: if so be ye have tasted that the Lord is gracious" (I Peter 2:2-3).

The Lord Jesus even spoke of God's Word as spiritual food, "It is written, Man shall not live by bread alone, but by every word that proceedeth out of the mouth of God" (Matthew 4:4).

"Every word that proceedeth out of the mouth of God" is different from any other word or book. The world has only the words of human beings, but the Bible is the WORD OF GOD! Although you may not understand a certain passage, you are still nourished through reading His Word. Thus, the Scriptures become spiritual food by which the spiritual life is sustained, "nourished up in the words of faith" (I Timothy 4:6).

NOTE:
18:26 **froward** means evil; 18:45 **close** means caves and strongholds; 22:5 **confounded** means shamed.

Psalm 18:49: *See Rom. 15:9.* **19:4:** *See Rom. 10:18.* **22:1:** *See Matt. 27:46; Mk. 15:34.* **22:6:** *See Matt. 2:23.* **22:8.** *See Matt. 27:43.* **22:18:** *See Matt. 27:35; John 19:24.* **22:22:** *See Heb. 2:12.*

"He shall feed his flock like a shepherd; he shall gather the lambs with his arm." Isa. 40:11

JUNE 29: Read Psalms 23-30.

Psalm 23: 1,3: "The Lord is my shepherd; I shall not want . . . He restoreth my soul: he leadeth me in the paths of righteousness for his name's sake."

David, the old shepherd king, looked upon himself as nothing more than a sheep that had to be led by the Great Shepherd in the paths of righteousness.

No other livestock requires so much attention as sheep. Left alone, sheep follow the same trails until those trails become ruts.

MEMORY VERSE FOR THE WEEK: Psalm 1:6

"For the Lord knoweth the way of the righteous: but the way of the ungodly shall perish."

One sheep may become so engrossed in following its own eating path that it becomes separated from the flock and is lost.

We, by nature, are like sheep, blindly and habitually following the same paths that we have seen ruin the lives of others or becoming so wrapped up in our own affairs that we lose our way.

There is something almost terrifying about the destructive self-determination of those who are not willing to be led "in paths of righteousness'—actually going their own way, even though it has taken others straight into trouble.

How many times have we prayed, "lead me in the paths of righteousness," while in our day-by-day conduct, we still refuse to deny ourselves, give up our "rights," and yield our own interests to the interests of others?

If we truly want God's will, then the offer of the Great Shepherd is still open: ". . . I will lead them in paths that they have not known: I will make darkness light before them, and crooked things straight . . ." (Isaiah 42:16).

NOTE:
23:1 **I shall not want** means I shall not lack anything; 28:3 **chief** means

malice, evil. **Psalm 24:1:** *See I Cor. 10:26.*

JUNE 30: Read Psalms 31-35.

Psalms 35:11-12: "False witnesses did rise up; they laid to my charge things that I knew not. They rewarded me evil for good . . ."

Throughout most of David's life, he had many enemies. When his son Absalom declared himself king, David was heartbroken. Fearing for the safety of Jerusalem, he fled barefooted over the hills of Mt. Olivet and wept.

In that dark hour of sorrow, he was confronted by Shimei, who cursed him, saying, "Come out, come out, thou bloody man, and thou man of Belial: the Lord hath returned upon thee all the blood of the house of Saul, in whose stead thou hast reigned."

Shimei's lies, insults, and stoning of David was more than Abishai could bear; he reacted by saying, "Why should this dead dog curse my lord the king?" Yet, David graciously refused to permit Abishai to slay Shimei, saying, ". . . let him curse . . ." (See II Samuel 15:30; 16:5-10.)

The principle of the Christian life is ". . . Avenge not yourselves, but rather give place unto wrath: for it is written, Vengeance is mine; I will repay, saith the Lord. Therefore if thine enemy hunger, feed him; if he thirst, give him drink . . ." (Romans 12:19-20).

Once again, the Lord said, "Love your enemies, bless them that curse you, do good to them that hate you, and pray for them which despitefully use you, and persecute you; that ye may be the children of your Father which is in heaven . . ." (Matthew 5:44-45).

NOTE:
31:4 **privily** means secretly; 32:2 **guile** means deceit.
Psalm 31:5: *See Luke 23:46.* **34:8:** *See I Pet. 2:3.* **34:20:** *See John 19:36.* **35:11:** *See Matt. 26:60.* **35:19:** *See John 15:25.*

MEMORY VERSE FOR THE WEEK: Psalm 1:6

"For the Lord knoweth the way of the righteous: but the way of the ungodly shall perish."

PRAYERS IN EZRA AND NEHEMIAH

B.C.	KING	EVENT	SCRIPTURE	PROPHETS
559-530	Cyrus	Return from exile	Ezra 1	End of Daniel's life (1:21; 10:1)
530-522	Cambyses	Not mentioned		Haggai and Zechariah
522-486	Darius I	Temple rebuilt	Ezra 4:5; 24:5	
486-465	Xerxes I (Ahasuerus)	The king who made Esther his queen and Mordecai his chief minister	Esther	
464-423	Artaxerxes I	The king who sponsored the return of Ezra and of Nehemiah; walls of Jerusalem rebuilt; reforms	Ezra 4:7-23; 7:1; Nehemiah 2:1	Malachi

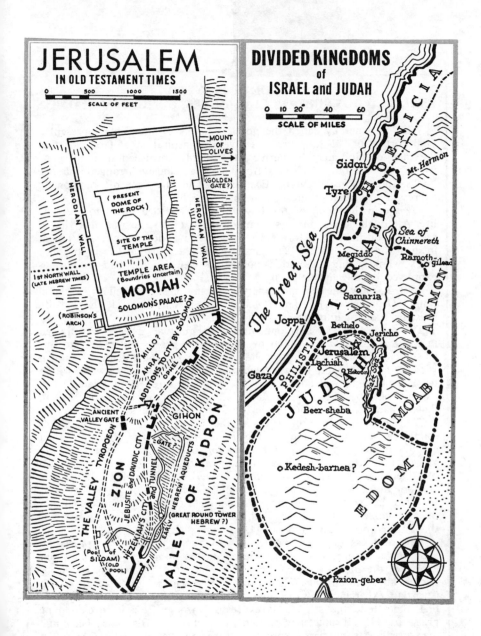

JERUSALEM
IN OLD TESTAMENT TIMES

0 500 1000 1500
SCALE OF FEET

MOUNT
OF
OLIVES

(GOLDEN
GATE?)

HERODIAN WALL

(PRESENT
DOME OF
THE ROCK)

SITE OF THE
TEMPLE

HERODIAN WALL

1st NORTH WALL
(LATE HEBREW TIMES)

TEMPLE AREA
(Boundries Uncertain)
MORIAH

SOLOMON'S PALACE?

(ROBINSON'S
ARCH)

MILLO?
AKRA?
OPHEL
ADDITIONS TO CITY BY SOLOMON

ANCIENT
VALLEY GATE

GIHON

THE VALLEY
TYROPOEON

ZION

JEBUSITE and DAVIDIC CITY

GATE?

HEZEKIAH'S CITY
and TUNNEL

EARLY HEBREW AQUEDUCTS

VALLEY
OF
KIDRON

(GREAT ROUND TOWER
HEBREW?)

(Pool of
SILOAM)
(OLD
POOL)

DIVIDED KINGDOMS
of
ISRAEL and JUDAH

0 10 20 40 60
SCALE OF MILES

PHOENICIA

Sidon

Tyre

Mt. Hermon

The Great Sea

Sea of
Chinnereth

Megiddo

Ramoth-
gilead

ISRAEL

Samaria

AMMON

Joppa

Bethel

Jericho

PHILISTIA

Jerusalem

Lachish

Salt Sea

Gaza

Hebron

JUDAH

MOAB

Beer-sheba

Kedesh-barnea?

EDOM

N

Ezion-geber

INTRODUCTION TO
PSALMS, PROVERBS, ECCLESIASTES, SONG OF SOLOMON

What is generally called the poetical books of the Bible represent a vital portion of *"all scripture . . . given by inspiration of God . . . that the man of God may be perfect, thoroughly furnished unto all good works"* (II Timothy 3:16-17). God has marvelously arranged the five books, Job, Psalms, Proverbs, Ecclesiastes, and the Song of Solomon, to express the spiritual progress of the believer's life.

We see in the *Book of Job* how he experienced a death to the self-life. Although he was the best man on earth (1:8), he was also viewed as a man on his face before God, praying, "I abhor myself, and repent in dust and ashes" (42:6). This first step in the spiritual life is to abhor one's whole being—his good points as well as his bad points—as expressed by the apostle Paul.

"For I know that in me (that is, in my flesh,) dwelleth no good thing" (Romans 7:18). The *Book of Job* reveals how all the self-life must be brought into submission to Gods' ways.

The *second* step of development in our spiritual growth is expressed in the *Book of Psalms,* which overflows with praise and prayer to our all-sufficient Lord. When the believer recognizes the fallacy of human wisdom and strength, he will begin to praise Him who dwells within us ". . . both to will and do of his good pleasure" (Philippians 2:13). Throughout the book, the psalmist admitted as did the apostle Paul, that he had ". . . no confidence in the flesh" (Philippians 3:3).

The believer then progresses in the practical discipline of God's school of spiritual wisdom in the *Book of Proverbs.* Not until then can the believer appreciate the *Book of Ecclesiastes,* where Solomon viewed all earthly treasures as nothing more than the worthless trash of time. The wisdom spoken of in Proverbs is that of God, but the wisdom in Ecclesiastes portrays the highest concept of human reasoning. The believer is led to firmly declare, "Let us hear the conclusion of the whole matter: Fear God, and keep his commandments: for this is the whole duty of man" (Ecclesiastes 12:13).

This progress in the Christian growth as set forth in the preceding four books is to prepare us to appreciate the *Song of Solomon,* which expresses the intimate relationship that binds the believer to His wonderful Lord in all the fullness of His precious love. Never can a Christian experience this precious fellowship with Christ until there is first a death to the self-life as expressed through Job; a revelation of praise for His all-sufficiency as told in the Psalms; His Word becoming the Christian's supreme treasure, ". . . for she is thy life" (Proverbs 4:13); and then, a full rejection of all earth's vanities (Ecclesiastes 1:2).

The fifth and final experience is that joy unspeakable and full of glory as the believer enjoys his fellowship with Christ as experienced in the Song of Solomon. Instead of complaining and being frustrated, one finds himself rejoicing in the wisdom of God's marvelous ways.

"The entrance of thy words giveth light; it giveth understanding unto the simple."

Psalm 119:130

JULY 1: Read Psalms 36-39.

Psalm 36:9: "For with thee is the fountain of life: in thy light shall we see light."

Not only is God the source of our *life*, but He is the source of *light* as well.

Unless God speaks there is no light—either physical or spiritual. Just as it was in the beginning when God said, "Let there be light," and the darkness that had concealed the world vanished, so today His "light shineth in darkness" (John 1:5) through Jesus, who is the Light of the world. He has brought to light God's marvelous love.

Jesus said, "I am the light of the world: he that followeth me shall not walk in darkness, but shall have the light of life" (John 8:12). To refuse to accept Christ as your personal Savior is to live in darkness and eventually be cast into outer darkness for all eternity. But it is a glorious fact "we who were sometimes in darkness are now children of light." (See 1 Peter 2:9 and Colossians 1:13.)

When "we walk in the light, as he is in the light, we have fellowship" with Him and with others who have also received Christ as their Savior. (See 1 John 1:7.)

Just as the psalmist acknowledged to God: "Thy word is a lamp unto my feet and a light unto my path," so we are totally dependent upon the Bible to reveal Christ, who is the *Living* Word. No other revelation of God reveals how "God, who commanded the light to shine out of darkness, hath shined in our hearts, to give the light of knowledge of the glory of God in the face of Jesus Christ" (II Corinthians 4:6).

NOTE:
36:11 **remove** *means drive me away; 37:9* **cut off** *means destroyed; 37:26* **seed** *means descendants; 37:28* **judgment** *means justice; 38:8* **roared** *means groaned.*
Psalm 36:1: *See Rom. 3:18.*

JULY 2: Read Psalms 40-45.

Psalm 40:1-2 "*I waited patiently* for the Lord; and he inclined unto me, and heard my cry. He brought me up also out of a horrible pit, out of the miry clay, and set *my feet upon a rock*, and *established my goings.*"

Looking back upon the past, the psalmist recalled how he had experienced a hopeless situation to which there seemed to be no end. It was like being encased in a pit where he continued to sink in the mire of hopelessness. David confessed his helplessness and his great need for God to lift him out of the mire of earth's problems. As the God of great mercy answered his prayer and lifted him up, his faith became firm as a rock.

MEMORY VERSE FOR THE WEEK: Psalm 1:6

"For the Lord knoweth the way of the righteous: but the way of the ungodly shall perish."

171

The word "patiently" means more than quietly enduring; in a sense, it also carries the thought of a doctor's patient—one who is suffering and needs a physician.

The psalmist felt assured that he was under the watchful care and the wisdom of the Great Physician, who is capable of caring for the most hopeless patient. He could "wait patiently for the Lord" with complete confidence, knowing the Great Physician had chosen the very hour for his restoration.

God does not prolong our suffering one moment beyond the wisdom of His great love. Only the one who waits patiently for the Lord experiences the deeper walk by *faith* and not by sight.

"For since the beginning of the world men have not heard, nor perceived by the ear, neither hath the eye seen, O God, beside thee, what he hath prepared for him that waiteth for him" (Isaiah 64:4; compare 1 Corinthians 2:9).

NOTE:
40:12 **compassed** *means surrounded;* *41:3* **languishing** *means sickness;* **make all his bed** *means restore him;* *44:20* **stretched out our hands** *means worshiped;* *45:1* **inditing** *means overflowing with;* *45:4* **terrible** *means wonderful.*
Psalm 40:6-8: *See Heb. 10:5-7.* **41:9:** *See Luke 22:47,48; John 13:18.* **44:22:** *See Rom. 8:36.* **45:6,7:** *See Heb. 1:8,9.*

". . . let them sing praises unto him with the timbrel and harp." Psalm 149:3

JULY 3: Read Psalms 46-51.
Psalm 50:23: "Whoso offereth praise glorifieth me: and to him that ordereth his conversation aright will I shew the salvation of God."

God is glorified when we praise Him. "From the rising of the sun unto the going down of the same the Lord's name is to be praised" (Psalm 113:3).

God bestows all of life's blessings—"he loadeth us with benefits." How often we take for granted our good health, sound mind, physical well-being, and all our possessions! Not only do we tend to take these things for granted, but even worse, we sometimes complain, as if we think we deserve more.

Failing to praise God is perhaps our greatest neglect. However, when we openly praise Him and let others know that all we have comes from God rather than "good luck," we glorify Him.

We cannot sincerely praise Him and be truly thankful without being satisfied with His arrangement of the affairs of our life. When we face disappointments, it is not necessary that we know why or that we understand what

MEMORY VERSE FOR THE WEEK: Psalm 119:9

"Wherewithal shall a young man cleanse his way? by taking heed thereto according to thy word."

172

God is working in our life. The secret of "rejoicing evermore" is confidently trusting in Him who knows what is best. Therefore, our praise must go beyond being thankful for what is pleasing to us, for we are taught to "Rejoice evermore. Pray without ceasing. In every thing give thanks: for this is the will of God in Christ Jesus concerning you" (I Thess. 5:16-18).

NOTE:
Psalm 51:4: *See Rom. 3:4.*

JULY 4: Read Psalms 52-59.
Psalm 55:6, 12-14: "And I said, Oh that I had wings like a dove! For then would I fly away, and be at rest . . . For it was not an enemy that reproached me; then I could have borne it: neither was it he that hated me that did magnify himself against me; then I would have hid myself from him: But it was thou, a man *mine equal, my guide,* and mine acquaintance. We took sweet counsel together, and walked unto the house of God in company."

Since David had experienced brokenheartedness because of the revolt and rebellion of his own son, Absalom, who turned the people's hearts against King David and declared himself king, David probably was not too surprised to discover that some of his friends had also deceived him. But when he discovered that Ahithophel, his most trusted advisor, not only had joined Absalom but had asked to personally execute David, he was shaken with grief. He expressed his deep disappointment in the hypocrisy and treachery of this one he called "mine equal, my guide."

David's first reaction was a cry of helpless desperation. "Oh that I had wings like a dove! For then would I fly away, and be at rest" (verse 6). But David did not have wings like a dove, and he could not fly away; even if he could, there would not have been rest in doing so. Instead, by committing his problem to the Lord and trusting in Him, he knew that his God was able to sustain him under every trial and to accomplish His purpose for his life. Therefore, he concluded that Psalm by saying, "Cast thy burden upon the Lord, and he shall sustain thee: he shall never suffer the righteous to be moved" (55:22).

Every servant of God probably has had a similar experience. Since we are the Lord's servants, we should not be greatly surprised when we are disappointed, deceived, or even betrayed by others, for our Lord has foretold: ". . . If they have persecuted me, they will also persecute you" (John 15:20).

NOTE:
55:4 **sore** *means grievously; 55:9* **divide their tongues** *means bring confusion; 56:5* **wrest** *means distort; 56:8* **tellest** *means hast taken account of; 59:10* **prevent** *means precede.*

MEMORY VERSE FOR THE WEEK: Psalm 119:9

"Wherewithal shall a young man cleanse his way? by taking heed thereto according to thy word."

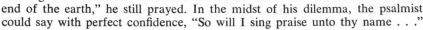

JULY 5: Read Psalms 60-66.

Psalm 61:1-2: "Hear my cry, O God; attend unto my prayer. From the end of the earth will I cry unto thee, when my heart is overwhelmed. Lead me to the rock that is higher than I."

King Saul had forced David to retreat to the country east of the Jordan River. It was not part of the Promised Land, and the psalmist felt exiled from God's presence in this foreign country. Although that desolate location seemed like "the end of the earth," he still prayed. In the midst of his dilemma, the psalmist could say with perfect confidence, "So will I sing praise unto thy name . . ." (verse 8).

Every person has burdens, and each one often thinks his own are the heaviest. The Lord never promised to take away our burdens, but He did promise "I will sustain thee." When some burden seems too heavy to bear or a problem seems to severe to face, just remember that all these are appointed by our Lord in love as gracious necessities in perfecting our spiritual life. "And we know that all things [must] work together for good . . ." (Romans 8:28). There can be no failure, for God has ordained it. This promise should dispel every trace of doubt or impatience and instill confidence that God in His wisdom truly cares.

The child of God never needs to fear. His chief concern should be to please Christ and bring honor to His name.

". . . Most gladly therefore will I rather glory in my infirmities, that the power of Christ may rest upon me . . . for when I am weak, then am I strong" (II Corinthians 12:9-10).

NOTE:
64:2 **insurrection** *means violence; 65:8* **tokens** *means evidence of your presence.*

JULY 6: Read Psalms 67-71.

Psalm 71:5, 18: "For thou art my hope, O Lord God: thou art my trust from my youth. . . . Now also when I am old and gray-headed, O God, forsake me not; until I have shewed thy strength unto this generation, and thy power to every one that is to come."

Over the years God had blessed and answered many of David's prayers, but now that the psalmist was old and sick, he was almost powerless to control the government. More than at any other time in his life, he realized that he must depend upon God.

MEMORY VERSE FOR THE WEEK: Psalm 119:9

"Wherewithal shall a young man cleanse his way? by taking heed thereto according to thy word."

Although the psalmist prayed, "Cast me not off in time of old age" (verse 9), this prayer was dictated by the Holy Spirit as part of the inspired Word of God. Therefore, you can be sure that it was more than a prayer; it was a *promise*. What God prompted to be written He will also fulfill.

It is as though He is saying, Although society may cast us aside, friends may forsake us, even our children may forget us, we can be sure that our heavenly Father will never "forsake" anyone who remains faithful to Him. Each day becomes a new opportunity to lean upon His Everlasting Arms.

Retirement years provide an opportunity to spend many hours with the Lord in His Word and in prayer. All who do so "shall still bring forth fruit in old age" (Psalm 92:14).

The more we become acquainted with God's Word year after year, the more effective we become in prayer. "As thy days, so shall thy strength be" (Deuteronomy 33:25). So old age presents a priceless privilege to devote oneself to Christ, praying for His ministries.

"Anna . . . was of a great age, . . . but [she] served God with fastings and prayers night and day" (Luke 2:36,37).

NOTE:
Psalm 68:18: *See Mk. 16:19; I Cor. 15:4; Eph. 4:8.* **69:9:** *See John 2:17; Rom. 15:3.* **69:21:** *See Matt. 27:34,38.* **69:22:** *See Rom. 11:9,10.* **69:25:** *See Acts 1:20.*

"I made sackcloth also my garment; and I became a proverb to them."   Psalm 69:11

JULY 7: Read Psalms 72-77.

Psalm 73:2-3: "But as for me, my feet were almost gone; my steps had well-nigh slipped. For I was envious at the foolish, when I saw the prosperity of the wicked."

In self-pity the psalmist had complained, "For all the day long have I been plagued, and chastened every morning" (verse 14). During one point in his life, David was critical as he saw those who blasphemed God enjoying life while those who worshiped God were having great difficulties. This has been a stumbling block for many weak Christians who don't understand enough about God, His Word, and His ways.

Keep in mind that the psalmist was not describing the facts, but rather what *seemed to him* to be the facts. He could not understand why the wicked were not plagued with sufferings.

He may have heard a scribe reading the book of Job and discovered that God has a marvelous purpose for the servant whom He can trust to suffer for Him. His faith could also have been strengthened as he heard how the great lawgiver chose ". . . to suffer affliction with the people of God, [rather] than to enjoy the pleasures of sin for a season" (Hebrews 11:25). But his words testify that he gained a true perspective of life's problems when he

MEMORY VERSE FOR THE WEEK: Psalm 119:9

"Wherewithal shall a young man cleanse his way? by taking heed thereto according to thy word."

went to the house of God to hear His Word: ". . . I went into the sanctuary of God; then understood I their end" (Psalm 73:17).

NOTE:
73:10 **waters of a full cup** *means fruits of prosperity; 74:4* **roar** *means threaten; 74:13* **dragons** *means crocodiles; 75:10* **horns** *means strength; 77:2* **my sore ran** *means my heart ached.*

JULY 8: Read Psalms 78-80.

Psalm 78: 60,67-68: "So that he forsook the tabernacle of Shiloh, the tent which he placed among men; . . . Moreover he refused the tabernacle of Joseph, and chose not the tribe of Ephraim: But chose the tribe of Judah, the mount Zion which he loved."

Throughout the wilderness journey, God had made known His presence in the tent tabernacle. After the children of Israel entered the Promised Land, the tabernacle was permanently established at Shiloh. It remained there during the 400-year period of the Judges, up to the time of Eli the priest when God forsook the ark because of the sins of Israel and permitted it to be taken by the Philistines (1 Samuel 4:17). Although the Philistines returned the ark to the Israelites, it was never again taken back to Shiloh. It was taken first to Nob, then to Gibeon, and finally, David took it to Jerusalem.

The ark was called "his [God's] strength" (verse 61) because it was a symbol of His saving presence and His power to protect His people. It was called *His beauty* or honor because it marked the place where God chose to manifest His presence.

The tribe of Ephraim was rejected because "They kept not the covenant of God, and refused to walk in his laws" (verse 10), "but [God] chose the tribe of Judah . . . which he loved."

The Ephraimites led the tribes in criticism, complaint, and unbelief. In the long history of the tribe of Ephraim, not one word of praise or thankfulness is recorded.

The ancient sin of discontent in Ephraim has many counterparts today. Many are following the reasoning of Ephraim and cannot understand why they experience so little of His abiding presence. "Turn us again, O God of hosts, and cause thy face to shine . . ." (Psalm 80:7).

NOTE:
78:15 **clave** *means split; 80:13* **waste** *means eat.*
Psalm 78:2: *See Matt. 13:35.* **78:24:** *See John 6:31.*

MEMORY VERSE FOR THE WEEK: Psalm 119:9

"Wherewithal shall a young man cleanse his way? by taking heed thereto according to thy word."

JULY 9: Read Psalms 81-87.

Psalm 84:2,10,11: "My soul longeth, yea, even fainteth for the courts of the Lord: my heart and my flesh crieth out for the living God. . . . For a day in thy courts is better than a thousand . . . no good thing will he withhold from them that walk uprightly."

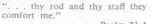
". . . thy rod and thy staff they comfort me."

Psalm 23:4

Oh, for more of the intense desire of David when he said, "A day in the Lord's presence is better than a thousand" days anywhere else! David enjoyed a peace with God which no rebellion in his kingdom could shake. He had unconditional confidence that "no good thing will he [God] withhold," or permit him to miss out on or be deprived of because God could and would direct each step of life's way.

David's practical and everyday experience should show us that God usually gives guidance one day at a time. We tend to want guidance as far in advance as possible instead of trusting God one day at a time.

Most of our frustrations come from our wanting to know all about our tomorrows. The child of God must learn to trust Him as Abraham did when he went forth, "not knowing whither he went"; but he had confidence in his Guide.

Do you doubt God's day-by-day guidance for the future? Then look back to the day He saved you from sin and how He has kept you since that day. Yes, God provides guidance each step of the way.

"Whereas ye know not what shall be on the morrow . . . ye ought to say, if the Lord will, we shall live, and do this, or that" (James 4:14,15).

NOTE:
81:2 **psaltery** *means book of Psalms; 83:2* **lifted up the head** *means exalted themselves.*

Psalm 82:6: *See John 10:34.*

JULY 10: Read Psalms 88-91.

Psalm 91:5-6,11: "Thou shalt not be afraid for the terror by night; nor for the arrow that flieth by day; nor for the pestilence that walketh in darkness; nor for the destruction that wasteth at noonday. For he shall give his angels charge over thee, to keep thee in all thy ways.

The precious promises of this entire chapter are dependent upon one's meeting all the conditions of the first two verses of this Psalm: "He that dwelleth in the secret place of the Most High shall abide under the shadow of the Almighty. I will say of the Lord, He is my refuge and my fortress: my God; in him will I trust." These principles teach us to live in complete faith in God.

MEMORY VERSE FOR THE WEEK: Psalm 119:10

"With my whole heart have I sought thee: O let me not wander from thy commandments."

The central point of this Psalm is that no matter what disaster we face, we can have confidence that God cares and controls every situation in our life. On the other hand, the psalmist did not imply that trusting in God provides a guaranteed immunity from all adversity, nor did he suggest that God will rescue the foolish one who violates principles of faith. Some adversity is the result of the troubles we make for ourselves.

Satan actually misinterpreted this Psalm when he urged Jesus to jump off the pinnacle of the Temple and to trust God to protect Him from injury (Matthew 4:6). But our Lord, in full dependence upon the Father, said, "It is written again, Thou shalt not tempt the Lord thy God" (Matthew 4:7).

NOTE:
89:14 **habitation** *means an abode; 89:41* **spoil** *means plunder and rob; 91:3* **noisome pestilence** *means epidemic or plague.*
Psalm 89:20: *See Acts 13:22.* **91:11,12:** *See Matt. 4:6; Luke 4:10,11.*

"And at midnight Paul and Silas prayed, and sang praises unto God: and the prisoners heard them."

Acts 16:25

JULY 11: Read Psalms 92-100.

Psalm 92:1-2: "It is a good thing to give thanks unto the Lord, and to sing praises unto thy name, O Most High: to shew forth thy loving-kindness in the morning, and thy faithfulness every night."

Christ is the Alpha and the Omega, so each day can begin and end with singing His praises. Singing should be an expression of enjoying His presence, and singing hymns of praise honors the Most High God.

Some people think that when they have problems they have a right to complain, but this is only self-pity that leads to additional gloom. Since we cannot praise God and complain at the same time, singing His praises often brings a release from sorrow.

Our song should never cease. The Lord's presence can turn even a prison into a paradise. The apostles, after being beaten and thrown into prison, sang praises to the Lord at midnight.

Although we may find it hard to reconcile some disappointments with the truth of God's Word, it is still a fact that "all things work together for good . . ." (Romans 8:28).

Singing God's praises is a testimony of our absolute confidence that every event in our life is love's message sent from heaven. No longer will we be guilty of faultfinding, dissatisfaction, and unhappiness.

Serving the Lord with gladness begins with unconditional confidence in His unchanging Word.

"Speaking to yourselves in psalms and hymns and spiritual songs, singing and making melody in your heart to the Lord" (Ephesians 5:19).

MEMORY VERSE FOR THE WEEK: Psalm 119:10

"With my whole heart have I sought thee: O let me not wander from thy commandments."

NOTE:
92:6 **brutish** *means senseless; 92:10* **unicorn** *means wild ox; 94:4* **hard** *means arrogant.*

Psalm 94:11: *See I Cor. 3:20.* **95:7-11:** *See Heb. 3:7-11.* **95:11:** *See Heb. 4:3.* **97:7:** *See Heb. 1:6.*

JULY 12: Read Psalms 101-105.

Psalm 103:7: "He made known *his ways* unto Moses, *his acts* unto the children of Israel."

His *ways* and His *acts* are not the same thing. In the long wilderness journey from Egypt to the Promised Land, Moses discerned "his [God's] ways"—His purpose in arranging the many trials and disappointments.

However, the children of Israel could only see "his acts," such as the bitter waters of Marah and the fiery serpents, as just another obstacle to reaching their destination.

In discerning "his ways," Moses not only could see God as the Faithful One responsible for every situation, but he could also see that His purpose on each occasion was to bring Israel to totally trust in His wisdom.

Moses' insight into the ways of the Almighty did not come easily. His problems, perplexities, and deep distress had led him to pray, "If I have found grace in thy sight, shew me now thy way, that I may know thee." As a result, God replied, "My presence shall go with thee, and I will give thee rest" (Exodus 33:13-14).

The Lord continues to permit circumstances to arise in each of our lives that we too may be led to pray, "Shew me now thy way, that I may know thee."

Like the multitude, we can be so intent on self-satisfaction and obtaining answers to our selfish prayers that we, too, become ". . . a people that do err in their heart, . . . [that] have not known my ways" (Psalm 95:10).

NOTE:
101:4 **know** *means recognize; 101:5* **privily** *means secretly.*

Psalm 102:25-27: *See Heb. 1:10-12.* **104:4:** *See Heb. 1:7.*

The keeper of the gate was responsible for keeping out enemies and warning of danger.

JULY 13: Read Psalms 106-107.

Psalm 107:20-21: "He sent his word, and healed them, and delivered them from their destructions. Oh that men would praise the Lord for his goodness, and for his wonderful works to the children of men!"

The psalmist could have said, "*The Lord* delivered them." Instead, it is specifically stated, "He sent *his word*, and healed them." It simply means that His Word is the means by which God

---

MEMORY VERSE FOR THE WEEK: Psalm 119:10

"With my whole heart have I sought thee: O let me not wander from thy commandments."

---

has chosen to supply and satisfy every need. Furthermore, there is no other reliable source of counsel for the inner emotional conflicts that seek to control our minds. Throughout the Bible we are taught the absolute necessity of relying on God's Word for every problem and in every situation—without exception.

Yes, His Word does give direction to solve any problem that confronts us. "He sent his word . . ." Yes, the *Word* by which the heavens were made (see Psalm 33:6) is the *same Word* by which God ". . . is able to do exceeding abundantly above all that we ask or think, according to *the power* that worketh in us" (Ephesians 3:20).

Through daily Bible reading we obtain the power that helps us have the faith to trust God in prayer to fulfill His promises (Hebrews 4:12). How much of this power do you make available for Him to use in your life?

Experience has taught us that we are prone to view our weakness in the light of our abilities and fail to recognize the greatness of God's gift—His Word that supplies the answer for every need.

Christ said, "Ye shall know the truth, and the truth shall make you free" (John 8:32).

NOTE:
106:30 **stayed** *means ceased; 107:11* **contemned** *means spurned, despised.*

JULY 14: Read Psalms 108-118.

Psalm 110:1,4-5: "The Lord said unto my Lord, Sit thou at my right hand, until I make thine enemies thy footstool . . . The Lord at thy right hand shall strike through kings in the day of his wrath."

Jesus asked the Pharisees ". . . What think ye of Christ? whose son is he?" They answered him, "The son of David." Then, in order to show Himself as Messiah, Jesus quoted this Psalm. (See Matthew 22:42-44; also see Luke 20:41-44.)

Our Lord combined this Psalm with the prophecy in Daniel 7:13 as He replied to the high priest, saying, ". . . Hereafter shall ye see the Son of man sitting on the right hand of power, and coming in the clouds of heaven" (Matthew 26:64; also see Acts 2:34-36).

This Psalm is a prophecy of the Christ who is the true King. "Sit thou at my right hand" is the same as saying "Be associated with me and participate in my universal dominion of all the earth."

By inspiration of God, David was able to foretell the true greatness of the Savior as King of kings.

MEMORY VERSE FOR THE WEEK: Psalm 119:10

"With my whole heart have I sought thee: O let me not wander from thy commandments."

". . . Thou sayest that I am a king. To this end was I born, and for this cause came I into the world, that I should bear witness unto the truth. Every one that is of the truth heareth my voice" (John 18:37).

NOTE:
111:7 **verity** *means trustworthiness.*

Psalm 109:4: *See Luke 23:34.* **109:8:** *See Acts 1:20.* **110:1:** *See Matt. 22:44;* **Mk.** *12:36;* **Luke** *20:42,43; Acts 2:34,35; I Cor. 15:25;* **Heb.** *1:13; 10:12,13.* **110:4:** *See Heb. 5:6; 7:17.* **112:9:** *See II Cor. 9:9.* **116:10:** *See II Cor. 4:13.* **117:1:** *See Rom. 15:11.* **118:6:** *See Heb. 13:6.* **118:22:** *See Acts 4:11; I Pet. 2:6,7.* **118:22,23:** *See Matt. 21:42; Mk. 12:10-11; Luke 20:17.* **118:26:** *See Matt. 21:9; 23:39; Mk. 11:9; Luke 13:35; John 21:13.*

JULY 15: Read Psalm 119.

"But his delight is in the law of the Lord; and in his law doth he meditate day and night."
Psalm 1:2

Psalm 119:14-15: "I have rejoiced in *the way* of thy testimonies, as much as in all riches. I will *meditate* in thy precepts, and have respect unto *thy ways.*"

God does not reveal His will and satisfy our needs when we read the Bible unless we seriously intend to live in harmony with it—to have "respect unto thy ways." To rejoice "in the way of thy testimonies" means to live each day as a living expression of His Word. To *meditate* is to prayerfully apply to our life what we read. This means that we should prayerfully read the Bible with an intense desire to do His will.

Many regular Bible readers tend to hurriedly read the chapters, gaining historical facts but missing the life-giving, transforming purpose God intended. Because of this many cannot say, as did Jeremiah: "Thy words were found and I did eat them; and thy word was unto me the joy and rejoicing of mine heart" (Jeremiah 15:16).

If we are to rejoice in His ways "as much as in all riches," then it is of utmost importance that we give sufficient time to reading His Word each day. We should be conscious of His presence; then His Word will bring the joy that comes from fellowship with God.

Our daily Bible reading can either be a mechanical accumulation of knowledge or it can be the expression of this 119th Psalm, where the Word of God is preeminent in every verse.

"Thy word is a lamp unto my feet, and a light unto my path" (Psalm 119:105).

NOTE:
119:28 **melteth** *means faints;* **heaviness** *means discouragement; 119:80* **sound** *means truthful.*

MEMORY VERSE FOR THE WEEK: Psalm 119:10

"**With my whole heart have I sought thee: O let me not wander from thy commandments.**"

JULY 16: Read Psalms 120-131.

Psalm 130: 5-6: "I wait for the Lord, my soul doth wait, and in *his word* do I hope. My soul waiteth for the Lord more than they that watch for the morning: I say, more than they that watch for the morning."

There is something beautiful in the repetition and emphasis given to the thought, "I say, more than they that watch for the morning." The psalmist compared his being on guard with that of the night watchman on the walls of Jerusalem watching over the city. The watchman was obligated to stay awake because of his responsibility to alert others in case the enemy were to attack the city.

With far more alertness and concern than that of a night watchman, the psalmist guarded his life from sin (verse 3). "In his Word" he enjoyed the security of the Lord's "plenteous redemption" (verse 7).

Those who value the Lord's presence will have, throughout the night of this world's experiences, the same alertness as that of the psalmist. The enemy of sin finds easy entrance into the life left unguarded through neglect of "his word."

This "waiting upon the Lord" is a true expression of our faith in His Word. "Waiting on the Lord" means studying the Word, believing the Word, and living the Word—all because it is *His Word*.

"Hear instruction, and be wise, and refuse it not. Blessed is the man that heareth me, watching daily at my gates, waiting at the posts of my doors. For whoso findeth me findeth life, and shall obtain favor of the Lord" (Proverbs 8:33-35).

NOTE:
131:1 **high** *means difficult.*

"That their hearts might be comforted, being knit together in love . . ."

Colossians 2:2

JULY 17: Read Psalms 132-138.

Psalm 133:1,3: "Behold, how good and how pleasant it is for the brethren to dwell together in unity! . . . upon the mountains of Zion: for there the Lord commanded the blessing, even life for evermore."

The Israelites went to Jerusalem three times a year to worship, singing this Psalm as they went. There were all kinds of people on that road—rich and poor, young and old—but they were united in one thing—they were all going to the City of David to worship God.

The unity of the Spirit is like the unity of many musicians in a great orchestra. There are many instruments; yet, there is perfect harmony. Unity is not obtained by rules and regulations but by the working of the Holy Spirit in the lives of those who have been born into the family of God.

MEMORY VERSE FOR THE WEEK: Psalm 119:11
"Thy word have I hid in mine heart, that I might not sin against thee."

This unity is the result of "the precious ointment" (verse 2). The oil represents the Holy Spirit. There is one "holy anointing oil," the Spirit of God Himself, flowing from the Head to every part of the body. Christ is the Head of the body—the mind, the voice. Christians make up the body of Christ. Therefore, when we obey Him—the Head—in all things, we will be in harmony and united with others who also worship the Lord. "If we walk in the light . . . we have fellowship one with another" (I John 1:7).

In sharp contrast to our Lord's intercessory prayer in John 17, " . . . that they may be one, as we are," is the warning, "he that soweth discord among brethren" is an abomination unto the Lord" (compare John 17:11 and Proverbs 6:19).

"Endeavoring to keep the unity of the Spirit in the bond of peace. There is one body . . ." (Ephesians 4:3-4).

JULY 18: Read Psalms 139-143.

Psalm 139:23-24: "Search me, O God, and know my heart: try me, and know my thoughts: and see if there be any wicked way in me, and lead me in the way everlasting."

The psalmist prayed to the great Revealer of hearts. He was aware that everything in his life, both past and present, was an open book to God, and he knew that it was impossible for him to see the evils of his own heart.

This prayer expresses a sincere willingness to forsake anything in his life that would hinder his prayer or fellowship with God. He knew, as did Jeremiah, that "it is not in man that walketh to direct his own steps," so he prayed, "lead me in the way everlasting." He was willing to forsake self-interest or anything else that was opposed to God's principles.

He declared his hatred for the wicked ways of sinners and was "grieved with those that rise up against thee" (verse 21). He knew that is human nature to hate the sins of others and overlook ones own faults. His desire was for God to let him see himself as God saw him. We may never realize the evil in our heart until we pray, as did the psalmist, "Search me, O God, and know my heart."

"The heart is deceitful above all things, and desperately wicked: who can know it?" only God (Jeremiah 17:9).

NOTE:
139:13 **reins** *means mind as the inner self.* *141:9* **gins** *means traps.*

MEMORY VERSE FOR THE WEEK: Psalm 119:11

"Thy word have I hid in mine heart, that I might not sin against thee."

". . . the word of the Lord is tried: he is a buckler to all them that trust in him . . . my shield, and he in whom I trust . . ."

II Sam. 22:31; Psalm 144:2

JULY 19: Read Psalms 144-150.

Psalm 146:3,5: "Put not your trust in princes, nor in the son of man, in whom there is no help. Happy is he that hath the God of Jacob for his help, whose hope is in the Lord his God."

In situations that baffle us, we are prone to place our faith and confidence in the wisdom and abilities of men. Even our closest friends may fail us at times. But if our "hope is in the Lord," we should begin each day by seeking Him—having fellowship with Him through prayer and Bible reading. Then, by having our hope in the Lord and not in men, there will be no need for disappointment.

When we are "putting no confidence in the flesh," our faith is greatly strengthened. As we wholeheartedly turn from the world to read His Word and wait on the Lord, He will always meet our needs.

When we are seeking advancement at work, by human nature we tend to cater to the influential ones who can have a part in promoting us. However, the psalmist declared that no man, regardless of how powerful he may be, is able to advance us to *permanent* security and prestige. All that a man will eventually possess on this earth will be his grave, whether he is a prince, a president, or a millionaire.

Therefore, ". . . Cursed be the man that trusteth in man . . ." (Jeremiah 17:5). So the Lord reveals that man's lasting eternal values are in "the God of Jacob" (verse 5).

"And again, The Lord knoweth the thoughts of the wise, that they are vain. Therefore let no man glory in men . . ." (I Corinthians 3:20-21).

JULY 20: Read Proverbs 1-3.

Proverbs 1:22: "How long, ye *simple* ones, will ye love simplicity? and the *scorners* delight in their scorning, and fools hate knowledge?"

The simple are not the ignorant, but rather, those who permit their natural desires for self-pleasure to be the motivating force in their lives. Over a period of time the simple ones become more fixed in sin and scorn the truth. The scorner eventually becomes more hardened in sin and then God calls him a "fool [for he] hates knowledge" (verse 22).

"I have called," says wisdom, but they reject that wisdom. They do not heed the warning that would awaken them to the fear of God. Therefore, when they ignore His truth, His wisdom will be powerless to deliver them when "destruction cometh as a whirlwind" (verse 27). It will be too late to reverse their life then.

MEMORY VERSE FOR THE WEEK: Psalm 119:11

"Thy word have I hid in mine heart, that I might not sin against thee."

How terrifying to think of those who are eternally lost in hell! They are reminded throughout eternity that they missed heaven because they "hated knowledge, and did not choose to fear the Lord" (verse 29).

Christ is "not willing that any should perish, but that all should come to repentance" (II Peter 3:9).

Anyone can mock (ignore) God's Word now, but the day will come when His words of wisdom will mock their misery. The Scriptures do not say that God Himself "will laugh at your calamity" (Proverbs 1:26), but it is His words of wisdom that they have rejected that will haunt them in hell throughout all eternity. Yes, our Lord has said, "He that rejecteth me, and receiveth not my words, hath one that judgeth him: the word that I have spoken, the same shall judge him in the last day" (John 12:48).

NOTE:
1:18 **privily** *means secretly; 1:21* **concourse** *means public affairs; 1:22* **simple** *means foolish; 2:7* **buckler** *means shield; 3:8* **marrow** *means strength.*
Proverbs 3:11,12: *See Heb. 12:5,6.* **3:34:** *See Jas. 4:6; I Pet. 5:5.*

> "A man that beareth false witness against his neighbour is a maul, and a sword, and a sharp arrow."   Proverbs 25:18

JULY 21: Read Proverbs 4-7.

Proverbs 6:16-19: "These six things doth the Lord hate: yea, seven are an abomination unto him: a proud look, a lying tongue, and hands that shed innocent blood, an heart that deviseth wicked imaginations, feet that be swift in running to mischief, a false witness that speaketh lies, and he that soweth discord among brethren."

Maul is a heavy war club with a metal head used as a armor-breaking weapon.

These seven things which God hates are completely opposite to the things He likes, as we find in the Beatitudes of Jesus. The first and the seventh in both lists deal with the same issue. The Lord hates a proud look, and in contrast, He said, "Blessed are the poor in spirit." The seventh one, "he that soweth discord among brethren," is in contrast to "the peacemaker." Our eyes, our tongue, our hands, and our feet are instruments to be used to declare God's glory, and we dare not use them dishonorably.

Four of these deadly sins pertain to an undisciplined tongue. Some Christians destroy their usefulness for Christ because of their careless conversation. Think for a moment. What kind of talk do you like to hear? The kind of talk you enjoy hearing indicates the kind of person you are.

We reveal our hearts by what we say. Every Christian is obligated to use his mouth as an overflow of the Spirit-filled life.

MEMORY VERSE FOR THE WEEK: Psalm 119:11

"Thy word have I hid in mine heart, that I might not sin against thee."

"A good man out of the good treasure of the heart bringeth forth good things: and an evil man out of the evil treasure bringeth forth evil things. For by thy words thou shalt be justified, and by thy words thou shalt be condemned" (Matthew 12:35,37).

NOTE:
5:6 **movable** *means unstable; 5:19* **ravished** *means delighted; 6:1* **surety** *means guarantee.*

JULY 22: Read Proverbs 8-11.

Proverbs 11:25: "The liberal soul shall be made fat: and he that watereth shall be watered also himself."

One of the greatest privileges in spiritual service is that of man cooperating with God. We often hear someone say, "I believe God can do it," yet they themselves make no effort to cooperate with the Lord.

When we use our time and money to share God's Truth with those who are hungry for reality, God sees to it that we gain much, "The liberal soul *shall* be made fat."

These great promises of God can only become a reality when the gift was given in the right spirit—whether it be money, sympathy, or kind words. Everything depends upon the motive. If you give, expecting to receive as much in return, that is exchange. If you give to receive more, that is covetousness. If you give expecting thanks, that is vanity. If you give to be seen, that is vainglory. If you give to cover ulterior motives, it is bribery. If you give from a heart of compassion, it is love.

Those who give with the right motive are always receiving and always have more to give.

". . . Freely ye have received, freely give" (Matthew 10:8).

NOTE:
10:9 **surely** *means safely.*
Proverbs 10:12: *See I Pet. 4:8.*

JULY 23: Read Proverbs 12-15.

Proverbs 13:24: "He that spareth his rod hateth his son: but he that loveth him chasteneth him betimes."

The rod is a symbol of correction, a symbol of authority which God has committed to parents for training their children.

To apply the *rod* literally means to exercise authority. It must be administered firmly but prayerfully. It certainly does not mean shouting demands or acting violently, such as slapping a child in the face, withholding meals, or other acts of child abuse.

In disciplining children, we should consider the question: Is the correction for the child's benefit, or is it only a release for the pleasure of a frustrated parent who may selfishly be thinking of their own peace of mind?

MEMORY VERSE FOR THE WEEK: Psalm 119:11

"Thy word have I hid in mine heart, that I might not sin against thee."

God's Word clearly says, "He that spareth the rod hateth his son." Sparing the rod is not a sign of love but a lack of spiritual insight—a sickly sentimentalism of a parent who is also living in rebellion to God's authority. Consequently, they permit the child to develop a stubborn, defiant self-will. The temper tantrums of your little one may cause you to smile today, but it will bring heartbreak tomorrow. Even worse, it will be a curse to your child in later years.

In the book of Hebrews, God tells us that "whom the Lord loveth he chasteneth . . . no chastening for the present seemeth to be joyous, but grievous: nevertheless afterward it yieldeth the peaceable fruit of righteousness . . ." (Hebrews 12:6,11). God does not chasten for His own pleasure but for our good. So it is with Christian parents who truly love their children.

The blessing of discipline far exceeds the pain inflicted. The psalmist expressed it in these words, "Before I was afflicted I went astray: but now have I kept thy word" (Psalm 119:67).

NOTE:
13:24 **betimes** *means diligently;* *15:17* **stalled** *means fattened.*

JULY 24: Read Proverbs 16-19.

"The sleep of a labouring man is sweet, whether he eat little or much: but the abundance of the rich will not suffer him to sleep."
Ecclesiastes 5:12

Proverbs 16:27-28: "An ungodly man diggeth up evil: and in his lips there is as a burning fire. A froward man soweth strife: and a whisperer separateth chief friends."

The judgment day of Christ may reveal that the damage done by careless gossip far exceeds the damage done by crimes that have sent others to prison. The destructive force of slander never ends. Once words have escaped the lips they cannot be recovered. Thoughtless gossip releases a cruel stream that flows on and on, spreading death wherever it goes. The psalmist's prayer should be ours, "Set a watch, O Lord, before my mouth; keep the door of my lips" (Psalm 141:3).

Many words of criticism that were spoken in the past as idle conversation are no longer "idle." They are *very busy* now, undermining the helpless victim. That is why Jesus so strongly condemned this vicious evil, saying "That *every idle word* that men shall speak, *they shall give an account* thereof in the day of judgment. For by thy words thou shalt be justified, and by thy words thou shalt be condemned" (Matthew 12:36-37).

We should flee a gossiper and a talebearer as we would a snake. (See Proverbs 20:19.) Their "latest information" may be interesting and even true, but even if we don't "pass it on," we are still guilty by association and participation. We become like those with whom we associate, and by human nature, we develop some of their mannerisms, their thoughts, their character. We cannot afford to jeopardize our fellowship with the Lord.

MEMORY VERSE FOR THE WEEK: Psalm 119:12
"Blessed art thou, O Lord: teach me thy statutes."

187

"Not that which goeth into the mouth defileth a man: but that which cometh out of the mouth, this defileth a man" (Matthew 15:11).

NOTE:
16:2 **spirits** *means motives.*

JULY 25: Read Proverbs 20-22.

Proverbs 20:22: "Say not thou, I will recompense evil; but wait on the Lord, and he shall save thee."

It is not enough merely to forgive and then avoid the offender. In both the Old and New Testaments we find, "If thine enemy be hungry, give him bread to eat; and if he be thirsty, give him water to drink: for thou shalt heap coals of fire upon his head, and the Lord shall reward thee" (Proverbs 25:21-22; compare Romans 12:20).

To "heap coals of fire on his head" is not a means of revenge but just the opposite. It illustrates the high priest (Leviticus 16:12) who, on the Day of Atonement, took the censer and refilled it with "coals of fire" from the altar of burnt offerings and then put incense (a symbol of prayer) on the fire that ascended toward heaven, giving off a sweet-smelling fragrance.

In other words, it is not enough to pray that we overcome our injured feelings so we can have peace with our heavenly Father; that is merely self-love. We must pray just as intently for our enemy, that God's mercy be extended to him as well as to us.

Our offender is unconsciously our best friend, for their unwelcome acts test the sincerity of our faith and cause us to see the inward condition of our heart and thoughts. Even as the fire purifies the gold, our trials expose superficial self-love. They never destroy genuine love.

Feelings of revenge and demanding our rights are instilled by Satan, whereas the spirit of Christ prompts us to ". . . Love our enemies, bless them that curse you, do good to them that hate you, and pray for them which despitefully use you, and persecute you; that ye may be the children of your Father which is in heaven . . ." (Matthew 5:44-45).

NOTE:
20:10 **Divers** *means unequal;* *22:26* **strike hands** *means pledge themselves.*
Proverbs 20:9: *See I John 1:8.*

MEMORY VERSE FOR THE WEEK: Psalm 119:12

"Blessed art thou, O Lord: teach me thy statutes."

JULY 26: Read Proverbs 23-26.

Proverbs 25:24: "It is better to dwell in the corner of the housetop, than with a brawling woman and in a wide house."

"The corner of a housetop" is the flat roof of the average, one-story home in Palestine which was exposed to the heat of the day and the chill of the night.

But considering all the discomforts of living in the corner of the housetop, the writer, under inspiration of God, said that it would be more pleasant than occupying a "wide house" (prominent home) with a "brawling" woman—that is, one who is nagging, quarrelsome, and faultfinding.

God authorized her unhappy husband to be her head, but he lives under the constant dread that any calm in the chilly atmosphere merely gives her time for further investigation and contemplation for gathering additional accusations.

The dear wife who has an honest, legitimate complaint should commit her problems to the Lord and be willing to sacrifice her own self-interest and self-sufficiency. When this is done in a spirit of sincerely wanting to obey the Lord, she will experience much peace. She can praise the Lord for allowing her to be drawn closer to Him through placing her dependence in Him. She should trust the Lord and submit herself to God's authority over her—". . . the head of the woman is the man . . ." (I Corinthians 11:3).

His Word is without exception or excuse, "For after this manner in the old time the *holy* women also, who trusted in God, adorned themselves, being in subjection unto their own husbands: even as Sarah obeyed Abraham, calling him lord: whose daughters ye are, as *long as ye do well*, and are not afraid with any amazement" (I Peter 3:5-6).

NOTE:
24:26 **kiss** *means approve.*
Proverbs 24:21: *See I Pet. 2:17.* **26:11:** *See II Pet. 2:22.*

JULY 27: Read Proverbs 27-31.

"Thy wife shall be as a fruitful vine by the sides of thine house: thy children like olive plants round about thy table."
Psalm 128:3

Proverbs 31:10,30: "Who can find a virtuous woman? For her price is far above rubies . . . Favor is deceitful, and beauty is vain: but a woman that feareth the Lord, she shall be praised."

A beautiful picture of the virtuous woman is portrayed. In this Scripture "virtuous" means more than moral chastity. It describes the woman who not only fulfills her obligation of love to her husband but also assumes the responsibility of managing the home, the children, and obligations to others.

Created to be a helpmate, her business is to satisfy her husband. "She will do him good and not evil all the days of her life" (verse 12).

MEMORY VERSE FOR THE WEEK: Psalm 119:12

"Blessed art thou, O Lord: teach me thy statutes."

Note the contrast between personal beauty and the fear of the Lord (verses 30-31). Personal "beauty is vain" (verse 30). With all of its desirable attractions, it may cover a selfish life. Other women seem to possess many of her fine qualifications, but the *virtuous* wife "excellest them all" in that she "feareth the Lord." The one who "feareth the Lord," regardless of outward beauty, has an inward beauty and loveliness that makes "her price far above rubies." Her conduct is directed by the Lord.

"*Trust in the Lord* with all thine heart; and lean not unto thine own understanding. In all thy ways acknowledge him, and *he shall direct thy paths*" (Proverbs 3:5-6).

NOTE:
27:16 **bewrayeth** *means betrays; 27:22* **bray** *means beat upon.*

JULY 28: Read Ecclesiastes 1-4.

Eccleciastes 1:12-14: "I the Preacher was king over Israel in Jerusalem. And I gave my heart to seek and search out by wisdom concerning all things that are done under heaven: this sore travail hath God given to the sons of man to be exercised therewith. I have seen all the works that are done under the sun; and, behold, all is vanity and vexation of spirit."

King Solomon spoke with inexcusable confidence when he said, "I gave my heart to seek . . . wisdom." He blundered when he concluded that he knew all that was to be known. There was a whole realm which he chose to ignore, for he refused to walk in the spiritual wisdom of his father, David. Because of this, God said He was angry with Solomon. (See I Kings 11:9).

In all his searching for the meaning of life, he was unable to escape from the fact that God had set the world (eternity) in their hearts. (See Eccl. 3:11.) In other words, God has instilled within each person a hunger that can only be satisfied by the Bread of Life—a thirst that can only be quenched with the Living Water from the Rock of Ages.

This "wise man" said that he applied his mind to wisdom in his search for the meaning of life. How fatal that the wisest man tried to substitute man's wisdom for God's wisdom!

Jesus recognized the fame of Solomon; but He said that Solomon, in all of his human wisdom, did not equal the glory of one tiny lily of the field which God's wisdom had made.

"And yet I say unto you, That even Solomon in all his glory was not arrayed like one of these" (Matthew 6:29).

NOTE:
Eccl. 2:24: *See 1 Cor. 15:32.*

MEMORY VERSE FOR THE WEEK: Psalm 119:12

"Blessed art thou, O Lord: teach me thy statutes."

"Their land also is full of idols;
they worship the work of their
own hands . . ."

Isaiah 2:8

JULY 29: Read Ecclesiastes 5-8.

Ecclesiastes 8:15,17: "Then I commended mirth, because a man hath no better thing under the sun, that to eat, and to drink, and to be merry . . . Then I beheld all the work of God . . . though a man labour to seek it out, yet he shall not find it; yea further; though a wise man think to know it, yet he shall not be able to find it."

There is not one prayer in the book of Ecclesiastes. When man thinks he has all the answers, he never feels the need to pray. During Solomon's reign, the prophets were not honored or given any public recognition. Thus, it is not surprising that no mention of prayer or repentance is found in Ecclesiastes.

With all his wisdom, Solomon never discovered the true values of life. There is nothing in the entire book concerning love, joy, or peace. "But the wisdom that is from above is first pure, then peaceable, gentle, and easy to be entreated, full of mercy and good fruits . . ." (James 3:17). Solomon had pursued everything but the Lord.

God is mentioned 39 times in Ecclesiastes, but without exception, it is the Hebrew word "*Elohim.*" This word for God was used by believers, but it was also used by unbelievers and idolaters in referring to their false gods and idols. Throughout the book, not once is God recognized as Jehovah or Lord. The name *Jehovah*, by which our Father is known by His people in covenant relationship with Him, is never once mentioned.

This confirms the fact that a search after wisdom without God becomes one of "ever learning, and never able to come to the knowledge of the truth" (II Timothy 3:7).

NOTE:
Eccl. 7:20: *See I John 1:8.*

JULY 30: Read Ecclesiastes 9-12.

Ecclesiastes 12:13-14: "Let us hear the conclusion of the whole matter: Fear God, and keep his commandments: for this is the whole duty of man. For God shall bring every work into judgment, with every secret thing, whether it be good, or whether it be evil."

Solomon lived to please himself. Consequently, he sought to satisfy every physical desire. As he pursued the vanities of life, he forever forfeited his opportunities to exalt the great name of Jehovah in his kingdom. But after pursuing all these vanities, his conclusion was, "I have no pleasure in them." In fact, he finally confessed, "I hated life" (2:17). What's more, he ended the book with the inevitable fact that he must face God, who ". . . shall bring every work into judgment . . ."

MEMORY VERSE FOR THE WEEK: Psalm 119:12

"Blessed art thou, O Lord: teach me thy statutes."

With all his wisdom, Solomon did not find the meaning of life for himself. Although he knew he must face God, we have no record of his repentance or asking God to forgive him for promoting idolatry in his kingdom.

Notice in this book that there is no mention of prayer, thanksgiving or praise to God. Ecclesiastes certainly was not written to satisfy an Israelite, much less a Christian. It was given to expose the empty vanities that keep so many from seeking the Lord.

King Solomon, a symbol of all the wisdom of this world, failed to satisfy man's need. We must go to the One who is greater than Solomon. Our Lord Jesus Christ, the King of kings, alone can satisfy.

". . . a greater than Solomon is here" (Matthew 12:42).

"I am my beloved's, and my beloved is mine: he feedeth among the lilies."
Song of Solomon 6:3

JULY 31: Read Song of Solomon 1-8.

Song of Solomon 1:2-4; 7:10: "Let him kiss me with the kisses of his mouth: for thy love is better . . . thy name is as ointment poured forth . . . Draw me . . . I am my beloved's, and his desire is toward me."

This song of songs not only expresses the love of King Solomon for a shepherdess maid in Northern Palestine whose beauty and gracious character had captivated the great king's heart, but it also honors the sacredness of married love.

This song far surpasses any historic experience. It illustrates the covenant relationship of God with His people. (See Isaiah 5:50-62; Malachi; Ephesians 5; Jesus' Parable of Ten Virgins; Revelation 21,22.)

From the day of Pentecost, we know the meaning of "thy name is as ointment poured forth." The Holy Spirit has been poured out upon His bride, the Church (Acts 2:18). No matter how poverty-stricken a Christian may be, he is rich, for he can say, "I am my beloved's, and His desire is toward me." The King of kings left His throne in glory to come to a distant place—the earth—to love worthless servants.

"Rise up my beloved" was the prayer of the shepherdess maid. She waited for the happy hour when her king, the one whom she loved, would return.

As the shepherdess maid longed to see her beloved, the Church now loves an unseen Savior. We long for our absent Lord to whom we are joined in a covenant marriage relationship, "the bride, the Lamb's wife" (Rev. 21:9).

The Church looks forward to her King, who will gather His saints as a bride and take them to be with Him forever.

The world's vanity has no power to occupy the attention of those who are in love with Him. "Herein is love, not that we loved God, but that he loved us, and sent his son to be the propitiation for our sins" (I John 4:10).

NOTE:

1:12 **spikenard** *means perfume; 1:14* **camphire** *means flowers; 2:5* **sick of love** *means love sick; 2:12* **turtle** *means turtle dove; 2:14* **comely** *means lovely; 5:4* **bowels** *means heart; 6:6* **barren** *means childless.*

MEMORY VERSE FOR THE WEEK: Isaiah 55:6

"Seek ye the Lord while he may be found, call ye upon him while he is near:"

BIBLICAL REFERENCE INDEX

PRAYERS IN PSALMS*

David—when he fled from his son Absalom ....Psalm 3

David—after Nathan the prophet confronted David with his sin
with Bathsheba ....:Psalm 51

David—for help when the Philistines took him in Gath ....Psalm 56

David—for help in his old age ....Psalm 71

Prayer of Moses ....Psalm 90

David—concerning God's Word ....Psalm 119

* There are many prayers in Psalms, but space does not permit us to itemize each prayer separately.

QUOTATIONS IN PSALMS WHICH CHRIST SPOKE

Psalm		Reference
6: 8	"Depart from me, all ye workers of iniquity; for the Lord hath heard the voice of my weeping."	Matt. 7:23
8: 2	"Out of the mouth of babes and sucklings hast thou ordained strength because of thine enemies, that thou mightest still the enemy and the avenger."	Matt. 21:16
22: 1	"My God, my God, why hast thou forsaken me?"	Matt. 27:46; Mark 15:34
31: 5	"Into thine hand I commit my spirit: thou hast redeemed me, O Lord God of truth."	Luke 23:46
35:19	"Let not them that are mine enemies wrongfully rejoice over me: neither let them wink with the eye that hate me without a cause."	John 15:25
41: 9	"Yea, mine own familiar friend, in whom I trusted, which did eat of my bread, hath lifted up his heel against me."	Luke 22:48
82: 6	"I have said, Ye are gods; and all of you are children of the Most High."	John 10:34
109: 4	"For my love they are my adversaries: but I give myself unto prayer."	Luke 23:34
110: 1	"The Lord said unto my Lord, Sit thou at my right hand until I make thine enemies thy footstool."	Matt. 22:44; Mark 12:36; Luke 20:42-43
118:22	"The stone, which the builders refused is become the head stone of the corner."	Matt. 21:42
118:26	"Blessed be he that cometh in the name of the Lord: we have blessed you out of the house of the Lord."	Matt. 23:39; Luke 13:35

Psalm		*N.T. Ref.*
2: 7	"Thou art my Son; this day have I begotten thee."	Matt. 3:17; Acts 13:33
8: 6	". . . Thou hast put all things under his feet."	Heb. 2:6-10
16:10	"For thou wilt not leave my soul in hell; neither wilt thou suffer thine Holy One to see corruption."	Mk. 16:67; Acts 2:27
22: 8	"He trusted on the Lord . . . let him deliver him."	Matt. 21:43; Luke 12:35
22:16	"They pierced my hands and feet."	John 20:25
22:18	"They part my garments among them, and cast lots upon my vesture."	Matt. 19:24
34:20	"He keepeth all his bones: not one of them is broken."	John 19:32,33
35:11	"False witnesses did rise up; they laid to my charge things that I knew not."	Mark 14:57-58
40: 7	". . . Lo, I come . . . to do thy will, O my God."	Heb. 10:7
41: 9	"Yea, mine own familiar friend, in whom I trusted, which did eat of my bread, hath lifted up his heel against me."	Luke 22:47-48
45: 6	"Thy throne, O God, is for ever and ever."	Heb. 1:8
49:15	"But God will redeem my soul from the power of the grave: for he shall receive me."	Mark 16:7
68:18	"Thou hast ascended on high, thou hast led captivity captive: thou hast received gifts for men; yea, for the rebellious also, that the Lord God might dwell among them."	Eph. 4:8
69: 9	"For the zeal of thine house hath eaten me up . . ."	John 2:17
69:21	"They gave me also gall for my meat; and in my thirst they gave me vinegar to drink."	Matt. 27:34,48
109: 4	"For my love they are adversaries; but I give myself unto prayer."	Luke 23:34
110: 4	"The Lord hath sworn, and will not repent, Thou art a priest for ever after the order of Melchizedek."	Heb. 5:5; 7:17

INTRODUCTION TO ISAIAH

Isaiah lived in the kingdom of Judah during the reign of Uzziah (6:1 about 740 B.C.) His ministry continued through the reigns of Jotham, Ahaz, Hezekiah, and possibly Manasseh, covering between 50 and 60 years.

It was an age of luxury, and only a few in Judah remained faithful to the old distinctive worship which had made the kingdom great. The sister kingdom of Israel, under Jereboam II, was also rich and prosperous; but it was socially, politically, and morally corrupt.

Samaria, the capital of Israel, was attacked by the Assyrians in 722 B.C., and the people were conquered and deported by the Assyrians, thus fulfilling Isaiah's prophecy.

Israel had "left all the commandments of the Lord their God, and made them molten images, even two calves . . ." Because of this, the Lord destroyed them, and ". . . there was none left but the tribe of Judah only" (II Kings 17:16,18).

In the beginning of Isaiah's ministry, Assyria dominated the world. During this time Jerusalem was a strong fortress on the trade route through which Assyria and Egypt had to pass.

Isaiah not only prophesied the fall of the Northern Kingdom of Assyria, but he also told of a greater enemy, Babylon, that was to come.

Prophecies from the book of Isaiah are quoted more times in the New Testament than any other book except Psalms.

The prophetic details that Isaiah wrote concerning an ideal King who would reign over both Jews and Gentiles in peace and love were so accurate that one might think they were written by one who lived during the time of Christ rather than 700 years earlier.

The last date recorded by Isaiah is the death of the Assyrian monarch, Sennacherib, who invaded Judah; but because of the prayers of Isaiah, the angel of God destroyed 185,000 Assyrian soldiers and Sennacherib had to return home, where he was assassinated by two of his sons (Isaiah 37:36-38; compare II Kings 19:35-37).

An oil lamp similar to those in Bible times. God's Word is compared to a lamp and is "a light unto our path." Psalm 119:105

AUGUST 1: Read Isaiah 1-4.

Isaiah 2:5: "O house of Jacob, come ye, and let us walk in the light of the Lord."

Seeing their blinded condition, Isaiah said of the nation, ". . . My people are gone into captivity, because they have no knowledge [no revelation of God's Word]" (5:13; compare Hosea 4:6).

The prophet revealed to the Israelites how clearly God had made known His will through His Word, pleading with them as he said, ". . . come ye, and let us walk in the light of the Lord."

Without light man cannot see where to walk and will eventually stumble in the darkness; and without the light of God's Word, it is impossible to live according to God's will.

Only God can say, "Let there be light" (Genesis 1:3), and only as God speaks His Word to your understanding *is* there light. It is not something that man decides, but it is discernment that only the Holy Spirit gives to those who live in dependence upon God. Apart from His speaking, we walk in darkness. But when we walk in the light of His Word, God carefully protects us from the snares Satan has placed in our path.

So as we read our Bible today it is vital that we pray for God to enlighten our hearts so that we may apply His truth.

"For ye were sometimes darkness, but now are ye light in the Lord: walk as children of light" (Ephesians 5:8).

NOTE:
1:25 **purely** means thoroughly; 1:31 **tow** means like chaff; **the maker of it** means his works; 2:9 **mean** means common; 2:11 **lofty** means proud; 2:15 **fenced** means fortified; 3:3 **artificer** means craftsman; 3:16 **mincing** means tripping; 3:18 **bravery** means beauty; **cauls** means netting for the hair; 3:20 **tablets** means perfume boxes; 3:22 **wimples** means a woman's veil headpiece; **crisping pins** means handbags; 3:23 **glasses** means mirrors; 3:24 **rent** means rope; **stomacher** means robe; 4:6 **covert** means shelter.

Isaiah 1:9: See Rom. 9:29.

AUGUST 2: Read Isaiah 5-9.

Isaiah 7:11-12: "*Ask* thee a sign of the Lord thy God; *ask* it either in the depth, or in the height above. But Ahaz said, I will not ask, neither will I tempt the Lord."

MEMORY VERSE FOR THE WEEK: Isaiah 55:6

"Seek ye the Lord while he may be found, call ye upon him while he is near:"

196

The kingdoms of Israel and Syria joined forces and declared war against the kingdom of Judah. This was done in revenge when Ahaz, king of Judah, refused to join them in a war against Assyria.

It was during this time that God sent Isaiah to tell King Ahaz that his kingdom would *not* be defeated by these two nations. To assure him of victory, God told Ahaz, "Ask for a sign." But Ahaz refused to accept any sign of assurance concerning the outcome of the war. He did not have faith in God's Word and proceeded with his own scheme to seek help from the king of Assyria.

Even though the king was unfaithful to God, in this hour of national crisis God gave them further insight concerning the supernatural nature of the coming Messiah, saying, ". . . his name shall be called Wonderful, Counselor, The mighty God, The everlasting Father, The Prince of Peace" (Isaiah 9:6; compare 10:21).

When we accept Christ and begin to read and believe God's Word, we soon realize that former fears no longer exist. This is to be expected since "Faith cometh by hearing, and hearing by the word of God" (Romans 10:17).

NOTE:
6:1 **his train** means his robe; 7:6 **vex** means attack; **make a breach** means force an entrance; 7:14 **Immanuel** means God with us; 7:16 **abhorrest** means hate; 7:25 **lesser cattle** means sheep; 8:3 **went unto** means married; 8:19 **peep** means whisper; 8:21 **hardly bestead** means sorely distressed; 9:8 **lighted** means come to be known; 9:9 **stoutness** means arrogance.

Isaiah 5:1, 2: See Mat. 21:33; Mk. 12:1; Lk. 20:9. **6:2, 3:** See Rev. 4:8. **6:9-10:** See Mat. 13:14-15; Mk. 4:12; Lk. 8:10; John 12:39-41; Acts 28:26-27; Rom. 11:18. **7:14:** See Mat. 1:23; Gal. 4:4. **8:14-15:** See Lk. 2:34; Rom. 9:33; I Pet. 2:8. **8:18:** See Heb. 2:13. **9:1-2:** See Mat. 4:15-16. **9:2:** See Lk. 1:79.

". . . There shall be a root of Jesse, and he that shall rise to reign over the Gentiles; in him shall the Gentiles trust."
Romans 15:12

AUGUST 3: Read Isaiah 10-14.

Isaiah 11:1-2: "And there shall come forth a rod out of the stem of Jesse, and a Branch shall grow out of his roots: And the spirit of the Lord shall rest upon him, the spirit of wisdom and under-standing, the spirit of counsel and might, the spirit of knowledge and of the fear of the Lord."

God miraculously preserved the lineage of the Messiah through the covenant with King David— "a Branch shall grow out of his roots." This was later confirmed "as a root out of a dry ground" (Isaiah 53:2). But He was more than a descendant of David, for "the spirit of the Lord shall rest upon

MEMORY VERSE FOR THE WEEK: Isaiah 55:6

"Seek ye the Lord while he may be found, call ye upon him while he is near:"

him." This prophecy reveals that Christ did not derive His wisdom from His own intellect, but He had an inward "spirit of counsel and might."

This source of Life is likened unto a "root." A tree cannot live and grow without roots.

To live thus "out of a dry ground" shows us that nothing merely circumstantial—no drought—can destroy this Life.

So amid barren and hostile conditions of our times, God provides His children with His "wisdom . . . and might" to become more than conquerors—yes, even with the same source of eternal life that was in Christ, for "your life is hid with Christ in God" (Colossians 3:3). Let us make this day a day when Christ will be seen in our lives.

"Rooted and built up in him, and stablished in the faith, as ye have been taught, abounding therein with thanksgiving" (Colossians 2:17).

NOTE:
10:4 **under** means among; 10:20 **stay** means rely; 10:22 **consumption** means destruction; 10:33 **lop** means cut off; 11:5 **reins** means waist; 11:8 **cockatrice'** means vipers'; 11:10 **an ensign** means a standard; 13:4 **mustereth** means calls together; 14:8 **feller** means tree cutter; 14:11 **viols** means musical instruments; 14:23 **bittern** means hedgehog; **besom** means broom.

Isaiah 10:22-23: See Rom. 9:27-28. **11:1, 10:** See Mat. 2:23; Rom. 15:12. **12:3:** See John 7:38. **13:10:** See Mat. 24:29; Mk. 13:24-25; Lk. 21:26. **14:13, 15:** See Mat. 11:23; Lk. 10:15.

AUGUST 4: Read Isaiah 15-21.
Isaiah 19:12-14: ". . . Where are thy wise men? . . . The princes of Zoan are become fools, the princes of Noph [Memphis, Capital of Egypt] are deceived . . . The Lord hath mingled a perverse spirit in the midst thereof and they have caused Egypt to err . . ."

Isaiah's revelation concerning the counselors of Egypt was given to Hezekiah and his advisors to prevent them from going to Egypt for help against the Assyrians. Isaiah foretold that all the ancient glory of the Pharaohs would soon vanish. It seemed impossible that the prophecy against the great and powerful nation could ever be fulfilled, but it was fulfilled in every detail.

These things were given as examples, that we should place our confidence in God rather than the power, prestige, or preeminence of men. (See I Corinthians 10:6.)

There is no reason for any of us to become ensnared with the wisdom of the world and lose our sense of spiritual values. Most of the Bible deals with human problems—every conceivable problem that anyone will ever face. Furthermore, the answers from God's point of view are unmistakably clear and always applicable to every generation.

MEMORY VERSE FOR THE WEEK: Isaiah 55:6

"Seek ye the Lord while he may be found, call ye upon him while he is near:"

Our Bible contains many examples of those who refused to be guided by His will, and the results were always disastrous. It is of little importance that we excel in the wisdom of the world, but it is of utmost importance that we study His Word. For His life-giving Book illuminates our understanding to the answers of life's complicated problems that we face from day to day.

". . . they have rejected the word of the Lord; and what wisdom is in them?" (Jeremiah 8:9).

NOTE:
16:3 **bewray** means betray; 16:5 **hasting** means prompt in; 16:14 **contemned** means despised; 17:11 **a heap** means a ruin; 18:7 **scattered and peeled** means widespread and obstinate; 19:8 **angle** means line and hook; 21:7 **chariot** means wagon; 21:8 **ward** means guard post.

Isaiah 19:2: See Mat. 24:7; Mk. 13:8; Lk. 21:10.

"there be gods many, and lords many, but to us there is but one God . . ." I Corinthians 8:5, 6

AUGUST 5: Read Isaiah 22-26.

Isaiah 26:13: "O Lord our God, other lords besides thee have had dominion over us: but by thee only will we make mention of thy name."

With every defeat of God's people—first by the Assyrians, then by Egypt, and finally by Babylon—Isaiah confessed how these nations "had dominion" over the Israelites. Each of them attempted to force the Hebrews to accept pagan worship.

Because of their faith and loyalty to God, Daniel, Shadrach, Meshach, and Abednego would not participate in pagan worship. Therefore, Daniel was thrown into a den of lions, and the other three Hebrew children were cast into a fiery furnace. But God miraculously delivered all four of them. (Read Daniel 1-3.)

These could say with Isaiah, "other lords besides thee have had dominion over us: but by thee only will we make mention of thy name."

God's people in every generation have faced similar enemies of God who seek to force them to accept pagan ways.

Evil influences are constantly seeking to corrupt those who are loyal to Christ. Christ is to be the Lord of our life. Other lords cannot have dominion over us. "For sin shall not have dominion over you . . ." (Romans 6:14).

"Neither yield ye your members as instruments of unrighteousness unto sin: but yield yourselves unto God, as those that are alive from the dead, and your members as instruments of righteousness unto God" (Romans 6:13).

MEMORY VERSE FOR THE WEEK: Isaiah 55:6

"Seek ye the Lord while he may be found, call ye upon him while he is near:"

AUGUST 6: Read Isaiah 27-31.

Isaiah 29:13: "Wherefore the Lord said, . . . this people draw near me with their mouth, and with their lips do honour me, but have removed their heart far from me, and their fear toward me is taught by the precept of men."

The prophet Isaiah exposed the fact that the backslidden Israelite nation was accepting the right doctrine, saying the right prayers, and offering the right sacrifices, but their hearts were far from God. Their worship was hypocritical and insincere. The Word of God was taught but not practiced. Therefore, God said that the wisdom of their wise men would perish.

Our Lord quoted this passage to the scribes and Pharisees who were in Jerusalem, saying, "Thus have ye made the commandment of God of none effect by your tradition. Ye hypocrites, well did Esaias [Isaiah] prophesy of you, saying, This people draweth nigh unto me with their mouth, and honoureth me with their lips; but their heart is far from me. But in vain they do worship me, teaching for doctrines the commandments of men" (Matthew 15:6-9).

When there is a lack of loyalty and obedience from the heart, man seeks to fill this emptiness with outward works in order to satisfy his conscience. Not only did an overwhelming majority of people worship God in the days of Isaiah with their lips rather than with their heart, but many today have "a form of godliness, but [are] denying the power thereof . . ." (II Timothy 3:5).

"Be ye doers of the word, and not hearers only, deceiving your own selves" (James 1:22).

MEMORY VERSE FOR THE WEEK: Isaiah 55:6

"Seek ye the Lord while he may be found, call ye upon him while he is near:"

AUGUST 7: Read Isaiah 32-37.

Isaiah 36:1, 15: "Now it came to pass in the fourteenth year of king Hezekiah, that Sennacherib king of Assyria came up against all the defenced cities of Judah, and took them . . . Thus saith the king, . . . Neither let Hezekiah make you trust in the Lord, saying, the Lord will surely deliver us: this city shall not be delivered into the hand of the king of Assyria."

Just eight years after he invaded and destroyed the Northern Kingdom, Sennacherib, king of Assyria, attacked Judah. (Compare II Kings 18:13-17 and II Chronicles 32:1-8.) It was during this time that King Hezekiah trusted in God and told his nation, ". . . with us is the Lord our God . . ." (II Chronicles 32:8).

Hezekiah, in desperation, sought to lead his people to trust in God alone as their only hope of survival against Assyria. When he read the letter which the Assyrian ambassador had brought from Sennacherib, Hezekiah took the letter to the Temple and spread it before the Lord. Then he sent an urgent message to Isaiah, asking the prophet to pray for the nation. (See II Kings 19:15-19; II Chronicles 32:20.)

The prayer was short and simple, but sincere. The faithful Christian is one who prays even in the best of times. Therefore, he instinctively turns to prayer when anything goes wrong because he is accustomed to turning to God when all things go right. If we truly live in fellowship with God, we will look to Him for all our needs.

". . . in every thing by prayer and supplication with thanksgiving let your requests be made known unto God" (Philippians 4:6).

NOTE:
32:2 **tempest** means storm; 32:5 **churl** means crafty; 33:23 **tacklings** means hoisting ropes; 34:11 **cormorant** means pelican.

Isaiah 34:4: See Heb. 1:10-12. **35:3:** See Heb. 12:12.

AUGUST 8: Read Isaiah 38-42.

Isaiah 42:1: "Behold my servant, whom I uphold; mine elect, in whom my soul delighteth; I have put my spirit upon him: he shall bring forth judgment to the Gentiles."

MEMORY VERSE OF THE WEEK: Isaiah 55:7
"Let the wicked forsake his way, and the unrighteous man his thoughts: and let him return unto the Lord, and he will have mercy upon him; and to our God, for he will abundantly pardon."

201

These prophetic words concerning Christ are quoted by our Lord, "That it might be fulfilled which was spoken by Esaias [Isaiah] the prophet, saying, Behold my servant, whom I have chosen" (Matthew 12:17, 18).

Even though the words "my servant" in this verse specifically apply to the Messiah, they equally apply to all who are born into the family of God.

I can't think of a higher calling than to be a "servant of the Lord." Many have said, "Well, I'm waiting for the Lord to call me to do some special work." But even the Son of God was called only a "servant."

Since the ascension of Christ, the Holy Spirit has continued His ministry of guiding men and women into a selfless ministry on behalf of a lost and dying world. The Holy Spirit empowers us to be faithful *servants* of the Lord.

Does your life daily reflect the guidance of the Holy Spirit as His servant?

"And whosoever of you will be the chiefest, shall be servant of all. For even the Son of man came not to be ministered unto, but to minister, and to give his life a ransom for many" (Mark 10:44-45).

NOTE:
38:13 **reckoned** means composed my soul; 40:2 **comfortably** means kindly; 40:12 **span** means 9 inches.

Isaiah 40:3-5: See Mat. 3:3; Mk. 1:2-3; Lk. 3:4-6; John 1:23. **40:6-8:** See I Pet. 1:24-25. **40:8:** See Mk. 13:31. **40:13:** See Rom. 11:34; I Cor. 2:16. **41:8-9:** See Lk. 1:54-55; Jas. 2:23. **42:1-4:** See Mat. 12:18-21. **42:6-7:** See Mat. 4:15-16; Lk. 2:32.

". . . Jerusalem, Thou shalt be built; and to the temple, Thy foundation shall be laid."
Isaiah 44:28

AUGUST 9: Read Isaiah 43-46.

Isaiah 44:24, 26-28: "Thus saith the Lord, . . . I will raise up the decayed places thereof: that saith to the deep, Be dry, and I will dry up thy rivers: That saith of Cyrus, He is my shepherd, and shall perform all my pleasure: even saying to Jerusalem, Thou shalt be built; and to the temple, Thy foundation shall be laid."

Only the Spirit of God could have given Isaiah such amazing details about a man named Cyrus 130 years before he was born.

No prophecy seemed more unlikely to be fulfilled. The Temple was still standing; the walls were in perfect condition; and the nation was still enjoying freedom when Isaiah foretold, "I [the Lord] will raise up the decayed places." This undoubtedly sounded ridiculous because there were no decayed places to be raised up at that time. Furthermore, it would have seemed unreasonable to believe that a world conqueror would release the Jews and then

---

MEMORY VERSE FOR THE WEEK: Isaiah 55:7

"Let the wicked forsake his way, and the unrighteous man his thoughts: and let him return unto the Lord, and he will have mercy upon him; and to our God, for he will abundantly pardon."

urge them to return to Jerusalem to rebuild the Temple for "the God of heaven." Yet, all these things happened exactly as Isaiah foretold.

Not one detail of any prophecy made by God's prophets has ever failed to be fulfilled. You can depend upon God's promises, for they cannot fail.

"O the depth of the riches both of the wisdom and knowledge of God! how unsearchable are his judgments, and his ways past finding out!" (Romans 11:33).

NOTE:
44:9 **delectable** means desirable; 46:4 **hoar hairs** means gray hairs.

Isaiah 44:3: See John 7:39. **45:9:** See Rom. 9:20. **45:21:** See Acts 15:18. **45:23:** See Rom. 14:11; Phil. 2:10.

AUGUST 10: Read Isaiah 47-51.

Isaiah 49:6: ". . . I will also give thee for a light to the Gentiles, that thou mayest be my salvation unto the end of the earth."

We see this prophecy carried out in the New Testament in Luke 2:25-32. At the exact moment when Mary and Joseph were approaching the Temple with the Baby Jesus, Simeon ". . . came by the Spirit into the temple." It had been revealed to Simeon that he would not die before he had seen the consolation of Israel.

How easily he could have missed the greatest moment of his life if he had been out of touch with the Divine Spirit of God! God so arranged the circumstances of Joseph and Mary that they would approach the Temple at the exact moment Simeon arrived that particular day, waiting for the "light to lighten the Gentiles" (Luke 2:32).

When he met the peasant parents, there were no outward circumstances to attract his attention—only two humble peasants presenting their Child to God and offering the sacrifice of the poor.

Equally unpretentious was Simeon, who greeted them. He was not the high priest; he was not even a priest. He was only a devout Jew. His only distinction was that he was waiting for the "consolation of Israel." And, holding the Baby Jesus, he announced the fulfillment of the prophecy which was written 700 years before our Savior's birth, saying, "For mine eyes have seen thy salvation, which thou has prepared before the face of all people; a light to lighten the Gentiles, and the glory of thy people Israel" (Luke 2:30-32).

NOTE:
48:4 **sinew** means muscle.

Isaiah 49:6: See Acts 13:47. **49:8:** See 2 Cor. 6:2. **50:6:** See Mat. 26:67. **51:6:** See Mat. 24:35.

MEMORY VERSE FOR THE WEEK: Isaiah 55:7

"Let the wicked forsake his way, and the unrighteous man his thoughts: and let him return unto the Lord, and he will have mercy upon him; and to our God, for he will abundantly pardon."

". . . ye are my witnesses, saith
the Lord, that I am God."
Isaiah 43:12

AUGUST 11: Read Isaiah 52-57.

Isaiah 53:1, 5: "Who hath believed our *report?*
and to whom is the arm of the Lord revealed? . . .
he was wounded for our transgressions, he was
bruised for our inquities: the chastisement of our
peace was upon him; and with his stripes we are
healed."

Thank God for His Word. It is His *report* to
us. Isaiah said, "Who hath believed our *report?*"
After all, the report was given about 700 years
before the birth of Christ. The beating and scourging, the suffering that the
Messiah was to endure to redeem sinful man was foretold by Isaiah.

As we read the four Gospels, we realize that these *reports* of Isaiah were
all fulfilled—from the naming of the place of His birth to the details of His
sacrificial death.

Christ miraculously fed the multitudes, healed the sick, and raised the dead,
but not one soul would ever have been saved had not Christ suffered and
died on the cross. It was made possible at that moment, by some unknown
mystery of His love and mercy, that all sins could be forgiven. Isaiah was
included when he said Christ "was wounded for our transgressions." The
salvation of those before Christ's death was dependent upon the forthcoming
crucifixion and resurrection.

Let us earnestly endeavor to *report* faithfully His message of salvation to
a lost and dying world. As this *report* came to us, it is our responsibility to
take it to all the world. The day will come when He will call us to make a
report to Him.

"For we must all appear before the judgment seat of Christ; that every one
may receive the things done in his body, according to that he hath done,
whether it be good or bad" (II Corinthians 5:10).

NOTE:
52:10 **made bare his holy arm** means revealed his power; 52:15 **sprinkle** means
startle; 57:3 **companies** means collection of idols.

Isaiah 52:5: See Rom. 2:24. 52:7: See Rom. 10:15. 52:10-11: See Lk. 2:30-31;
2 Cor. 6:17. 52:15: See Rom. 15:21. 53:1: See John 12:38; Rom. 10:16. 53:4: See
Mat. 8:17; I Pet. 2:24. 53:5: See Lk. 24:46. 53:7-9: See Mat. 26:54-56; Acts 8:28,
30, 32, 33. 53:9: See Mat. 27:60; I Pet. 2:22. 53:11: See Acts 10:43. 53:12: See Mk.
15:28; Lk. 22:37. 54:1: See Lk. 23:29; Gal. 4:27. 54:13: See John 6:45. 55:1: See
John 7:37. 55:3: See Acts 13:34. 56:7: See Mat. 21:13; Mk. 11:17; Lk. 19:46.

MEMORY VERSE FOR THE WEEK: Isaiah 55:7

"Let the wicked forsake his way, and the unrighteous man his thoughts:
and let him return unto the Lord, and he will have mercy upon him; and to
our God, for he will abundantly pardon."

AUGUST 12: Read Isaiah 58-63.

Isaiah 63:10: "But they rebelled, and vexed his holy spirit: therefore he was turned to be their enemy, and he fought against them."

When recalling Israel's failure, Isaiah reminded the nation that each time they complained, they were rebelling against God, which in turn, "vexed his holy spirit."

The children of Israel complained against God and Moses ten specific times "and have not hearkened to my voice" (Numbers 14:22). Unbelief resulted in 38 wasted years of wandering in the wilderness.

But with all of God's provisions to the children of Israel in the desert, the kingdom of Judah failed to relate God's miraculous provisions in the past to their present needs. The great kingdom was as guilty of unbelief as were the children of Israel in the desert, for "they rebelled, and vexed his holy spirit."

Having personal plans interrupted cause many to complain, believing they deserve better things. Complaining about our circumstances does "vex his holy spirit," and we forfeit His blessings.

Far too many fail to see the seriousness of discontent. It is actually questioning the wisdom and ability of the loving Father to guide His children. Let us graciously submit to His arrangements and under no circumstances grieve the Holy Spirit.

"And grieve not the holy Spirit of God . . ." (Ephesians 4:30).

NOTE:
58:11 **fat** means make strong; 60:6 **dromedaries** means young camels; 60:17 **exactors** means oppressors; 62:4 **Beulah** means Married; 63:15 **the sounding of thy bowels** means the stirring of thy heart.

Isaiah 58:11: See John 7:38. **59:7-8:** See Rom. 3:15-17. **59:17:** See Eph. 6:17. **59:20-21:** See Rom. 11:26-27. **60:1:** See Eph. 5:14. **61:1-2:** See Lk. 4:18-19; Heb. 1:8-9. **62:11:** See Mat. 21:5.

"O that thou hadst hearkened to my commandments! then had thy peace been as a river . . ."
Isaiah 48:18

AUGUST 13: Read Isaiah 64-66.

Isaiah 66:12: "For thus saith the Lord, Behold, I will extend peace to her like a river, and the glory of the Gentiles like a flowing stream . . ."

There is a peace of God that "passeth all understanding"—as never ending as a great and mighty river. Futhermore, "God is no respector of persons" (Acts 10:34), and His peace is the rightful inheritance of every Christian.

There is no promise of freedom from sorrows in this verse, nor is it a promise of success and prosperity. But it is a promise of inward contentment which outward circumstances cannot alter.

MEMORY VERSE FOR THE WEEK: Isaiah 55:7

"Let the wicked forsake his way, and the unrighteous man his thoughts: and let him return unto the Lord, and he will have mercy upon him; and to our God, for he will abundantly pardon."

Believers in every generation have been able to say that His indwelling presence has lifted them above all adverse circumstancs. His peace is an actual reality—the outcome of becoming familiar with His Word and His arrangement of the events in our lives.

It is ignorance of God's wisdom and His ways that causes a Christian to fear the unknown future. Peace does not exist because external affairs are satisfactory, nor is His peace the result of "positive thinking," but it is the power of His presence. To enjoy His unending peace "like a flowing stream," we should become thoroughly acquainted with Him. "These things I have spoken unto you, that in me ye might have peace. In the world ye shall have tribulation: but be of good cheer; I have overcome the world" (John 16:33).

NOTE:
Isaiah **64:4:** See I Cor. 2:9. **65:1-2:** See Rom. 10:20-21. **65:16:** See 2 Cor. 10:17. **65:17:** See 2 Pet. 3:13. **66:14:** See John 16:22. **66:24:** See Mk. 9:44.

INTRODUCTION TO JEREMIAH

Jeremiah prophesied during the last 40 years of the kingdom of Judah's history. The time interval between Isaiah and Jeremiah was about 70 years.

Assyria had already destroyed the ten-tribed nation of Israel. But since that time, Assyria had been weakened considerably by a battle with Nebuchadnezzar. Babylon was continuing to emerge as the world ruler.

Jeremiah pleaded in vain for the nation of Judah to repent and serve the Lord. He then made a strong plea for them to submit to Babylon or else be defeated. Because of this message, most of the people in Jerusalem assumed that Jeremiah was unpatriotic.

About this time the Babylonian king, Nebuchadnezzar, and his army attacked Judah. They defeated Jerusalem and carried about 10,000 captives to Babylon, including all the craftsmen and talented Israelites. (See II Kings 24:14.)

After eleven years, Zedekiah—the last king to sit on the throne of David—revolted against Babylon's control, and Nebuchadnezzar once again attacked the strong, fortified city of Jerusalem. After 18 months, King Zedekiah lost all hope and attempted to escape. He was captured, his eyes put out, and he was taken to Babylon as one of the exiles in the second major deportation.

A few remaining people in Judah fled to Egypt, taking Jeremiah with them as a captive. The last record we have of the old prophet Jeremiah, he was preaching against the Jewish women worshipping "the queen of heaven" (see Jeremiah 44:15-30).

Jeremiah foresaw all these events and looked even beyond them; he predicted that even great Babylon, after 70 years, would fall and a new power would take its place.

On occasions, the sequence of events is difficult to follow because the book of Jeremiah is not written in chronological order. Its chief purpose is not a chronology of historic events, but an arrangement in the order that served the purposes of God.

AUGUST 14: Read Jeremiah 1-3.

Jeremiah 2:11-13: ". . . my people have changed their glory for that which doth not profit. Be astonished, O ye heavens, at this . . . For my people have committed two evils; they have forsaken me the fountain of living waters, and hewed them out cisterns, broken cisterns, that can hold no water."

Israel, the only people in the world having a revelation of God and His will, was the very nation that exchanged their God "for that which doth not profit" (2:11). What an astounding example of ingratitude and mockery! Their sin was rejecting the real for the unreal.

In the desert climate of Palestine, water was the first necessity of human existence. Men fought and died over wells. No man in his right mind would leave an artesian well where there was a great supply of water to dig his own well and just hope for some miraculous spring of water. We would consider such a man foolish indeed.

"Be astonished," saith the Lord. Here is an amazing fact—God was theirs; yet, they deserted Him.

This is also a picture of many who reject the Bible as the *fountain of living waters*. Many have turned to the easy-to-read substitutes written by men, but they are little more than "cisterns that can hold no water" compared to the Word of God. Many writings of men may be helpful in life, but they should not be used as a substitute for Bible study.

"But whosoever drinketh of the water that I shall give him shall never thirst; but the water that I shall give him shall be in him a well of water springing up into everlasting life" (John 4:14).

NOTE:
2:31 **lords** means independent; 3:10 **feignedly** means falsely; 3:16 **visit** means miss it.

"Whoso looketh into the perfect law of liberty, and continueth therein . . . this man shall be blessed"
James 1:25

AUGUST 15: Read Jeremiah 4-6.

Jeremiah 5:31; 6:10: "The prophets prophesy falsely, and the priests bear rule by their means; and my people love to have it so: . . . behold, the *word* of the Lord is unto them a *reproach; they have no delight in it.*"

It was deplorable and unthinkable that the kingdom of Judah had *"no delight"* in the "word of the Lord."

If those who call themselves Christians live day after day without reading the Word of God—year after year without ever reading the Bible through—it is quite apparent that they also "have no delight in it."

MEMORY VERSE FOR THE WEEK: Isaiah 55:8-9

"For my thoughts are not your thoughts, neither are your ways my ways, saith the Lord. For as the heavens are higher than the earth, so are my ways higher than your ways, and my thoughts than your thoughts."

Turning away from God's message is a trend toward apostasy, but reading and upholding every word of God as pure and true (Proverbs 30:5) is a mark of sonship. A true Christian delights in His words and believes the Scriptures, ". . . more to be desired are they than gold" (Psalm 19:10).

The trend in our secular society is away from the "word of the Lord." The Thessalonica Christians thought the day of the Lord shall not come except the falling away (literally, "the apostasy") come first, and the man of sin be revealed.

Many who call themselves Christians will forsake the Lord, as did Demas (II Timothy 4:10), and will manifest evidence of apostasy, as foretold in the book of Jude.

"For there are certain men crept in unawares, who were before of old ordained to this condemnation, ungodly men, turning the grace of our God into lasciviousness, and denying the only Lord God, and our Lord Jesus Christ" (Jude 4).

NOTE:
4:22 **sottish** means stupid; 6:22 **sides** means remote areas.

AUGUST 16: Read Jeremiah 7-10.

Jeremiah 10:23: "O Lord, I know that the way of man is not in himself: it is not in man that walketh to direct his steps."

The more we read the Bible, the more we realize that God's ways are not our ways. "For as the heavens are higher than the earth, so are my ways higher than your ways, and my thoughts than your thoughts" (Isaiah 55:9).

The more time we spend with a person, the more we become familiar with his way of thinking and doing things. So it is with our relationship with God. It is only as we become familiar with God's Word that we can more clearly discern His will for our daily life.

Jeremiah saw himself as a *child,* ". . . Ah, Lord God! behold, I cannot speak; for I am a child" (1:6). Most of us feel we are too *grown up;* we know too many answers. We are like the Biblical people of Jerusalem, resting in a false sense of security.

Even with all our technological advances in education, it is just as true today as it was when God spoke through Jeremiah, that "It is not in man that walketh to the direct his steps."

Unless we are guided by a *full knowledge* of God's Word, it may appear that we have an answer to prayer, when in reality, we were able to *physically* accomplish the task we "prayed about." We didn't actually know how to discern His will in the matter.

"But the natural man receiveth not the things of the Spirit of God: for they are foolishness unto him: neither can he know them, because they are spiritually discerned" (I Corinthinas 2:14).

NOTE:
7:33 **fray** means frighten; 8:14 **water of gall** means bitter water; 10:22 **noise of the bruit** means sound of a rumor.

Jeremiah 7:11: See Mat. 21:13; Mk. 11:17; Lk. 19:46. **9:23-24:** See I Cor. 1:31; 2 Cor. 10:17.

MEMORY VERSE FOR THE WEEK: Isaiah 55:8-9

"For my thoughts are not your thoughts, neither are your ways my ways, saith the Lord. For as the heavens are higher than the earth, so are my ways higher than your ways, and my thoughts than your thoughts."

AUGUST 17: Read Jeremiah 11-14.

Jeremiah 13:9-10: "Thus saith the Lord, After this manner will I *mar the pride* of Judah, and *the great pride of Jerusalem*. This evil people, which refuse to hear my words, . . . shall even be as this girdle, which is good for nothing."

The Hebrew men wore a loose tunic (dress-like garment) which went down near their ankles. The girdle was a sash-like belt that was an essential article of clothing to be worn when they were running or working.

The nation of Judah rejected the Word of God given by His prophet Jeremiah, and God exposed their sin as "the great pride of Jerusalem." The inevitable result was that God would "mar the great pride of Judah." God illustrated this by telling Jeremiah to bury a linen girdle near Babylon, about 250 miles from Jerusalem. (In the Scriptures, the girdle symbolizes being equipped and prepared for service, and linen stands for righteousness.)

After allowing the girdle to decay for a while, Jeremiah dug it up and wore it back to Jerusalem to illustrate that Judah's unrighteous condition made the nation unworthy to be God's servants. The kingdom of Judah would soon be "buried and forsaken," as was the girdle in Babylon—worthless captives for 70 years.

"The great pride" that destroyed Jerusalem was the original sin of Satan (I Timothy 3:6). It deceives the heart (Jeremiah 49:16), hardens the mind (Daniel 5:20), and is hated of God (Proverbs 16:5; also 6:16-17).

Pride describes the man who ignores the authority of God over him by attempting to control his own present life (I John 2:16) and to shape his own future (James 4:16).

"Humble yourselves in the sight of the Lord, and he shall lift you up" (James 4:10).

NOTE:
12:13 **revenues** means harvest; 13:1 **girdle** means waistband, belt; 13:9 **mar** means ruin.

Jeremiah 12:7: See Mat. 23:38; Lk. 13:35. **12:15:** See Acts 15:16-18.

MEMORY VERSE FOR THE WEEK: Isaiah 55:8-9

"For my thoughts are not your thoughts, neither are your ways my ways, saith the Lord. For as the heavens are higher than the earth, so are my ways higher than your ways, and my thoughts than your thoughts."

AUGUST 18: Read Jeremiah 15-18.

Jeremiah 18:3, 4, 6: "Then I went down to the potter's house, . . . and the vessel that he made of clay was marred in the hand of the potter: so he made it again another vessel, as seemed good to the potter to make it . . . O house of Israel, cannot I do with you as this potter? . . ."

The potter was not satisfied with the first vessel. The clay may not have been the right consistency to retain the shape that the potter had in mind, so he reshaped it.

This is the story of God's chosen people. God is the Potter, Israel is the clay, history is the wheel. As a nation, Israel resisted the will of God and was miserably marred by sin. Therefore, the "vessel"—Israel—was broken by Assyria and the kingdom of Judah was taken to Babylon as slaves.

After seventy years in exile, God made of the "same clay" yet another "vessel" as Ezra returned with a remnant of Jews and rebuilt the Temple.

God wants our will to be as submissive to His will as clay is in the potter's hands—"as seemed good to the potter to make it" (18:4). The Master has a plan for your life as a *vessel* to honor Him. "For it is God which worketh in you both to will and to do of his good pleasure" (Philippians 2:13).

Every Christian is an earthen vessel—the container for "His good pleasure," and "we look for the Saviour, the Lord Jesus Christ: who shall change our vile body, that it may be fashioned like unto his glorious body, according to the working whereby he is able even to subdue all things unto himself" (Philippians 3:20-21).

NOTE:
16:7 **tear themselves** means prepare food; 17:10 **try the reins** means test the mind. **Jeremiah 18:6:** See Rom. 9:21.

AUGUST 19: Read Jeremiah 19-22.

Jeremiah 21:7, 8: ". . . I will deliver Zedekiah king of Judah . . . into the hand of Nebuchadrezzar . . . thus saith the Lord; Behold, I set before you the way of life, and the way of death."

About eighteen months before the final fall of the kingdom of Judah, Jerusalem was attacked by the Babylonians. But Judah became optimistic when the Egyptian armies intercepted the Babylonians. About that time, King Zedekiah sent messengers to Jeremiah, asking him to pray. Instead, Jeremiah

MEMORY VERSE FOR THE WEEK: Isaiah 55:8-9

"For my thoughts are not your thoughts, neither are your ways my ways, saith the Lord. For as the heavens are higher than the earth, so are my ways higher than your ways, and my thoughts than your thoughts."

prophesied that the Egyptian help would be temporary and that Nebucha-drezzar would soon return and destroy the city. Jeremiah then urged them to choose "the way of life" and surrender to the Chaldeans (Babylon). Because of this unfavorable advice, Jeremiah was misunderstood as a traitor and was cruelly beaten and put in prison.

The kingdom of Judah had rejected "the way of life"; consequently, they chose "the way of death" by famine and war in the final attack on Jerusalem.

There are but two ways to travel through life. There is no neutral position. Either you are in the way of life, having received Christ as Lord of your life, or you are choosing the way of death—eternal hell. And to one of these two eternal destinies you are advancing every day.

"Blessed are they that do his commandments, that they may have right to the tree of life, and may enter in through the gates into the city. For without are dogs, and sorcerers, and whoremongers, and murderers, and idolaters, and whosoever loveth and maketh a lie" (Revelation 22:14-15).

NOTE:
19:9 **straitness** means confinement; 20:10 **halting** means fall; 22:24 **signet** means ring.

Jeremiah 19:13: See Acts 7:42-43. **22:5:** See Mat. 23:38. **22:25:** See Lk. 13:35.

AUGUST 20: Read Jeremiah 23-25.

Jeremiah 23:1, 4: "Woe be unto the pastors that destroy and scatter the sheep of my pasture! saith the Lord. . . . I will set up shepherds over them which shall feed them. . . ."

The word *pastor* was first used when referring to David because he was called from taking care of his father's sheep and anointed to be the shepherd-king over God's people.

Why did God choose David rather than his brothers? Perhaps because David risked his life on two occasions to save his father's sheep—once when they were being attacked by a lion and another time by a bear. He knew that he was accountable to his father for the care of the sheep. But more than this, he loved his sheep.

We, too, have a place of service in God's plan for caring for His sheep. If we are truly concerned over the spiritual welfare of others, the Holy Spirit will guide us in our giving, praying, and our serving.

"Feed the flock of God which is among you . . ." (I Peter 5:2).

NOTE:
23:10 **swearing** means the curse.

MEMORY VERSE FOR THE WEEK: Isaiah 55:8-9

"For my thoughts are not your thoughts, neither are your ways my ways, saith the Lord. For as the heavens are higher than the earth, so are my ways higher than your ways, and my thoughts than your thoughts."

"When they heard these things, they were cut to the heart . . . And cast him (Stephen) out of the city, and stoned him . . . And he kneeled down, and cried with a loud voice, Lord, lay not this sin to their charge . . ."
Acts 7:54-60

AUGUST 21: Read Jeremiah 26-28.

Jeremiah 26:6: "Then will I make this house like *Shiloh,* and will make this city a curse to all the nations of the earth."

Shiloh was the capital city of Canaan where Joshua set up the tabernacle when they first entered the Promised Land. This city became distinguished because the tabernacle was located there for about 400 years (I Samuel 4:3). But because the Israelites did not remain faithful to God, He "forsook the tabernacle of Shiloh" (Psalm 78:60), and in Jeremiah's time, Shiloh was in ruins—only a small, insignificant city (Jeremiah 7:12, 14).

About twenty-two years before the first destruction of Jerusalem, God commanded Jeremiah to "speak unto all the cities of Judah which come to worship in the Lord's house." He warned that "this house"—the Temple—would be left as empty as Shiloh—leaving nothing more than a memory.

After Jeremiah faithfully delivered the message, the priests who were serving in the Temple arrested him, saying, "This man is worthy to die; for he has prophesied against this city, as ye have heard with your ears" (26:11). In fact, we are told that ". . . *all* the people were gathered against Jeremiah in the house of the Lord" (verse 9).

The popular crowd seldom has the leading of God. If we choose to walk in the path that our Lord has chosen, we will often find that we stand alone. The path to the cross is not crowded.

But we can be assured that "if we suffer, we shall also reign with him . . ." (II Timothy 2:12).

NOTE:
26:14 **meet** means right.

AUGUST 22: Read Jeremiah 29-31.

Jeremiah 29:7: "And seek the peace of the city whither I have caused you to be carried away captives, and pray unto the Lord for it: for in the peace thereof shall ye have peace."

God is true to His Word. Jeremiah prophesied the destruction of Jerusalem, the slavery of the people, and their return to Jerusalem after being in captivity for exactly seventy years.

These prophecies were all fulfilled as recorded in the book of Ezra, ". . . that the word of the Lord by the mouth of Jeremiah might be fulfilled . . ." (Ezra 1:1).

MEMORY VERSE FOR THE WEEK: Isaiah 55:10

"For as the rain cometh down, and the snow from heaven, and returneth not thither, but watereth the earth, and maketh it bring forth and bud, that it may give seed to the sower, and bread to the eater:"

In Babylon, the place of captivity and oppression, Jeremiah taught the people how to react to their situation—not by stirring up a useless revolt or sitting down in sullen despondency. He showed them a better way, "Seek the peace"—that is, be content and seek the best interest of the oppressors, "for in the peace thereof shall ye have peace."

This is a principle of conduct by which Christians are to live. Many people are dissatisfied with their present circumstances and are waiting until some time in the future to really enjoy living. Perhaps they are waiting until they get another promotion, recover from an illness, have a better home, or retire. But they are always waiting for release from their present situation—often with bitter resentment.

True enjoyment is only found in seeking His peace, His love, to be bestowed upon our oppressors in our "captive situation" wherever we may be.

"Rejoice in the Lord always: and again I say, Rejoice" (Philippians 4:4).

NOTE:
31:14 **satiate** means satisfy fully; 31:21 **high heaps** means guideposts.

Jeremiah 29:8: See Mk. 13:5. **31:15:** See Mat. 2:18. **31:31-34:** See John 6:45; Acts 10:43; Heb. 8:8-12; 10:16-17.

". . . I have loved thee with an everlasting love: therefore with loving-kindness have I drawn thee." Jeremiah 31:2

AUGUST 23: Read Jeremiah 32-33.

Jeremiah 32:17-19: "Ah Lord God! behold, . . . Thou showest loving-kindness unto thousands, and recompensest the iniquity . . . to give every one according to his ways, and according to the fruit of his doings."

Jeremiah could say almost the exact words that David uttered when he wrote, "How excellent is thy loving-kindness, O God! Therefore the children of men put their trust under the shadow of thy wings" (Psalm 36:7).

In the midst of suffering and final defeat, the prophet Jeremiah proclaimed that God, in loving-kindness, was waiting to bless the nation of Judah if they would turn from their sins. But they would not heed his warning.

Whether we are accepted or rejected as we tell others about His Word, we should faithfully remind them of His loving-kindness that He bestows upon all who put their trust in Him.

Every adverse circumstance is an opportunity to manifest His loving-kindness—a privilege to bless those who offend us. In the words of the Psalmist we can say, "It is a good thing . . . to shew forth [talk about] thy loving-kindness . . ." (Psalm 92:1-2).

MEMORY VERSE FOR THE WEEK: Isaiah 55:10

"For as the rain cometh down, and the snow from heaven, and returneth not thither, but watereth the earth, and maketh it bring forth and bud, that it may give seed to the sower, and bread to the eater:"

213

When the Christian yields himself to the influence and guidance of the Holy Spirit, there will be no room in our hearts for jealousy, bitterness, or hatred.

"A new commandment I give unto you, That ye love one another; as I have loved you . . ." (John 13:34).

NOTE:

Jeremiah 32:17: See Mat. 19:26.

AUGUST 24: Read Jeremiah 34-36.

Jeremiah 36:22-23: "Now the king sat in the winter house in the ninth month: and there was a fire on the hearth burning before him. And it came to pass, that when Jehudi had read three or four leaves, he [the king] cut it with the penknife, and cast it into the fire that was on the hearth, until all the roll was consumed in the fire that was on the hearth."

The king of Egypt had defeated the kingdom of Judah and placed Eliakim, the second son of godly Josiah, on the throne, changing Eliakim's name to Jehoiakim and demanding that he pay heavy taxes to Egypt. After four years Nebuchadrezzar, king of Babylon, invaded Jerusalem. He took some captives, including Daniel and his three friends, and the golden vessels from the Temple to Babylon (Daniel 1:1-6). Jehoiakim was forced to surrender the kingdom to Babylonian control.

Jeremiah wrote on a scroll in protest to the ruthless and cruel reign of Jehoiakim and announced that the king of Babylon would come again and destroy the kingdom (see 36:29). When Jehudi (the king's official reader) read Jeremiah's prophecy, Jehoiakim's anger became uncontrollable. He stopped the reader, cut the scroll with his penknife, and cast it into the fire. He then issued a warrant for Jeremiah's arrest.

Unknown to himself, Jehoiakim sealed his death when he destroyed the Word of God. All who reject the Bible will one day be judged by the very Word they have rejected. Jesus said, "He that rejecteth me, and receiveth not my words, hath one that judgeth him: the word that I have spoken, the same shall judge him in the last day" (John 12:48).

"Then he put out the eyes of Zedekiah, . . . bound him in chains, and carried him to Babylon, and put him in prison till the day of his death."
Jeremiah 52:11

AUGUST 25: Read Jeremiah 37-40.

Jeremiah 39:2, 4, 5, 7: "And in the eleventh year of Zedekiah . . . the city was broken up . . . Zedekiah the king of Judah . . . fled, and went, forth out of the city by night, . . . But the Chaldeans' army pursued after them, and overtook Zedekiah in the plains of Jericho: . . . Moreover he put out Zedekiah's eyes, and bound him with chains, to carry him to Babylon."

The Hebrew nation almost 500 years old, but

MEMORY VERSE FOR THE WEEK: Isaiah 55:10

"For as the rain cometh down, and the snow from heaven, and returneth not thither, but watereth the earth, and maketh it bring forth and bud, that it may give seed to the sower, and bread to the eater:"

---

because the people ignored the prophets, their downfall was inevitable. The capture of Israel's last king, Zedekiah, took place in the same area where Joshua had won the first victory in gaining the Promised Land.

The eyes of King Zedekiah, the last son of Josiah, were put out, and he was taken in chains to Babylon, thus fulfilling the two prophecies that foretold the details of his horrifying experience.

Ezekiel had prophesied, ". . . I [the Lord] will bring him to Babylon . . . yet shall he *not see* it [he was blinded], though he shall die there" (Ezekiel 12:13). (See II Kings 25:7, Jeremiah 32:4, 39:7.) He was a compromiser who did not have faith to do what the prophet recommended.

This blinded and imprisoned king is an example of what spiritually happens to every person who yields to the opinions of men and fails to follow the will of God.

"In whom the God of this world hath blinded the minds of them which believe not . . ." (II Corinthians 4:4).

NOTE:
37:12 **separate himself thence** means receive his portion there; 37:16 **cabins** means cells.

AUGUST 26: Read Jeremiah 41-44.

Jeremiah 43:4-7: ". . . and all the people obeyed not the voice of the Lord, to dwell in the land of Judah . . . and all the captains of the forces . . . took Jeremiah the prophet . . . so they came into the land of Egypt. . . ."

Nebechadrezzar blinded King Zedekiah and appointed Gedaliah as governor over the remaining Jews, who were "the poor people left in the land." Gedaliah ruled as governor for only two months and was assassinated (41:1). The remaining Jewish people who were loyal to Egypt feared the revenge of Nebuchadrezzar; therefore, they took Jeremiah as a prisoner and escaped to Egypt. Jeremiah was forced into the very land where he had warned the people that if they were to go there for protection, it would mean their extinction (see 44:12).

Some would assume that surely this great prophet deserved better treatment for his loyalty than death in Egypt. But Jeremiah was living to please the Lord—not himself.

Our personal enjoyments in life will be sacrificed again and again if we remain faithful to His Word. There is a great need for more Jeremiahs today who will give up their own interests in order to live for Christ.

"Looking unto Jesus the author and finisher of our faith; who for the joy that was set before him endured the cross, despising the shame, and is set down at the right hand of the throne of God. For consider him that endured such contradiction of sinners against himself, lest ye be wearied and faint in your minds" (Hebrews 12:2-3).

NOTE:
41:14 **cast about** means deserted; 42:20 **dissembled** means were deceitful.

MEMORY VERSE FOR THE WEEK: Isaiah 55:10

"For as the rain cometh down, and the snow from heaven, and returneth not thither, but watereth the earth, and maketh it bring forth and bud, that it may give seed to the sower, and bread to the eater:"

AUGUST 27: Read Jeremiah 45-48.

Jeremiah 48:10: "Cursed be he that doeth the work of the Lord deceitfully, and cursed be he that keepeth back his sword from blood."

"Cursed be he that doeth the work of the Lord deceitfully" refers not only to the insincere hypocrite, but in this case, it also includes those Christians who are slothful, idle, and lukewarm. This curse rests upon much of Christendom today. It is upon those who serve the Lord only to the extent of satisfying their own interests. Those who do the work of the Lord deceitfully avoid becoming too involved in the Lord's work; and much of the time, their enthusiasm for the Lord's work is not equal to their interest in worldly affairs.

The curse is a condemnation against those who are indifferent to their opportunities and responsibilities. It reminds us of Judges 5:23, "Curse ye, Meroz, said the angel of the Lord, curse ye bitterly the inhabitants thereof; because they came not to the help of the Lord, to the help of the Lord against the mighty."

Christians who recognize their indebtedness to God's redeeming grace will see the eternal tragedy of wasting time or postponing opportunities to minister to a needy world. They will take seriously the Scripture that says, "Not slothful in business; [but] fervent in spirit; serving the Lord" (Romans 12:11).

NOTE:
46:4 **furbish** means polish; **brigandines** means armor; 48:6 **heath** means forsaken person; 48:19 **espy** means watch.

AUGUST 28: Read Jeremiah 49-50.

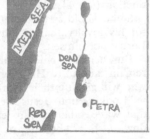

Jeremiah 49:16-17: "Thy terribleness hath deceived thee, and the pride of thine heart, O thou that dwellest in the clefts of the rock . . . I will bring thee down from thence, saith the Lord. Also Edom shall be a desolation: every one that goeth by it shall be astonished . . ."

Every word of this fearful, prophetic description was fulfilled. There is no trace of the history of Edom, for God had said, "Edom shall be a desolation: every one that goeth by it shall be astonished."

The Edomites were descendants of Esau and have remained enemies of Israel. (See Genesis 36:8, Numbers 20:21.) Their country was considered

---

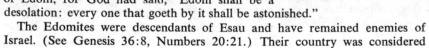

MEMORY VERSE FOR THE WEEK: Isaiah 55:11

"So shall my word be that goeth forth out of my mouth: it shall not return unto me void, but it shall accomplish that which I please, and it shall prosper in the thing whereto I sent it."

---

to be an impenetrable fortress, high in the rocky, deep gorges "in the clefts of the rock." The pillars of its temples, tombs, and dwellings were wholly protected by the solid rock mountains. The ancient capital of Edom was a major thoroughfare for world trade—a center of weath—and held a position of great military strength. In their pride the Edomites cherished the delusion that no power on earth could ever defeat her. But God said, "I will bring thee down."

The ruins of the rose-red city of Petra in the Hashemite kingdom of Jordan today seems to fit the description of the ancient kingdom of Edom, but no one is certain.

Although kings reigned over the Edomites from the time of Moses (Compare Numbers 20:14-21 and Genesis 36:31-39), every trace of its history, is culture, its kings, and its greatness has been destroyed. Edom is one more testimony to the absolute accuracy of prophecy.

"Heaven and earth shall pass away, but my words shall not pass away" (Matthew 24:35).

NOTE:
50:36 **dote** means become fools.

AUGUST 29: Read Jeremiah 51-52.
Jeremiah 51:60, 62: "So Jeremiah wrote in a book all the evil that should come upon Babylon, even all these words that are written against Babylon . . . Then shalt thou say, O Lord, thou hast spoken against this place, to cut it off, that none shall remain in it, neither man nor beast, but that it shall be desolate for ever."

The great nation of Babylonia—"the land of the Chaldeans" (Jeremiah 24:5; 25:12)—was enjoying its greatest power as a one-world government when God declared that "it shall be desolate for ever" and "Thus shall Babylon sink, and shall not rise . . ." (51:62, 64).

Its capital, Babylon, has stood throughout the ages as a symbol of the political and religious, God-defying forces of this world.

The term "MYSTERY, BABYLON . . ." (Revelation 17:5) does not mean something unknown, but rather something revealed only to believers who will listen and read with the aid of the Holy Spirit. (Read Revelation 14:16-18; and compare Isaiah 13-14; 21:1-47; and Jeremiah 50-51.)

Behind all worldly activities is a power that seeks to defeat and destroy the work of God—a satanic system that controls "the world [that] knew not God" (I Corinthians 1:21) and "hated" Christ (John 15:18).

Beware! lest you become involved by its attractions, pulled along with its popularity and controlled by its power. The time draws near for the final termination of this world's system of things.

The irrevocable doom upon "Babylon" has been pronounced, and the righteous judgments of God are about to be fulfilled. "And a mighty angel took up a stone like a great millstone, and cast it into the sea, saying, Thus

MEMORY VERSE FOR THE WEEK: Isaiah 55:11
"So shall my word be that goeth forth out of my mouth: it shall not return unto me void, but it shall accomplish that which I please, and it shall prosper in the thing whereto I sent it."

with violence shall that great city Babylon be thrown down, and shall be found no more at all" (Revelation 18:21).

NOTE:
52:22 **chapiter** means upper part.
Jeremiah 51:45: See 2 Cor. 6:17.

AUGUST 30: Read Lamentations 1-2.

Lamentations 2:9: "Her gates are sunk into the ground; he hath destroyed and broken her bars; her king and her princes are among the Gentiles; the law is no more; her prophets also find no vision from the Lord."

Jerusalem had been destroyed by the Babylonians. Jeremiah was grief-stricken over the total destruction. He first saw the loss of all the material things. (The walls were torn down, Solomon's world-famed Temple was gone, her priests had been murdered and its rulers slaughtered.)

But then he thought upon the greater loss. God had withdrawn His protection and rejected His people. Even the prophets could "find no vision from the Lord." So on behalf of the scattered slaves who once made up a powerful nation, the prophet confessed the sins of the people and their leaders. He then prayed that God would again restore His people to Jerusalem.

When God ceases to reveal His Word to us, life soon becomes the empty calculation of the human mind. Since our faith is based on how much of the Word is revealed to us, our real strength comes from daily reading His Word.

The knowledge and love of God's truth is essential if God's presence is to be expected. His presence does more than provide our material blessings, for it encompasses every need of man.

"My people are destroyed for lack of knowledge: because thou hast rejected knowledge, I will also reject thee, that thou shalt be no priest to me: seeing thou has forgotten the law of thy God, I will also forget thy children" (Hosea 4:6).

NOTE:
1:1 **tributary** means a forced laborer; 2:22 **swaddled** means tenderly cared for.

"For I have no pleasure in the death of him that dieth, saith the Lord God: wherefore turn yourselves, and live ye."
Ezekiel 18:32

AUGUST 31: Read Lamentations 3-5.

Lamentations 5:2, 21: "Our inheritance is turned to strangers, our houses to aliens. . . . Turn thou us unto thee, O Lord, and we shall be turned . . ."

This prayer is the conclusion of a pathetic, historic event. Jerusalem had been satisfied with outward things. Everywhere they looked, there was an abundance of material things. This caused their hearts to be puffed up with pride. Now

MEMORY VERSE FOR THE WEEK: Isaiah 55:11

"So shall my word be that goeth forth out of my mouth: it shall not return unto me void, but it shall accomplish that which I please, and it shall prosper in the thing whereto I sent it."

that material things had been removed, they had an ever-deepening realization of their loss and humiliation. There was nowhere to turn but to the Lord.

The Great Shepherd of Jerusalem had no delight in permitting their misery and defeat, but it was necessary in order to humble their hearts that they might seek Him.

This last petition in prayer, "Turn thou us unto thee," is the one supreme thing to be desired. It is not a restoration of external possessions and comforts that should concern us most, but it is us turning to God and Him turning to us. The results that come from our being turned to God will be worth all the loss and pain that we have suffered.

"Forasmuch then as Christ hath suffered for us in the flesh, arm yourselves likewise with the same mind: for he that hath ceased from sin; That he no longer should live the rest of his time in the flesh to the lusts of men, but to the will of God" (I Peter 4:1-2).

NOTE:
4:10 **sodden** means boiled.

BIBLICAL REFERENCE INDEX
PRAYERS IN JEREMIAH

PROPHETIC REFERENCES TO CHRIST

Isaiah 7:14	To be born of a virgin	Luke 1:26, 27, 30, 31
Isaiah 9:1, 2	Galilean ministry	Matthew 4:13-16
Isaiah 9:7	Heir to the throne of David	Luke 1:32, 33
Isaiah 11:2	Some of His characteristics	Luke 2:52
Isaiah 50:6	Spat upon and smitten	Matthew 26:67
Isaiah 53:3	Rejected by His own people, the Jews	John 1:11; Luke 23:18
Isaiah 53:5	Vicarious sacrifice	Romans 5:6, 8
Isaiah 53:7	Silent to accusations	Mark 15:4, 5
Isaiah 53:9	Buried with the rich	Matthew 27:57-60
Isaiah 53:12	Crucified with sinners	Mark 15:27, 28
Isaiah 61:1, 2	To heal the brokenhearted	Luke 4:18, 19
Jeremiah 31:15	Slaughter of the innocents	Matthew 2:16-18

MEMORY VERSE FOR THE WEEK: Isaiah 55:11
"So shall my word be that goeth forth out of my mouth: it shall not return unto me void, but it shall accomplish that which I please, and it shall prosper in the thing whereto I sent it."

INTRODUCTION TO THE PROPHETS

Prophets were men whom God "raised up" during the times of spiritual apostasy and moral decline of the kingdoms of Israel and Judah. They cover a period of about 400 years, beginning with Elijah during the days of Ahab and ending with Malachi.

The words of the prophets were the very words of God Himself who said, "I will raise them up a Prophet . . . and will put my words in his mouth; and he shall speak unto them all that I shall command him" (Deuteronomy 18:18). These words of Moses concerning the Messiah Savior was true of all His prophets who "spake as they were moved by the Holy Ghost" (II Peter 1:21).

After the Northern Kingdom was defeated by the Assyrians, little remained of the kingdom of Judah. After the Assyrian kingdom was conquered by the Chaldeans (Babylonians), the kingdom of Judah was also conquered and ruled by Nebuchadrezzar. When King Jehoiakim rebelled against Babylonian domination, Nebuchadnezzar went to Jerusalem and captured the king and many other prominent leaders in Jerusalem (II Chronicles 36:2-7; Jeremiah 45:1; Daniel 1:1-3). Among them was Daniel, who later became a prophet. The sacred vessels from the Temple were also taken to Babylon. (See Daniel 5:3, compare II Chronicles 36:6.)

Eight years later, Nebuchadnezzar again invaded Jerusalem and captured King Jehoiachin and deported more than 10,000 people to Babylon. Among them was the prophet Ezekiel (II Kings 24:14-16).

Eleven years later, Nebuchadnezzar captured Zedekiah, the last king of Judah. In this seige, they burned the Temple, destroyed the city of Jerusalem, and deported all but the poorest people into Babylonia. (II Kings 25:2-21). A final group was taken to Babylon five years after the destruction of the city (Jeremiah 52:30).

INTRODUCTION TO EZEKIEL

By the time Ezekiel was deported to Babylon, Daniel had been there eight years and held a prominent position in the palace.

Ezekiel probably was a student under Jeremiah in Jerusalem while he was preparing to become a priest; however, God called him to be a prophet. His prophecies cover a period of 22 years.

In order to correctly interpret the book of Revelation, the visions and parables of Ezekiel require diligent, prayerful study.

The Book of Ezekiel is of utmost importance in revealing the terrible power of sin to overthrow, tear down, and destroy men and nations. But beyond the acts of men is the sovereign hand of God who will fulfill His promises to the future remnant of Israel.

SEPTEMBER 1: Read Ezekiel 1-4.

Ezekiel 2:7-9; 3:2-3: "And thou shalt speak my words unto them, whether they will hear, or whether they will forbear; for they are most rebellious. But thou, son of man, hear what I say unto thee; . . . open thy mouth, and eat that I give thee . . . and, lo, a roll of a book was therein; . . . so I opened my mouth, and he caused me to eat that roll . . . it was in my mouth as honey for sweetness."

The truth of God's Word not only must be studied, but we must feed on it as "the bread of life." The Lord explained to the prophet that His message would not be welcome and informed him of the opposition and rejection of that message, saying, ". . . they are most rebellious."

Ezekiel enjoyed the Word of God by meditating upon it, inwardly digesting it, thus making it a living reality in his life.

This has always been true of God's servants. Jeremiah said, "Thy words were found, and I did eat them; and thy word was unto me the joy and rejoicing of mine heart . . ." (Jeremiah 15:16).

Job testified, ". . . I have esteemed the words of his mouth more than my necessary food" (Job 23:12; see also Revelation 10:9-11). Only as we feed on the Word can we become strong in the Lord and in the power of His might.

Many have a certain amount of head knowledge—an intellectual acquaintance of the truth of the Scriptures—but they have never really made it their very life.

God never expects anyone to proclaim His Word in their own strength nor to be guided by their own wisdom.

"I have given them thy word; and the world hath hated them, because they are not of the world, even as I am not of the world" (John 17:14).

NOTE:
1:4 **infolding itself** means flashing continually; 1:20 **up over against** means close beside; 2:4 **impudent** means stubborn; 2:10 **within and without** means front and back; 3:9 **an adamant** means a stone; 3:14 **heat** means anger; 4:16 **care** means anxiety.

SEPTEMBER 2: Read Ezekiel 5-9.

Ezekiel 8:4, 9:3: "And, behold, *the glory* of the God of Israel was there, according to the vision that I saw in the plain . . . And *the glory* of the God of Israel was gone up from the cherub, whereupon he was, to the threshold of the house . . ."

MEMORY VERSE FOR THE WEEK: Isaiah 55:11

"So shall my word be that goeth forth out of my mouth: it shall not return unto me void, but it shall accomplish that which I please, and it shall prosper in the thing whereto I sent it."

Just preceding the destruction of Jerusalem, Ezekiel, a captive in Babylon, was "lifted . . . up between the earth and the heaven, and brought . . . in the visions of God to Jerusalem . . ." (8:3). There he beheld the cloud—the visible manifestation of God's presence, "the glory of the Lord."

He also observed to one side an idol, which is referred to as the "image of jealousy" (8:5). Then he saw seventy elders facing the sanctuary but secretly worshiping the idols of Israel. Another group of twenty-five men, with their backs turned from the Lord, were worshiping the rising sun.

Following this, Ezekiel beheld the mysterious cloud, the symbol of the presence of God, rising from over the Holy of Holies and slowly moving toward the exit of the Temple. The glory of the Lord then departed from the city and went to the Mount of Olives, lingering there for a time, as if waiting to see if Israel would repent and return to Him. But no one seemed to recognize that the Lord had withdrawn His presence.

It was vital that the captives in Babylon realize why the nation was being destroyed—they had turned to various other forms of worship, and were no longer worshiping only God.

Without submission to His Word our worship may become just empty idol worship. Many become an easy victim to satanic deceptions because they have "changed the truth of God into a lie, and worshiped and served the creature more than the Creator, who is blessed for ever. Amen" (Romans 1:25).

NOTE:
8:12 **imagery** means imagination; 8:14 **Tammuz** means a Babylonian idol.

> ". . . bound in affliction and iron;
> Because they rebelled against the
> words of God . . ."
> Psalm 107:10,11

SEPTEMBER 3: Read Ezekiel 10-13.

Ezekiel 12:12,13: "And the prince that is among them shall bear upon his shoulder in the twilight, and shall go forth: they shall dig through the wall to carry out thereby: . . . My net also will I spread upon him, and he shall be taken in my snare: and I will bring him to Babylon to the land of the Chaldeans; *yet shall he not see it, though he shall die there.*"

When Zedekiah, king of Judah, rebelled at being under Babylonian control, it brought about the final war and destruction of the Holy City. Zedekiah escaped from Jerusalem by digging through its wall, but he was captured near Jericho by Nebuchadnezzar (see II Kings 25:1-7).

They "put out the eyes of Zedekiah," thus fulfilling the strange prophecy of Ezekiel that Zedekiah would be taken to Babylon, "yet shall he not see it, though he shall die there [in Babylon]."

MEMORY VERSE FOR THE WEEK: Isaiah 55:11

"So shall my word be that goeth forth out of my mouth: it shall not return unto me void, but it shall accomplish that which I please, and it shall prosper in the thing whereto I sent it."

Ezekiel faithfully foretold the coming judgments of God to King Zedekiah and the nation. But "they mocked the messengers of God, and despised his words, and misused his prophets, until the wrath of the Lord arose against his people, till there was no remedy" (II Chronicles 36:16).

Even though it may not be popular, we too should faithfully make known the Father's will as given in His Word. The unfailing mark of a true Christian is a humble submission to the Word of God.

". . . but the word preached did not profit them, not being mixed with faith in them that heard it" (Hebrews 4:2).

SEPTEMBER 4: Read Ezekiel 14-16.

Ezekiel 14:1,3: "Then came certain of the elders of Israel unto me, and sat before me. . . . Son of man, these men have set up their idols in their heart, and put the stumbling block of their iniquity before their face. . . ."

God revealed to Ezekiel that these elders were not sincerely seeking Him but that they, like the other elders, were intent on worshiping idols. They sincerely believed that God should, and would, deliver them from Babylonian slavery, but they were deceived. Sin destroys spiritual discernment.

Anyone who refuses to live according to God's Word will be deceived into drawing false conclusions. For instance, (1) "Be ye doers of the word, and not hearers only, *deceiving* your own selves" (James 1:22). Many who call themselves Christians know the right answers, but they do otherwise. (2) "If any man among you seem to be religious, and bridleth not his tongue, but *deceiveth* his own heart, this man's religion is vain [worthless]" (James 1:26). (3) "Be not *deceived:* evil communications corrupt good manners" (I Corinthians 15:33).

Jesus quoted the prophet Isaiah when He said, "This people draweth nigh unto me with their mouth, and honoreth me with their lips; but their heart is far from me. But in vain they do worship me, teaching for doctrines the commandments of men" (Matthew 15:8-9; compare Isaiah 29:13).

NOTE:
14:15 **noisome** means wild; 15:4 **meet** means useful; 16:4 **supple** means cleanse; 16:30 **imperious whorish** means bold, domineering; 16:31 **eminent place** means pagan shrine; 16:43 **fretted** means angered.

SEPTEMBER 5: Read Ezekiel 17-19.

Ezekiel 18:29: "Yet saith the house of Israel, The way of the Lord is not equal [fair or just]. O house of Israel, are not my ways equal? are not your ways unequal?"

The people of Judah endured much suffering during the final days of Jerusalem when they were taken as slaves to Babylon. Consequently, they were bitter and accused God of being unjust in allowing them to be disgraced and defeated by the Chaldeans (Babylonians).

MEMORY VERSE FOR THE WEEK: I John 1:6

"I we say that we have fellowship with him, and walk in darkness, we lie, and do not the truth."

223

Why didn't God come to their rescue? Surely they were not as evil as Nebuchadnezzar and his cruel heathen armies. How could God permit the wicked Chaldeans to prosper and control the earth?

Ezekiel told them not to blame their fathers, but to examine their own conduct, to turn to God with ". . . a new heart and a new spirit . . . and live" (18:31-32). Some think the ways of the Lord are not fair, but in reality His ways seem unfair only because our own ways are perverted or misdirected.

God's concern has always been that man should turn from his sins and enjoy His protection and provisions.

"The Lord is . . . not willing that any should perish, but that all should come to repentance" (II Peter 3:9).

NOTE:
18:8 **usury** means interest.

SEPTEMBER 6: Read Ezekiel 20-21.

Ezekiel 20:13: "But the house of Israel rebelled against me in the wilderness: they walked not in my statutes, and they despised my judgments, which if a man do, he shall even live in them; and my sabbaths they greatly polluted: then I said, I would pour out my fury upon them in the wilderness, to consume them."

"The elders" (in Babylonian captivity) went to Ezekiel "to inquire of the Lord" on three occasions. (See 8:1; 14:1; 20:1.)

On the first occasion, the prophet revealed their sins and foretold Jerusalem's doom because of idolatry. At the second meeting, God pointed the finger directly to the elders before Ezekiel, revealing to the prophet that "these men have set up their idols in their heart" (14:3). Eleven months later the elders again came to the prophet "to inquire of the Lord." On this third occasion, Ezekiel told them that the destruction of the Holy City and the doom of the guilty people was imminent.

It is significant that eight times in the two chapters of today's reading God said, "They might know that I am the Lord." In fact, this phrase occurs more than sixty times in the 48 chapters of Ezekiel.

The downfall of the nation and the humiliation of Babylonian captivity were necessary that "they might know that I am the Lord."

God demands that we accept Him as Sovereign Ruler—as Lord. Have you made a decision to turn your life and your will over to His care?

"God, who at sundry [different] times and in divers manners [various ways] spake in time past unto the fathers by the prophets, hath in these last days spoken unto us by his Son . . ." (Hebrews 1:1-2).

NOTE:
20:5 **lifted up mine hand** means promised; 20:6 **espied** means searched out; 20:40 . **oblations** means gifts; 21:9 **furbished** means polished; 21:31 **brutish** means cruel. **Ezekiel 20:33,34,42:** See II Cor. 6:17.

MEMORY VERSE FOR THE WEEK: I John 1:6

"If we say that we have fellowship with him, and walk in darkness, we lie, and do not the truth."

Ezekiel 24:1,2: "Again in the ninth year, in the tenth month, in the tenth day of the month, the word of the Lord came unto me, saying, . . . the king of Babylon set himself against Jerusalem this same day."

Ezekiel foretold the exact historic date of Jerusalem's destruction as recorded in II Kings 25:1. How could Ezekiel know this? The Lord gave him the information and told him to record the date, saying, "Son of man, write thee the name of the day, even of this selfsame day: the king of Babylon set himself against Jerusalem this same day." It was also revealed to Ezekiel that on that same date, the one he loved most, "the desire of thine eyes," would be taken from him.

Ezekiel was instructed not to express any sorrow when his wife died—not even to shed a tear. His personal grief was to be insignificant compared to his sorrow for the destruction of Jerusalem and the Temple.

Are you as concerned over eternal treasures as was Ezekiel? Our Lord's highest calling is given to those whose hearts are set on satisfying Him.

"Herein is our love made perfect, that we may have boldness in the day of judgment: because as he is, so are we in this world" (I John 4:17).

NOTE:
22:5 **vexed** means confused; 23:16 **doted upon** means lusted after; 24:17 **tire** means turban.

SEPTEMBER 8: Read Ezekiel 25-28.

Ezekiel 26:2,3,14: "Son of man, because that Tyrus [Tyre] hath said against Jerusalem, Aha, she [Jerusalem] is broken . . . I shall be replenished, now she is laid waste [by Nebuchadnezzar]. Therefore thus saith the Lord God; Behold, I am against thee, O Tyrus . . . And I will make thee like the top of a rock: thou shalt be a place to spread nets upon; thou shalt be built no more: for I the Lord have spoken it, saith the Lord God."

The stronghold of the city of Tyrus [Tyre] was on an island, but much of the city was on the mainland of the Mediterranean seacoast, just north of Mt. Carmel. Including its coastal territorial possessions, it was the greatest commercial metropolis of the world at the time of Ezekiel.

The inhabitants of Tyrus were anxious to see Jerusalem destroyed, for they could satisfy their greedy and heartless desire for full control of world commerce. Because of this, God foretold their complete destruction.

Nebuchadnezzar battled against Tyrus for thirteen years and finally defeated them. But after 70 years, Tyrus was rebuilt, as prophesied by Isaiah (Isaiah 23:17-18).

History records that Alexander the Great destroyed the walls, towers, and buildings on the *mainland* Tyrus and used the material to build a rock

---

MEMORY VERSE FOR THE WEEK: I John 1:6

"If we say that we have fellowship with him, and walk in darkness, we lie, and do not the truth."

225

road to the *island* fortress of Tyrus, thus fulfilling the strange words of Ezekiel, ". . . and they shall lay thy stones and thy timber and thy dust in the midst of the water" (26:12).

As a witness to the infallible prophecy of Ezekiel, this "indestructible" island was never rebuilt. Since that time, the area that was once Tyrus has been used only by fishermen as a "place to spread nets."

The island of ancient Tyre is a testimony that "Thy word is true from the beginning: and every one of thy righteous judgments endureth for ever" (Psalm 119:160).

NOTE:
25:5 **couching place** means resting place; 26:17 **haunt it** means dwelt there.

". . . I also made you contemptible and **base** before all the people, according as ye have not kept my ways . . ." Malachi 2:9

SEPTEMBER 9: Read Ezekiel 29-32.
Ezekiel 29:12-16: "And I will make the land of Egypt desolate . . . and her cities . . . that are laid waste shall be desolate forty years: . . . At the end of forty years will I gather the Egyptians from the people whither they were scattered: . . . It shall be the basest of the kingdoms; . . . that they . . . shall be no more the confidence of the house of Israel, . . . but they shall know that I am the Lord God."

For centuries Egypt was a prominent world power and had become famous for its art, literature, and achievements. Consequently, this shocking prediction by Ezekiel seemed the most unlikely of all his prophecies—that Egypt would be defeated, then rebuilt in 40 years, but forever remain as a base kingdom—never to regain world prominence.

The prophecy that Tyre was *never* to be rebuilt and that equally great nations like Assyria and Babylon were to become extinct was a striking contrast to the prophecy that Egypt was to continue as a *base kingdom*.

Nebuchadnezzar did not know that God was preparing him and his Babylonian armies to fulfill prophecy. But after Babylon accomplished God's purpose, it was forever destroyed.

God sometimes uses men with selfish interests as well as godly men to fulfill His Word. This vital truth is often overlooked by the self-seeker who prides himself in popularity and success.

"Every man's work shall be made manifest: for the day shall declare it, because it shall be revealed by fire; and the fire shall try every man's work of what sort it is" (I Corinthians 3:13).
NOTE:
29:6 **staff of reed** means weak support; 30:21 **roller** means bandage.
Ezekiel 32:7-8: See Mat. 24:29; Mk. 13:24,25; Lk. 21:26.

MEMORY VERSE FOR THE WEEK: I John 1:6

"If we say that we have fellowship with him, and walk in darkness, we lie, and do not the truth."

SEPTEMBER 10: Read Ezekiel 33-36.

Ezekiel 34:23,31: "And I will set up one shepherd over them, and he shall feed them, even my servant David; he shall feed them, and he shall be their shepherd. . . . And ye my flock, the flock of my pasture, are men, and I am your God, saith the Lord God."

The Israelites understood the meaning of a shepherd, for they knew the nature of sheep and the problems of their care. They also understood the qualifications of a good shepherd and his value.

In the hopeless hour following the prophecy concerning the fall of Jerusalem, the exiled Jews were given this compassionate message of mercy in which the coming of the true Shepherd of Israel was foretold.

All those who have been scattered will be reunited as sheep with their Shepherd. A new David—the Messiah—will care for His true sheep. Under His care, they will experience "showers of blessing" (34:26).

The true Shepherd can only be the Messiah, our Lord Jesus Christ. He came down from heaven to earth almost 2,000 years ago to seek the lost sheep (people) of Israel. He was rejected by His own nation and people, and went back to heaven. But one day He will return to earth to once again deliver His people. (See Isaiah 9:6-7; Luke 1:31-33; Acts 1:9-11; 3:19-21; 15: 14-18.)

"I am the good shepherd: the good shepherd giveth his life for the sheep" (John 10:11).

NOTE:
34:14 **fat** means rich; 34:17 **cattle** means sheep.
Ezekiel 34:5: See Mat. 9:36; Mk. 6:34. **34:16:** See Lk. 19:10. **34:23:** See John 10:16.

"They burnt the house of God, and brake down the wall of Jerusalem . . . and destroyed all the goodly vessels."
(II Chron. 36:19)
But Ezekiel foretold that God would save a remnant and it shall live again.

SEPTEMBER 11: Read Ezekiel 37-39.

Ezekiel 37:1,11: "The hand of the Lord . . . set me down in the midst of the valley which was full of bones . . . Then he said unto me, Son of man, these bones are the whole house of Israel: behold, they say, Our bones are dried, and our hope is lost: we are cut off for our parts."

In Ezekiel's vision, he saw a valley full of scattered, disjointed bones. It looked as though a great battle had been fought and the slain left unburied.

Those bleached, dislocated skeletons had been exposed to the sun and wind and were "very dry" bones, slowly burying themselves in their progressive

---

MEMORY VERSE FOR THE WEEK: I John 1:7

"But if we walk in the light, as he is in the light, we have fellowship one with another, and the blood of Jesus Christ his Son cleanseth us from all sin."

227

decay as they crumbled into dust. It seemed impossible that these bones could ever come together to be so much as a skeleton, much less a living body.

The Jewish captives had been in Babylon for about 25 years and had lost all hope of ever again becoming a nation. They said, "Our bones are dried, and our hope is lost. . . ." But these exiled Jews were dead only in the sense that their sins had destroyed their faith in the promises of God which the prophet had told them.

Just as God was the only One who could restore life to the dry bones, He was saying to Israel, ". . . I shall put my spirit in you, and ye shall live . . ." (37:14). Israel was made to live again, and her return as a nation is told in the books of Ezra and Nehemiah.

Every defeated believer can be assured that the life-giving Word of God can, and will, transform and restore the most hopeless situation. Renew your faith by reading His promises and pray the prayer of David, ". . . Quicken thou me according to thy word" (Psalm 119:25).

NOTE:
39:6 **carelessly** means securely; 39:14 **sever out** means set apart; **passengers** means those passing by.
Ezekiel 37:27: See II Cor. 6:16.

SEPTEMBER 12: Read Ezekiel 40-42.
Ezekiel 40:1,4: ". . . the hand of the Lord was upon me . . . behold with thine eyes, and hear with thine ears, and set thine heart upon all that I shall show thee; . . . declare all that thou seest to the house of Israel."

These comforting promises were given to assure the captives that they would return to their own land, restore the nation, rebuild the Temple, and once again participate in "the most holy things" (42:13).

These chapters climax the entire book, for they look beyond the return from captivity to Jerusalem, where God would forever dwell with them. The beauty of the new Temple is the fact that "the Lord is there" (48:35).

Ezekiel viewed, in the distant future, a very remarkable feature of the Temple. A stream flowed from its threshold. It is this mysterious stream that transforms all things it touches with new life. It is shallow at first, but this ever-rising stream becomes the *river of life*, the Word and the Spirit of the Lord.

As Christians begin reading the Scriptures, some verses and chapters are easily understood, but others will require much study in order to understand them. Still others are beyond our depth of comprehension. However, the Holy Spirit reveals deeper meanings to all who continue to walk in the stream of His life-giving Word.

"For the Lamb which is in the midst of the throne shall feed them, and shall lead them unto living fountains of waters. . . ." (Revelation 7:17).

NOTE:
40:9 **inward** means faced inward; 40:16 **inward** means facing the court; 40:23 **over against** means opposite; 41:12 **separate** place means temple yard; 42:6 **building** means upper chambers; **straitened** means reduced.

MEMORY VERSE FOR THE WEEK: I John 1:7

"But if we walk in the light, as he is in the light, we have fellowship one with another, and the blood of Jesus Christ his Son cleanseth us from all sin."

SEPTEMBER 13: Read Ezekiel 43-45.

Ezekiel 43:5: "So the spirit took me up, and brought me into the inner court; and, behold, the glory of the Lord filled the house."

One of the most serious errors of the people during the time of Ezekiel was that they had much worship that did not conform to God's Word. For this reason, the elders in authority at Jerusalem could neither discern the presence of the Lord nor hear Him speak.

It is the *heart* and not the *head* which makes God's servants capable of doing His will. In fact, it is only with a heart full of love in obedience to His Word that we can serve God acceptably.

Our body is the temple of the Holy Spirit, and we are constructing a temple each day with every act and thought. This construction of the temple is either according to His plan or our own human intellect. God has made available a blueprint (His Word) for building this temple to prepare us for eternity.

Although he would probably live in it less than 50 years, the most qualified builder would refuse to erect a mere $50,000 home without carefully following the blueprint. How much more we should be concerned about carefully building our eternal temple.

We cannot afford to neglect His Word, for it is a Master Plan for building our life according to His design.

"Except the Lord build the house, they labor in vain that build it: except the Lord keep the city, the watchman waketh but in vain" (Psalm 127:1).

NOTE:
43:20 **settle** means ledge; 44:22 **put away** means divorced; 44:25 **come at** means go near; 45:20 **simple** means ignorant.

SEPTEMBER 14: Read Ezekiel 46-48.

Ezekiel 47:1,8: "Afterward he brought me again unto the door of the house . . . Then said he unto me, These waters issue out toward the east country, and go down into the desert, and go into the sea: which being brought forth into the sea, the waters shall be healed."

God has a pure river of life in store for His redeemed people. As Ezekiel continued to look, he saw the waters of life reach the Dead Sea. As this river poured into the Dead Sea it brought forth fresh, life-giving water. Where there had been only death and desolation before, great schools of fish could be seen. We are told that, "every thing shall live whither the river cometh" (47:9).

The river of the Water of Life has its source in Him whose glory filled the Temple. All the blessings of life are the result of the stream of eternal life that begins at the throne and flows through every Christian. Christ is the

---

MEMORY VERSE FOR THE WEEK: I John 1:7

"But if we walk in the light, as he is in the light, we have fellowship one with another, and the blood of Jesus Christ his Son cleanseth us from all sin."

---

source of the Water of Life which flows in Gospel channels, spreading and deepening among nations throughout the world. Similarly, the growth of grace in the individual life is a progressive work. It begins with a small stream from Christ, the Fountainhead, and continues to increase in depth and preciousness as we walk in the light of His Word.

". . . Whosoever will, let him take the water of life freely" (Revelation 22:17).

NOTE:
46:22 **of one measure** means the same size; 47:12 **according to his months** means every month.

INTRODUCTION TO DANIEL

Because of Daniel's faithfulness and obedience to God, he became a high governmental official in Babylon. The Book of Daniel goes beyond the destiny of the Jews and reveals the four great world empires that would succeed each other and rule the world until the coming of the "Messiah the Prince" (Daniel 9:25).

Daniel looked beyond all the great kingdoms to the day of resurrection (Daniel 12:2-3) and showed how the events of history are unmistakably determined by God.

Jesus quoted Daniel's prophecy when He referred to the fearful times just preceding the Great Tribulation (Matthew 24:15,21).

SEPTEMBER 15: Read Daniel 1-3.
Daniel 2:31: "Thou, O king, sawest, and behold a great image. This great image, whose brightness was excellent, stood before thee; and the form thereof was terrible."

A dazzling giant image representing four great world empires that would rule successively over the earth appeared in King Nebuchadnezzar's dream. This great human-like figure represented the rule of Babylon (with Nebuchadnezzar as head), followed by the Medo-Persian kingdom, Greece, and finally the Roman empire. As prophesied, these four nations ruled the world in succession from Daniel to Christ.

This image appeared with glorious luster in the mind of Nebuchadnezzar, whose life was wholly taken up with the admiration of worldly greatness. The same monarchies were represented later to Daniel from a spiritual point of view as fierce, wild animals intent on controlling the hearts of men in defiance to God (chapter 7).

Then it was revealed that a fifth kingdom would arise and conquer all other nations (2:44-45). It appeared as a stone that was cut from the mountain without human intervention, and it broke the whole image into pieces

---

MEMORY VERSE FOR THE WEEK: I John 1:7

"But if we walk in the light, as he is in the light, we have fellowship one with another, and the blood of Jesus Christ his Son cleanseth us from all sin."

and scattered it to the winds. The fact that it was "cut out of the mountain without hands" reveals the source of its king, the Messiah (Daniel 7:13-14). His smiting the great image confirms the power of God in overturning world empires in preparation for that day when His saints will reign with Him.

". . . The kingdoms of this world are become the kingdoms of our Lord, and of his Christ; and he shall reign for ever and ever" (Revelation 11:15).

NOTE:
1:10 **sort** means age; 1:12 **pulse** means vegetable diet; 2:31 **terrible** means magnificent; 3:19 **the form of his visage** means his facial expression; **wont** means usually; 3:28 **changed** means violated.

Daniel 3:27: See Heb. 11:34.

SEPTEMBER 16: Read Daniel 4-6.
Daniel 4:30: "The king spake, and said, Is not this great Babylon, that *I* have built for the house of the kingdom by the might of *my* power, and for the honour of *my* majesty?"

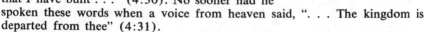

Successful wars and immense construction in Babylon had produced for Nebuchadnezzar the most magnificent capital in world history. He was now worshiping his *idol*—"this great Babylon, that I have built . . ." (4:30). No sooner had he spoken these words when a voice from heaven said, ". . . The kingdom is departed from thee" (4:31).

The great king, who in the morning had ruled over millions of people in his kingdom, became mentally deranged. He was forced from his throne "and did eat grass as oxen" for seven years (4:33).

Pride is the root of all sin that ruined our race. Pride reached out its hand in the Garden of Eden when Eve saw ". . . a tree to be desired to make one wise" (Genesis 3:6).

It is possible, even in Christian work, to achieve great things and be admired and respected, but still possess a heart like Nebuchadnezzar's.

When God restored Nebuchadnezzar's mind, he humbly acknowledged, "I praised and honoured him . . . whose dominion is an everlasting dominion . . . and those that walk in pride he is able to abase" (4:34,37).

God in mercy seeks to bring every Christian to humbly acknowledge and be "clothed with humility: for God resisteth the proud, and giveth grace to the humble" (1 Peter 5:5).

NOTE:
4:37 **abase** means humble.
Daniel 4:3: See Lk. 1:33: **4:12,21:** See Mat. 13:32; Mk. 4:32; Lk. 13:19. **6:22:** See Heb. 11:33.

MEMORY VERSE FOR THE WEEK: I John 1:7

"But if we walk in the light, as he is in the light, we have fellowship one with another, and the blood of Jesus Christ his Son cleanseth us from all sin."

231

Daniel 9:3-4: "And I set my face unto the Lord God, to seek by prayer and supplications, with fasting, and sackcloth, and ashes: And I prayed unto the Lord my God, and made my confession, and said, O Lord, the great and dreadful God, keeping the covenant and mercy to them that love him, and to them that keep his commandments."

Daniel was about thirteen when he was taken captive. When he prayed the above prayer, he was over eighty years old.

The remarkable career of Daniel as a government administrator and prophet of God can be directly linked with his prayer life. It was no secret that Daniel "kneeled upon his knees three times a day, and prayed, and gave thanks before his God" (Daniel 6:10; Daniel 9:1-19).

Daniel knew from reading the prophecy of Jeremiah that the "seventy years in the desolations of Jerusalem" was nearing an end (9:2; compare Jeremiah 25). He "understood by books the number of the years" (9:2). (The "books" refer to the Hebrew Scriptures, particularly the writings of the prophets.)

This led Daniel to say, "I set my face unto the Lord God, to seek by prayer and supplications, with fasting, and sackcloth, and ashes."

Daniel's prayer was not a rambling recital of generalities, mentioning everything and claiming nothing. He could pray with confidence and assurance because he knew the Word of God.

Pray according to the promises of God, and God will answer you as He did Daniel.

"If ye abide in me, and my words abide in you, ye shall ask what ye will, and it shall be done unto you" (John 15:7).

NOTE:
7:28 **cogitations** means thoughts; 8:7 **choler** means anger.
Daniel 7:13: See Mat. 24:30; Mk. 13:26; Lk. 21:27. **7:14**: See Mat. 28::18. **9:24**: See Acts 10:43. **9:27 and 12:11**: See Mat. 24:15; Mk. 13:14.

Daniel 12:2-3: "And many of them that sleep in the dust of the earth shall awake, some to everlasting life, and some to shame and everlasting contempt. And they that be wise shall shine as the brightness of the firmament; and they that turn many to righteousness as the stars for ever and ever."

Daniel presented, in vivid contrast, the resurrection of life and the resurrection of damnation. The Bible clearly states that our destiny after death is for all eternity, ". . . it is appointed unto men once to die, but after this the judgment" (Hebrews 9:27).

When our Lord spoke of the resurrection of life and the resurrection of damnation, He confirmed the prophecy of Daniel, that they who "sleep in the dust of the earth shall awake, some to everlasting life, and some to shame and everlasting contempt . . ."

Our life here is a preparation for eternity. The Christian is a "light" in a world of darkness. "Let your light so shine before men, that they may see

MEMORY VERSE FOR THE WEEK: I John 1:8
"If we say that we have no sin, we deceive ourselves, and the truth is not in us."

your good works, and glorify your Father which is in heaven" (Matthew 5:16).

To the extent we instruct others by His Word and by our witness and example, we shall "shine as stars." We shall receive a glorious eternal reward when Christ returns.

". . . He that winneth souls is wise. Behold the righteous shall be recompensed in the earth . . ." (Proverbs 11:30-31).

NOTE:
10:3 **pleasant bread** means tasty food; 11:15 **most fenced** means best fortified; 11:24 **forecast his devices** means devise plans; 11:34 **holpen** means helped.

Daniel 11:31 and 12:11: See Mat. 24:15; Mk. 13:14. **11:36:** See 2 Thess. 2:4. **12:1:** See Mat. 24:21; Mk. 13:19. **12:2:** See Mat. 25:46; Mk. 13:14. **12:11:** See Mat. 24:15.

INTRODUCTION TO HOSEA

Hosea was the only prophet from the ten-tribed kingdom of Israel. His ministry was in Israel during the reigns of Zechariah, Shallum, and Menahem. At the same time, Micah, Amos, and Israel were prophets in Judah. This was about 40 years before the Northern Kingdom was defeated by Assyria.

Under Jeroboam II the Northern Kingdom experienced great economic prosperity, but their religious life degenerated with the immoral and pagan Baal and Ashtoreth worship.

At Mt. Sinai, Israel became united to God through a covenant relationship. Hosea stressed that Israel had broken her covenant relationship with God—as an unfaithful bride with her divine lover (see Hosea 2:19).

"For the Son of man is come to seek and to save that which was lost."
Luke 19:10

SEPTEMBER 19: Read Hosea 1-6.
Hosea 3:1-2: "Then said the Lord unto me, Go yet, love a woman beloved of her friend, yet an adulteress, according to the love of the Lord toward the children of Israel, who look to other gods, and love flagons of wine. So I bought her to me . . ."

With the Lord's help, Hosea was able to do what few men would have done. He loved his unfaithful wife who had disgraced his name by becoming a prostitute. When she was no longer wanted by other men, she was taken to the slave market. Hosea found her there, bought her, and took her back home.

God could use Hosea to reveal His love to the unfaithful nation of Israel only because Hosea could love an unlovely woman. As a result of his forgiving spirit, he had the privilege of being an example of God's unfailing love toward Israel.

MEMORY VERSE FOR THE WEEK: I John 1:8
"If we say that we have no sin, we deceive ourselves, and the truth is not in us."

The Israelites had forsaken God and committed spiritual adultery by turning to idols. But God in mercy continued to plead with them to return to Him. Oh, what love!

The same love that Hosea expressed should be manifest in every Christian. Has someone offended you and hurt your pride? Don't wait for them to come to you and apologize. It is always the responsibility of the innocent person to be forgiving—even "seventy times seven," if need be.

The necessity of this fully forgiving spirit is clearly stated by Christ in a parable of the *unforgiving* servant who was "delivered to the tormentors." Jesus concluded by saying, "So likewise shall my heavenly Father do also unto you, if ye from your hearts forgive not every one his brother their trespasses" (Matthew 18:35).

NOTE:
4:12 **staff** means diviners wand; 5:15 **early** means earnestly.

Hosea 1:10: See Rom. 9:26; I Pet. 2:10. **2:23:** See Rom. 9:25,26. **6:2:** See I Cor. 15: 4. **6:6:** See Mat. 9:13; 12:7.

SEPTEMBER 20: Read Hosea 7-14.
Hosea 11:1,4: "When Israel was a child, then I loved him, and called my son out of Egypt. I *drew them with cords of a man,* with *bands of love:* and I was to them as they that take off the yoke on their jaws, and I laid meat unto them."

The Scripture, "When Israel was a child, then I loved him and called my son out of Egypt," not only refers to the Hebrew slaves being led by Moses from the land of bondage, but it also refers to Christ.

The Holy Spirit leads us in seeing how far-reaching the Old Testament Scriptures are in revealing Christ. The angel of the Lord guided Joseph to take the young child into Egypt, ". . . that it might be fulfilled which was spoken of the Lord by the prophet, saying, "Out of Egypt have I called my son" (Matthew 2:15). This confirms how vital the Old Testament is to our spiritual comprehension of the whole Bible.

Not only were the Hebrews delivered from slavery, but every Christian has been delivered from an even worse bondage than Egypt slavery. We were brought to a saving knowledge of Christ and freed from the power of Satan through God's tender love. To the weakest Christian, God is still saying, "I drew them [not drove them] . . . with bands of love." When He drew us from our sins to Himself, it was indeed "the cords of man"—the Man, Christ Jesus.

"But God commendeth his love toward us, in that, while we were yet sinners, Christ died for us" (Romans 5:8).

NOTE:
7:15 **bound** means taught; 9:7 **visitation** means judgment; 9:8 **hatred in** means opposed to; 11:8 **repentings** means compassions; 12:10 **similitudes** means parables; 13:8 **rend the caul** means tear the fat; 13:12 **hid** means stored up; 14:2 **calves** means our thanks.

Hosea 10:8: See Lk. 23:30; Rev. 6:16. **11:1:** See Mat. 2:15. **13:14:** See I Cor. 15:55. **14:2:** See Heb. 13:15.

MEMORY VERSE FOR THE WEEK: I John 1:8
"If we say that we have no sin, we deceive ourselves, and the truth is not in us."

INTRODUCTION TO JOEL

The prophet Joel described a severe locust plague that swept through the country, devouring the crops and stripping every leaf from the trees. This was followed by a severe drought which left the land desolate. After this incident, God gave Joel a vision of the future day of Jehovah when God would pour out His spirit upon His servants, ". . . whosoever shall call on the name of the Lord shall be saved" (Acts 2:21; compare Joel 2:32).

"But when the Comforter is come, whom I will send unto you from the Father, even the Spirit of truth, which proceedeth from the Father, he shall testify of me." John 15:26

SEPTEMBER 21: Read Joel 1-3.

Joel 2:28: "And it shall come to pass afterward, that I will pour out my spirit upon all flesh; and your sons and your daughters shall prophesy, your old men shall dream dreams, your young men shall see visions."

Other prophets had foretold of the coming Messiah, but the prophet Joel was the first to foretell of the coming of the Holy Spirit.

Joel had foretold that the day would come when God's people would "know . . . that I am the Lord your God, . . . and my people shall never be ashamed" (Joel 2:27). This confidence became a reality with the indwelling Holy Spirit.

The outpouring of the Holy Spirit was accompanied by remarkable signs, but one of the most thrilling things was that it brought about a marvelous change in the lives of the believers. There was a marked contrast between Peter's outright denial of Christ before the Holy Spirit indwelled him and his holy boldness to confess Christ after the Holy Spirit came on the day of Pentecost.

Many Jews scoffed at the miraculous things that had happened so suddenly in their midst, and the Holy Spirit directed Peter to say, "But this is that which was spoken by the prophet Joel" (Acts 2:16).

Peter could also say, "Whereby are given unto us exceeding great and precious promises: that by these ye might be partakers of the divine nature, having escaped the corruption that is in the world through lust" (II Peter 1:4).

NOTE:
1:7 **barked** means chewed off the bark; 1:12 **languisheth** means waste away; 2:6 **blackness** means sorrow; 2:20 **ill savor** means foul smell.

Joel 2:10 and 3:15: See Mat. 24:29. **2:28-30:** See Acts 2:17-21. **2:32:** See Rom. 10:13. **3:13:** See Mk. 4:29.

MEMORY VERSE FOR THE WEEK: I John 1:8

"If we say that we have no sin, we deceive ourselves, and the truth is not in us."

INTRODUCTION TO AMOS

The prophet Amos was not trained in the religious schools (7:14-15). He was a herdsman in the small mountain village of Tekoa in the kingdom of Judah. (Compare II Chronicles 11:6; Jeremiah 6:1).

His message was one of doom upon the surrounding nations (chapters 1,2) and upon the kingdom of Israel (chapters 3-9).

He foretold the destruction of the nation "as if a man did flee from a lion, and a bear met him" (5:19). Then at the close, he foretold the greatness of the Messianic kingdom (9:11-15).

SEPTEMBER 22: Read Amos 1-5.

Amos 5:10,22-23: "They hate him that rebuketh in the gate, and they abhor him that speaketh uprightly . . . Though ye offer me burnt offerings and your meat offerings, I will not accept them: neither will I regard the peace offerings of your fat beasts. Take thou away from me the noise of thy songs; for I will not hear the melody of thy viols."

The prophecy of Amos seems to have been delivered in Bethel about 30 years before the fall of Israel. Bethel was the religious center of the Northern Kingdom.

From outward appearance, it seemed that the nation of Israel was worshiping God, but in reality, their hearts were far from Him. The Lord spoke through Amos to show them how sadly deceived they had been and appealed to them to "Seek good, and not evil, that ye may live" (5:14). But Amos's message was unwelcome.

Both Amos and Isaiah foretold that vile men would ". . . lay a snare for him [the faithful messenger of God] that reproveth in the gate . . ." (Isaiah 29:21).

"The gate" was a well-known center of business where the elders sat and judged the people. (Compare Jeremiah 17:19; 19:2.) The "faithful messengers" are always a target of much criticism as they make known the terribleness of sin.

It is only through the power of God's Word that we will seek good and not evil. Loving the Lord means loving His Word. Those who receive Him find in His Word the source of their strength.

"He that rejecteth me, and receiveth not my words, hath one that judgeth him: the word that I have spoken, the same shall judge him in the last day" (John 12:48).

NOTE:
3:5 **gin** means trap; 4:1 **kine** means cows; 4:3 **breaches** means breaks in the wall; **smell** means delight; 5:23 **viols** means harps.

Amos 5:25-27: See Acts 7:42,43.

MEMORY VERSE FOR THE WEEK: I John 1:8
"If we say that we have no sin, we deceive ourselves, and the truth is not in us."

INTRODUCTION TO OBADIAH

Obadiah, the shortest book in the Old Testament, reveals God's judgment upon the nation of Edom. It is said that they "rejoiced over the children of Judah in the day of their destruction" and ". . . stood in the crossway, to cut off those . . . that did escape" (verses 12,14). Because of the many attacks which the Edomites made against God's chosen people (see II Chronicles 28:17), the prophet Obadiah foretold that they would be "cut off forever" and "they shall be as though they have not been" (verses 9,16).

Within four years after Jerusalem was defeated, Edom was destroyed.

SEPTEMBER 23: Amos 6-9 through Obadiah 1.
Amos 7:8: "And the Lord said unto me, Amos, what seest thou? And I said, A plumbline. Then said the Lord, Behold, I will set a plumbline in the midst of my people Israel: I will not again pass by them any more."

"The Lord stood upon a wall . . . with a plumbline in his hand" (verse 7).

The plumbline is a line with a weight at one end. The mason (a craftsman who builds with

A PLUMBLINE

stone or brick) uses it to make sure the walls are exactly vertical or upright as they lay the stones one upon another.

God's Word is our plumbline. It must be our guide to make sure our thoughts and ways are upright and in line with God's will. God has said, "Study to show thyself approved unto God, a workman that needeth not to be ashamed, rightly dividing the word of truth" (II Timothy 2:15). Just as a mason uses a plumbline to make sure the wall is straight, the Christian must be just as precise in "rightly dividing" (accurately applying) Bible truths to himself as he would to others, as if Christ Himself held the plumbline of His Word to measure the correctness of our life.

The *wall* was a symbol of separation of the kingdom of Israel from the world, and His prophets were the "plumbline"—ever cutting a straight path for the message of the Truth.

Once again Amos saw the Lord with a plumbline (verse 8). But this time, He was standing on the wall—not to build the wall but to announce its destruction. The wall had become so hopelessly off-center that destruction was the only answer.

How does your life measure up to the Word of God? God's Word is the only accurate "plumbline" for our life, for it reveals God's viewpoint to us.

MEMORY VERSE FOR THE WEEK: I John 1:8
"If we say that we have no sin, we deceive ourselves, and the truth is not in us."

237

"Not every one that saith unto me, Lord, Lord, shall enter into the kingdom of heaven; but he that doeth the will of my Father which is in heaven" (Matthew 7:21).

NOTE:
Obadiah 1:21 **saviours** means deliverers.
Amos 8:9: See Mat. 24:29; Mk. 13:24,25; Lk. 21:26. **9:11-12:** See Acts 15:16-18.

INTRODUCTION TO JONAH
The ministry of Jonah is evidence that it is impossible to escape from God. Jonah expressed deep regret over the salvation of Nineveh. His selfishness and human nature is in contrast to God's mercy and love. Many miss these great lessons by focusing their attention upon the great fish. Christ confirms the story as history as recorded in the Gospels. (See Matthew 12:38-41; 16:4; Luke 11:29-32.)

"But Jonah rose up to flee unto Tarshish from the presence of the Lord, and went down to Joppa. . . ." Jonah 1:3

SEPTEMBER 24: Read Jonah 1-4.
Jonah 1:2: "Arise, go to Nineveh, that great city, and cry against it; for their wickedness is come up before me."

The prophet Jonah had been a good influence in Israel. He had foretold the great military success of King Jeroboam II over the Syrians. These victories resulted in the largest expansion of Israelite territory since the days of King David (see II Kings 14:25).

When God told Jonah to preach His Word in Nineveh, the capital city of Assyria, he ignored Him (1:1-3). Jonah closed his mind to God's command and fled instead to Joppa, Jerusalem's seaport.

Instead of having a pleasant time "getting away from it all," a great storm arose, and the ship in which the prophet was sleeping almost wrecked. Because he was not living according to God's will, he was a cause of confusion and trouble.

The Lord had to bring Jonah through many terrifying experiences before he was willing to do God's will.

Then when the word of the Lord came unto Jonah the second time (see 3:1), he made no objections that the journey to Nineveh was too long, too unpleasant, or too dangerous. Nor did he "flee . . . from the presence of the Lord" (Jonah 1:3).

A successful Christian life can only be lived on the basis of continued obedience to God's revealed Word (Jonah 3:1).

"The men of Nineveh shall rise in judgment with this generation, and shall condemn it: because they repented at the preaching of Jonah; and, behold, a greater than Jonah is here" (Matthew 12:41).

NOTE:
Jonah 1:17: See Mat. 12:39-41; 16:4; Lk. 11:29-30. **2:10:** See Lk. 11:30. **3:5,10:** See Mat. 12:41; Lk. 11:32.

MEMORY VERSE FOR THE WEEK: I John 1:8
"If we say that we have no sin, we deceive ourselves, and the truth is not in us."

INTRODUCTION TO MICAH

Micah prophesied to both Samaria (the capital of Israel) and Jerusalem (the capital of Judah). He lived in Judah during the reigns of Jothan, Ahaz, and Hezekiah. Micah prophesied during the same time as Isaiah; and together, they greatly influenced King Hezekiah in his spiritual reformation (see Jeremiah 26:18). (During this time, Hosea was preaching in the Northern Kingdom.) Micah foretold the fall of Samaria because of their idolatrous ways. The Book of Micah closes with a message of faith in the fulfillment of God's covenant of blessings to Abraham (7:20).

SEPTEMBER 25: Read Micah 1-7.

Micah 5:2: "But thou Bethlehem Ephratah though thou be little among the thousands of Judah, yet out of thee shall he come forth unto me that is to be ruler in Israel; whose goings forth have been from of old, from everlasting."

The birthplace of our Lord was foretold by Micah 700 years before Jesus was born. Micah was the only prophet who specifically said that Christ would be born in Bethlehem. His message to both Judah and Israel looked beyond the judgment to the day when Christ, the Messiah, will reign, and peace will cover the earth.

This is one of the four most significant prophecies relating to the coming Messiah: (1) The Shiloh prophecy designates that the Messiah would come through the tribe of Judah (Genesis 49:10); (2) Nathan said He would be of the family of David (II Samuel 7:26); (3) Daniel announced the exact year (Daniel 9:25); and (4) the fourth prophecy was the answer given to Herod by the scribes when he demanded *where* Christ was to be born (Matthew 2:3-6).

Bethlehem in the Hebrew literally means "House of Bread." *Ephratah* signifies fruitfulness or abundance. So our Lord not only is the *Bread of Life,* but He always satisfies *abundantly.*

The size of Bethlehem is also significant—"little among thousands of Judah." Christ is always born among the "little" ones—in hearts humble enough to confess sin and acknowledge Him as Lord. It is to the meek and lowly in heart that Jesus comes.

"Blessed are the poor in spirit: for theirs is the kingdom of heaven" (Matthew 5:3).

NOTE:

1:6 **discover** means lay bare; 1:7 **hires** means earnings; 1:8 **dragons** means jackals; 1:14 **lie** means deception; 1:16 **poll thee** means cut off your hair; 2:8 **securely** means peaceably; 2:13 **breaker** means destroyer; 4:6 **halteth** means the lame; 6:9 **hear ye the rod** means pay attention to the ruler.

Micah 4:2: See John 6:45. **5:2:** See Mat. 2:5-6; John 7:42. **6:15:** See John 4:37. **7:6:** See Mat. 10:35; Mk. 13:12; Lk. 12:53. **7:18:** See Acts 10:43. **7:20:** See Lk. 1:55,72.

MEMORY VERSE OF THE WEEK: I John 1:9

"If we confess our sins, he is faithful and just to forgive us our sins, and to cleanse us from all unrighteousness."

INTRODUCTION TO NAHUM

Nahum foretold the destruction of Nineveh, the capital of Assyria, which was the greatest military power of his day. Within 50 years, the mighty world empire of Assyria that had destroyed the Northern Kingdom of Israel was conquered by the Babylonians and never again rose to power, as foretold by Nahum.

INTRODUCTION TO HABAKKUK

At the time Habakkuk prophesied, the Temple was still standing (2:20), but he foretold of the rise of the Chaldean power (Babylon) (1:5-6). So it is very likely that Habakkuk witnessed the decline and fall of the Assyrian empire and Babylon's threat to the weak kingdom of Judah.

Habakkuk wondered *why* God did not judge the kingdom of Judah for its idol worship and sinful disobedience to His Word. But he certainly didn't understand *how* God could permit the Chaldeans, who were even more wicked, to punish His people.

In response God revealed that man's limited observation was not capable of seeing how all evildoers would finally perish (2:6-9). So the faithful prophet expressed praise and thanksgiving to God for every situation, knowing that God's righteousness would prevail.

SEPTEMBER 26: Read Nahum 1-3; Habakkuk 1-3.

Nahum 3:7: "And it shall come to pass, that all they that look upon thee shall flee from thee, and say, Nineveh is laid waste: who will bemoan her? Whence shall I see comforters for thee?"

God sent Jonah to Nineveh with the message of judgment about 150 years before Nahum prophesied. Through Jonah's message, Nineveh turned to the Lord. When Nahum prophesied he foretold not only the complete destruction of Nineveh (the capital) but also of the entire Assyrian empire that had ruled for over 500 years.

Nahum boldly proclaimed God's Word, for he recognized God's sovereign control over nations and history. Even though his warning was more severe than Jonah's, the people did not change their sinful ways.

It all happened exactly as Nahum had foretold. Ninevah was destroyed by the armies of the Medes and Babylonians.

"For verily I say unto you, Till heaven and earth pass, one jot or one tittle shall in no wise pass from the law, till all be fulfilled" (Matthew 5:18).

MEMORY VERSE FOR THE WEEK: I John 1:9

"If we confess our sins, he is faithful and just to forgive us our sins, and to cleanse us from all unrighteousness."

240

NOTE:

1:5 **burned** means upheaved; 1:10 **folden together** means as bundles; 1:14 **be sown** means bear children; 2:7 **lead** means mourn; 2:12 **ravin** means torn flesh; 3:19 **bruit** means report.

Habakkuk 1:15 **angle** means hook; 2:6 **thick clay** means pledges; 2:16 **shameful spewing** means disgrace.

Habakkuk **1:5:** See Acts 13:41. **2:3-4:** See Rom. 1:17; Gal. 3:11; Heb. 10:37-38. **2:6:** See Heb. 12:26.

INTRODUCTION TO ZEPHANIAH

Zephaniah was the third cousin of the three kings Jehoahaz, Jehoia-kim, and Zechariah; thus, the prophet had a familiar relationship with the court to which God's message was specifically directed (1:8). His principal work seems to have been in Josiah's reign. Though he dreaded the day of Jehovah which he saw fast approaching, he could look beyond and rejoice in the restoration message. He was among the last prophets before Judah's 70 years of captivity by Nebuchadnezzar.

INTRODUCTION TO HAGGAI AND ZECHARIAH

Both Haggai and Zechariah were undoubtedly born in Babylon during the exile and came to Jerusalem after the decree of King Cyrus.

Haggai and Zechariah turned the nation from their indifference and inspired the people to complete the Temple. (See Ezra 3-6, see also Jeremiah 29:10-11.)

SEPTEMBER 27: Read Zephaniah 1-3; Haggai 1-2.

Haggai 1:1,6: "In the second year of Darius the king, in the sixth month, in the first day of the month, came the word of the Lord by Haggai the prophet unto Zerubbabel . . . saying, . . . Ye have sown much, and bring in little; ye eat, but ye have not enough; ye drink, but ye are not filled with drink; ye clothe you, but there is none warm; and he that earneth wages earneth wages to put it into a bag with holes."

The Israelites who went to Jerusalem because of Cyrus' decree got off to a good start on rebuilding the Temple. During the first year they built the altar and laid the foundation of the Temple.

Then the opposition, ridicule, and plotting by their enemies seemed to have caused the people to give up. But in reality, their devotion to self-interest took the place of their devotion to the Lord. They excused themselves from the work by claiming that the time was not right.

It was not the opposition that had kept them from rebuilding the Temple earlier, but it was the lack of sacrificial devotion to God.

The people of Haggai's day gave the same excuses for not doing the Lord's work that many Christians give today, but the principle is still the same.

We should be devoted to Christ and His interest if we expect the Lord's blessings. (See Matthew 6:33 and Colossians 3:1.) When we do, we can rest assured that He will take care of us.

MEMORY VERSE FOR THE WEEK: I John 1:9

"If we confess our sins, he is faithful and just to forgive us our sins, and to cleanse us from all unrighteousness."

"But seek ye first the kingdom of God, and his righteousness; and all these things shall be added unto you" (Matthew 6:33).

NOTE:
1:7 **bid** means consecrated; 1:9 **leap on the threshhold** means entering houses to steal; 1:14 **hasteth greatly** means coming quickly; 2:3 **wrought** means kept; 2:14 **bittern** means porcupine.

> ". . . If ye have faith as a grain of mustard seed, ye shall say unto this mountain, Remove hence to yonder place; and it shall remove; and nothing shall be impossible unto you."
> Matthew 17:20

SEPTEMBER 28: Read Zechariah 1-7.

Zechariah 4:6-7: "Then he answered and spake unto me, saying, This is the word of the Lord unto Zerubbabel, saying, Not by might, nor by power, but by my spirit, saith the Lord of hosts. Who art thou, *O great mountain?* before Zerubbabel thou shalt become a plain: and he shall bring forth the headstone thereof with shoutings, crying, Grace, grace unto it."

The foundation of the Temple that lay desolate for 14 years was a testimony of incomplete obedience and an unfinished task. Therefore, God raised up the prophets Haggai and Zechariah (Ezra 5:1) to rebuke the Jews for their complacency and to challenge them to finish rebuilding the Temple (Haggai 1:3-11). "And the elders of the Jews builded, and they *prospered* through the prophesying of Haggai . . . and Zechariah . . ." (Ezra 6:14). This time they ignored the threats of their enemies and completed the Temple.

The word *mountain* is a symbol of the great obstacles and powers that face Christians. (Note Isaiah 40:4; 49:11; Daniel 2:35,45.) All the mountain-like obstacles vanished as the people believed and obeyed God's Word.

God revealed to Zerubbabel the source of power by which any work of God is accomplished. It is "not by might, nor by power, but by my spirit, saith the Lord of hosts." The words *might* and *power* express human strength —such as well-trained and skilled leadership. But God is not dependent upon numbers or human wisdom.

God's Spirit can perfect *His* strength in the weakest believer. This He made clear to the apostle Paul saying, ". . . My grace is sufficient for thee: for my strength is made perfect in weakness . . ." (II Corinthians 12:9; see also Hosea 1:7; Hebrews 11:34).

NOTE:
1:21 **fray** means terrify; 6:3 **grizzled and bay** means active and strong. **Zechariah 3:8:** See Mat. 2:23. **6:12:** See John 1:45.

SEPTEMBER 29: Read Zechariah 8-14.

Zechariah 9:9: *"Rejoice greatly,* O daughter of Zion; shout, O daughter of Jerusalem: behold, thy King cometh unto thee: he is just, and having *salvation;* lowly, and riding upon an ass, and upon a colt the foal of an ass."

MEMORY VERSE FOR THE WEEK: I John 1:9

"If we confess our sins, he is faithful and just to forgive us our sins, and to cleanse us from all unrighteousness."

The words "Behold, thy king cometh" abound in every chapter of the book of Zechariah's prophecy. His prophetic message extends far beyond the restoration of the small Jewish nation to the coming of the King of kings when all "nations shall be joined to the Lord" (2:11).

In the Gospel of Matthew we read, "All this was done, that it might be fulfilled which was spoken by the prophet" (Matthew 21:4).

Zechariah's prophecy was fulfilled in part when Jesus entered Jerusalem, "riding upon an ass, and upon a colt the foal of an ass." It was His formal presentation as their King. But the Messianic cry "Hosanna" was soon changed to "the prophet from Nazareth," and that was soon changed to the final cry of rejection—"Crucify Him!"

It is the second coming of Christ the King, in all His glory, that will complete the fulfillment of His dominion from sea to sea, even to the ends of the earth. (Reread Zechariah 9:9-10.)

"Tell ye the daughter of Zion, Behold, thy King cometh unto thee, meek, and sitting upon an ass, and a colt the foal of an ass" (Matthew 21:5).

NOTE:
14:2 **rifled** means robbed; 14:8 **former** means eastern; **hinder** means western; 14:21 **seethe** means boil.

Zechariah 8:16: See Eph. 4:25. **9:9:** See Mat. 21:5; John 12:15. **9:11:** See Mat. 26: 28; Mk. 14:24; Lk. 22:20. **11:12-13:** See Mat. 27:9-10. **12:10:** See John 19:37. **12:12:** See Mat. 24:30. **13:1:** See Acts 10:43. **13:7:** See Mat. 26:31; Mk. 14:27. **14:5:** See Jude 14. **14:8:** See John 7:38.

INTRODUCTION TO MALACHI

Malachi was the final voice of the Old Testament prophets. Probably several generations had passed since the days of Haggai and Zechariah, who also had returned to Jerusalem as recorded in Ezra and Nehemiah.

The early zeal for rebuilding the Temple had died out. Religious indifference, mixed marriages (2:10-12), and failure to pay tithes (3:8-10) were conditions that developed during the time of Ezra and Nehemiah (Ezra 7, Nehemiah 13) but had continued to grow worse.

The spiritual decline probably arose from the disappointment of the people for an immediate, glorious Messianic kingdom. Malachi appealed to the people to return to their faith in God's Word and confirmed a future Messianic kingdom.

SEPTEMBER 30: Read Malachi 1-4.
Malachi 3:1-2: "Behold, I will send my messenger, and he shall prepare the way before me: and the Lord, whom ye seek, shall suddenly come to his temple, even the messenger of the covenant, whom ye delight in: behold, he shall come, saith the Lord of hosts. But who may abide the day of his coming? and who shall stand when he appeareth? for he is like a refiner's fire, and like fullers' soap."

MEMORY VERSE FOR THE WEEK: I John 1:9
"If we confess our sins, he is faithful and just to forgive us our sins, and to cleanse us from all unrighteousness."

Malachi had foretold of a coming messenger (John the Baptist) "who would prepare the way" for the "messenger of the covenant"—meaning the Messiah. (See Matthew 11:10; Mark 1:2; Luke 1:76; 7:27.)

Malachi announced that Christ "shall suddenly come to his temple." The sudden coming means that He would come in a way that the people would not expect. They assumed he would deliver the Jews from Roman control and set up His earthly kingdom.

The Messiah's mission would be like "a refiner's fire," separating the godly from the ungodly, beginning at Christ's first coming to earth and continuing to the Second Coming (Matthew 25:31-46).

John the Baptist announced this purging of His people saying, "Whose fan is in his hand, and he will thoroughly purge his floor, and gather his wheat into the garner; but he will burn up the chaff with unquenchable fire" (Matthew 3:12).

NOTE:
3:13 stout means arrogant.

Malachi 1:2-3: See Rom. 9:13. **3:1:** See Mat. 11:10; Mk. 1:2-3; Lk. 1:76; 7:27. **4:2:** See Lk. 1:78. **4:5-6:** See Mat. 11:14; 17:10-11; Mk. 9:11-12; Lk. 1:17.

BIBLICAL REFERENCE INDEX
PRAYERS OF THE PROPHETS

PROPHETIC REFERENCES TO CHRIST

Daniel 9:25	The time of the Messiah's birth	Matt. 2:1,2
Hosea 11:1	His flight into Egypt	Matt. 2:15
Micah 5:1	Christ to be smitten	Matt. 27:30
Micah 5:2	To be born in Bethlehem	Luke 2:4-7
Zech. 9:9	Triumphal entry to be on an ass	Mark 11:7-11
Zech. 11:12	Christ to be sold for 30 pieces of silver	Matt. 26:15
Zech. 12:10	His side, hands, and feet to be pierced	John 19:34; 20:27
Zech. 13:7		Matt. 26:31,56

THE PROPHETS

The entire period of the Prophets covers about 400 years.

There are 17 books of the Prophets and 16 prophets (Jeremiah wrote two—Jeremiah, and Lamentations).

Amos, Hosea .... To Israel
Jonah, Nahum .... To Nineveh
Daniel .... To Babylon
Ezekiel .... To the captives in Babylon
Obadiah .... To Edom
Isaiah, Jeremiah, Joel, Micah, Habakkuk,
Zephaniah, Haggai, Zechariah, Malachi .... To Judah

INTRODUCTION TO THE GOSPELS

Not one of the Gospels can be omitted, nor could they be united without serious loss to the greatness of our wonderful Lord.

MATTHEW

Matthew, a Jew, was writing to the Jews about their Messiah-King. He alone told of the wise men inquiring, "Where is he that is born King?" (2:2). He was the only writer who presented Jesus as being legally entitled to the throne of David and fulfilling the Messiah requirements concerning the Abrahamic covenant. As evidence, he established the genealogy back to David and on to Abraham.

More of what Jesus said is recorded in Matthew than in the other Gospels because the words of a king are of utmost importance. Throughout the Gospel of Matthew, the kingdom of heaven is prominent. Both John the Baptist and our Lord began by proclaiming, "The kingdom of heaven is at hand"; yet, neither explained what the kingdom was because the Jews were familiar with the Old Testament prophets who foretold of the Messiah's reign over a reunited kingdom. The phrase "That it might be fulfilled" is recorded thirty-eight times, referring to the Old Testament prophets to confirm that Jesus was the Messiah-Savior of the world. With all this undisputable evidence, they crucified their King.

MARK

Mark was part Jew and part Gentile, as his name, John Mark, indicates. He portrayed the rapid activities of Jesus as the servant of God. Since the genealogy is of little interest to a servant, Mark did not record one.

There is nothing in Mark concerning the wise men seeking a king or of angels announcing the birth of the new King. Nothing is mentioned of His denounciation of the cities of Galilee, or of the scribes and Pharisees for rejecting their King. The word "straightway," showing His actions, occurs 43 times since the *work* of Jesus rather than His *words* is the qualification of a servant.

Only in Mark are the hands of Jesus prominent, portraying the actions of a servant. When the Lord healed Peter's mother-in-law, he "took her by the hand" (1:31). At Bethany He took the blind man by the hand and afterwards put His hands on him (8:23). In healing the demoniac son, Jesus took him by the hand (9:27). In healing the deaf and dumb, He put His fingers in his ears.

Although the title "Lord" is addressed to Christ more than 70 times in the other three Gospels, Mark never mentioned it once until after His resurrection. The only exceptions are the Syrophoenician woman, which carries the thought of "Sir" rather than "Lord" (7:24-28), and the blind man, where the meaning is "Rabbi" (10:51). Not until The Servant had finished His work on earth was Christ called "Lord" in the book of Mark.

LUKE

Luke, a Gentile, addressed his book to a Gentile named Theophilus. He gave special attention to the Man Jesus. No other Gospel gives the details of the many human aspects of Jesus as did Luke, who told us about the parents and the birth of Christ's cousin, John the Baptist. Luke gave the details of the journey of Mary and Joseph to Bethlehem for Christ's birth (2:1-7), and how He was "laid in a manger" (2:7).

Only the book of Luke tells how the baby Jesus was presented for circumcision in the Temple (2:21-24), of His conversation with the doctors at the age of twelve (2:42-46), and how He "increased in wisdom and stature, and favor with God and man" (2:52).

Luke gave us the genealogy of Christ—not only back to Abraham, father of the Jews, but back to Adam, the first man. Through the actual, physical genealogy of Mary, Christ is linked with *all* the human race.

In Luke we see Jesus' human dependence upon the Father in prayer (3:21; 5:16; 6:12; 9:16, 18, 28, 29; 10:21; 11:1; 22:17, 19; 23:46; 24:30).

Matthew presented Him as King; Mark, as a Servant of God; Luke, as the Son of Man; and John, as the preexistent God.

"... we are come to worship him." Matthew 2:2

OCTOBER 1: Read Matthew 1-4.

Matthew 2:1, 2: ". . . behold, there came wise men from the east to Jerusalem, saying, Where is he that is born King of the Jews? for we have seen his star in the east, and are come to worship him."

The wise men made the long, difficult journey from the east to Jerusalem in search for the promised Messiah. They were probably surprised and disappointed that no one in the City of the Kings was aware of the Messiah's birth. Perhaps it was an even greater surprise that, although the chief priests and scribes knew of the prophecy that Christ would be born in Bethlehem, they were unimpressed with what had taken place.

We find no record of any of the chief priests or scribes following the wise men to the home of Mary and Joseph. But the wise men did not hesitate to present their gifts of wealth as they knelt in that poor, peasant abode.

Until the heart is right, man's reasoning will always misguide him, regardless of how much he may know. Most people react as did Herod—"troubled" about any special interest we may give to Christ. Others, like the chief priests, are satisfied by merely reciting historic facts. But the "wise men" of today will be satisfied with nothing less than His presence. They will gladly sacrifice personal pleasure and all else for the privilege of giving their very best for Him.

MEMORY VERSE FOR THE WEEK: I John 1:9

"If we confess our sins, he is faithful and just to forgive us our sins, and to cleanse us from all unrighteousness."

"... His name shall be called Wonderful, Counselor, The mighty God, The everlasting Father, The Prince of Peace" (Isaiah 9:6).

NOTE:

1:18 **espoused** means engaged; 1:19 **privily** means secretly; 2:6 **rule** means feed; 3:8 **fruits meet for repentance** means a life conforming to true repentance; 3:12 **garner** means barn; 3:15 **suffered** means permitted; 4:24 **divers** means various.

Matthew 1:23: See Isa. 7:14. **2:6:** See Mic. 5:2. **2:15:** See Hos. 11:1. **2:18:** See Jer. 31:15. **3:3:** See Isa. 40:3. **4:4:** See Deu. 8:3. **4:6:** See Ps. 91:11-12. **4:7:** See Deu. 6:16. **4:10:** See Deu. 6:13. **4:15-16:** See Isa. 9:1-2; 42:7.

OCTOBER 2: Read Matthew 5-6.

Matthew 5:39, 44: "But I say unto you, That ye resist not evil: but whosoever shall smite thee on thy right cheek, turn to him the other also. . . . But I say unto you, Love your enemies, bless them that curse you, do good to them that hate you, and pray for them which despitefully use you, and persecute you."

Revenge and hatred are always wrong because God has reserved for Himself the right of vengeance. When we avenge our wrongs, we take God's authority away from Him. Instead, we are to be willing to suffer injury and commit our injustices to Him, who is the Judge of all earth.

When Christ said, "resist not evil," He was not forbidding lawful means of protecting our rights or apprehending and punishing illegal acts by offenders. Officers of the law are the ministers of God to maintain justice and arrest violaters (see Romans 13:3-4). Furthermore, He did not mean that we should not take a stand against the evils of sin and the temptations of Satan.

When you are faced with unjustified injury, pray that your reactions will harmonize with the example of Christ, "Who, when he was reviled, reviled not again; when he suffered, he threatened not; but committed himself to him that judgeth righteously" (I Peter 2:23).

Christ solemnly warned us that if we forgive not men their trespasses, neither will God forgive ours (see Matthew 6:15).

"Dearly beloved, avenge not yourselves, but rather give place unto wrath: for it is written, Vengeance is mine; I will repay, saith the Lord" (Romans 12:19).

NOTE:

5:13 **savor** means strength; 5:18 **one jot or one tittle** means dot of the i or cross of the t; 5:22 **Raca** means vain fellow; 5:23 **aught** means anything; 5:26 **farthing** means fraction of a penny; 5:31 **put away** means divorce; 5:47 **salute** means greet; 6:1 **alms** means gifts to the poor and needy; 6:7 **vain repetitions** means meaningless words; 6:25 **Take no thought** means Do not worry.

Matthew 5:21: See Ex. 20:13. **5:27:** See Ex. 20:14. **5:31:** See Deu. 24:1. **5:33:** See Lev. 19:12. **5:38:** See Ex. 21:24. **5:43:** See Lev. 19:18. **5:48:** See Gen. 17:1.

MEMORY VERSE FOR THE WEEK: Matthew 5:3-4

"Blessed are the poor in spirit; for theirs is the kingdom of heaven. Blessed are they that mourn: for they shall be comforted."

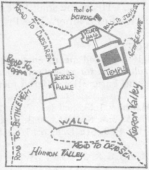

OCTOBER 3: Read Matthew 7-9.

Matthew 7:13, 14: "Enter ye in at the strait gate: for wide is the gate, and broad is the way, that leadeth to destruction, and many there be which go in thereat: Because strait is the gate, and narrow is the way, which leadeth unto life, and few there be that find it."

It is generally assumed that heaven can be obtained on much easier terms than those prescribed by our Lord. Many in this twentieth-century generation believe they can be good Christians without being born again (note John 3:3, 5). Not many people believe that if they 'live after the flesh they shall die: but if they through the Spirit do mortify the deeds of the body, they shall live' (Romans 8:13). "The broad way" is filled with those who live under the control of their earthly nature. The few are "led by the Spirit of God" (Romans 8:14).

Many falsely believe they *can* serve two masters or *can* succeed in "making the best of two worlds." They do not believe the way is as "narrow" as Christ declared it to be. They are on the broad way. The gate is "wide," and those who enter that gate reject His Word, insisting that as long as they are sincere, it doesn't really matter what they believe.

"There is a way which seemeth right unto a man; but the end thereof are the ways of death" (Proverbs 14:12).

NOTE:
7:2 **mete** means hand it out; 7:5 **mote** means speck; 7:13 **strait** means narrow; 9:9 **receipt of custom** means tax collector's office; 9:10 **at meat** means eating.

Matthew 7:23: See Ps. 6:8. **8:17:** See Isa. 53:4. **9:13; 12:7:** See Hos. 6:6.

OCTOBER 4: Read Matthew 10-11.

Matthew 11:10-11: "For this is he, of whom it is written, Behold, I send my messenger before thy face, which shall prepare thy way before thee. Verily I say unto you, Among them that are born of women there hath not risen a greater than John the Baptist . . ."

In prison John the Baptist evidently began wondering if Jesus were indeed the Messiah. He therefore sent two of his remaining disciples to ask Jesus if He really was the Messiah "or do we look for another?" (11:3).

Jesus answered John's question, saying, "Go and shew John again those things which ye do hear and see: The blind receive their sight . . . the lepers are cleansed, and the deaf hear . . . and blessed is he, whosoever shall not be offended in me" (11:4-6).

It seems that many of the people rejected John because he was stern and crude. At the same time they rejected Jesus because He was just the opposite —too sociable, "a friend of publicans and sinners" (Matthew 11:19; Luke 7:34). The fact is, a vast majority reject the message of God's love, no

MEMORY VERSE FOR THE WEEK: Matthew 5:3-4

"Blessed are the poor in spirit; for theirs is the kingdom of heaven. Blessed are they that mourn: for they shall be comforted."

matter how it is presented. It is always so. God's message is to the few humble and lowly who are willing to confess their sins and respond to God's message of love.

". . . Verily I say unto you, Except ye be converted, and become as little children, ye shall not enter into the kingdom of heaven" (Matthew 18:3).

NOTE:
10:35 **at variance** means in conflict.

Matthew 11:10: See Mal. 3:1.

OCTOBER 5: Read Matthew 12.

Matthew 12:40: "For as Jonah was three days and three nights in the whale's belly; so shall the Son of man be three days and three nights in the heart of the earth."

Christ, who knew the truth about all things, quoted from the book of Jonah as the very Word of God and declared unhesitatingly that Jonah had been in the belly of the great fish.

The Lord not only acknowledged the validity of Jonah's experience of being swallowed by a great fish, but He used it as a prophecy of His own death, burial, and resurrection.

The people of Nineveh believed Jonah the prophet and repented, but the people of Israel would not repent, even though there was One greater than Jonah who preached to them.

The ministry of Christ was saturated with the words of the Old Testament. He revealed how "all the scriptures" speak of Him, thus removing any doubt as to whether the Old Testament is the Word of God.

How great is the foolishness of those who question the Scriptures and profess to be wiser than Jesus Christ Himself!

"And beginning at Moses and all the prophets, he expounded unto them in all the scriptures the things concerning himself" (Luke 24:27).

NOTE:
12:29 **spoil his goods** means take away his possessions; 12:44 **garnished** means put in order.

Matthew 12:18-21: See Isa. 42:1-4.

OCTOBER 6: Read Matthew 13-14.

Matthew 13:3-8: ". . . Behold, a sower went forth to sow; . . . some seed fell by the wayside, . . . some fell upon stony places, . . . some fell among thorns; . . . But other fell into good ground . . ."

Great multitudes were gathered to hear Jesus, and in order to reveal the spiritual condition of their hearts, Jesus told a parable. He told of four kinds

MEMORY VERSE FOR THE WEEK: Matthew 5:5-6

"Blessed are the meek: for they shall inherit the earth. Blessed are they which do hunger and thirst after righteousness: for they shall be filled."

of responses to hearing His Word, and then explained why so few were receptive.

Some react with a self-destroying indifference to His Word—the seed fell "by the wayside" (13:19).

Others seem so receptive to His Word—"straightway it sprang up." Oh, what joyful enthusiasm! How swift the growth! The "convert" appears so promising, so full of life. But within a few months, or even a matter of days, it is difficult to detect any sign of life, for it fell "into stony places" (13:20). Since there was no true depth, all interest vanished when they were faced with "tribulation or persecution . . . because of the Word" (13:21).

Still others are deceived by "the care of this world, and the deceitfulness of riches" (13:22). This conflict of seed among the thorns exposes a double-minded man who is neither indifferent like the first nor shallow like the second, but other interests hold equal devotion within his heart. The tragic result is the "word of God" is choked and becomes unfruitful.

The devil, the flesh, and the world are portrayed as the three hindrances that destroy fruitfulness among three types of people who hear the Word.

But some "fell into good ground." These "received with meekness the engrafted word, which is able to save the soul." Our fruitfulness is dependent upon how much of His Word controls our life to accomplish His will.

"No man can serve two masters. . . . Ye cannot serve God and mammon" (Matthew 6:24).

NOTE:
13:5 **waxed gross** means become callous; 13:25 **tares** means weeds; 14:8 **charger** means platter.

Matthew 13:14-15. See Isa. 6:9-10. **13:35:** See Ps. 78:2.

OCTOBER 7: Read Matthew 15-17.
Matthew 15:7-8: "Ye hypocrites, well did Esaias (Isaiah) prophesy of you, saying, This people draweth nigh unto me with their mouth, and honoreth me with their lips; but their heart is far from me."

More than 700 years had passed since the prophet Isaiah had exposed the worship of the backslidden Israelite nation as hypocritical and insincere. God was accepted in theology, but sincere worship was no longer practiced (see Isaiah 29:13).

The Lord quoted the same harsh words that Isaiah spoke when they asked Him, "Why do thy disciples transgress the tradition of the elders?" He told them there was another question which must be answered first. "Why do ye also transgress the commandment of God by your tradition?" (15:3). Our

---

Lord exposed the hypocrisy of the scribes and Pharisees who were more concerned with backing their philosophies than they were in teaching the true Word of God, saying, "But in vain they do worship me, teaching for doctrines the commandments of men" (15:9).

Religion as practiced by many today is not too different from the position of those Christ rebuked. They go to church, go through the rites and rituals, but their heart isn't in it.

Notice as you read the Gospels that our Lord did not choose doctors of the law or scribes to be His apostles. They were convinced that they already had all the answers—too much to *unlearn* to be useful. The Lord can only teach those whose hearts are hungry and willing to listen to Him.

"Therefore if any man be in Christ, he is a new creature: old things are passed away; behold, all things are become new" (II Corinthians 5:17).

NOTE:
16:6 **leaven** means teaching; 16:23 **savorest not** means understand not.

Matthew 15:4: See Ex. 20:12. **15:4:** See Ex. 21:17. **15:8-9:** See Isa. 29:13.

OCTOBER 8: Read Matthew 18-20.

Matthew 18:34-35: "And his lord was wroth, and delivered him to the tormentors . . . So likewise shall my heavenly Father do also unto you, if ye from your hearts forgive not every one his brother their trespasses."

Peter thought there should be a reasonable limitation to forgiving another's persistent sins against him. But Christ replied that his forgiving spirit was not to be limited to seven offenses, but should extend seventy times seven (meaning, without limitation—see 18:21-22).

The Lord's response was a parable that exposed how small someone else's trespasses are against us compared to how much we have been forgiven by God. When we hold resentment, hatred, or jealousy in our hearts, we tend to forget our own great sinfulness against the Lord.

God knows us as we really are, not as we want to see ourselves. In view of this, how can we not forgive others?

Even in prayer the Lord taught us to pray, "Father . . . forgive us . . . as we forgive . . ." (Matthew 6:9, 12). It is a very serious thing of eternal consequence to hold *any* unforgiveness in our hearts. If we see a sin being committed, we must realize that it is the sin that is to be condemned. We are admonished to forgive the sinner.

When we truly see how much we have been forgiven, see ourselves for what we really are, there will be an unlimited spirit of compassion and forgiveness toward everyone for anything.

"If a man say, I love God, and hateth his brother, he is a liar: for he that loveth not his brother whom he hath seen, how can he love God whom he hath not seen?" (I John 4:20).

MEMORY VERSE FOR THE WEEK: Matthew 5:5-6
"Blessed are the meek: for they shall inherit the earth. Blessed are they which do hunger and thirst after righteousness: for they shall be filled."

NOTE:
19:8 **suffered** means permitted; 20:3 **third hour** means nine a.m.; 20:26 **minister** means servant.

Matthew 19:4: See Gen. 1:27. **19:5:** See 2:24. **19:18:** See Ex. 20:13. **19:19:** See Ex. 20:12; Lev. 19:18.

OCTOBER 9: Read Matthew 21-22.

"And when they came nigh to Jerusalem, unto Bethphage and Bethany, at the mount of Olives, he sendeth forth two of his disciples . . . And they brought the colt to Jesus, and cast their garments on him; and he sat upon him."   Mark 11:1, 7

Matthew 21:4-5: "All this was done, that it might be fulfilled which was spoken by the prophet, saying, Tell ye the daughter of Zion, Behold, thy King cometh unto thee, meek, and sitting upon an ass, and a colt the foal of an ass."

More than five hundred years before this event, the prophet Zechariah had foretold that the King of Kings would one day appear, "riding upon an ass" (Zechariah 9:9). How different from what

most kings would expect! The garments of the disciples and the branches of the multitude could not compare to the gorgeous array with which other kings might display their power. Even the animal on which the Messiah-King made His royal entry into Jerusalem was lowly. Indeed, nothing could be plainer or less pretentious than this memorable event that fulfilled prophecy! How seldom humility and meekness are recognized as essential principles of true greatness!

We will find a new joy in our Christian life when we learn to yield our will to the care of God as His submissive servants. If this seems difficult, it is often because of a false pride of self-importance which still exists.

Jesus said, ". . . learn of me; for I am meek and lowly in heart . . ." (Matthew 11:29). Then, on another occasion, He went a step further in teaching humility, saying, "And whosoever will be chief among you, let him be your servant: Even as the Son of man came not to be ministered unto, but to minister . . ." (Matthew 20:27-28).

NOTE:
21:8 **strewed** means spread; 21:33 **husbandmen** means tenants; 22:6 **remnant** means others; 22:20 **superscription** means likeness; 22:25 **issue** means children.

Matthew 21:5: See Isa. 62:11; Zec. 9:9. **21:9:** See Ps. 118:26. **21:13:** See Isa. 56:7; Jer. 7:11. **21:16:** See Ps. 8:2. **21:42:** See Ps. 118:22-23. **22:24:** See Deu. 25:5. **22:32:** See Ex. 3:6. **22:37:** See Deu. 6:5. **22:39:** See Lev. 19:18. **22:44:** See Ps. 110:1.

MEMORY VERSE FOR THE WEEK: Matthew 5:7-8
    "Blessed are the merciful: for they shall obtain mercy. Blessed are the pure in heart: for they shall see God."

OCTOBER 10: Read Matthew 23-24.

Matthew 24:35: "Heaven and earth shall pass away, but my words shall not pass away."

Much of what man creates or writes today will be of little or no value in a few years. Everything around us will soon be gone, and in this age of uncertainties, the Bible is the reliable and unchanging guide for our lives. God has made it emphatically clear that His Word "shall not pass away."

"All scripture is given by inspiration of God . . ." (II Timothy 3:16). This removes any basis for comparing the Scriptures to any other writings. ". . . It is written, Man shall not live by bread alone, but by every word that proceedeth out of the mouth of God" (Matthew 4:4). As we read His Word, it *proceedeth* (not *has* proceeded, but *proceedeth,* and is still proceeding) out of His mouth—alive and fresh to all who hunger and thirst to know His will. We must recognize this fact, for it removes all doubt of the importance of *every word,* from Genesis to Revelation. The living God has fellowship with His children, and He speaks to them in living power through His Word.

"Who also hath made us able ministers of the new testament; not of the letter, but of the spirit: for the letter killeth, but the spirit giveth life" (II Corinthinas 3:6).

NOTE:

23:5 **phylacteries** means small boxes containing religious texts; 23:15 **proselyte** means convert; 24:43 **suffered** means allowed; 24:45 **meat in due season** means food at the right time.

Matthew 23:39: See Ps. 118:26.

OCTOBER 11: Read Matthew 25-26.

Matthew 26:39: "And he went a little farther, and fell on his face, and prayed, saying, O my Father, if it be possible, let this cup pass from me: nevertheless not as I will, but as thou wilt."

Night (New Testament)	
First Watch, **evening**	= 6 to 9 p.m.
Second Watch, **midnight**	= 9 to 12 p.m.
Third Watch, **cock-crow**	= 12 to 3 a.m.
Fourth Watch, **morning**	= 3 to 6 a.m.
Day (New Testament)	
Third hour	= 6 to 9 a.m.
Sixth hour	= 9 to 12 midday
Ninth hour	= 12 to 3 p.m.
Twelfth hour	= 3 to 6 p.m.

From beginning to end, Christ's life, as well as this prayer, was in perfect submission to the heavenly Father. God did not answer His prayer by removing the cup, but by supplying the strength to bear it, and ultimately by being resurrected (see Hebrews 5:7).

After His prayer, Jesus returned to the sleeping disciples. Perhaps Jesus singled out Peter for particular counsel because of his recent, self-confident boasting and urged him to "watch and pray." He knew that Peter's spirit was willing, but He also knew the flesh was weak (see Matthew 26:41).

Obedience to His Word and dependence upon prayer is a means God uses to strengthen us in the hour of testing. There may come a time when the Lord will say to anyone who has ignored His Word and failed to pray, "Sleep

MEMORY VERSE FOR THE WEEK: Matthew 5:7-8

"Blessed are the merciful: for they shall obtain mercy. Blessed are the pure in heart: for they shall see God."

on now." This was not said in irony. He simply meant that the opportunity to pray about a particular given crisis often passes before we are willing to take action to pray about it.

On the last night of His earthly life, Jesus did not sleep. Instead, "he went a little farther" apart from His disciples and prayed alone, first kneeling, then falling upon His face. He prayed intensely, ". . . Not as I will, but as thou wilt." How long He remained in prayer we do not know, but His prayer was no mere ritual, for "his sweat was as it were great drops of blood falling down to the ground" (see Luke 22:41-44).

"Be careful for nothing; but in every thing by prayer and supplication with thanksgiving let your requests be made known unto God" (Philippians 4:6).

NOTE:
25:27 **usury** means interest; 26:4 **subtilty** means trickery; 26:63 **I adjure thee** means I command thee under oath.

Matthew 26:31: See Zec. 13:7.

OCTOBER 12: Read Matthew 27-28.
Matthew 28:6: "He is not here: for he is risen, as he said. Come, see the place where the Lord lay."

As Mary Magdalene and others approached the tomb, the angel of the Lord rolled back the stone from the entrance. The triumphant resurrection of Jesus Christ had already taken place when the angel announced to the astounded women, "He is risen, as he said." Jesus Christ is alive and reigning in the midst of His disciples today.

When Jesus rose from the dead, He did not go to those who had crucified Him so He could prove how wrong they had been, but He went to those who loved Him. Would we have done the same, or would we have wanted to prove to Pilate and the Pharisees how wrong they were? Christ sought fellowship with His believers. They needed His encouragement, comfort, and confidence to tell others whose hearts were open to God's love.

As we recognize His authority, we will obey His last command: "Go ye therefore, and teach all nations, baptizing them in the name of the Father, and of the Son, and of the Holy Ghost: Teaching them to observe all things whatsoever I have commanded you." Then we can be assured of His pleasure and presence as He said, "Lo, I am with you always, even unto the end of the world. Amen" (Matthew 28:19-20).

NOTE:
27:15 **wont** means accustomed; 27:24 **tumult** means riot.

Matthew 27:9-10: See Zec. 11:12-13. **27:35:** See Ps. 22:18. **27:46:** See Ps. 22:1.

MEMORY VERSE FOR THE WEEK: Matthew 5:7-8
"Blessed are the merciful: for they shall obtain mercy. Blessed are the pure in heart: for they shall see God."

OCTOBER 13: Read Mark 1-3.

Mark 1:40-41: "And there came a leper to him, beseeching him, and kneeling down to him, and saying unto him, If thou wilt, thou canst make me clean. And Jesus, moved with compassion, put forth his hand, and touched him, and saith unto him, I will; be thou clean."

At least thirty-four of the miracles which Jesus performed were recorded in detail in the Gospels. He healed many victims of fever, leprosy, palsy, withered limbs, restored speech, hearing, and sight, and cast out many demons. But perhaps the most touching of all His miracles was the healing of this leper. No disease was assumed to be more absolutely incurable, so loathsome and dreaded, as leprosy. Lepers were known as "untouchables," and if anyone went near them, they had to cry out, "Unclean, unclean."

Of all the Gospel writers, only Mark tells us that Jesus was "moved with compassion" and out went the loving hand to the decayed flesh to this leper. Jesus could have healed him by just speaking a word, but instead, He *touched* this lonely, miserable man who was "full of leprosy" (Luke 5:12).

Throughout the entire Biblical times, only a miracle of God could heal this terrible disease of leprosy (Numbers 12:13). Just one touch of the Master's hand and the leper's entire body was cleansed. Even so, the Master alone can touch the sinner and cleanse him from sin.

". . . They that are whole have no need of the physician, but they that are sick. I came not to call the righteous, but sinners to repentance" (Mark 2:17).

NOTE:
1:26 **torn** means thrown; 1:43 **straitly charged** means strictly directed; 2:15 **publicans** means tax collectors; 2:19 **children** means guests; 2:26 **showbread** means bread dedicated for worship.

Mark 1:2: See Mal. 3:1. **1:3:** See Isa. 40:3.

OCTOBER 14: Read Mark 4-5.

Mark 5:15: "And they come to Jesus, and see him that was possessed with the devil, and had the legion, sitting, and clothed, and in his right mind: and they were afraid."

This man had been dwelling among the tombs, the burial places of the dead. To even touch a grave polluted a person (Numbers 19:16), so the unclean spirits had driven this man into the place of defilement.

MEMORY VERSE FOR THE WEEK: Matthew 5:7-8
"Blessed are the merciful: for they shall obtain mercy. Blessed are the pure in heart: for they shall see God."

When Jesus cast out the demons from this man, He permitted them to enter a herd of swine, which in turn caused the swine to run violently into the sea and be killed. This was a vivid illustration of how Satan destroys whatever he touches, of how this man was being violently destroyed until he was set free by our Lord's Word.

At the words of Christ, this demon-possessed man ran to Jesus and worshiped Him, and his life was transformed. This demon-controlled person presents a picture of every unsaved person who, in some way, is under the control and mastery of Satan and his evil forces.

Men sometimes think that a single individual doesn't count for very much, but God and the devil both think differently. The devil thought it worthwhile to let a whole legion of demons take possession of one man. Christ considered this man so precious that He was willing to be rejected by an entire city in order to deliver him from Satan's stronghold. What a transformation takes place when we respond to the Word of the Prince of Peace!

"The Lord is not slack concerning his promise, as some men count slackness; but is long-suffering to us-ward, not willing that any should perish, but that all should come to repentance" (II Peter 3:9).

NOTE:
Mark 4:12: See Isa. 6:9-10.

> "Let this mind be in you, which was also in Christ Jesus: Who . . . made himself of no reputation, and took upon him the form of a servant . . . Wherefore God also hath highly exalted him . . ." Phil. 2:5-9

OCTOBER 15: Read Mark 6-7.
Mark 7:21-23: "For from within, out of the heart of men, proceed evil thoughts, adulteries, fornications, murders, thefts, covetousness, wickedness, deceit, lasciviousness, an evil eye, blasphemy, pride, foolishness: all these evil things come from within, and defile the man."

We deceive ourselves when we say there is no harm in evil thoughts that are never expressed, for "as he thinketh in his *heart, so is he*" (Proverb 23:7). Christ solemnly declared that deceit, pride, and covetousness in the heart defile the man just as much as adulteries and murders.

We have the responsibility of keeping our hearts with diligence, "for out of it are the issues of life" (Proverbs 4:23). "To keep the heart" is to "bring" into captivity *every* thought to the obedience of Christ" (II Corinthians 10:5) so that our lives are a practical expression of the indwelling Christ.

MEMORY VERSE FOR THE WEEK: Matthew 5:7-8
"Blessed are the merciful: for they shall obtain mercy. Blessed are the pure in heart: for they shall see God."

Not only is the Word of God the *life-giving* factor, ("being born again . . . by the word of God"—I Peter 1:23), but it is also a *life-keeping* factor. Through the Word of God we can experience spiritual growth and stability (I Peter 2:1-2; II Timothy 3:16-17). Faith for our salvation, as well as our Christian growth, comes from hearing the Word of God (see Romans 10:17).

Spiritual cleansing of the mind can be accomplished through submission to His Word (see II Corinthians 10:5).

"Now ye are clean through the word which I have spoken unto you" (John 15:3).

NOTE:
6:8 **scrip** means wallet; 7:19 **purging** means making clean; 7:27 **meet** means proper.

Mark 7:6-7: See Isa. 29:13. **7:10:** See Ex. 20:12; 21:17.

OCTOBER 16: Read Mark 8-9.

Mark 9:7-8: "And there was a cloud that overshadowed them: and a voice came out of the cloud, saying, This is my beloved Son: hear him. And suddenly, when they had looked round about, they saw no man any more, save Jesus only with themselves."

Jesus and His three disciples withdrew from the crowds and He "leadeth them up into a high mountain apart by themselves" (verse 2). Suddenly the disciples beheld Moses (representing the law) and Elijah (representing the prophets) "talking with Jesus" (verse 4).

Peter wanted to build three tabernacles, but Christ has no equals, for He represents the fulfillment of both the law and the prophets. The Voice from Heaven left no doubt, saying, "This is my beloved Son: hear him" (verse 7).

Peter made a second mistake when he wanted to remain on the mountain. There was a cross to be borne and a lost world to be redeemed. In fact, at that very moment, a desperate man was in the valley awaiting their return in order that his son might be relieved of an evil spirit.

Like Peter, so many have missed the Savior's best. They have placed too much importance on great speakers and popular books instead of seeking Christ and His will through His Word. Oh, how we need to declare that Christ is sufficient, seeing "no man any more, save Jesus only!"

"But we see Jesus . . . crowned with glory and honor . . ." (Hebrews 2:9).

NOTE:
9:3 **fuller** means laundry man; 9:12 **set at anought** means treated with contempt; 9:13 **listed** means desired; 9:18 **teareth** means convulses; 9:43 **maimed** means crippled.

Mark 9:44: See Isa. 66:24.

MEMORY VERSE FOR THE WEEK: Matthew 5:9-10

"Blessed are the peacemakers: for they shall be called the children of God. Blessed are they which are persecuted for righteousness' sake: for theirs is the kingdom of heaven."

"... Moses suffered to write a bill of divorcement, and to put her away. And Jesus answered and said unto them, For the hardness of your heart he wrote you this precept." Mark 10:4, 5

OCTOBER 17: Read Mark 10-11.

Mark: 10:9: "What therefore God hath joined together, let not man put asunder."

The husband and wife relationship is inseparably linked together with their mutual relationship with Christ. Often a husband tends to feel that his wife belongs to him and overlooks the fact that she belongs to the Lord. As a result, he often fails to recognize his stewardship responsibility of caring for the one who truly belongs to the Lord.

It is the husband's duty to provide for her physical needs and care for her spiritual life, to "nourish and cherish" his wife, "even as Christ also loved the church" (see Ephesians 5:22-31).

God created the world and put Adam in charge of it before He created woman. Eve was not created as an equal partner but as a helpmate, an assistant, under Adam's authority. No home that ignores God's plain Word "that the head of every man is Christ; and the head of the woman is the man" (I Corinthians 11:3) has ever been successful and happy.

Many Christian wives also fail to perceive that "holy women also, who trusted in God, [were] in subjection unto their own husbands: Even as Sarah obeyed Abraham . . ." Oh, that we would rely upon the mercy and wisdom of God rather than upon our own reasoning (I Peter 3:5-6).

Most divorces are the outcome of one party or both rejecting these God-given principles for a happy home. You cannot separate submission to one another from submission to Christ.

"Submitting yourselves one to another in the fear of God" (Ephesians 5:21).

NOTE:
Mark 10:6: See Gen. 1:27. 10:7-8: See Gen. 2:24. 10:19: See Ex. 20:13-14. 11:19: See Ps. 118:26. 11:17: See Isa. 56:7; Jer. 7:11.

Mark 12:30-31: "And thou shalt love the Lord thy God with all thy heart, and with all thy soul, and with all thy mind, and with all thy strength: this is the first commandment. And the second is like, namely this, Thou shalt love thy neighbor as thyself. There is none other commandment greater than these."

Love is the one distinguishing characteristic of the Christian (see John 13:35). Not only are we to love God with our entire being, but we must express an equal sincerity of love toward others because love is an integral part of God's nature that indwells every Christian.

MEMORY VERSE FOR THE WEEK: Matthew 5:9-10

"Blessed are the peacemakers: for they shall be called the children of God. Blessed are they which are persecuted for righteousness' sake: for theirs is the kingdom of heaven."

This love fulfills two functions in our lives. First, it is the visible evidence that Christ dwells within us. ". . . As he is, so are we in this world" (I John 4:17). By expressing loving words and deeds toward others, the Christian becomes the means by which the invisible God is seen. Second, when we practice love, God's love is "perfected in us" (I John 4:12).

The extent and strength of our love toward others will be in exact proportion to His love that has become a living reality in our life. The degree to which we refuse to love others is the same degree to which we reject Him: "If a man say, I love God, and hateth his brother, he is a liar: for he that loveth not his brother whom he hath seen, how can he love God whom he hath not seen?" (I John 4:20).

When Christians turn from their pride and self-love (demanding their rights) they too will love the unlovely, even those who would despitefully use them.

We must determine in our hearts to obey His New Commandment ". . . That ye love one another; as I have loved you, that ye also love one another" (John 13:34).

NOTE:
12:1 **let** means rented; 12:17 **Render** means Pay; 12:34 **durst** means dared; 12:41 **over against** means opposite.

Mark **12:10-11:** See Ps. 118:22-23. **12:19:** See Deu. 25:5. **12:26:** See Ex. 3:6. **12:29:** See Deu. 6:4. **12:30:** See Deu. 6:5. **12:31:** See Lev. 19:18: **12:36:** See Ps. 110:1.

> **Buried Opportunities**
> "I . . . went and hid thy talent in the earth: . . . His lord answered and said unto him, Thou wicked and slothful servant, thou knewest that I reap where I sowed not, and gathered where I have not strewed."
> Matthew 25:25-26

OCTOBER 19: Read Mark 14-16.
Mark 14:3-4: ". . . there came a woman having an alabaster box of ointment of spikenard very precious; and she brake the box, and poured it on his head. And there were some that had indignation within themselves, and said, Why was this waste . . . ?"

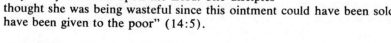

Six days before the Passover, Jesus returned to Bethany where Lazarus' sister, Mary, sacrificed very costly ointment upon the Lord. The disciples thought she was being wasteful since this ointment could have been sold "and have been given to the poor" (14:5).

MEMORY VERSE FOR THE WEEK: Matthew 5:9-10
"Blessed are the peacemakers: for they shall be called the children of God. Blessed are they which are persecuted for righteousness' sake: for theirs is the kingdom of heaven."

Judas, of course, who is a type of the unsaved world, would have thought that anything poured out upon Jesus was a waste. What a great contrast to Mary's sacrificial act of love. She could have used it to purchase many luxuries for herself, or kept it as a security for some future need.

Little could she realize that her gift was the anointing of our Lord's body for burial (see 14:8), for Jesus said, ". . . Wheresoever this gospel shall be preached . . . this also that she hath done shall be spoken of for a memorial of her" (14:9). The influence of her gift extended far beyond what she could possibly have comprehended!

This reveals how our gifts of love are far more sacred and far reaching than any of us can possibly comprehend.

All earthly values that seem so appealing today will soon vanish. The day will come when all material accumulations will be seen for their true value—worthless. (See I Corinthians 3:12-13.)

Dearest Lord, I waste myself upon Thee;
  Loving Thee, I'm deeply satisfied.
Love outpoured from hidden depths within me,
  Costly oil, dear Lord, I would provide.

NOTE:
14:3 **spikenard** means perfume; 14:31 **vehemently** means earnestly; 14:43 **staves** means clubs; 14:44 **token** means sign; 14:65 **buffet him** means hit him with their fists; 15:15 **scourged** means whipped.

Mark 14:27: See Zec. 13:7. **15:28:** See Isa. 53:12. **15:34:** See Ps. 22:1.

OCTOBER 20: Read Luke 1.
Luke 1:46: "And Mary said, My soul doth magnify the Lord."

This joyous outburst of praise from the lips of Mary is a beautiful outflow of the Scriptures she had within her heart (note Psalm 34:2-3). It compares to the inspired song of Hannah recorded in 1 Samuel 2. Hannah declared, "My heart rejoiceth in the Lord," and Mary said, "My soul doth magnify the Lord." She praised the Lord with all that was within her.

The angel had told Mary that her baby would be the "Son of the Highest" and that His name should be called Jesus, which means Jehovah-Savior.

It had been foretold by the prophet Micah that the Messiah would be born in Bethlehem (Micah 5:2). But Mary, His mother, lived in Nazareth. Little did the Roman emperor realize when he gave the order that all should return to the city of their birth to pay taxes that he was the person God would use to bring Mary and Joseph from Nazareth to Bethlehem to fulfill prophecy (2:1-3).

". . . My heart rejoiceth in the Lord, mine horn is exalted in the Lord: my mouth is enlarged over mine enemies; because I rejoice in thy salvation" (I Samuel 2:1).

MEMORY VERSE FOR THE WEEK: Matthew 5:9-10
"Blessed are the peacemakers: for they shall be called the children of God. Blessed are they which are persecuted for righteousness' sake: for theirs is the kingdom of heaven."

NOTE:
Luke 1:17: See Mal. 4:6.

OCTOBER 21: Read Luke 2-3.
Luke 3:21-22: "Now when all the people were baptized it came to pass, that Jesus also being baptized, and praying, the heaven was opened, and the Holy Ghost descended in a bodily shape like a dove upon him, and a voice came from heaven, which said, Thou art my beloved Son; in thee I am well pleased."

The Gospel of Luke emphasizes the human Jesus. Matthew and Mark told of Jesus being baptized, but Luke added "and praying." Standing in the Jordan River, Jesus prayed and the Spirit came upon Him and God announced, "Thou art my beloved Son." Just as Jesus needed to pray, you and I need to pray. We have the same Satan to combat and the same need to pray.

As we study the prayer life of Jesus, we discover that prayer releases spiritual power from Heaven. The place of prayer is the place of power.

Just as we feed our bodies systematically, we also need to pray systematically. He taught us to have a daily time of prayer, "Give us this *day* our daily bread."

The effectiveness of prayer is vitally connected with Bible reading. Your prayers become more meaningful and effective as you prayerfully read the Bible. Then you can pray according to His will: "If ye abide in me, and my words abide in you, ye shall ask what ye will, and it shall be done unto you" (John 15:7).

NOTE:
2:46 **doctors** means teachers; 3:1 **tetrarch** means governor.

Luke 2:23: See Ex. 13:2, 12. **2:24:** See Lev. 12:8. **3:4-6:** See Isa. 40:3-5.

OCTOBER 22: Read Luke 4-5.
Luke 4:18: "The Spirit of the Lord is upon me because he hath anointed me to preach the gospel to the poor; he hath sent me to heal the broken-hearted, to preach deliverance to the captives, and recovering of sight to the blind, to set at liberty them that are bruised."

As Jesus read that great prophetic passage of Scripture from Isaiah (61:1-2), He implied that this Scripture referred to Himself by saying, "This day is this scripture fulfilled in your ears" (verse 21).

He knew exactly what to read and where to stop reading. His ministry at His first coming was to "heal the broken-hearted and to preach deliverance to the captives." His Second Coming will be "the day of vengeance of our Lord."

They could not accept Him as the Messiah because they thought He was only a *carpenter's* son (see 4:22). In anger they "rose up," interrupting the

---

MEMORY VERSE FOR THE WEEK: Matthew 5:9-10
"Blessed are the peacemakers: for they shall be called the children of God. Blessed are they which are persecuted for righteousness' sake: for theirs is the kingdom of heaven."

---

synagogue service, and dragged Him to a cliff, intending to throw Him over it but "he passing through the midst of them went his way" (Luke 4:30).

Since many have heard stories about the Bible from the time they were children, they may think they are familiar with the Bible and are, therefore, equally blind to their desperate need of a daily personal relationship with the Lord. Read the Scriptures just to "know him, and the power of his resurrection, and the fellowship of his sufferings, being made conformable unto his death" (Philippians 3:10).

NOTE:
4:29 **brow** means edge; 5:9 **draught** means catch.

Luke 4:4: See Deu. 8:3. **4:8:** See Deu. 6:13. **4:10-11:** See Ps. 91:11-12. **4:12:** See Deu. 6:16. **4:18-19:** See Isa. 58:6; 61:1-2.

"And above all these things put on charity, which is the bond of perfectness." Colossians 3:14

OCTOBER 23: Read Luke 6-7.

Luke 7:37, 38: ". . . a woman in the city, which *was* a *sinner*, . . . stood at his feet behind him weeping, and began to wash his feet with tears, and did wipe them with the hairs of her head, and kissed his feet, and anointed them with the ointment."

An influencial Pharisee named Simon invited Christ as a guest to his home. But Simon apparently did not look upon Christ very highly. He did not extend to Jesus the customary courtesy of washing His feet or greeting Him with a kiss as was common to an honored guest. He apparently decided not to treat Him as an honored guest until he was sure Jesus deserved such an honor.

Now there came an uninvited guest also, "a woman in the city" who had a bad reputation. She brought an alabaster box of ointment and stood at Jesus' feet, weeping and washing His feet with her tears.

As Simon was observing all this he thought, "If this man were a prophet, He would have known what kind of woman this is, for she *is* a *sinner* (probably a prostitute). But Jesus, knowing his thoughts and seeing what was in his heart said, "Simon, I have somewhat to say unto thee."

Simon had misjudged her attention to Christ. He had misread those tears and the affection this woman was showing Christ. In fact, Simon had misjudged her when he said, she IS a SINNER—No, she WAS a sinner, but she had found the Savior.

The extent of our love for Christ is revealed by the spirit of compassion or condemnation we have toward another. Yes, Christ was known as "a friend of publicans and sinners" (see Matthew 11:19; Luke 7:34).

NOTE:
Luke 7:27: See Mal. 3:1.

MEMORY VERSE FOR THE WEEK: Matthew 5:11-12
"Blessed are ye, when men shall revile you, and persecute you, and shall say all manner of evil against you falsely, for my sake. Rejoice, and be exceeding glad: for great is your reward in heaven: for so persecuted they the prophets which were before you."

OCTOBER 24: Read Luke 8-9.

Luke 9:57-58: "And it came to pass, that, as they went in the way, a certain man said unto him, Lord, I will follow thee whithersoever thou goest. And Jesus said unto him, Foxes have holes, and birds of the air have nests; but the Son of man hath not where to lay his head."

The Lord tested the sincerity of this would-be disciple who volunteered to follow Him by saying that to follow Him, he could expect to accumulate less that he could call his own than the animals and the birds. When Jesus said, 'The Son of man has nowhere to lay His head,' He meant more than not having a place to sleep because there were homes of friends to which He would have been welcome. But he had no time to settle down and enjoy life. His life was occupied with eternal values, and His disciples were "strangers and pilgrims on the earth" (Hebrews 11:13).

A true disciple is far more than a casual follower. The path for a disciple requires daily dying to self. To avoid suffering, humiliation, and self-denial, many like this would-be disciple substitute beliefs about Jesus for commitments to follow Him.

Discipleship demands self-denial. This does not mean the self-denial so commonly spoken of (denying oneself of *certain things*), but it means denying self, giving up self-love and self-will.

"Lay up for yourselves treasures in heaven, where neither moth nor rust doth corrupt, and where thieves do not break through nor steal" (Matthew 6:20).

NOTE:
9:3 **staves** means walking stick.

Luke 8:10: See Isa. 6:9.

"My sheep wandered through all the mountains, and upon every high hill: yea, my flock was scattered upon all the face of the earth, and none did search or seek after them . . . Behold, I, even I, will both search my sheep, and seek them out."
Ezekiel 34:6, 11

OCTOBER 25: Read Luke 10-11.

Luke 10:33: "But a certain Samaritan, as he journeyed, came where he was: and when he saw him, he had compassion on him."

In reply to the lawyer's question, "And who is my neighbor?," Jesus gave this most touching parable of a destitute sufferer who had been beaten and robbed and left "half dead."

The priest and the Levite should have been first to show compassion, but they both avoided

---

this helpless man and each could have *justified* their cruel indifference because they were on their way to *serve God* in the Temple and could not risk becoming defiled. For all they knew the unconscious man could have been *dead!* Touching a dead man, even a Jew, would have made them ceremonially unclean (see Numbers 19:11-19).

It is one thing to serve God but quite another to live for Him in humble submission to His Word. The priest and the Levite both knew the law taught "Thou shalt not see thy brother's ass or his ox fall down by the way, and hide thyself from them; thou shalt surely help him to lift them up again" (Deuteronomy 22:5).

Christ is that good Samaritan, who came from Heaven and saw the lost and dying, lying helpless in the road of this world, stripped and left half dead by Satan. He bound up our wounds, poured in the oil of the Holy Spirit and the wine of His own cleansing and sanctifying blood, and lifted us up. He Himself bore our griefs and our sins in His own body on the tree. He has given us to the keeping of the host until He comes again.

". . . The Lord hath laid on him the iniquity of us all" (Isaiah 53:6).

NOTE:
10:40 **cumbered** means burdened.

Luke 10:27: See Deu. 6:5; Lev. 19:18.

OCTOBER 26: Read Luke 12-13.
Luke 12:15: "And he said unto them, Take heed, and beware of covetousness: for a man's life consisteth not in the abundance of the things which he possesseth."

The Lord illustrated the deceptiveness of covetousness by saying that ". . . the ground of a certain rich man brought forth plentifully." This successful farmer, by hard work and good management in the innocent occupation of farming, became wealthy. There is no indication that his wealth was gained by dishonest methods.

This successful farmer made several false assumptions. First, he unconsciously confessed how little satisfaction his wealth had brought him when he said "Take thine ease." It is a confession there had not yet been any ease in his life.

Far more serious is the fact that he spent a lifetime accumulating for self, and God called him a fool, and then added, "So is he that layeth up treasure for himself, and is not rich toward God" (12:21). A little later Jesus explained, "Ye cannot serve God and mammon [wealth]" (Luke 16:13).

Jesus said, "A man's life consisteth not in the abundance of things." Many people would be prone to disagree with the Lord and say that a man's life

---

does consist in the abundance of things he possesses. Many are deceived into believing that earthly things will bring satisfaction or that "gain is godliness" (I Timothy 6:5).

Christian friend, whoever you are, and regardless of how much or how little you may possess, God in mercy has revealed that "the love of money is the root of all evil: which while some coveted after, they have erred from the faith, and pierced themselves through with many sorrows" (I Timothy 6:10).

NOTE:
12:50 **straightened** means distressed; 13:11 **had a spirit of infirmity** means had been crippled.

Luke 13:35: See Ps. 118:26.

> "Let the wicked forsake his way, and the unrighteous man his thoughts: and let him return unto the Lord, and he will have mercy upon him; and to our God, for he will abundantly pardon."
> Isaiah 55:7

OCTOBER 27: Read Luke 14-16.
Luke 15:13-18: ". . . the younger son . . . took his journey into a far country, and there wasted his substance . . . and he began to be in want . . . and no man gave unto him . . . and when he came to himself, he said, . . . I perish with hunger! I will arise and go to my father, and will say unto him, Father, I have sinned against heaven, and before thee."

The self-centered prodigal son insisted on being free from his father's authority and from any responsibility to him.

Eventually he was destitute, and for a while he struggled with his sense of emptiness and shame of a wasted life rather than confess his sin. But at last he "came to himself" and returned to his father. When one comes to himself he will always come to the Father.

This is a story of the human race in its self-will and self-sufficiency demanding to live independent of God, to be a god to himself—abandoning himself to his own will and to his own pleasure.

In contrast to "Give me the portion of goods" (verse 12) is the daily prayer of every Christian, "Give us this day our daily bread." The Christian acknowledges that his desire is to wait upon the Father for the supply of all his needs—both bodily and spiritually.

MEMORY VERSE FOR THE WEEK: Matthew 5:11-12
"Blessed are ye, when men shall revile you, and persecute you, and shall say all manner of evil against you falsely, for my sake. Rejoice, and be exceeding glad: for great is your reward in heaven: for so persecuted they the prophets which were before you."

We are inclined to believe that the word "prodigal" means one who has wandered away from the father, but it has quite a different meaning. A prodigal is more than a wanderer; he is a waster, "he wasted his substance."

Just as the penniless prodigal found that his father's compassion and love was deeper than he had ever dared dream, so today the heavenly Father is waiting to transform the "wasted lives" of all who say, "I will arise and go to my father . . ." (Luke 15:18).

NOTE:
14:10 **worship** means honor; 14:32 **an ambassage** means a delegation; 15:16 **would fain** means longed to; 16:11 **mammon** means riches; 16:14 **derided** means ridiculed.

OCTOBER 28: Read Luke 17-18.
Luke 18:1: "And he spake a parable unto them to this end, that men ought always to pray, and not to faint."

The parable of the destitute widow urges Christians not to lose faith in God, even when it seems that He does not hear or answer our prayers. "Though he bear long with them" (verse 7) means that God is long-suffering and will meet the need when His children continue to pray.

Perhaps this unjust judge was a Roman official who had no personal interest in the needs of a Jewish widow, but *she came* (verse 3), implying that she kept on, day after day, pleading for protection from her adversary. Because he anticipated the widow's persistence, the judge yielded to her request.

Jesus expects His followers to trust Him with both their present and future needs, thus freeing themselves from worry and fear. Many are so despondent over experiences of the past or so afraid of the disastrous outcome of the future that they cannot enjoy the present—all because they fail to pray.

If any unjust judge would respond to the request of a widow whom he did not know, certainly we can depend upon the heavenly Judge to grant the requests of His own children who call upon Him. God never fails the faithful.

"For every one that asketh receiveth; and he that seeketh findeth; and to him that knocketh it shall be opened" (Matthew 7:8).

NOTE:
18:1 **faint** means give up; 18:3 **Avenge** means Defend; 18:30 **manifold** means many times.

Luke 18:20: See Ex. 20:12-16.

MEMORY VERSE FOR THE WEEK: Matthew 5:11-12
"Blessed are ye, when men shall revile you, and persecute you, and shall say all manner of evil against you falsely, for my sake. Rejoice, and be exceeding glad: for great is your reward in heaven: for so persecuted they the prophets which were before you."

OCTOBER 29: Read Luke 19-20.

Luke 19:1-2: "And Jesus entered and passed through Jericho. And, behold, there was a man named Zaccheus, which was the chief among the publicans, and he was rich."

This was the Lord's last journey, just fifteen miles and a few days before Calvary. As far as we know, Zaccheus was the last one to experience salvation before the crucifixion.

Zaccheus, a Jew, was a tax collector and was looked upon by his fellow countrymen as a thief and a servant of the enemy. His position indicated to his countrymen that he had sold his soul for wealth, for "he was rich" (verse 2). But buried beneath his wealth, he deeply longed for something that money could not buy. Because of his desperation and faith, he overcame all hindrances to obtain this treasure. Although he was probably ridiculed, in desperation he climbed into a sycamore tree in his determination to see Jesus. When Jesus called to him saying, "Zaccheus, come down," he made haste and came down and received Him joyfully.

A new love permeated his life and opened his eyes to the needs of others, and he spontaneously announced his first gift to be half of all his possessions. It was an expression of gratitude for the heavenly gift of salvation.

"Every man according as he purposeth in his heart, so let him give; not grudgingly, or of necessity: for God loveth a cheerful giver" (II Corinthians 9:7).

NOTE:
19:3 **Occupy** means Manage my business; 19:21 **austere** means exacting; 20:20 **feign** means pretend.

Luke 19:46: See Isa. 56:7; Jer. 7:11. **20:17:** See Ps. 118:22-23. **20:28:** See Deu. 25:5. **20:42-43:** See Ps. 110:1.

OCTOBER 30: Read Luke 21-22.

Luke 22:19-20: "And he took bread, and gave thanks, and brake it, and gave unto them, saying, This is my body which is given for you: this do in remembrance of me. Likewise also the cup after supper, saying, This cup is the *new testament in my blood,* which is shed for you."

The Passover was the most sacred feast of the Jewish religious year. It was in celebration of the deliverance of the children of Israel from bondage in Egypt.

MEMORY VERSE FOR THE WEEK: I Corinthians 13:1
"Though I speak with the tongues of men and of angels, and have not charity (love), I am become as sounding brass, or a tinkling cymbal."

267

This was the last Passover. The Messiah, the Lamb of God, had come to fulfill the true meaning of the Passover (Exodus 12:7; compare I Corinthians 5:7).

As the blood of the Passover lamb had been the sacrifice that was instrumental in accomplishing the redemption from Egypt, so Christ was "the Lamb of God, which taketh away the sin of the world" (John 1:29). Through His death "Christ hath redeemed us from the curse of the law" (Galatians 3:13) and established a new covenant relationship with His redeemed people, saying, "This is the new testament [covenant] in my blood."

The new covenant is the assurance that our Redeemer will come the second time—not to bear sin, but to meet sinners whose sins are washed away in His atoning blood. The redeemed of God look forward to His coming and that day when we enter into the actual presence of God.

". . . he is the mediator of a better covenant, which was established upon better promises" (Hebrews 8:6).

NOTE:
21:4 **penury** means poverty; 21:34 **surfeiting** means overeating.

Luke 22:37: See Isa. 53:12.

> "As soon as he (Pilate) heard that he belonged unto Herod's jurisdiction, he sent him to Herod . . . and Pilate and Herod were made friends together: for before they were at enmity between themselves." Luke 23:7, 12

OCTOBER 31: Read Luke 23-24.
Luke 23:23: "And they were instant with loud voices, requiring that he might be crucified. And the voices of them and of the chief priests prevailed."

After cross-examining Jesus, Pilate "said unto them the third time, I have found no cause of death in him" (23:22). Unable to persuade the Jews to set Christ free, Pilate attempted to clear himself from the consequences of condemning an innocent man.

In the book of Matthew we read of the strange and tragic event of Pilate washing his hands, thus claiming that he would have no part in crucifying Christ (Matthew 27:24). But throughout eternity Pilate will bear his guilt, along with others, for the crucifixion of Christ (note Acts 4:27-28).

Lacking moral courage and acting as an irresponsible judge, Pilate said, *"What shall I do then with Jesus which is called Christ?"* (Matthew 27:22).

MEMORY VERSE FOR THE WEEK: I Corinthians 13:1
"Though I speak with the tongues of men and of angels, and have not charity (love), I am become as sounding brass, or a tinkling cymbal."

It was Pilate who was on trial rather than Jesus when the Lord stood befor him. Every person comes to a cross-road in his life when he must answer the quest.on, *What shall I do then with Jesus?* No one can avoid, postpone, or blame others for the decision that must be made concerning Christ. You alone must decide either to receive Christ as your personal Savior or reject Him. You cannot ignore Him.

"That at the name of Jesus every knee should bow, of things in heaven, and things in earth, and things under the earth" (Philippians 2:10)

NOTE:
23:16 **chastise** means whip; 23:19 **sedition** means riot; 24:27 **expounded** means explained.

Luke 23:30: See Hos. 10:8. **23:46:** See Ps. 31:5.

BIBLICAL REFERENCE INDEX

PRAYERS IN MATTHEW, MARK, AND LUKE

MEMORY VERSE FOR THE WEEK: I Corinthians 13:1
"Though I speak with the tongues of men and of angels, and have not charity [love], I am become as sounding brass, or a tinkling cymbal."

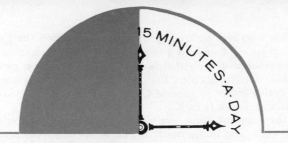

INTRODUCTION TO JOHN

The Gospel of John does not begin like Matthew with Christ as the descendant of Abraham or like Luke, tracing His genealogy back to Adam. John emphasized that Jesus' beginning preceded human history. He was equal with God the Father—the preexistent, eternal Divine Word who became flesh.

The book of John is a Gospel of love, revealing Christ as God, as the Fountain of Living Water that forever satisfies the thirsty soul. John presents Christ as the Light of the World that illuminates the darkness of sin in the earth; as the resurrection life that conquers death and imparts eternal life; and as the Good Shepherd who cares for His sheep. This Gospel was written ". . . that ye might believe that Jesus is the Christ, the Son of God; and that believing, ye might have life through his name" (John 20:31).

There are eight miracles of our Lord in the book of John, six of which are recorded *only* in John. (Note *)

Turning the water into wine	2: 1*
Healing the nobleman's son of fever	4:46*
Healing the impotent man at Bethesda	5: 1*
Feeding the five thousand	6: 5
Walking on the Sea of Galilee	6:19
Healing the man born blind	9: 1*
Raising of Lazarus from death	11:43*
Draught of fishes	21: 1*

There are no parables recorded in the book of John.

Our Lord's message was not merely to *preach* a Gospel—He *is* the Gospel:

"I AM the Bread of Life"—not come merely to *give* bread
(6:35, 41, 48, 51)

"I AM the Light of the World"—not come merely to *shed* light (8:12)

"I AM the Door of the Sheep"—not come merely to *show* the door
(10:7, 9)

"I AM the Good Shepherd"—not come merely to *name* a shepherd
(10:11, 14)

"I AM the Resurrection and the Life"—not come only to *die* for sinners
(11:25)

"I AM the Way, the Truth, the Life"—not come merely to *point* the way
(14:6)

"I AM the true Vine"—not come merely to *plant* a vine (15:1, 5)

(Additional references to Christ as the, "I AM": 4:26; 6:20; 8:24, 28, 58; 13:19; 18:5, 6, 8)

"Verily, verily, I say unto you, He that heareth my word, and believeth on him that sent me, hath everlasting life, and shall not come into condemnation; but is passed from death unto life."
John 5:24

NOVEMBER 1: Read John 1-3.
John 1:4-5: "In him was life; and the life was the light of men. And the light shineth in darkness; and the darkness comprehended it not."

Only Christ has the power to transform the human heart and create within us a new life. Change of environment plus training can never solve the sin problem. Only Christ—the Living Word, the Light of the World—can deliver us from sin and impart within us His nature.

Darkness represents the kingdom of Satan, and wherever the Gospel is received, darkness disappears. If we are to experience life in Christ, our hearts must first be exposed to the light of His Word. Then we will see the Light of Life. The Christ-rejecting world hates this light because it exposes what they really are. "The light" of His eternal life "shineth in darkness," but those who love their evil ways (darkness) do not "comprehend it" (1:5).

The supreme difference between a Christian and all other religious persons is that a Christian has obediently trusted in and received a personal Savior rather than merely changed some of his ways of living. Christianity is a *new birth*—a vast difference from accepting new beliefs.

"Which were born, not of blood, nor of the will of the flesh, nor of the will of man, but of God" (John 1:13).

NOTE:
1:28 **Bethabara** means Bethany; 1:47 **guile** means dishonesty; 2:15 **scourge** means whip; 3:20 **reproved** means exposed; 3:25 **purifying** means religious washing.

John 1:23: See Isa. 40:3. **2:17:** See Ps. 69:9.

NOVEMBER 2: Read John 4-5.
John 5:17-18: "But Jesus answered them, My Father worketh hitherto, and I work. Therefore the Jews sought the more to kill him, because he not only had broken the sabbath, but said also that God was his Father, making himself equal with God."

It is no accident that the Lord chose to heal a man who had been helplessly crippled for 38 years. It illustrates how the children of Israel had wandered in the wilderness for 38 years—only because they refused to believe and obey God's command to enter the Promised Land.

MEMORY VERSE FOR THE WEEK: I Corinthians 13:1
"Though I speak with the tongues of men and of angels, and have not charity [love], I am become as sounding brass, or a tinkling cymbal."

271

When Christ commanded the helpless, crippled man at the pool of Bethesda to "Rise, take up thy bed, and walk," the man neither questioned Christ's authority nor concerned himself with the opinions of the religious leaders. He immediately believed and he was healed. What a striking picture of how a helpless sinner is transformed!

The hatred of the religious leaders against Christ was first expressed because "he had done these things on the sabbath day" (5:16). But their hatred turned to a violent rage when Christ said, *My Father* worketh hitherto, and *I work.*" Jesus not only spoke of God as "my Father," but He united Himself as one with the Father in His ministry. In order to remove any remaining doubt as to His relationship with God, He went on to say, ". . . He that honoureth not the Son honoureth not the Father which hath sent him" (5:23).

NOTE:
4:6 **sixth hour** means noon; 5:3 **impotent** folk means **invalids;** 5:21 **quickeneth** means makes alive.

NOVEMBER 3: Read John 6-8.

John 8:7: "So when they continued asking him, he lifted up himself, and said unto them, He that is without sin among you, let him first cast a stone at her."

The woman had been caught in the very act of adultery. She was taken to Jesus and forced to stand before Him while the scribes and Pharisees hurled their accusations, saying, "Moses in the law commanded us, that such should be stoned: but what sayest thou?" (8:5).

Spiritual darkness had covered her life, but now she stood before "the Light of the World" (8:12). The religious leaders who had insisted on keeping the Law slipped away when the Light exposed *their* sin, too.

Jesus did not suggest that what she had done was not a serious sin. No, He merely said, "He that is without sin among you, let him first cast a stone at her." She had indeed sinned, and according to the Law, she should have been stoned. "For the law was given by Moses, but *grace* and *truth* came by Jesus Christ" (John 1:17). Notice the double emphasis—truth on the one hand and grace on the other. Truth says, Stone her! but grace says, "Neither do I condemn thee: go, and sin no more" (8:11).

To share His grace, we must do more than say, "I will forgive, but I will never forget"; or, "I trusted you once, but I will never trust you again!" We receive as much grace from the Lord as we are willing to show others. ". . . forgiving one another, even as God for Christ's sake hath forgiven you" (Ephesians 4:32).

NOTE:
6:52 **strove** means argued.

John 6:31: See Ps. 78:24. **6:45:** See Isa. 54:13.

MEMORY VERSE FOR THE WEEK: I Corinthians 13:1
"Though I speak with the tongues of men and of angels, and have not charity [love], I am become as sounding brass, or a tinkling cymbal."

"Go, wash in the pool of Siloam
. . . He went his way therefore,
and washed, and came seeing."
John 9:7

NOVEMBER 4: Read John 9-10.

John 9:1, 39: "And as Jesus passed by, he saw a man which was blind from his birth. . . . And Jesus said, For judgment I am come into this world, that they which see not might see; and that they which see might be made blind."

After declaring Himself to be "the Light of the World" (8:12), Jesus was confronted with a man who had been born blind. This man illustrates a world that is spiritually blind—stumbling through the darkness of sin.

THE POOL OF SILOAM
(John 9:7)

After Jesus healed the blind man, the religious leaders did their utmost to turn the healed man against Christ. They attempted to convince him that Jesus was a fraud—a sinner. The man replied that he didn't know if Jesus was a sinner or not, but "whereas I was blind, now I see' (9:25).

The healed man witnessed even more strongly when he said, ". . . herein is a marvelous thing, that ye know not from whence he is, and yet he hath opened mine eyes . . . If this man were not of God, he could do nothing" (vss. 30, 33). Although this man had always been blind, he revealed through his witnessing that, even in his blindness, he had more understanding of the *truth* and *light* than did the Pharisees, who could see.

The blind man first believed in Christ as a friend who helped him (9:11), then as a prophet and teacher (9:17, 30-33). But a man can believe all this and not be saved, so Jesus asked him a very personal and important question, "Dost thou believe on the Son of God?" And when he knew who Jesus was, he said, "Lord, I believe. And he worshipped him" (John 9:35, 38).

NOTE:
9:28 **reviled** means criticized.

John 10:34: See Ps. 82:6.

"And I am glad for your sakes that I was not there, to the intent ye may believe . . ."
John 11:15

NOVEMBER 5: Read John 11-12.

John 11:21: "Then said Martha unto Jesus, Lord, if thou hadst been here, my brother had not died."

The death of Lazarus was a great loss to Mary and Martha, but our Lord revealed to His disciples the true significance of what was occurring. He told them that as in the case of the man blind from birth this was "for the glory of God" (vs. 4).

Jesus intentionally waited two days, then said,

MEMORY VERSE FOR THE WEEK: I Corinthians 13:1

"Though I speak with the tongues of men and of angels, and have not charity [love], I am become as sounding brass, or a tinkling cymbal."

"Let us go into Judaea again . . . Lazarus sleepeth; but I go, that I may awake him . . ." (vss. 7, 11). Then Jesus plainly stated, "Lazarus is dead. And I am glad for your sakes that I was not there . . ." (vss. 14, 15). He clearly revealed that, although His arrival might appear to men to be too late, there was a master plan behind the events as they occurred. It was done ". . . that the Son of God might be glorified thereby" (vs. 4).

God is never late for an appointment, and He never forgets one. Although we often think otherwise, He is always on time. When we complain, we imply that our wisdom is greater than that of our all-wise Father, that our love is more perfect than His. So we need to be careful with our complaints as to what God should do and when He should do it.

His loving-kindness allows rejection, sorrow, and disappointments in order to bring a better understanding and appreciation of our Lord. "Then many of the Jews which came to Mary, and had seen the things which Jesus did, believed on him" (John 11:45).

NOTE:
John 12:13: See Ps. 118:26. **12:15:** See Zec. 9:9. **12:38:** See Isa. 53:1. **12:40:** See Isa. 6:9, 10.

NOVEMBER 6: Read John 13-16.

John 13:34: "A new commandment I give unto you, That ye love one another; as I have loved you, that ye also love one another."

God's message to the world is love. When we accept His love, we in turn are expected to express His love to everyone we encounter each day. ". . . God is love, and he that dwelleth in love dwelleth in God, and God in him" (I John 4:16).

All too often, Christians have ignored "the new commandment" and have continued to express their old nature of strife, bitterness, envy, and even hatred. They have tried to justify these actions with the excuse they were only defending their rights. Even though they may hold a spirit of ill-will against only one person, it must be recognized for what it is, "Whosoever hateth his brother is a murderer" (I John 3:15).

Our Lord brings situations into our lives to test the depth and fullness of our love for Him. It doesn't take the love of Christ to love those who love us. Jesus said that even the worldly man or woman can do this (Matthew 5:46). It is because Christ's love is in us that we are able to love the unlovely. Remember, dear friend, His love does not come from our efforts—its source is the indwelling Christ.

I love my God, but with no love of mine,
    For I have none to give;
I love Thee, Lord, but all that love is Thine,
    For by Thy life I live.
                    Madame Guyon (1648-1717)

MEMORY VERSE FOR THE WEEK: I Corinthians 13:2
"And though I have the gift of prophecy, and understand all mysteries, and all knowledge; and though I have all faith, so that I could remove mountains, and have not charity [love], I am nothing."

"... He that loveth not his brother whom he hath seen, how can he love God whom he hath not see?" (I John 4:20).

NOTE:
13:30 **sop** means bite of bread; 14:8 **sufficeth** means will satisfy; 15:2 **purgeth** means prunes; 15:22 **cloak** means excuse.

John 13:18: See Ps. 41:9. 15:25: See Ps. 35:19; 69:4.

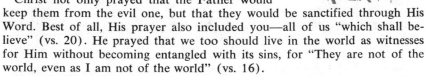

"But I have prayed for thee, that thy faith fail not . . ."
Luke 22:32

NOVEMBER 7: Read John 17-18.

John 17:15-17: "I pray not that thou shouldest take them out of the world, but that thou shouldest keep them from the evil."

Jesus' prayer for His disciples excels all other prayers in the Scriptures. He acknowledged that God had entrusted Him with each of the apostles and then prayed to the Father to keep them from the evil in the world as they took His place.

Christ not only prayed that the Father would keep them from the evil one, but that they would be sanctified through His Word. Best of all, His prayer also included you—all of us "which shall believe" (vs. 20). He prayed that we too should live in the world as witnesses for Him without becoming entangled with its sins, for "They are not of the world, even as I am not of the world" (vs. 16).

Our chief importance in the world rests in the fact that we have received His Word; and the more we read His Word, the more like Christ we become and the more united we will be with each other. Let us pray for one another as He prayed—to be united in a spirit of love, "that they all may be one" (vs. 21). His Word is our only basis for unity. And His prayer for His disciples and for us is our assurance as well as our challenge to live each day to honor Him.

"That they all may be one; as thou, Father, art in me, and I in thee, that they also may be one in us: that the world may believe that thou hast sent me" (John 17:21).

NOTE:
18:2 **resorted** means met there; 18:30 **malefactor** means criminal.

MEMORY VERSE FOR THE WEEK: I Corinthians 13:2
"And though I have the gift of prophecy, and understand all mysteries, and all knowledge; and though I have all faith, so that I could remove mountains, and have not charity [love], I am nothing."

John 19:17, 18, 30: "And he bearing his cross went forth into a place called the place of a skull . . . where they crucified him . . . he said, It is finished: and he bowed his head, and gave up the ghost."

The simple statement, "They crucified him," describes the most painful and brutal way of execution. The condemned man was placed on a cross, his arms outstretched, and nails driven through the palms of his hands and feet. The cross was raised and dropped into a hole which had been dug for it, and then he was left suspended there until death came.

It was during that time of suffering, thirst, and fever that Christ prayed for His tormentors, saying, "Father, forgive them; for they know not what they do" (Luke 23:34).

Some only consider Christ as a great example to be followed, but they disregard the fact that everything in His life pointed to His death on the cross. It was not until then that he cried out, "It is finished" (speaking of His work). Furthermore, the never-to-be-forgotten crucifixion of Christ was not the death of a hero or a faithful martyr. No, it was the death of God's *only* begotten Son—the Lamb of God "who gave himself for our sins, that he might deliver us from this present evil world . . ." (Galatians 1:4). His great work for our salvation "is finished."

"But this man, after he had offered one sacrifice for sins for ever, sat down on the right hand of God; . . . For by one offering he hath perfected for ever them that are sanctified" (Hebrews 10:12, 14).

NOTE:
19:29 **hyssop** means a hyssop branch; 19:41 **sepulcher** means tomb; 21:7 **girt** means put on.

John 19:24 See Ps. 22:18. **19:36:** See Ex. 12:46; Ps. 34:20. **19:37:** See Zec. 12:10.

INTRODUCTION TO ACTS

The book of Acts is a continuation of the Gospel of Luke. It contains the history of the first thirty years of the church. The church began with 120 disciples whom Jesus had told to "tarry at Jerusalem and wait for the promise of the Father"—the Holy Spirit.

The ministry of the Holy Spirit is referred to about 70 times in the book of Acts. The Holy Spirit indwelt and empowered the small group of believers to reach the world with His Word in their generation.

"The acts" of only two of the apostles are recorded. Peter and the church in Jerusalem are most notable in the first twelve chapters. Following the death of Stephen, intense persecution forced the church to spread from Jerusalem "unto the uttermost part of the earth" (1:8). After the conversion of Saul (Paul) of Tarsus, Antioch became the central city of worldwide evangelism, reaching into Asia and Europe. Paul and the events of his three missionary tours are prominent in chapters 13 through 28.

The book of Acts abruptly ends with the imprisonment of Paul in Rome.

NOVEMBER 9: Read Acts 1-3.

Acts 2:38: "Then Peter said unto them, Repent, and be baptized every one of you in the name of Jesus Christ for the remission of sins, and ye shall receive the gift of the Holy Ghost."

During those days of waiting "for the promise of the Father," something wonderful happened. Look at the change that took place in Peter's life!

Less than two months before the day of Pentecost, Peter had boastfully said, "Though all men

JERUSALEM, JUDAEA, SAMARIA
(Acts 1:8)

shall be offended because of thee, yet will I never be offended" (Matthew 26:33). Then just hours after that statement, he cowardly denied ever having known the Lord. He even swore a little in order to convince his questioner that he was not a follower of Christ.

But after the Holy Spirit indwelled Peter, he faced a hostile, cynical crowd and boldly preached about Jesus' resurrection.

"The Holy Ghost" is not a "thing" or "an experience," but it is *a Person* of the Godhead—the Holy Spirit. Without His indwelling presence, our ministry would be cold, lifeless, and fruitless, lacking any eternal value.

". . . Now if any man have not the Spirit of Christ, he is none of his" (Romans 8:9).

NOTE:

1:1 **treatise** means book of Luke; 1:12 **sabbath day's journey** means little over ½ mile; 2:3 **cloven** means tongues distributing among them; 2:40 **untoward** means wicked; 3:17 **wot** means know.

Acts 1:20: See Ps. 69:25; 109:8. **2:17-21:** See Joel 2:28-32. **2:25-28:** See Ps. 16:8-11. **2:34, 35:** See Ps. 110:1. **3:22, 23:** See Deu. 18:18, 19. **3:25:** See Gen. 12:3; 22:18.

"Can two walk together, except they be agreed?"   Amos 3:3

NOVEMBER 10: Read Acts 4-6.

Acts 4:31-32: "And when they had prayed, . . . they spake the word of God with boldness. And the multitude of them that believed were of one heart and of one soul . . ."

The 120 believers in the upper room prayed "in one accord" and the Holy Spirit changed them from self-seekers to Christ-pleasers. Old King Pride had been overcome and they were reigning with Christ in a new and living way.

One of the greatest privileges Christians have is praying—not only for ourselves but for *others*. Our Lord promised to be in our midst "where two or three are gathered together" in His name (Matthew 18:20). He taught us to

---

MEMORY VERSE FOR THE WEEK: I Corinthians 13:2

"And though I have the gift of prophecy, and understand all mysteries, and all knowledge; and though I have all faith, so that I could remove mountains, and have not charity [love], I am nothing."

---

pray, *"Our* Father," not *"My* Father"; furthermore, we are "to carry *one another's* burdens."* Many Christians do not realize the purpose and power in united prayer, but whenever we meet together in the name of Jesus, the presence of the Lord Himself is there. It is the living presence of Christ in fellowship with His loving, praying disciples that gives united prayer its power.

"Behold, how good and how pleasant it is for brethren to dwell together in unity!" (Psalm 133:1).

NOTE:
4:17 **straitly** means sternly; 5:12 **wrought** means performed; 5:13 **durst** means dared; 5:16 **vexed** means afflicted; 5:17 **indignation** means jealousy; 6:11 **suborned** means bribed.

Acts 4:11: See Ps. 118:22. **4:25, 26:** See Ps. 2:1, 2.

NOVEMBER 11: Read Acts 7-8.
Acts 7:59-60: "And they stoned Stephen, calling upon God, and saying, Lord Jesus, receive my spirit. And he kneeled down, and cried with a loud voice, Lord, lay not this sin to their charge. And when he had said this, he fell asleep."

Stephen, filled with the Holy Spirit, preached the Word of God at great length. In fact, this longest sermon recorded in the New Testament was never finished.

As Stephen stood before them as a witness to the Light of the World, these rulers refused to see their wickedness exposed by the Light; and in an effort to put out this light, they stoned Stephen to death. With the hostile crowd was Saul (Paul), who was also "consenting unto his death" (Acts 8:1).

The impact of Stephen's sermon and dying prayer must have had a tremendous influence upon Paul, for years later, he testified that he had stood with the crowd as Stephen was martyred. (See Acts 22:20.) It is a fearful thing to see the Light of His Word and reject His will.

The believer who knows the Word of God and the God of the Word will remain faithful, even when confronted by the satanic hatred of those who oppose the truth.

The pain we may suffer from the cruel stones of the unbelieving world is of little importance if it will lead another to believe on Christ. ". . . Be thou faithful unto death, and I will give thee a crown of life" (Revelation 2:10).

NOTE:
7:6 **sojourn** means stay; 7:11 **dearth** means famine; 7:19 **subtilly** means deceitfully; 7:38 **lively oracles** means living words; 8:2 **lamentation** means weeping; 8:3 **haling** means arresting; 8:9 **sorcery** means witchcraft.

Acts 7:3: See Gen. 12:1. **7:27, 28:** See Ex. 2:14. **7:32:** See Ex. 3:6. **7:33, 34:** See Ex. 3:5, 7, 8, 10. **7:37:** See Deu. 18:15. **7:40:** See Ex. 32:1. **7:42, 43:** See Am. 5:25-27. **7:49, 50:** See Isa. 66:1, 2. **8:32, 33:** See Isa. 53:7, 8.

MEMORY VERSE FOR THE WEEK: I Corinthians 13:2
"And though I have the gift of prophecy, and understand all mysteries, and all knowledge; and though I have all faith, so that I could remove mountains, and have not charity [love], I am nothing."

NOVEMBER 12: Read Acts 9-10.

Acts 9:36: "Now there was at Joppa a certain disciple, named Tabitha, which by interpretation is called Dorcas: this woman was full of good works and almsdeeds which she did."

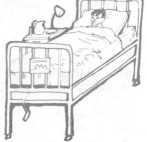

Don't make the mistake of underestimating the importance of a modest, unpretentious Christian whose life is dedicated to helping others in whatever way they can. Often, the people who are being used of God to make the greatest influence do not appear exceptionally outstanding, but in an inconspicuous way, they "do good, and lend, hoping for nothing again" (Luke 6:35).

When the love of Christ captured the heart of Dorcas, she did what she could through her deeds of compassion and helpfulness. Her good works and generosity did not make her a Christian, but they reflected the genuineness of her faith. She was a true servant of the One whom the Bible says, "went about doing good" (Acts 10:38).

There are needy, lonely, elderly people in rest homes; others are sick, longing to have someone pray with them; shut-ins who wonder if anyone cares what happens to them. God cares, but perhaps He needs you to share His comfort and love through reading the Bible and praying with them, or by providing some physical necessity.

It is natural for the unsaved person to live by the principle, "What's in it for me?" But the Christian has a new nature, and it should be natural for him "to do good and to communicate (meaning, to be generous and share what he has), . . . for with such sacrifices God is well pleased" (Hebrews 13:16).

NOTE:
9:43 **tanner** means leather worker; 10:1 **centurion** means captain; 10:14 **common** means outside the regulations of the Law; 10:29 **gainsaying** means objection.

NOVEMBER 13: Read Acts 11-13.

Acts 13:2, 5, 13: "As they ministered to the Lord, and fasted, the Holy Ghost said, Separate me Barnabas and Saul for the work whereunto I have called them . . . and they had also John [John Mark] to their minister . . . they came to Perga in Pamphylia: and John departing from them returned to Jerusalem."

God calls certain dedicated "servants" to every ministry to work many long, hard hours behind the scenes. They will not receive as much recognition as the one who is speaking, but their work is just as vital and equally anointed.

MEMORY VERSE FOR THE WEEK: I Corinthians 13:3
"And though I bestow all my goods to feed the poor, and though I give my body to be burned, and have not charity [love], it profiteth me nothing."

Paul and Barnabas had chosen to take John Mark "to their minister"—meaning, the position of service or servant. He had been chosen mainly to help Paul in the things pertaining to their travel—perhaps to help earn their support—thus allowing Paul and Barnabas to devote themselves more fully to the ministry of preaching and teaching. He started out with the man whom God had anointed to preach the Gospel to the Gentiles, but he didn't last long and soon returned home.

Many are not prepared to endure the hardship of the work, the criticism, the opposition of Satan, and the long and difficult hours that usually are hidden from the view of the crowd. In the midst of difficulties, many give up and go back to their easier way of life. Only a few Christians are willing to be a lowly, humble servant. But what a privilege it is to be a servant! Even our Lord Himself "came not to be ministered unto, but to minister" (Mark 10:45; compare John 13:2-17 and Philippians 2:5-8).

NOTE:
12:4 **four quaternions** means sixteen; 12:21 **oration** means speech; 13:17 **a high arm** means power; 13:18 **suffered** means patiently endured; 13:43 **proselytes** means Gentile converts from Judaism.

Acts **13:22:** See Ps. 89:20. **13:33:** See Ps. 2:7. **13:34:** See Isa. 55:3. **13:35:** See Ps. 16:10. **13:41:** See Hab. 1:5. **13:47:** See Isa. 49:6.

"Great peace have they which love thy law: and nothing shall offend them." Psalm 119:165

NOVEMBER 14: Read Acts 14-16.
Acts 16:23, 25: "And when they had laid many stripes upon them, they cast them into prison, charging the jailer to keep them safely: . . . And at midnight Paul and Silas prayed, and sang praises unto God: and the prisoners heard them."

Mark had gone home during the first missionary journey of Paul and Barnabas, so Paul refused to let Mark accompany them on their second trip. Barnabas was displeased with Paul's decision and returned to the island of Cypress, where he formerly lived (4:36-37; compare 15:39).

In defending his nephew, Barnabas had forsaken God's anointed leader in the ministry. He had let personal feelings keep him from fulfilling the task that the Holy Spirit had directed him to do (see Acts 13:2). After this event, we have no record of Barnabas ever having done anything for Christ.

The Apostle Paul then chose Silas to be his helper. They suffered many hardships together, but there is not a single hint that Silas was ever sorry he accepted the opportunity to be a servant of Christ. Even when God permitted

MEMORY VERSE FOR THE WEEK: I Corinthians 13:3
"And though I bestow all my goods to feed the poor, and though I give my body to be burned, and have not charity [love], it profiteth me nothing."

280

them to be beaten and put in jail, they did not protest. As a result of their imprisonment, the jailer and his family heard the Gospel and accepted Christ as their Savior (see Acts 16:32-33). Paul and Silas rejoiced because "they were counted worthy to suffer shame for his name" (Acts 5:41).

NOTE:
15:2 **dissension** means argument; 15:10 **yoke** means burden; 15:24 **subverting** means misleading; 15:30 **epistle** means letter; 16:7 **assayed** means attempted; 16:13 **wont** means accustomed.

Acts 15:16, 17: See Am. 9:11, 12.

> "But exhort one another daily, while it is called To-day; lest any of you be hardened through the deceitfulness of sin."
> Hebrews 3:13

NOVEMBER 15: Read Acts 17-19.
Acts 17:11: "These were more noble than those in Thessalonica, in that they received the word with all readiness of mind, and searched the scriptures daily, whether those things were so."

The people at Berea listened very carefully as Paul compared the Old Testament Scriptures with the facts of Jesus' life. He proved beyond doubt that Jesus of Nazareth truly fulfilled the prophecies concerning the Messiah. So they studied the Scriptures carefully to determine if Jesus actually was the promised Messiah. Then "with all readiness of mind," they gave up their preconceived opinions and accepted the authority of God's Word.

Through daily Bible reading, Christians can know the will of God for their lives because the Spirit of Truth has promised to "guide you [the reader of God's Word] into all truth" (John 16:13).

One of the signs of the last days is that many "shall turn away their ears from the truth, and shall be turned unto fables" (II Timothy 4:4). By failing to read *all the Scriptures,* it is easy to believe false doctrines and be persuaded by the "enticing words" of man's wisdom (Colossians 2:4).

"Study to shew thyself approved unto God, a workman that needeth not to be ashamed, rightly dividing the word of truth" (II Timothy 2:15).

NOTE:
17:3 **alleging** means giving evidence; 17:4 **consorted** means associated; 17:5 **lewd** means evil; 17:19 **Areopagus** means Mars' Hill; 19:9 **divers** means some; 19:13 **exorcists** means witch doctors; 19:19 **curious arts** means magical; 19:27 **set at nought** means regarded as worthless; 19:35 **appeased** means quieted; 19:38 **implead** means bring charges.

MEMORY VERSE FOR THE WEEK: I Corinthians 13:3
"And though I bestow all my goods to feed the poor, and though I give my body to be burned, and have not charity [love], it profiteth me nothing."

NOVEMBER 16: Read Acts 20-22.

Acts 21:31: "And as they went about to kill him, tidings came unto the chief captain of the band, that all Jerusalem was in an uproar."

Jesus made a startling statement to His followers when He told them, "If any man will come after me, let him deny himself, and take up his cross *daily*, and follow me" (Luke 9:23).

It is no surprise then that Christ said of Saul (Paul) of Tarsus, "I will shew him how great things he must suffer for my name's sake" (Acts 9:16).

Immediately after he arrived in Jerusalem, the Apostle Paul faced serious opposition. His enemies created a riot that resulted in his being brutally beaten by the angry mob.

Many sing and talk about carrying a cross, but usually they are referring to the typical difficulties of life that all human beings experience. The cross that Jesus talked about was a different sort; it refers to a daily denial of certain pleasures, privileges, and necessities in order to help others come to know Him. Not everyone is martyred in order to bear his cross, but Christ does call us to bear any persecution that we may face for faithfully following Him.

It is the willingness to die daily to self-interests that will determine how much we really want to follow in the Master's footsteps.

"For even hereunto were ye called: because Christ also suffered for us, leaving us an example, that ye should follow his steps" (I Peter 2:21).

NOTE:
20:2 **exhortation** means encouraging words; 20:3 **abode** means stayed; 21:11 **girdle** means belt; 22:24 **scourging** means whipping.

"He sendeth forth his commandment upon earth: his word runneth very swiftly." Psalm 147:15

NOVEMBER 17: Read Acts 23-25.

Acts 23:11-12: "And the night following the Lord stood by him, and said, Be of good cheer, Paul: for as thou hast testified of me in Jerusalem, so must thou bear witness also at Rome. And when it was day, certain of the Jews banded together, and bound themselves under a curse, saying that they would neither eat nor drink till they had killed Paul."

We have no record that members of the Jerusalem church tried to encourage, comfort, or defend Paul while he was imprisoned in their city (contrast Acts 21:17-20). But the Lord stood by him, offering the comforting words, "Be of good cheer."

The following day, Paul was told that forty men had vowed not to eat until they had murdered him. Paul did more than just "pray about the situation." He used every possible means to get word to the proper authorities in an effort to avoid the attack by his conspirators.

MEMORY VERSE FOR THE WEEK: I Corinthians 13:3
"And though I bestow all my goods to feed the poor, and though I give my body to be burned, and have not charity [love], it profiteth me nothing."

There are times when we are not in a position to do anything about our situation except pray and then wait in full confidence for the Lord to answer. But there are other times, probably more numerous, when the Lord does not answer our prayers until we, by faith, do what we can to accomplish His will. He may not use the means we would expect, and friends that we may have counted on may let us down, but as we remain faithful to Him, we see that His ways are always best.

"Fight the good fight of faith, lay hold on eternal life whereunto thou art also called, and hast professed a good profession before many witnesses" (I Timothy 6:12).

NOTE:
23:3 **whited wall** means hypocrite; 24:4 **clemency** means fair consideration; 24:18 **tumult** means riot; 25:16 **license** means opportunity.

Acts 23:5: See Ex. 22:28.

> "And now I exhort you to be of good cheer: for there shall be no loss of any man's life among you, but of the ship . . . Fear not, Paul . . . lo, God hath given thee all them that sail with thee."
> Acts 27:22, 24

NOVEMBER 18: Read Acts 26-28.

Acts 27:20-25: ". . . all hope that we should be saved was then taken away. . . . And now I exhort you to be of good cheer . . . For there stood by me this night the angel of God, whose I am, and whom I serve, saying, Fear not, . . . Wherefore, sirs, be of good cheer: for I believe God, that it shall be even as it was told me."

After Paul had been imprisoned in Caesarea for two years, Festus, the new governor of Judea, placed Paul in the custody of a centurion soldier who was to take him to Rome where he would stand trial.

Shortly after their departure on a cargo ship, a storm at sea caused their ship to eventually sink. During that fearful ordeal, Paul stated, "All hope that we should be saved was then taken away" (27:20).

No matter how hopeless your situation may become, a Christian can carry on. Never lose hope! Never give up! "The things which are impossible with men are possible with God" (Luke 18:27).

One of the great blessings of being a Christian is the assurance that although life's stormy voyages may be rough, there will come a day when the tempest we have weathered will seem unimportant compared to what God was able to accomplish through our suffering.

God had placed the Apostle Paul on that particular ship to accomplish His own Divine purpose. Paul could never have preached the Gospel on that island if it had not been for that storm.

MEMORY VERSE FOR THE WEEK: I Corinthians 13:3
"And though I bestow all my goods to feed the poor, and though I give my body to be burned, and have not charity [love], it profiteth me nothing."

Thank God for your next disaster, for it may be the means of someone else coming to know the Lord.

"Therefore I take pleasure in infirmities, in reproaches, in necessities, in persecutions, in distresses for Christ's sake: for when I am weak, then am I strong" (II Corinthians 12:10).

NOTE:
27:30 **under color** means under the pretense.

Acts 28:26, 27: See Isa. 6:9, 10.

INTRODUCTION TO ROMANS

The plan of salvation is progressively developed from chapter to chapter through the book of Romans.

The book first ". . . proved both Jews and Gentiles, that they are all under sin; as it is written, There is none righteous, no, not one" (3:9-10). It continues by saying that even after man has done everything in his power in an effort to earn salvation, the Word of God still says, "By the deeds of the law there shall no flesh be justified" (3:20).

The foundation of this book is Christ—"Who was delivered for our offenses, and was raised again for our justification" (4:25).

Having died to the old life of sin, the believer is ". . . buried with him by baptism into death: that like as Christ was raised up from the dead . . . even so we also should walk in newness of life" (6:4).

In the following chapters the believer discovers how to be led by the Spirit (8:14) and to know "that good, and acceptable, and perfect, will of God" (12:1-2).

The book of Romans can be summed up in one verse: "For I am not ashamed of the gospel of Christ: for it is the power of God unto salvation to every one that believeth; to the Jew first, and also to the Greek" (1:16).

NOVEMBER 19: Read Romans 1-3.

Romans 3:20,24: "Therefore by the deeds of the law there shall no flesh be justified in his sight: for by the law is the knowledge of sin. . . . Being justified freely by his grace through the redemption that is in Christ Jesus."

Down through the ages, "the law and the prophets" all pointed to the Messiah, who was to bear our sins. Because of His death on the cross, He made it possible for you and me to be "justified in his sight." The altars, the priestly sacrifices, the Temple services with their ceremonies of shewbread, candlesticks, and altar of incense that had been practiced for centuries were made useless "through the redemption that is in Christ Jesus."

The vilest sinner can be saved from all sin—"justified freely by his [Christ's] grace" when he believes that Christ is indeed the Lamb, the sacrifice for our sin.

The real sacrifice for sin was complete when Jesus cried from the cross, "It is finished."

MEMORY VERSE FOR THE WEEK: I Corinthians 13:3
"And though I bestow all my goods to feed the poor, and though I give my body to be burned, and have not charity [love], it profiteth me nothing."

The pride of human works has nothing to offer to earn or deserve salvation, for it is "by his grace" that He has separated us from an ungodly world and made us "partakers of his divine nature."

"'Therefore we conclude that a man is justified by faith without the deeds of the law" (Romans 3:28).

NOTE:
1:13 **let** means hindered; 1:21 **vain** means stupid; 1:27 **meet** means fitting.

Romans 1:17: See Hab. 2:4. **2:24:** See Isa. 52:5. **3:4:** See Ps. 51:4. **3:10:** See Ps. 14:1, 3. **3:11:** See Ps. 14:2. **3:12:** See Ps. 14:3. **3:13:** See Ps. 5:9; 140:3. **3:14:** See Ps. 10:7. **3:15:** See Isa. 59:7. **3:16, 17:** See Isa. 59:7, 8. **3:18:** See Ps. 36:1.

> ". . . If ye continue in my word, then are ye my disciples indeed; And ye shall know the truth, and the truth shall make you free."
> John 8:31, 32

NOVEMBER 20: Read Romans 4-7.

Romans 6:5-7. "For if we have been planted together in the likeness of his death, we shall be also in the likeness of his resurrection: knowing this, that our old man is crucified with him, that the body of sin might be destroyed, that henceforth we should not serve sin. For he that is dead is freed from sin."

All believers have been united with the Lord Jesus in His death, but better still, we are united with Him in His resurrection. As a result, the power of the sin nature has been broken, and we can experience daily victories over temptations to sin. For this to become a practical reality, there are two facts that every Christian should accept by faith. The believer is to "reckon" (accept as a fact) that he is indeed dead to sin and should no longer live a sinful life. Furthermore, it is also a fact that he is "alive unto God"—and now "the servants of righteousness" (6:18).

Through the first Adam in the Garden of Eden, we inherited a sinful nature with its condemnation and death. Through the last Adam—the Lord Jesus Christ—God's *justice* was satisfied. This means that by His death on the cross, Christ made it possible for us to be justified—just as if we had never sinned. Every doubt is a devil's lie. Our old nature *was* crucified with Christ. His life now empowers us to live for God.

"Therefore being justified by faith, we have peace with God through our Lord Jesus Christ" (Romans 5:1).

NOTE:
5:11 **atonement** means reconciliation; 5:14 **similitude** means likeness; 7:8 **concupiscence** means lust.

Romans 4:3: See Gen. 15:6. **4:7, 8:** See Ps. 32:1, 2. **4:17:** See Gen. 17:5. **4:18:** See Gen. 15:5. **7:7:** See Ex. 20:17.

MEMORY VERSE OF THE WEEK: I Corinthians 13:4
"Charity [love] suffereth long, and is kind; charity [love] envieth not; charity [love] vaunteth not itself, is not puffed up."

NOVEMBER 21: Read Romans 8-10.

Romans 8:1: "There is therefore now no condemnation to them which are in Christ Jesus, who walk not after the flesh, but after the Spirit."

As a devout Jew, Paul realized that the Law was God's perfect living standard, but regardless how hard he tried to live in perfect obedience to the Law, it was impossible. Although he said, "I delight in the law" (7:22), he was unable to live up to all that he knew was right, and he was also unable to keep from doing things he knew were wrong. But "what the law could not do, in that it was weak through the flesh, God sending his own Son in the likeness of sinful flesh, and for sin, condemned sin in the flesh: that the righteousness of the law might be fulfilled in us . . ." (8:3-4).

Let us not be disillusioned. To become a Christian does not guarantee a safe retreat into some heavenly place where there are no trials or temptations. Instead, we may be confronted with Satan's most furious assaults of evil. At times, we will face what appear to be insurmountable temptations. But the child of God does not face these trials in his own strength.

With the indwelling Holy Spirit, we are able to withstand the influences of evil and to maintain our separation from the world. But when we fail, "Who is he that condemneth? It is Christ that died, yea rather, that is risen again, who is even at the right hand of God, who also maketh intercession for us" (Romans 8:34).

NOTE:
9:3 **accursed** means cut off.

Romans **8:36:** See Ps. 44:22. **9:7:** See Gen. 21:12. **9:9:** See Gen. 18:10. **9:12:** See Gen. 25:23. **9:13:** See Mal. 1:2, 3. **9:15:** See Ex. 33:19. **9:17:** See Ex. 9:16. **9:25:** See Hos. 2:23. **9:26:** See Hos. 1:10. **9:27, 28:** See Isa. 10:22, 23. **9:29:** See Isa. 1:9. **9:33:** See Isa. 28:16. **10:5:** See Lev. 18:5. **10:6, 7:** See Deu. 30:12, 13. **10:8:** See Deu. 30:14. **10:11:** See Isa. 28:16. **10:13:** See Joel 2:32. **10:15:** See Isa. 52:7. **10:16:** See Isa. 53:1. **10:18:** See Ps. 19:4. **10:19:** See Deu. 32:21. **10:20:** See Isa. 65:1. **10:21:** See Isa. 65:2.

"So teach us to number our days, that we may apply our hearts unto wisdom."   Psalm 90:12

NOVEMBER 22: Read Romans 11-13.

Romans 13:12,14: "The night is far spent, the day is at hand: let us therefore cast off the works of darkness, and let us put on the armour of light. . . . put ye on the Lord Jesus Christ, and make not provision for the flesh, to fulfil the lusts thereof."

This present age is like nighttime from which we must be awakened to see the urgency of our opportunities to serve Him. Life is too short to be "dreaming" over material advantages and worldly

MEMORY VERSE OF THE WEEK: I Corinthians 13:4
"Charity [love] suffereth long, and is kind; charity [love] envieth not; charity [love] vaunteth not itself, is not puffed up."

attractions. We have a responsibility to tell others of the love of Christ, and our lives should express the will of Christ who said, "I must work the works of him that sent me, while it is day: the night cometh, when no man can work" (John 9:4).

Although we are *in* the night, we are not *of* the night. Therefore, we are to "cast off the works of darkness." Everything that is characteristic of the darkness of this evil world is to be cast aside. Only in the light of God's Word can we do this. Christians must be Christ-clothed, prepared to meet Him. He alone is to be seen in our lives (II Corinthians 3:3; Galatians 3:27; Ephesians 4:24).

". . . Awake thou that sleepest, and arise from the dead, and Christ shall give thee light" (Ephesians 5:14).

NOTE:
11:14 **emulation** means jealousy; 12:9 **dissimulation** means hypocrisy.

Romans 11:3: See 1 Kn. 19:10, 14. **11:4:** See 1 Kn. 19:18. **11:8:** See Isa. 29:10. **11:9, 10:** See Ps. 69:22. **11:26, 27:** See Isa. 59:20, 21. **11:34:** See Isa. 40:13. **11:35:** See Job 41:11. **12:19:** See Deu. 32:35. **12:20:** See Prov. 25:21, 22. **13:9:** See Ex. 20:13-17; Lev. 19:18.

> "Shouldest not thou also have had compassion on thy fellow-servant, even as I had pity on thee?" Matthew 18:33

NOVEMBER 23: Read Romans 14-16.

Romans 14:4: "Who art thou that judgest another man's servant? To his own master he standeth or falleth. Yea, he shall be holden up: for God is able to make him stand."

One of the greatest temptations in the world is to judge others. But the Holy Spirit clearly reveals in these verses that every believer is responsible to the Lord, who alone has the authority to pass judgment. God does not need our spoken opinion as to his servants' spiritual status. Regardless of a person's years of Christian experience (or lack of it), all criticism, condemnation, and judging others is simply a self-righteous pride—un-Christian conduct of which we must rid ourselves.

If we judge our brother, we assume our Lord's role and, in effect, place ourselves above Him. To play the role of "Holy Spirit" in that person's life is a very dangerous thing to do. Oh, how much contention, bitterness, and trouble would be avoided among Christians if we left all judging of others to God.

"But dost thou judge thy brother? or why dost thou set at nought thy brother? for we shall all stand before the judgment seat of Christ . . . every one of us shall give account of himself to God. Let us not therefore judge one another any more . . ." (Romans 14:10,12,13).

NOTE:
16:2 **succourer** means helper; 16:23 **chamberlain** means treasurer.
Romans 14:11: See Isa. 45:23. **15:3:** See Ps. 69:9. **15:9:** See Ps. 18:49. **15:10:** See Deu. 32:43. **15:11:** See Ps. 117:1. **15:12:** See Isa. 11:1, 10. **15:21:** See Isa. 52:15.

MEMORY VERSE OF THE WEEK: I Corinthians 13:4
"Charity [love] suffereth long, and is kind; charity [love] envieth not; charity [love] vaunteth not itself, is not puffed up."

INTRODUCTION TO I AND II CORINTHIANS

Paul wrote the first letter to the church at Corinth to correct many serious problems that existed among its members. The church was split into various divisions, as well as having other sins that seriously hindered the spiritual growth of the church. He said they were immature Christians —merely "babes" who were unable to comprehend spiritual judgment.

One of the most treasured chapters of the New Testament is I Corinthians 13, giving a comprehensive definition of love. The concluding highlight is chapter 15, one of the most beautiful explanations of the resurrection found in the New Testament.

The book of *II Corinthians* was written to commend the church for correcting its errors. Some parts of this letter are joyous because most of the people had repented as a result of Paul's first letter. But in other parts of the letter, Paul was stern and rebuking because a few of them were suspicious and critical, seeking to damage the apostle's character.

He challenged each believer to separate themselves from all worldly evils, saying, "Wherefore come out from among them, and be ye separate, saith the Lord, and touch not the unclean thing" (6:17).

Paul again told about the absolute certainty of life after death. "For we know that if our earthly house of this tabernacle were dissolved, we have a building of God, an house not made with hands, eternal in the heavens" (5:1).

NOVEMBER 24: Read I Corinthians 1-4.

I Corinthians 3:5-8: "Who then is Paul, and who is Apollos, but ministers by whom ye believed, even as the Lord gave to every man? I have planted, Apollos watered; but God gave the increase. So then neither is he that planteth any thing, neither he that watereth; but God that giveth the increase. Now he that planteth and he that watereth are one . . ."

To "rate" one Christian above another shows a lack of spiritual understanding. Several serious sins existed in the church at Corinth, which, in our opinion, may seem far more serious than the problem that received first attention—the division caused by the recognition given to certain ministers because of their abilities.

Apollos was a gifted preacher in the church at Corinth, but both Paul and Apollos were mere servants of Christ. As such, they could only do what the Lord called and enabled them to do. "Nay, much more those members of the body, which seem to be more feeble, are necessary" (I Corinthians 12:22).

MEMORY VERSE OF THE WEEK: I Corinthians 13:4
"Charity [love] suffereth long, and is kind; charity [love] envieth not; charity [love] vaunteth not itself, is not puffed up."

So the effectiveness and true worth of every Christian's service is only known by God. Since each gift and ability is given by God, He alone can determine their eternal values. Furthermore, except for His blessing, the most well-performed and most earnest work will be ineffective and fruitless insofar as spiritual results are concerned.

"Having then gifts differing according to the grace that is given to us, whether prophecy . . . ministry . . . teaching . . . exhortation: he that giveth, let him do it with simplicity; he that ruleth, with diligence . . ." (Romans 12:6-8).

NOTE:
4:5 **counsels** means motives; 4:11 **buffeted** means mistreated.

I Corinthians 1:19: See Isa. 29:14. **1:31:** See Jer. 9:24. **2:16:** See Isa. 40:13. **3:19:** See Job 5:13. **3:20:** See Ps. 94:11.

NOVEMBER 25: Read I Corinthians 5-9.

I Corinthians 6:9-11: "Know ye not that the unrighteous shall not inherit the kingdom of God? Be not deceived: neither fornicators, nor idolators, nor adulterers, nor effeminate, nor abusers of themselves with mankind, nor thieves, nor covetous, nor drunkards, nor revilers, nor extortioners, shall inherit the kingdom of God. And such were some of you: but ye are washed, but ye are sanctified, but ye are justified in the name of the Lord Jesus, and by the Spirit of our God."

A marvelous change takes place when we are converted! God said, "Ye are justified." This means more than being forgiven for past sins; it means that we possess our Lord's Divine nature. The old life with its sin and condemnation is gone. We received a new life and have passed from death unto life (John 5:24; I John 3:14). This new life continues to grow in Christlikeness. Just as newborn babes are unable to care for themselves and fall many times before they learn to walk, the newborn in Christ can expect to make mistakes as he grows into Christian maturity.

But our justification as believers does not vary with the fluctuations of our feelings, but in His finished work as revealed in His perfect Word.

Satan often succeeds in implanting a guilt upon our conscience for our failures. And through our lack of understanding of Christ's sufficiency and of our justification, we often feel very "un-justified" to be a child of God.

Therefore, He assures us, "Who shall lay any thing to the charge of God's elect? It is God that justifieth" (Romans 8:33).

NOTE:
7:12 **put her away** means divorce her; 8:10 **emboldened** means encouraged; 9:17 **dispensation** means stewardship.

I Corinthians 6:16: See Gen. 2:24. **9:9:** See Deu. 25:4.

MEMORY VERSE OF THE WEEK: I Corinthians 13:4
"Charity [love] suffereth long, and is kind; charity [love] envieth not; charity [love] vaunteth not itself, is not puffed up."

NOVEMBER 26: Read I Corinthians 10-13.

I Corinthians 10:33: "Even as I please all men in all things, not seeking mine own profit, but the profit of many, that they may be saved."

All about us are people who have serious problems, broken hearts, and burdens too heavy to carry. They are searching—desperately searching —for answers, for someone who cares.

God's people today need a deeper awareness of Christ's mission—of our commission "to seek and to save that which was lost" (Luke 19:10). It will cause each of us to see more clearly the opportunities around us.

As we seek the spiritual welfare of others, we lay up precious treasures in Heaven. On the other hand, a self-centered life is a wasted and empty life.

No one can truly possess the life and nature of Christ and still live for himself. Selfishness is incompatible with true Christianity. Though Christ was rich, He became poor for our sakes (see II Corinthians 8:9). He was born to save others. Because of Him and through us, thirsty souls are satisfied with the Water of Life.

We have the privilege of using our time and material wealth that others might gain eternal treasures.

"For the Son of man is come to seek and to save that which was lost" (Luke 19:10).

NOTE:
10:25 **shambles** means market; 11:19 **heresies** means errors; 12:25 **schism** means division; 13:1 **charity** means love; 13:4 **vaunteth** means boasteth.

I Corinthians 10:7: See Ex. 32:6; **10:26:** See Ps. 24:1.

NOVEMBER 27: Read I Corinthians 14-16.

I Corinthians 15:47,49: "The first man is of the earth, earthly: the second man is the Lord from heaven. . . . And as we have borne the image of the earthly, we shall also bear the image of the heavenly."

What a privilege to "bear the image of the heavenly"—to possess His nature! From the moment we were saved, we should have a desire to please God because we love Him! "As newborn babes, desire the sincere milk of the word, that ye may grow thereby" (I Peter 2:2).

This new nature has given us a hunger to read His Word that we might think as He thinks, feel as He feels, and desire what He desires. It has given us a new love for others and a longing for our loved ones to also come to know our wonderful Lord.

Wherever there is a new birth, there is a beginning of oneness and likeness of Spirit, and the process of becoming like Christ continues each day.

MEMORY VERSE FOR THE WEEK: Ephesians 3:16
    "That he would grant you, according to the riches of his glory, to be strengthened with might by his Spirit in the inner man"

"But we all, with open face beholding as in a glass the glory of the Lord, are changed into the same image from glory to glory, even as by the Spirit of the Lord" (II Corinthians 3:18).

NOTE:
14:10 **signification** means meaning; 14:27 **by course** means in turn; 15:20 **slept** means have died; 15:40 **celestial** means heavenly; **terrestrial** means earthly; 16:22 **Anathema** means Accursed; **Maran-atha** means Our Lord cometh.

I Corinthians 14:21: See Isa. 28:11, 12. **15:25:** See Ps. 110:1. **15:27:** See Ps. 8:6. **15:32:** See Isa. 22:13. **15:45:** See Gen. 2:7. **15:54:** See Isa. 25:8. **15:55:** See Hos. 13:14.

"If a man therefore purge himself from these, he shall be a vessel unto honour, sanctified, and meet for the master's use, and prepared unto every good work."   II Timothy 2:21

NOVEMBER 28: Read II Corinthians 1-4.

II Corinthians 4:7: "But we have this treasure in earthen vessels, that the excellency of the power may be of God, and not of us."

A Christian is like an *earthen vessel* that contains a very precious *treasure*. This treasure is "Christ in you" (Colossians 1:27). But it is not simply a matter of a treasure or simply an earthen vessel, but the Christian is a vessel that contains the treasure of the Holy Spirit.

This means that without God, you can do nothing of lasting, spiritual good. Furthermore, it is more than God blessing your abilities and answering prayer for wisdom and strength. It literally means that the Lord wants you to be as yielded to Him as a glove is yielded to the hand that is with it. He wants control as King of your life.

Without Christ, we are as worthless as an earthen vessel. The power to manifest that inward treasure is not dependent upon human strength. It requires more than the efforts of man to be Christlike. Christ wants to be King. He is either Lord of all or He is not Lord at all.

"This treasure" has been placed in weak, earthen vessels to draw attention to our precious Lord. Our value is dependent upon how much of Him—His Word—possesses us.

"Not that we are sufficient of ourselves to think any thing as of ourselves; but our sufficiency is of God" (II Corinthians 3:5).

NOTE:
2:14 **savour** means fragrance.

II Corinthians 3:13: See Ex. 34:33. **4:13:** See Ps. 116:10.

MEMORY VERSE FOR THE WEEK: I Corinthians 13:5
"[Love] Doth not behave itself unseemly, seeketh not her own, is not easily provoked, thinketh no evil."

NOVEMBER 29: Read II Corinthians 5-8.

II Corinthians 5:14,19: "For the love of Christ constraineth us; . . . God was in Christ, reconciling the world unto himself, not imputing their trespasses unto them; and hath committed unto us the word of reconciliation."

The child of God has a changed attitude from hostility to love and obedience. So our enmity with God is gone, and we are at peace with Him. "We love him, because he first loved us" (I John 4:19).

Reconciliation began with God, who loved the world so much "that he gave his only begotten Son" so that sinners could be united with Him (see John 3:16).

The ministry of reconciliation is a sacred trust that "constraineth us." *Constraineth* means that He draws our energies into His channel of love. Because He "constraineth us," we too may reach out with the wonderful news of His marvelous love that others too will be reconciled to God. The love of Christ should so master us that our foremost ambition is to live for His glory. Every decision in life should be determined by this mighty constraint of His love.

"Now then we are ambassadors for Christ, as though God did beseech you by us: we pray you in Christ's stead, be ye reconciled to God" (II Corinthians 5:20).

NOTE:
6:12 **bowels** means emotions.

II Corinthians 6:2: See Isa. 49:8. **6:16:** See Lev. 26:11, 12. **6:17:** See Isa. 52:11. **8:15:** See Ex. 16:18.

"Make thy face to shine upon thy servant; and teach me thy statutes." Psalm 119:135

NOVEMBER 30: Read II Corinthians 9-13.

II Corinthians 10:17-18: "But he that glorieth, let him glory in the Lord. For not he that commendeth himself is approved, but whom the Lord commendeth."

By human instinct, we wish to be accepted and well thought of among our friends and associates. We naturally want to feel important. At the center of self is the big "I" that seeks recognition. The worldly minded often achieve that goal by the clothes they wear, the automobile they drive, or other status symbols, such as being a member of an exclusive club.

MEMORY VERSE FOR THE WEEK: I Corinthians 13:5
"[Love] Doth not behave itself unseemly, seeketh not her own, is not easily provoked, thinketh no evil."

292

Christians have sometimes been just as guilty in seeking recognition by saying oratorical prayers or in a display of vocal or musical abilities—"all to the glory of God." More often, the attempt to build one's spiritual image is done by downgrading the motives and actions of another. This was the way the Apostle Paul's persecutors attacked him. They ridiculed his appearance, his language, his ministry, and his authority. In reality, they were commending themselves before each other. How unfortunate! They had allowed themselves to forfeit the only approval that really mattered—the Lord's.

The Lord's approval is not based on one's abilities or popularity. The one whom the Lord commends sincerely acknowledges that Christ alone is worthy of all honor and praise—that all self-efforts are vain and worthless without Him. "He that glorieth, let him glory in the Lord" (II Corinthians 10:17).

NOTE:
13:6 **reprobates** means rejected.

II Corinthians 9:9: See Ps. 112:9. **10:17:** See Jer. 9:24. **13:1:** See Deu. 19:15.

BIBLICAL REFERENCE INDEX

PRAYERS

MEMORY VERSE FOR THE WEEK: I Corinthians 13:5
"[Love] Doth not behave itself unseemly, seeketh not her own, is not easily provoked, thinketh no evil."

INTRODUCTION

The New Testament is composed of 27 books which may be divided into four general sections:

1. The historic books, including Matthew, Mark, Luke, John, and Acts
2. The thirteen epistles of Paul
3. The general epistles, including three by John, two by Peter, one by James, one by Jude, and the book of Hebrews
4. The prophetic book of Revelation which describes in symbolic terms a fuller explanation of Christ's work within His Church and His judgment upon the unbelieving world.

The New Testament completes the "Scripture . . . given by inspiration of God, and is profitable for doctrine, for reproof, for correction, for instruction in righteousness: That the man of God may be perfect, throughly furnished unto all good works" (II Timothy 3:16-17).

GALATIANS—The book of Galatians exposes the dangers of thinking that Christ's death and resurrection is not sufficient for our salvation. The Israelite had been dependent upon fulfilling the Law for his salvation, but now, "by the works of the law shall no flesh be justified."

The new position was ". . . we have believed in Jesus Christ, that we might be justified by the faith of Christ . . ." (2:16).

Abraham is mentioned eight times in this book to remind us that faith in God's redeeming grace began with Abraham, and that through him would come the Savior through whom the whole earth would be blessed. God provided the written Law 430 years later and showed how the sacrifices were symbolic of the coming Christ, "And if ye be Christ's, then are ye Abraham's seed, and heirs according to the promise" (3:29).

The key thought is "if righteousness come by the law, then Christ is dead in vain" (2:21).

"... no man is justified by the
law ... The just shall live by
faith."   Galatians 3:11

DECEMBER 1: Read Galatians 1-3.

Galatians 3:13-14: "Christ hath redeemed us from the curse of the law, . . . that we might receive the promise of the Spirit through faith."

Certain teachers were misdirecting the people of Galatia by telling them that in addition to believing in Christ, they must also fulfill certain ceremonial works of the Law, such as being circumcized. But salvation in Christ is complete. His redemption is not dependent upon human efforts.

Four hundred and thirty years before the Law was given to Moses, God blessed Abraham because of his faith. If faith without the Law was sufficient for Abraham, why should we turn from faith to the Law?

Abraham is mentioned eight times in chapter three to assure us that "even as Abraham believed God, and it was accounted to him for righteousness" (3:6), so it is through our faith in the crucified Christ and not in keeping the Law or doing good works that we become a child of God.

The Law was given as ". . . our schoolmaster to bring us unto Christ . . ." (3:24).

A schoolmaster was a servant who was entrusted with the care of a child until he reached maturity. The Law, like a faithful schoolmaster, caused the sinner to realize how sinful he really was and how utterly impossible it is to be good enough to please God.

God's forgiveness, mercy, and love can only be experienced through a personal relationship with Christ. "For as many of you as have been baptized into Christ have put on Christ" (Galatians 3:27).

NOTE:
1:11 **certify** means assure; 1:13 **conversation** means manner of life; 2:13 **dissimulation** means insincerity.

Galatians 3:6: See Gen. 15:6. **3:8:** See Gen. 12:3. **3:10:** See Deu. 27:26. **3:11:** See Hab. 2:4. **3:12:** See Lev. 18:5. **3:13:** See Deu. 21:23.

DECEMBER 2: Read Galatians 4-6.

Galatians 4:5-6: "To redeem them that were under the law, that we might receive the adoption of sons. And because ye are sons, God hath sent forth the Spirit of his Son into your hearts, crying, Abba, Father."

In the Old Testament, if poverty had caused a person to go into slavery or to lose his inheritance, the head of the family could act as a "kinsman" *redeemer.* This kinsman could *redeem* the poverty-stricken relative by paying the required ransom for his release and the restoration of his property (see Ruth 3:13).

MEMORY VERSE FOR THE WEEK: Ephesians 3:16

"That he would grant you, according to the riches of his glory, to be strengthened with might by his Spirit in the inner man"

When God announced His plan to deliver Israel from bondage in Egypt, He said, "I will *redeem* you with a stretched out arm" (Exodus 6:6). Israel's release from Egyptian slavery and restoration of the Promised Land was symbolic of the spiritual deliverance whereby Christ, our "kinsman" Redeemer, delivers us from sin and restores us to fellowship with God. By His death on the cross, Christ paid the ransom to God the Father for our sins (Titus 2:14; Hebrews 9:12-14).

Through the redeeming work of Christ, the believer is no longer a slave to sin, but he is a child of God and joint-heir with Christ (Romans 8:17). Our Lord's two-fold purpose for redeeming us was to pay the penalty for our sins and to adopt us into the family of God.

"Forasmuch as ye know that ye were not redeemed with corruptible things, as silver and gold, from your vain conversation received by tradition from your fathers; but with the precious blood of Christ, as of a lamb without blemish and without spot" (I Peter 1:18-19).

NOTE:
4:24 gendereth to means is destined for.

Galatians 4:27: See Isa. 54:1. **4:30:** See Gen. 21:10. **5:14:** See Lev. 19:18.

EPHESIANS—Even before the foundation of the world, Christ's re-deemed church was in God's plan. All believers are spiritually united as members of that spiritual body of which Christ is the Head.

The key thought in this book is that the believer is "chosen in Christ" to be holy and blameless—a living witness of the power of Christ in his life. "According as he hath chosen us in him before the foundation of the world, that we should be holy and without blame before him in love" (1:4).

DECEMBER 3: Read Ephesians 1-3.
Ephesians 2:18: "For through him we both have access by one Spirit unto the Father."

After the exodus from Egypt, God provided a way for His people to offer acceptable prayer to Him. Only the high priest was allowed to enter into the presence of God in the holy of holies to offer the incense for prayer on behalf of the wor-shipers.

The Gentiles had absolutely no covenant agree-ment with God. But today, because of the atoning death of Christ, Jews and Gentiles alike who have accepted Christ as Savior have this wonderful privilege.

MEMORY VERSE FOR THE WEEK: Ephesians 3:16
"That he would grant you, according to the riches of his glory, to be strengthened with might by his Spirit in the inner man"

The Good News is that "God, who is rich in mercy, for his great love wherewith he loved us" not only has delivered us from sin, but He has made it possible for each of us to come to Him in prayer at any time. (See Ephesians 2:4; compare Hebrews 7:25.)

God is calling His people to set aside time to pray. Satan does not want us to pray, and he continually seeks to destroy the spirit of prayer in every possible way.

This sacred privilege is also a great responsibility. Failure to pray is more serious than mere negligence—it is sin! "God forbid that I should sin against the Lord in ceasing to pray . . ." (I Samuel 12:23).

NOTE:
1:8 **prudence** means practical insight; 1:10 **dispensation** means administration; 1:14 **earnest** means pledge.

DECEMBER 4: Read Ephesians 4-6.

Ephesians 5:19,21: "Speaking to yourselves in psalms and hymns and spiritual songs, singing and making melody in your heart to the Lord . . . Submitting yourselves one to another in the fear of God."

Within the heart of every believer is a joyfulness—a deep sense of thanksgiving. Since the love of Christ indwells every Christian, the life of each member of the family of God should reflect His Spirit. "Beloved, let us love one another: for love is of God; and every one that loveth is born of God, and knoweth God" (I John 4:7).

His love is a tremendous unifying power. The Christian who has a self-seeking, independent spirit must yield to the gentle and gracious Spirit of Christ.

The submission and respect we have for God will be manifested as we submit ourselves "one to another in the fear of God." This oneness of the members of the Body of Christ produces a natural desire to "bear ye one another's burdens" (Galatians 6:2) and to express this love "in deed and in truth" (I John 3:18).

Our fellow believer is a representative of the Lord Jesus Christ, and we should look upon his needs and welfare as if he were Christ Himself.

"But whoso hath this world's good, and seeth his brother have need, and shutteth up his bowels of compassion from him, how dwelleth the love of God in him?" (I John 3:17).

NOTE:
4:14 **sleight** means craftiness; 6:11 **wiles** means strategies; 6:14 **girt about** means belted around.

Ephesians 4:8: See Ps. 68:18. **4:25:** See Zec. 8:16. **4:26:** See Ps. 4:4. **5:31:** See Gen. 2:24. **6:2,3:** See Exod. 20:12; Deu. 5:16.

MEMORY VERSE FOR THE WEEK: Ephesians 3:17
"That Christ may dwell in your hearts by faith; that ye, being rooted and grounded in love,"

PHILIPPIANS—Christ is mentioned 40 times, and "joy" or "rejoice" is mentioned 16 times in these four short chapters to tell us that inward joy is experienced daily when Christ becomes preeminent in our lives. The key thought is "Rejoice in the Lord, alway: and again I say, Rejoice" (Philippians 4:4).

Paul was in prison and enduring bitter hardships when he wrote this letter, which reveals the Lord as our true source of joy, regardless of external circumstances.

In a cold Roman dungeon, Paul wrote most of our treasured epistles of the New Testament.

"Not that I speak in respect of want: for I have learned, in whatsoever state I am, therewith to be content."
Philippians 4:11

DECEMBER 5: Read Philippians 1-4.

Philippians 4:7: "And the peace of God, which passeth all understanding, shall keep your hearts and minds through Christ Jesus."

How can our "heart and minds" be kept by "the peace of God"?

Strange as it may seem, only a few Christians are enjoying the peace of God. Many are in turmoil, finding that their efforts only cause them to exchange one frustration for another. Too often, inner confusion results from not having fully confessed and forsaken some secret hate, envy, greed, or jealousy.

Our minds have been likened to a house where guests are entertained. Once we allow the demon thoughts of jealousy, lust, and other evils to enter our minds, they are like rude guests who insist on dominating our thoughts and time and refuse to leave. They are not satisfied to remain as guests, but they want to take up residency and destroy one's peace of mind.

Release from these enemies of God's peace and freedom from self-love can be accomplished through the indwelling power of God. He is able to provide His strength to prepare us for any situation. Allowing the Holy Spirit to control our personality through our knowledge of His Word is the secret of the Spirit-filled life.

The key to enjoying the peace of God that passes all understanding is revealed in the following verses: "Finally, brethren, whatsoever things are true, whatsoever things are honest, whatsoever things are just, whatsoever things are pure, whatsoever things are lovely, whatsoever things are of good report; if there be any virtue, and if there be any praise, think on these things. Those things, which ye have both learned, and received, and heard, and seen in me, do: and the God of peace shall be with you" (Philippians 4:8-9).

NOTE:
3:2 **the concision** means false circumcision; 4:5 **moderation** means forebearing spirit.

MEMORY VERSE FOR THE WEEK: Ephesians 3:17
"That Christ may dwell in your hearts by faith; that ye, being rooted and grounded in love,"

COLOSSIANS—This letter exalts the preeminence and deity of Christ. Special emphasis is given to the relationship of Christ with the Church. He is the Head and the Church is the body. As the physical body is subjected to the complete control of the Head, so ought also the body of Christ, the Church, be subject to Him in all things.

The epistle tells us that Christ is our life, and we are "complete in Him" (2:10). "For ye are dead, and your life is hid with Christ in God" (3:3).

The Christian life is not a "creed" or a "system of doctrine," but it is Christ's life within us. The key thought is ". . . that in all things he might have the preeminence" (Colossians 1:18).

DECEMBER 6: Read Colossians 1-4.

Colossians 3:16: "Let the word of Christ dwell in you richly in all wisdom; teaching and admonishing one another in psalms and hymns and spiritual songs, singing with grace in your hearts to the Lord."

In this epistle to the Colossians, we see the truly exalted position of the Christian's life with Christ. Instead of speaking of the Word of *God,* the Holy Spirit directed the Apostle Paul to write, "Let the word of *Christ* dwell in you richly . . ."

The Scriptures exalt and glorify Christ, who "is all, and in all" (3:11).

Those who do not avail themselves of "the knowledge of his will" often experience spiritual defeat. But by knowing His will, we can be in harmony with Christ.

Just think! Right now, as we consistently read through His Word, we have the privilege of having the Word of Christ dwell richly within us, and we are "strengthened with all might, according to his glorious power" (1:11).

". . . Christ in you, the hope of glory: . . . teaching every man in all wisdom; that we may present every man perfect in Christ Jesus" (Colossians 1:27-28).

NOTE:
3:5 **concupiscence** means desire.

I AND II THESSALONIANS—Jesus is presented 25 times in I Thessalonians as Lord—dying for us and giving us life through His death. This new life in Christ is expressed by brotherly love (I Thessalonians 4:1-12) and living "unblameable in holiness before God" (3:13).

I and II Thessalonians are principally concerned with preparing the believer for the return of Christ and what must take place before that day. The key thought is "For the Lord himself shall descend from heaven with a shout, with the voice of the archangel, and with the trump of God: and the dead in Christ shall rise first" (I Thess. 4:16).

MEMORY VERSE FOR THE WEEK: Ephesians 3:17
    "That Christ may dwell in your hearts by faith; that ye, being rooted and grounded in love,"

DECEMBER 7: Read I Thessalonians 1-5.

I Thessalonians 4:16: "For the Lord himself shall descend from heaven with a shout, with the voice of the archangel, and with the trump of God: and the dead in Christ shall rise first."

There are at least twenty references in I and II Thessalonians to the return of our Lord. It is obvious that the purpose of these two letters is to prepare the Christian for His return.

For nearly 2,000 years, Christians have anxiously awaited His return; still, the promise remains unfulfilled. But the Savior promised that He would come again and receive us unto Himself (John 14:1-3).

So the believer who is in fellowship with Christ is watching and waiting for the triumphant shout of his Redeemer, "For the Lord himself shall descend from heaven with a shout" (I Thessalonians 4:16).

The great Conqueror—the King of Kings—will soon return, "... and so shall we ever be with the Lord" (I Thessalonians 4:17).

NOTE:
2:2 **entreated** means insulted; 2:9 **chargeable** means an expense; 3:8 **fast** means firm; 4:4 **possess his vessel** means control his own body; 4:15 **prevent** means precede.

DECEMBER 8: Read II Thessalonians 1-3.

II Thessalonians 1:7: "And to you who are troubled rest with us, when the Lord Jesus shall be revealed from heaven with his mighty angels."

In the two short letters to the Thessalonians, Paul emphasized that all worldly interests are insignificant compared to our need to be prepared for the glorious event of our Lord's return.

Christ's first coming surprised the religious leaders of His time, and it is possible that His Second Coming will be an even greater surprise to many people, for "the day of the Lord so cometh as a thief in the night" (I Thessalonians 5:2).

Since the Lord's return is mentioned more than 300 times in the 260 chapters of the New Testament, the Christian who is diligent in reading the Bible soon discovers that the central theme of the New Testament is the second coming of Christ.

The time is drawing near "when he shall come to be glorified in his saints, and to be admired in all them that believe ..." (II Thessalonians 1:10).

All who love Christ are preparing themselves for His great and wonderful return, "And every man that hath this hope in him purifieth himself, even as he is pure" (I John 3:3).

MEMORY VERSE FOR THE WEEK: Ephesians 3:17
"That Christ may dwell in your hearts by faith; that ye, being rooted and grounded in love,"

I AND II TIMOTHY—reveal the importance of prayerfully studying the Scriptures and fervently preaching the Word as the only effective solution to every false way. The key thought is "Study to shew thyself approved unto God, a workman that needeth not to be ashamed, rightly dividing the word of truth" (II Timothy 2:15; see also II Timothy 3:14 through 4:5).

"Take my yoke upon you, and learn of me; for I am meek and lowly in heart: and ye shall find rest unto your souls. For my yoke is easy, and my burden is light." Matthew 11:29-30

DECEMBER 9: Read I Timothy 1-6.

I Timothy 2:1-2: "I exhort therefore, that, first of all, supplications, prayers, intercessions, and giving of thanks, be made for all men; For kings, and for all that are in authority; that we may lead a quiet and peaceable life in all godliness and honesty."

At the time Paul wrote the book of I Timothy, the Roman ruler, Nero, was cruelly persecuting Christians. Yet, the Bible emphasizes the importance of Christians praying for those who have authority over them, even though many rulers are ruthless, ungodly men.

Strange as it may seem, the Scriptures record occasions when God even used wicked rulers to accomplish His purpose. So we have an obligation to pray "for all that are in authority." The Lord would never have taught us to pray "Thy will be done in earth, as it is in heaven" if prayer had no influence on our nation's leaders.

Our prayers affect the unseen world more than we will ever know, and as we pray for others, our own needs are met in such a way ". . . that we may lead a quiet and peaceable life in all godliness and honesty" (I Timothy 2:2).

NOTE:
2:7 **verity** means truth; 2:12 **usurp** means claim; 3:1 **bishop** means spiritual overseer; 3:2 **vigilant** means self-controlled; 4:14 **presbytery** means board of elders; 5:11 **wax wanton** means draw away.

I Timothy 5:18: See Deu. 25:4.

DECEMBER 10: Read II Timothy 1-4.

II Timothy 3:16-17: "All scripture is given by inspiration of God, and is profitable for doctrine, for reproof, for correction, for instruction in righteousness: That the man of God may be perfect, throughly furnished unto all good works."

MEMORY VERSE FOR THE WEEK: Ephesians 3:17
"That Christ may dwell in your hearts by faith; that ye, being rooted and grounded in love,"

The Bible alone can thoroughly prepare a Christian "unto all good works" and fully equip him to do God's will.

The excuse many people use for not reading the Bible is, "I just don't have time." Actually, time is the one thing which God has distributed equally to every man, so it is really a matter of devoting our time to what we believe is most important.

We spend several years studying to gain an education for life's vocation, but when we neglect to make an equal commitment to reading God's Word, we are admitting that the attainments of this world mean more to us than pleasing the Lord.

Just as regularly eating good food is necessary to properly maintain the physical body, regular Bible reading is necessary to properly maintain the spiritual life. So we must not merely read the Bible *as time permits*.

Once we realize the importance of seeking the Lord for guidance, we will have no difficulty finding time to read His Word every day.

"But whoso looketh into the perfect law of liberty, and continueth therein, he being not a forgetful hearer, but a doer of the work, this man shall be blessed in his deed" (James 1:25).

NOTE:
2:4 **entangleth himself** means becomes involved; 2:5 **strive for masteries** means compete as an athlete; 2:17 **canker** means cancer; 2:23 **gender** means produce; 3:3 **incontinent** means without self-control.

II Timothy 2:19: See Num. 16:5.

TITUS—Special moral and spiritual fitness is set forth for the believer. The book of Titus particularly emphasizes having godly church leaders. They must be blameless both in their home life and in their personal life. They must be true to the Word (1:6-9), for there are many "vain talkers and deceivers . . . teaching things which they ought not, for filthy lucre's sake" who confess "that they know God; but in works they deny him" (1:10,11,16).

The key thought in Titus is that Christ, "gave himself for us, that he might redeem us from all iniquity, and purify unto himself a peculiar people, *zealous of good works*" (Titus 2:14).

PHILEMON—This book emphasizes Christian love and forgiveness, showing the power of the Gospel in winning a runaway slave to Christ. Christ has joined each individual Christian in Himself and thus created a spiritual brotherhood that will cause both master and slave to recognize that they are one in Christ. The key thought is "hearing of thy love and faith, which thou has toward the Lord Jesus, and toward all saints" (Philemon 5).

MEMORY VERSE FOR THE WEEK: Ephesians 3:17
"That Christ may dwell in your hearts by faith; that ye, being rooted and grounded in love,"

DECEMBER 11: Read Titus 1-3 and Philemon.
Titus 3:1-2: "Put them in mind to be subject to principalities and powers, to obey magistrates, to be ready to every good work, to speak evil of no man, to be no brawlers, but gentle, showing all meekness unto all men."

Where God and His Word are not recognized as man's supreme authority, there is a disregard for life and for law and order.

Just as Satan caused Eve to eat of the forbidden fruit in the Garden of Eden, still today, he is opposed to God's authority and instigates violence, rebellion, and lawlessness.

If our officials are incompetent or the government corrupt, there are orderly processes available to bring about the needed changes. Rioting and violence are never God's way to bring about healthy change.

When Peter cut off the ear of the high priest's servant, Christ admonished him by saying, "Put up again thy sword . . . they that take the sword shall perish with the sword" (Matthew 26:52).

The Christian does not have the right to choose which laws he will obey and which laws he will disobey.

"Submit yourselves to every ordinance of man for the Lord's sake: whether it be to the king, as supreme; or unto governors, as unto them that are sent by him for the punishment of evildoers, and for the praise of them that do well. For so is the will of God, that with well-doing ye may put to silence the ignorance of foolish men" (I Peter 2:13-15).

NOTE:
1:9 **gainsayers** means those who contradict and oppose; 1:11 **subvert** means mislead; **lucre** means money; Philemon 8 **enjoin** means give directions.

HEBREWS—The central person in Hebrews is Christ. He is presented as far superior to the prophets, the angels, and even Moses. Christ has cleansed us from our sins by His blood, and He sits at the right hand of God as the High Priest over all.

The key thought is "Wherefore, holy brethren, partakers of the heavenly calling, consider the Apostle and High Priest of our profession, Christ Jesus;" (Hebrews 3:1).

"Let us therefore come boldly unto the throne of grace, that we may obtain mercy, and find grace to help in time of need" (4:16). This book shows that the source of power to live the victorious Christian life is the Word. Christ is the Living Word of God, who is alive, "quick and powerful," all wise and all knowing (4:12).

MEMORY VERSE FOR THE WEEK: Ephesians 3:18
"May be able to comprehend with all saints what is the breadth, and length, and depth, and height;"

DECEMBER 12: Read Hebrews 1-4.

Hebrews 4:15-16: "For we have not an high priest which cannot be touched with the feeling of our infirmities; but was in all points tempted like as we are, yet without sin. Let us therefore come boldly unto the throne of grace, that we may obtain mercy, and find grace to help in time of need."

The high priest held a position of supreme importance in the Hebrew nation. Through him, they could secure and retain an acceptable relationship with God. The high priest was also a representative from God to the people.

Once every year, on the day of Atonement, Israel's high priest passed through the curtain that separated the holy place from the holy of holies where the glory of God's presence dwelt. This was symbolic of Christ, who passed from the presence of His disciples "into the heavens"—the holy place of God's presence.

Christ is our all-sufficient great High Priest who offered Himself on the cross as a sacrifice for the sins of those who accept Him as Savior. Therefore, we are invited to "come boldly unto the throne of grace"—into the presence of God—with our requests. "Let us therefore come" literally means that we may *keep on approaching* the throne of grace to receive wisdom and strength to meet every need.

Having these wonderful truths, we should never doubt that God will answer prayer! "Seeing then that we have a great high priest, that is passed into the heavens, Jesus the Son of God, let us hold fast our profession" (Hebrews 4:14)

NOTE:
2:17 **behoved** means was imperative for; 4:12 **quick** means living.

Hebrews 1:5: See Ps. 2:7; II Sam. 7:14. 1:6: See Ps. 97:7. 1:7: See Ps. 104:4. 1:8-9: See Ps. 45:6-7. 1:10-12: See Ps. 102:25-27. 1:13: See Ps. 110:1. 2:6-8: See Ps. 8:4-6. 2:12: See Ps. 22:22. 2:13: See Isa. 8:18. 3:7-11: See Ps. 95:7-11. 4:3: See Ps. 95:11. 4:4: See Gen. 2:2.

"Wherefore he is able also to save them to the uttermost that come unto God by him, seeing he ever liveth to make intercession for them." Hebrews 7:25

DECEMBER 13: Read Hebrews 5-7.

Hebrews 5:4: "And no man taketh this honour unto himself, but he that is called of God, as was Aaron."

Aaron, the first high priest, was not selected by the people—he was chosen of God. On *the day of Atonement,* God directed him to make an atonement first for his sins and then for the sins of his household. Following this, he was qualified to make an atonement for the sins of the people (Leviticus 16:11-15).

MEMORY VERSE FOR THE WEEK: Ephesians 3:18
"May be able to comprehend with all saints what is the breadth, and length, and depth, and height;"

By contrast, on the *Great Day of Atonement* at Calvary, there was no need for Christ to make a sin offering for Himself because He was the sinless Son of God. Christ assures us that He is *always* available to intercede for us before the throne of God. So in every respect, He was definitely superior to the priesthood of Aaron.

How comforting to know that any time, day or night, we can come to God "in Jesus' name," confessing our sins, and receive His gracious mercy through our great High Priest!

He has assured us, "Lo, I am with you alway, even unto the end of the world" (Matthew 28:20).

NOTE:
6:17 **immutability** means unchangeableness.

Hebrews 5:5: See Ps. 2:7. **5:6:** See Ps. 110:4. **6:14:** See Gen. 22:17

DECEMBER 14: Read Hebrews 8-10.
Hebrews 10:19,22: "Having therefore, brethren, boldness to enter into the holiest by the blood of Jesus, . . . Let us draw near with a ture heart in full assurance of faith, having our hearts sprinkled from an evil conscience, and our bodies washed with pure water."

The Aaronic priesthood, animal sacrifices, and Temple ceremonies were all fulfilled in Christ. Not only was Christ the one true sacrifice, but He is the one eternal High Priest.

When Jesus died on the cross, God caused the veil of the Temple to be torn from top to bottom. This act of God proclaimed that Christians have the blessed privilege of coming before the throne of God in prayer through Jesus, our eternal High Priest. Not only do we have access into His presence through prayer, but "Let us draw near" means that we have the privilege of living day by day in His presence.

The Israelite worshiper did not have the privilege of entering God's presence in the holy place, but through Christ, the believer may dwell in the presence of the Most High every moment of every day, in every circumstance, "by a new and living way, which he hath consecrated for us" (Hebrews 10:20).

NOTE:
10:33 **gazingstock** means object of ridicule; 10:39 **perdition** means destruction.

Hebrews 8:5: See Exod. 25:40. **8:8-12:** See Jer. 31:31-34. **9:20:** See Exod. 24:8. **10:5-7:** See Ps. 40:6-8. **10:12-13:** See Ps. 110:1. **10:16-17:** See Jer. 31:33-34. **10:30:** See Deu. 32:35-36. **10:37-38:** See Hab. 2:3-4.

MEMORY VERSE FOR THE WEEK: Ephesians 3:18
"May be able to comprehend with all saints what is the breadth, and length, and depth, and height;"

"Choosing rather to suffer affliction with the people of God, than to enjoy the pleasures of sin for a season;" Hebrews 11:25

DECEMBER 15: Read Hebrews 11-13.

Hebrews 11:36: "And others had trial of cruel mockings and scourgings, yea, moreover of bonds and imprisonment."

Ordinary men of faith "subdued kingdoms, wrought righteousness, obtained promises, stopped the mouths of lions" (11:33). But the *others* who are mentioned in this great list of heroes of faith had as much, if not more, faith. They were those "of whom the world was not worthy" (11:38). These *others* "wandered in deserts, and in mountains, and in dens and caves of the earth," and received "cruel mockings and scourgings."

They too remained faithful during persecution and suffering, "that they might obtain a better resurrection" (11:35). These *others* had so abandoned self-recognition and self-interests that we don't even know their names! Their faith wasn't dependent upon favorable circumstances, but it was grounded in the unseen One.

Those who really love the Lord and are living for Him must sometimes "suffer for his name's sake," but we have the assurance: "If we suffer, we shall also reign with him: if we deny him, he also will deny us" (II Timothy 2:12).

"I am crucified with Christ: nevertheless I live; yet not I, but Christ liveth in me: and the life which I now live in the flesh I live by the faith of the Son of God, who loved me, and gave himself for me" (Galatians 2:20).

NOTE:
11:29 **assaying** means attempting.

Hebrews 11:18: See Gen. 21:12. **12:5-6:** See Prov. 3:11-12. **12:12:** See Isa. 35:3. **12:26:** See Hag. 2:6. **13:5:** See Jos. 1:5. **13:6:** See Ps. 118:6.

JAMES—The book of James is a practical guide to the Christian life and conduct that declares: Faith without works is worthless. In both the first and last chapters, James urges Christians to pray (1:5-8; 5:13-18). The key thought that covers the many aspects of our Christian conduct is "if any of you lack wisdom, let him ask of God" (1:5). God is the source of all true wisdom, so we are to receive with meekness the engrafted Word and then pray that His Word will create the needed transformation to make us "doers of the word, and not hearers only . . ." (1:22).

MEMORY VERSE FOR THE WEEK: Ephesians 3:18
"May be able to comprehend with all saints what is the breadth, and length, and depth, and height;"

DECEMBER 16: Read James 1-5.

James 1:18-19,22: "Of his own will begat he us with the word of truth, that we should be a kind of firstfruits of his creatures. Wherefore, my beloved brethren, let every man be swift to hear, slow to speak, slow to wrath: . . . But be ye doers of the word, and not hearers only, deceiving your own selves."

Often when someone is talking to us, we are so preoccupied with our own thoughts that we don't pay attention to what they are saying. Therefore, we miss much of what they were trying to tell us.

One of the greatest hindrances to hearing God's voice in His Word is being so preoccupied with our own ideas that we do not listen to Him. So He cautions us, "Let every man be swift to hear, slow to speak."

When we read the Bible, are we "swift to hear," or do we also insult God by not paying attention to what He is trying to tell us?

If we are as swift to hear His voice as we are to express our opinions, the defeating forces within will vanish and we will be marvelously changed by the perfect law of liberty.

Most of us insist on doing things the way we want to and when we want to. But when the King of Kings speaks, we must humble ourselves and "receive with meekness the engrafted word, which is able to save your souls" (1:21). The "engrafted word" speaks of Christ as well as His Word. The original Greek uses the same word. Christ and His Word are inseparable.

"And the Word was made flesh, and dwelt among us, (and we beheld his glory, the glory as of the only begotten of the Father,) full of grace and truth" (John 1:14).

NOTE:

1:21 **superfluity** means excesses; 3:4 **listeth** means chooses; 5:3 **cankered** means rusted through; 5:16 **effectual** means unceasing.

James 2:8: See Lev. 19:18. **2:11:** See Exod. 20:13-14. **2:23:** See Gen. 15:6. **4:6:** See Prov. 3:34.

I AND II PETER—Suffering is mentioned fourteen times in these two epistles. Since the days of the early church when great presecution forced Christians to leave Jerusalem (Acts 8:1), Christians have been subjected to every conceivable kind of torture.

The presence of the Lord becomes even more precious to Christians during times of suffering, and the reappearing of our Lord becomes equally precious as the Christian's "blessed hope."

The key thought is, "That the trial of your faith, being much more precious than of gold that perisheth, though it be tried with fire, might be found into praise and honour and glory at the appearing of Jesus Christ" (I Peter 1:7).

MEMORY VERSE FOR THE WEEK: Ephesians 3:18

"May be able to comprehend with all saints what is the breadth, and length, and depth, and height;"

DECEMBER 17: Read I Peter 1-2.

I Peter 1:7: "That the trial of your faith, being much more precious than of gold that perisheth, though it be tried with fire, might be found unto praise and honour and glory at the appearing of Jesus Christ."

Sometimes we find ourselves in circumstances that are painful and against our own desires. Our natural reaction is to try to find a solution to our problems, but occasionally, they are beyond our ability to solve.

During these times, we often turn to God in prayer. When He does not answer according to our wishes, we sometimes feel that God has failed us. But the truly faithful Christian will realize that He will supply our needs and strengthen us when and how He chooses: "For my thoughts are not your thoughts, neither are your ways my ways, saith the Lord" (Isaiah 55:8).

The trial of our faith can be very precious when we place our problems in the hands of the Lord. So with every trial, let us not be so concerned about *how* our problem will be solved as we are in trusting Him. God has a reason for allowing our trials, and His way of resolving them will always be to our best interest.

His Word assures us that we "are kept by the power of God through faith unto salvation ready to be revealed in the last time" (I Peter 1:5).

NOTE:
1:1 **strangers** means exiles; 1:17 **sojourning** means temporary residence; 2:4 **disallowed** means rejected; 2:19 **thankworthy** means approved; 2:24 **stripes** means wounds.

I Peter 1:16: See Lev. 11:44. **1:24-25:** See Isa. 50:6-8. **2:6:** See Ps. 118:22; Isa. 28:16. **2:7:** See Ps. 118:22. **2:22:** See Isa. 53:9. **2:24:** See Isa. 53:4.

DECEMBER 18: Read I Peter 3-5.

I Peter 3:14; 4:1: "But and if ye suffer for righteousness' sake, happy are ye: and be not afraid of their terror, neither be troubled; . . . Forasmuch then as Christ hath suffered for us in the flesh, arm yourselves likewise with the same mind . . ."

At least sixteen times in this short letter, we are encouraged to remain faithful to Christ as we experience trials and testings.

Peter was the first to object when Jesus said that it was time for the Son of man to "suffer many things." Peter replied, ". . . Lord: this shall not be unto thee," thinking that suffering surely wasn't the will of God (see Matthew 16:21-22).

MEMORY VERSE FOR THE WEEK: Ephesians 3:19

"And to know the love of Christ, which passeth knowledge, that ye might be filled with all the fulness of God."

But the same Peter wrote this epistle many years later, emphasizing the importance of being willing to suffer for our Lord's sake.

His advice to the Lord on the first occasion was to avoid the cross (see Matthew 16:22). But now Peter recalls how his Lord suffered, "who, when he was reviled, reviled not again; when he suffered, he threatened not; but committed himself to him that judgeth righteously" (I Peter 2:23).

Through the years, Peter too had learned to endure many beatings and much suffering. He wrote to encourage and strengthen others by reminding them, ". . . arm yourselves likewise with the same mind"—be willing to suffer as Christ did.

"Looking unto Jesus the author and finisher of our faith; who for the joy that was set before him endured the cross, despising the shame, and is set down at the right hand of the throne of God. For consider him that endured such contradiction of sinners against himself, lest ye be wearied and faint in your minds" (Hebrews 12:2-3).

NOTE:
4:15 **busybody** means meddler.

I Peter 3:10-12: See Ps. 34:12-16. **5:5:** See Prov. 3:34.

"I must work the works of him that sent me, while it is day: the night cometh, when no man can work."
John 9:4

DECEMBER 19: Read II Peter 1-3.

II Peter 3:14-15: "Wherefore, beloved, seeing that ye look for such things, be diligent that ye may be found of him in peace, without spot, and blameless. And account that the longsuffering of our Lord is salvation . . ."

During the interval between Christ's ascension and His return, the unbelievers of the world "continue walking after their own lusts." They assume that the long delay is proof that Christ will never return. (See II Peter 3:3-4.) But the believer is preparing to meet Him.

Remember our Lord's parable of the virgins when He said, "Behold, the bridegroom cometh." His return will be so sudden that there will be no time to make preparation after He appears (see Matthew 25:1-13). It will be too late then to ask forgiveness of sins or to make things right with others, for the Word of God is clear, "Behold, I come quickly" (Revelation 22:12). If we are to be prepared like the five wise virgins were, we must make the necessary preparations now.

We must all watch, wait, work, and pray for the coming of the Lord. At the time appointed by God ". . . this same Jesus, which is taken up from you into heaven, shall so come in like manner as ye have seen him go into heaven" (Acts 1:11).

NOTE:
II Peter 2:22: See Prov. 26:11.

MEMORY VERSE FOR THE WEEK: Ephesians 3:19
"And to know the love of Christ, which passeth knowledge, that ye might be filled with all the fulness of God."

I JOHN—The word *love* appears forty-eight times in the first epistle of John. God's indwelling love causes a remarkable two-fold change in the life of a believer. It gives us a desire to please God and a concern for the welfare of others.

Love for others and our love for God are inseparably united as one.

DECEMBER 20: Read I John 1-3.

I John 2:28: "And now, little children, abide in him; that, when he shall appear, we may have confidence, and not be ashamed before him at his coming."

To "be ashamed" is different from the humiliations that result from making a mistake or by having tried and failed. Shame is caused by the consciousness of guilt. It is the result of intentionally doing wrong or the unwillingness to do that which we knew was right.

As we "abide in him" we will never be ashamed. Abiding in Him results from knowing Him through His Word.

As Christians, we should feel obligated to study the Bible. How else are we to learn God's will or how to abide in Him? We need to "Study to shew thyself approved unto God, a workman that needeth *not to be ashamed,* rightly dividing the word of truth" (II Timothy 2:15).

The word *study* means "to be devoted to the mastery of." So as we diligently read His Word to do His will, we will discover that His Word empowers us to accomplish His will.

When we set aside a definite time each day to read His Word and fellowship with Him in prayer, we need never fear being "ashamed" before Him at His coming.

"For whosoever shall be ashamed of me and of my words, of him shall the Son of man be ashamed, when he shall come in his own glory, and in his Father's, and of the holy angels" (Luke 9:26).

"For if any be a hearer of the word, and not a doer, he is like unto a man beholding his natural face in a glass: For he beholdeth himself, and goeth his way, and straightway forgetteth what manner of man he was."
James 1:23-24

DECEMBER 21: Read I John 4-5.

I John 4:17: "Herein is our love made perfect, that we may have boldness in the day of judgment: because as he is, so are we in this world."

Most of us talk a lot but say so little. In contrast, God has said very little—just one Book throughout all the history of mankind—but each word is vitally important.

A general rule to be remembered concerning the importance of what God has said is this:

When God says something once, it is important, but when He says it more than once, we must give it our utmost consideration.

In view of this, consider the seriousness of our responsibility as stewards of God's love, which is mentioned more than 25 times in chapter four. "Beloved, if God so loved us, we ought also to love one another" (4:11).

When a dispute arose between Abraham's herdsmen and Lot's herdsmen, Abraham immediately said, "Let there be no strife . . . for we be brethren . . . Is not the whole land before thee? . . . (Genesis 13:8-9).

Just as Abraham responded in love toward his greedy nephew, Lot, we must likewise respond when someone takes advantage of us. Expressing the nature of God's love was more important to Abraham than material gain.

It is not enough merely to speak of God's love, but we must manifest this love and long-suffering in our daily encounters with our fellowman.

"If a man say, I love God, and hateth his brother, he is a liar: for he that loveth not his brother whom he hath seen, how can he love God whom he hath not seen?" (I John 4:20).

II JOHN—The word *truth* is used five times in these thirteen verses. We must examine our opinions, our convictions, and our doctrines according to the Scriptures. Are we "walking in truth, as we have received a commandment from the Father"? (vs. 4). The truth of God's Word can only fulfill God's purpose in our lives to the extent that we read and adhere to "all Scripture." The key thought is "whosoever transgresseth, and abideth not in the doctrine of Christ, hath not God . . ." (vs. 9).

III JOHN—Two types of church members are presented. Gaius is generous and a helper in the Lord's work, but Diotrephes is a hindrance to the ministry. These men are examples of the two great classes of Christians, either helping or hindering the ministry of Christ. The key thought is "beloved, follow not that which is evil, but that which is good. He that doeth good is of God: but he that doeth evil hath not seen God" (vs. 11).

JUDE—Certain people had joined the church and were teaching false doctrines. "Woe unto them . . . to whom is reserved the blackness of darkness for ever" (vss. 11,13).

In contrast to the false teachers are those who will be presented "faultless before the presence of his glory" (vs. 24). Jude clearly states the key thought: "Beloved, when I gave all diligence to write unto you of the common salvation, it was needful for me to write unto you, and exhort you that ye should earnestly contend for the faith which was once delivered unto the saints" (vs. 3).

DECEMBER 22: Read II John, III John, and Jude.

Jude 3: "Beloved, when I gave all diligence to write unto you of the common salvation, it was needful for me to write unto you, and exhort you that ye should earnestly contend for the faith which was once delivered unto the saints."

The book of Jude was written to the "preserved in Jesus Christ and called" (vs. 1). It is the only book in the Bible that is devoted to the apostasy that will prevail throughout the world before our Lord's return.

MEMORY VERSE FOR THE WEEK: Ephesians 3:19
"And to know the love of Christ, which passeth knowledge, that ye might be filled with all the fulness of God."

An apostate may have received, to some degree, the *written* Word, but he has not received the *Living* Word, the Son of God. He has received light, but not life.

Rejecting revealed truth leads to apostasy. Jude makes this clear in referring to Cain, Balaam, and Core (vs. 11).

Christ was referring to this time when He said: "When the Son of man cometh, shall he find faith on the earth?" (Luke 18:8). The Scriptures tell us that "faith cometh by hearing, and hearing by the word of God" (Romans 10:17).

God's Word also tells us of the day when many "will not endure sound doctrine." Therefore, we are told to "preach the word" (II Timothy 4:1-4).

"But ye, beloved, building up yourselves on your most holy faith, praying in the Holy Ghost, Keep yourselves in the love of God, looking for the mercy of our Lord Jesus Christ unto eternal life" (Jude 20-21).

NOTE:
III John 10 **prating against** means unjustly accusing; Jude 4 **lasciviousness** means uncontrolled behavior.

REVELATION—This is the only book of prophecy in the New Testament. More than 300 symbolic terms describe the historic events concerning Christ and His Church. His glorious and eternal reign is the outstanding theme. All of God's promises will be fulfilled, and every judgment will come to pass. So remember the promise, "Blessed is he that readeth, and they that hear the words of this prophecy, and keep those things which are written therein: for the time is at hand" (1:3).

The last words of Christ in His Revelation are: "Surely I come"; and the response of every believer who is prepared to meet Him will be "Even so, come, Lord Jesus" (22:20).

DECEMBER 23: Read Revelation 1-2.
Revelation 1:1: "The Revelation of Jesus Christ, which God gave unto him, to shew unto his servants things which must shortly come to pass; and he sent and signified it by his angel unto his servant John."

Every child of God should desire to know more about Christ, and as we prayerfully read God's Word, we will discover that every book in the Bible is a revelation of our wonderful Savior.

The book of Revelation presents the personal Christ—His living relationship with His people today—and the unfolding of "things which must shortly come to pass."

MEMORY VERSE FOR THE WEEK: Ephesians 3:19
"And to know the love of Christ, which passeth knowledge, that ye might be filled with all the fulness of God."

Many Christians become so involved in trying to understand all the symbols, the mysteries, and the judgments that they fail to see that the book of Revelation is the unveiling of the Person, Jesus Christ, who is the center of everything. He is revealed as the "Alpha and Omega, the first and the last" (1:11); "A Lamb as it had been slain" (5:6); "the first begotten of the dead" (1:5,18; 2:8).

It is the Revelation of Christ's final triumph over all evil. It gives assurance that the living Lord Jesus rules and uses all the activities of men and all the calamities of nature to accomplish His purposes.

Jesus Christ, the faithful witness; the first begotten from the dead; the One who loved, washed, and lifted us into sonship—this is the risen Christ who is coming again!

"Blessed is he that readeth, and they that hear the words of this prophecy, and keep those things which are written therein: for the time is at hand" (Revelation 1:3).

NOTE:
1:8 **Alpha and Omega** means Beginning and End; 1:13 **girt** means wrapped; **paps** means chest; 2:19 **charity** means love.

DECEMBER 24: Read Revelation 3-5.

Revelation 3:20: "Behold, I stand at the door, and knock: if any man hear my voice, and open the door, I will come in to him, and will sup with him, and he with me."

Our Lord waits at the door, knocking and seeking admission into the heart of everyone who will open to Him.

"Stand" and "knock" can be translated "I have been standing" and "I have been knocking." Therefore, He has been and still is waiting for each person who will receive Him.

Although the appeal continues to be given, many continue to ignore His presence. Others are so preoccupied with worldly activities that they don't even realize He is knocking at the door of their heart. Just how carefully do we listen to what the Spirit has to say?

This glorious invitation is extended to everyone (see Revelation 22:17). Come before it is forever too late!

"But as many as received him, to them gave he power to become the sons of God, even to them that believe on his name" (John 1:12).

MEMORY VERSE FOR THE WEEK: Ephesians 3:19
"And to know the love of Christ, which passeth knowledge, that ye might be filled with all the fulness of God."

DECEMBER 25: Read Revelation 6-8.

Revelation 7:9: "After this I beheld, and, lo, a great multitude, which no man could number, of all nations, and kindreds, and people, and tongues, stood before the throne, and before the Lamb, clothed with white robes, and palms in their hands."

This white-robed, palm-bearing multitude has overcome Satan and at last is in the company of their Lord. With a joyfully loud voice, they are singing, "Salvation to our God which sitteth upon the throne, and unto the Lamb" (7:10). The angels, elders, and the living creatures who surround the throne of God are also worshiping Him in ceaseless praise. This privilege is given only to His own redeemed who are clothed in "white robes"—the righteousness of Christ. It means too that for all eternity, they will share in the honors given to the Lamb.

As children of God, we have a wonderful reason to shout with joy for our great salvation. He is worthy of more praise than we can ever give Him in this life or in the life to come.

God created us in such a way that we can be truly happy only when we are praising our wonderful Lord.

". . . and I heard the voice of many angels around about the throne and the beasts and the elders: . . . Saying with a loud voice, Worthy is the Lamb that was slain to receive power, and riches, and wisdom, and strength, and honour, and glory, and blessing" (Revelation 5:11,12).

NOTE:
6:13 **untimely** means unripe; 6:15 **bondman** means slave.

DECEMBER 26: Read Revelation 9-11.

Revelation 11:3,7: "And I will give power unto my two witnesses . . . And when they shall have finished their testimony, the beast that ascendeth out of the bottomless pit shall make war against them, and shall overcome them, and kill them."

Who are these two witnesses? What is their message? When will they appear? The answers have been many, but let us not become so concerned over who the witnesses are in this future event that we fail to recognize their significance to us.

The two witnesses are not a self-appointed committee. but they are commissioned by God to face the fierce opposition of those who hate God. Furthermore, they are empowered to fulfill their calling and will be invincible until they have "finished their testimony." Then and only then will these witnesses of God be martyred in the city "where also our Lord was crucified" (11:8).

MEMORY VERSE FOR THE WEEK: Ephesians 3:20
"Now unto him that is able to do exceeding abundantly above all that we ask or think, according to the power that worketh in us."

The message of God's Divine authority upon earth cannot be defeated.

We too are commissioned to be a faithful witness. Jesus said, ". . . ye shall be witnesses unto me" (Acts 1:8). If we are willing to live or die as faithful witnesses for Christ, we too will be "caught up together with them in the clouds, to meet the Lord in the air: and so shall we ever be with the Lord" (I Thessalonians 4:17).

NOTE:
9:11 **Apollyon** means a destroyer.

". . . Arise, and take the young child and his mother, and flee into Egypt, and be thou there until I bring thee word: for Herod will seek the young child to destroy him. When he arose, he took the young child and his mother by night, and departed into Egypt." Matthew 2:13-14

DECEMBER 27: Read Revelation 12-13.
Revelation 12:1,3,10,11: "And there appeared . . . a woman clothed with the sun . . . And there appeared another wonder . . . a great red dragon, having seven heads and ten horns . . . And I heard a loud voice saying . . . the accuser of our brethren is cast down . . . And they overcame him by the blood of the Lamb, and by the word of their testimony; and they loved not their lives unto the death."

The "woman clothed with the sun" is symbolic of Satan's hatred and violent efforts against all Christians.

The heads, horns, and crowns of the Dragon indicate the many forms of his malicious influence. Satan, the perpetual enemy of Christ, as "the dragon," is as determined to destroy the work of Christ as Pharaoh was to kill all the Hebrew male children during the time of Moses, and as Herod was to slaughter all the babies in Bethlehem in an effort to kill Christ.

But the vision of the man-child being caught up to God assures us that Christ and His followers in every generation will overcome the Dragon "by the blood of the Lamb." Satan cannot destroy those who are covered by the blood of Christ and who have the testimony of the Living Word within them.

The spiritual enemy continually seeks to destroy the likeness of Christ in every Christian, but we are assured of final triumph over all evil. This is the day for which we are praying!

". . . Now is come salvation, and strength, and the kingdom of our God, and the power of his Christ: for the accuser of our brethren is cast down, which accused them before our God day and night" (Revelation 12:10).

NOTE:
12:1 **wonder** means sign; 12:6 **threescore** means sixty; 12:17 **wroth** means furious.

MEMORY VERSE FOR THE WEEK: Ephesians 3:20
"Now unto him that is able to do exceeding abundantly above all that we ask or think, according to the power that worketh in us."

315

DECEMBER 28: Read Revelation 14-16.

Revelation 15:3: "And they sing the song of Moses the servant of God, and the song of the Lamb, saying, Great and marvellous are thy works, Lord God Almighty; just and true are thy ways, thou King of saints."

These Christians who die for Christ will one day stand beside a sea of glass mingled with fire, which symbolizes the fiery trials which they suffered (15:2; compare 4:6).

The terrible suffering, deprivation, and death that these faithful martyrs must face is not to be compared with the glorious, victorious eternal future that awaits them. The rejoicing martyrs have no complaint over their earthly troubles but stand by the sea of glass, praising God and saying, ". . . just and true are thy ways, thou King of saints."

They refuse to worship the last devil-inspired ruler of the satanic world's system, the Beast, the Antichrist. Their praise declares that God's judgments upon His enemies, as well as their personal sufferings, are all consistent with His infinite wisdom and holy and loving character. They will sing the new song of the redeemed (Revelation 13:1-10).

They remind us of the Israelites who passed victoriously through the Red Sea while their Egyptian enemies (a type of the satanic-controlled world system) were destroyed in the sea. Filled with praise to God, the Israelites victoriously sang the song of Moses for their deliverance from the Egyptians. (See Exodus 15.)

The King of the nations will soon complete His judgment upon His enemies and will reign supreme with the great family of God. "Here is the patience of the saints: here are they that keep the commandments of God, and the faith of Jesus" (Revelation 14:12).

NOTE:
14:5 **no guile** means no lie; 15:6 **girded** means wrapped; 15:7 **vials** means bowls.

> ". . . Babylon the great is fallen, is fallen, and is become the habitation of devils . . . Thus with violence shall that great city Babylon be thrown down, and shall be found no more at all."
> Revelation 18:2,21

DECEMBER 29: Read Revelation 17-18.

Revelation 17:5: "And upon her forehead was a name written, MYSTERY, BABYLON THE GREAT, THE MOTHER OF HARLOTS AND ABOMINATIONS OF THE EARTH."

One-eighth of the book of Revelation (more than 50 verses) is devoted to the judgment upon Babylon (see 14:8-10; 16:19; 18:5). Babylon is identified as both a harlot in chapter 17 and as a great city in chapter 18.

Babylon is symbolic of a vast religious system that has joined forces with the world.

MEMORY VERSE FOR THE WEEK: Ephesians 3:20
    "Now unto him that is able to do exceeding abundantly above all that we ask or think, according to the power that worketh in us."

She pretends to be a representative of God's Church, but she is spiritually false. In contrast to the True Church, her faith is in human power and human works. This Great Harlot has her heart set upon the luxuries of life (17:4). She is the oppressor of eternal truth, the deceiver of the "souls of men." All of her followers reflect her evil influence. This system is actually "the habitation of devils, and the hold of every foul spirit" (18:2).

It is not enough merely to be sincere or religious. We can be sincere, but sincerely wrong; we may be religious, but eternally lost.

We will not be led astray by the deceits of the world if we obey Christ's Word, ". . . Come out of her, my people, that ye be not partakers of her sins, and that ye receive not of her plagues" (Revelation 18:4).

NOTE:
17:8 **perdition** means destruction; 18:12 **thyine** means scented.

DECEMBER 30: Read Revelation 19-20.
Revelation 19:5-6: "And a voice came out of the throne, saying, Praise our God, all ye his servants, and ye that fear him, both small and great. And I heard as it were the voice of a great multitude, and as the voice of many waters, and as the voice of mighty thunderings, saying, Alleluia: for the Lord God omnipotent reigneth."

"The Battle of Armageddon" often receives the most attention in this chapter, but if we are going to feel at home with the great crowd of witnesses in Heaven, we should start expressing the language of Heaven.

So often, we hear people say, "Good luck!" Or when something disappointing happens, we hear "Oh, that's too bad," or "This isn't my day." What has happened to our *praise?*

The voice from the throne commands, "Praise our God, all ye his servants." And the multitude will respond, "Alleluia; Salvation, and glory, and honour, and power, unto the Lord our God" (19:1).

The word *Alleluia* is taken from the Hebrew and is made up of two words *Hallel*—meaning "praise"— and *Jah*—meaning "the Lord." The voice from the throne is saying, *"Praise the Lord . . . ye that fear him."*

Praise the Lord! We as Christians need to learn the value of praising the Lord in whatever circumstances we find ourselves.

"By him therefore let us offer the sacrifice of *praise to God continually,* that is, the fruit of our lips giving thanks to his name." (Hebrews 13:15— Note the word "continually.")

By doing so, we will soon discover that our inner life has taken on a fresh glow of supernatural satisfaction. There is no way to measure the true eternal value of saying aloud, "Praise the Lord!"—anywhere, about everything. It is an open declaration that we are really satisfied with His arrangements.

"Let every thing that hath breath praise the Lord. Praise ye the Lord" (Psalm 150:6).

NOTE:
19:6 **omnipotent** means all powerful; 19:13 **vesture** means robe; 20:9 **compassed** means surrounded.

MEMORY VERSE FOR THE WEEK: Ephesians 3:20
"Now unto him that is able to do exceeding abundantly above all that we ask or think, according to the power that worketh in us."

DECEMBER 31: Read Revelation 21-22.

Revelation 22:18-19: "For I testify unto every man that heareth the words of the prophecy of this book, If any man shall add unto these things, God shall add unto him the plagues that are written in this book: And if any man shall take away from the words of the book of this prophecy, God shall take away his part out of the book of life, and out of the holy city, and from the things which are written in this book."

We have come to the end of another year and to the end of THE BOOK OF BOOKS. Each time we read through the Bible, our relationship with our Lord is strengthened. Our lives will never be the same, for we "are changed into the same image from glory to glory, even as by the Spirit of the Lord" (II Corinthians 3:18).

One of these days, sooner than we think, we will be turning the last page in the book of our life, and one of our greatest regrets will be that we spent such little time each year in becoming more acquainted with Christ through His Word.

If you were asked what you believe should be added to the Bible, what would you say? On the other hand, what would you leave out? If you don't read every book in the Bible, then for all practical purposes, you have left out of your life that part of the Book of Life.

In your daily Bible reading, think and pray and believe that the Holy Spirit will mold your life to be like Him, whose name is "The Word of God" (Revelation 19:13). Let His Word fill your thoughts throughout each day, and you will become a living expression of His life.

Whatever time we fail to set aside for Bible study in preparation to meet Him will soon be eternally sealed. As you read this final chapter in Revelation, determine in your heart that you will listen more intently to Christ. Make a New Year's resolution to devote yourself more fully to the study of His Word.

"Thy word is a lamp unto my feet, and a light unto my path" (Psalm 119:105).

BIBLICAL REFERENCE INDEX

PRAYERS

	JANUARY	CHECK THIS COLUMN AS YOU READ EACH DAY		FEBRUARY	CHECK THIS COLUMN AS YOU READ EACH DAY		MARCH	CHECK THIS COLUMN AS YOU READ EACH DAY
1	Genesis 1-3		1	Leviticus 1-3		1	Deut. 1-2	
2	Genesis 4-6		2	Leviticus 4-6		2	Deut. 3-4	
3	Genesis 7-9		3	Leviticus 7-8		3	Duet. 5-7	
4	Genesis 10-12		4	Leviticus 9-10		4	Deut. 8-10	
5	Genesis 13-15		5	Leviticus11-13		5	Deut. 11-13	
6	Genesis 16-18		6	Leviticus 14-15		6	Deut. 14-16	
7	Genesis 19-21		7	Leviticus 16-18		7	Deut. 17-20	
8	Genesis 22-24		8	Leviticus 19-21		8	Deut. 21-23	
9	Genesis 25-27		9	Leviticus 22-23		9	Deut. 24-27	
10	Genesis 28-30		10	Leviticus 24-25		10	Deut. 28	
11	Genesis 31-33		11	Leviticus 26-27		11	Deut. 29-31	
12	Genesis 34-36		12	Numbers 1-2		12	Deut. 32-34	
13	Genesis 37-39		13	Numbers 3-4		13	Joshua 1-3	
14	Genesis 40-42		14	Numbers 5-6		14	Joshua 4-6	
15	Genesis 43-45		15	Numbers 7		15	Joshua 7-8	
16	Genesis 46-48		16	Numbers 8-9		16	Joshua 9-10	
17	Gen. 49-Exodus 1		17	Numbers 10-11		17	Joshua 11-13	
18	Exodus 2-4		18	Numbers 12-13		18	Joshua 14-16	
19	Exodus 5-7		19	Numbers 14-15		19	Joshua 17-19	
20	Exodus 8-10		20	Numbers 16-18		20	Joshua 20-21	
21	Exodus 11-13		21	Numbers 19-20		21	Joshua 22-24	
22	Exodus 14-16		22	Numbers 21-22		22	Judges 1-2	
23	Exodus 17-19		23	Numbers 23-25		23	Judges 3-5	
24	Exodus 20-22		24	Numbers 26-27		24	Judges 6-7	
25	Exodus 23-25		25	Numbers 28-29		25	Judges 8-9	
26	Exodus 26-28		26	Numbers 30-31		26	Judges 10-11	
27	Exodus 29-31		27	Numbers 32-33		27	Judges 12-14	
28	Exodus 32-34		28	Numbers 34-36		28	Judges 15-17	
29	Exodus 35-37					29	Judges 18-19	
30	Exodus 38-39					30	Judges 20-21	
31	Exodus 40					31	Ruth 1-4	

	APRIL	CHECK THIS COLUMN AS YOU READ EACH DAY		MAY	CHECK THIS COLUMN AS YOU READ EACH DAY		JUNE	CHECK THIS COLUMN AS YOU READ EACH DAY
1	I Samuel 1-3		1	II Kings 1-3		1	Ezra 1-2	
2	I Samuel 4-7		2	II Kings 4-5		2	Ezra 3-5	
3	I Samuel 8-11		3	II Kings 6-8		3	Ezra 6-7	
4	I Sam. 12-14:23		4	II Kings 9-10		4	Ezra 8-9	
5	I Sam. 14:24-16		5	II Kings 11-13		5	Ezra 10	
6	I Samuel 17-18		6	II Kings 14-15		6	Neh. 1-3	
7	I Samuel 19-21		7	II Kings 16-17		7	Neh. 4-6	
8	I Samuel 22-24		8	II Kings 18-20		8	Neh. 7-8	
9	I Samuel 25-27		9	II Kings 21-23:20		9	Neh. 9-10	
10	I Samuel 28-31		10	II Kings 23:21-25		10	Neh. 11-12	
11	II Samuel 1-2		11	I Chron. 1-2		11	Neh. 13	
12	II Samuel 3-5		12	I Chron. 3-5		12	Esther 1-3	
13	II Samuel 6-9		13	I Chron. 6-7		13	Esther 4-7	
14	II Samuel 10-12		14	I Chron. 8-10		14	Esther 8-10	
15	II Samuel 13-14		15	I Chron. 11-13		15	Job 1-4	
16	II Samuel 15-16		16	I Chron. 14-16		16	Job 5-8	
17	II Samuel 17-18		17	I Chron. 17-20		17	Job 9-12	
18	II Samuel 19-20		18	I Chron. 21-23		18	Job 13-16	
19	II Samuel 21-22		19	I Chron. 24-26		19	Job 17-20	
20	II Samuel 23-24		20	I Chron. 27-29		20	Job 21-24	
21	I Kings 1-2:25		21	II Chron. 1-3		21	Job 25-29	
22	I Kings 2:26-4		22	II Chron. 4-6		22	Job 30-33	
23	I Kings 5-7		23	II Chron. 7-9		23	Job 34-37	
24	I Kings 8		24	II Chron. 10-13		24	Job 38-40	
25	I Kings 9-11		25	II Chron. 14-17		25	Job 41-42	
26	I Kings 12-13		26	II Chron. 18-20		26	Psalms 1-9	
27	I Kings 14-15		27	II Chron. 21-24		27	Psalms 10-17	
28	I Kings 16-18		28	II Chron. 25-27		28	Psalms 18-22	
29	I Kings 19-20		29	II Chron. 28-30		29	Psalms 23-30	
30	I Kings 21-22		30	II Chron. 31-33		30	Psalms 31-35	
			31	II Chron. 34-36				

JULY | AUGUST | SEPTEMBER

Day	JULY	✓	Day	AUGUST	✓	Day	SEPTEMBER	✓
1	Psalms 36-39		1	Isaiah 1-4		1	Ezek. 1-4	
2	Psalms 40-45		2	Isaiah 5-9		2	Ezek. 5-9	
3	Psalms 46-51		3	Isaiah 10-14		3	Ezek. 10-13	
4	Psalms 52-59		4	Isaiah 15-21		4	Ezek. 14-16	
5	Psalms 60-66		5	Isaiah 22-26		5	Ezek.17-19	
6	Psalms 67-71		6	Isaiah 27-31		6	Ezek. 20-21	
7	Psalms 72-77		7	Isaiah 32-37		7	Ezek. 22-24	
8	Psalms 78-80		8	Isaiah 38-42		8	Ezek. 25-28	
9	Psalms 81-87		9	Isaiah 43-46		9	Ezek. 29-32	
10	Psalms 88-91		10	Isaiah 47-51		10	Ezek. 33-36	
11	Psalms 92-100		11	Isaiah 52-57		11	Ezek. 37-39	
12	Psalms 101-105		12	Isaiah 58-63		12	Ezek. 40-42	
13	Psalms 106-107		13	Isaiah 64-66		13	Ezek. 43-45	
14	Psalms 108-118		14	Jer. 1-3		14	Ezek. 46-48	
15	Psalm 119		15	Jer. 4-6		15	Daniel 1-3	
16	Psalms 120-131		16	Jer. 7-10		16	Daniel 4-6	
17	Psalms 132-138		17	Jer. 11-14		17	Daniel 7-9	
18	Psalms 139-143		18	Jer. 15-18		18	Daniel 10-12	
19	Psalms 144-150		19	Jer. 19-22		19	Hosea 1-6	
20	Proverbs 1-3		20	Jer. 23-25		20	Hosea 7-14	
21	Proverbs 4-7		21	Jer. 26-28		21	Joel 1-3	
22	Proverbs 8-11		22	Jer. 29-31		22	Amos 1-5	
23	Proverbs 12-15		23	Jer. 32-33		23	Amos 6-9	
24	Proverbs 16-19		24	Jer. 34-36			Obadiah 1	
25	Proverbs 20-22		25	Jer. 37-40		24	Jonah 1-4	
26	Proverbs 23-26		26	Jer. 41-44		25	Micah 1-7	
27	Proverbs 27-31		27	Jer. 45-48		26	Nahum 1-3	
28	Eccles. 1-4		28	Jer. 49-50			Habak. 1-3	
29	Eccles.5-8		29	Jer. 51-52		27	Zeph. 1-3	
30	Eccles. 9-12		30	Lam. 1-2			Haggai 1-2	
31	Song of Sol. 1-8		31	Lam. 3-5		28	Zech. 1-7	
						29	Zech. 8-14	
						30	Malachi 1-4	

OCTOBER | NOVEMBER | DECEMBER

Day	OCTOBER	✓	Day	NOVEMBER	✓	Day	DECEMBER	✓
1	Matthew 1-4		1	John 1-3		1	Galatians 1-3	
2	Matthew 5-6		2	John 4-5		2	Galatians 4-6	
3	Matthew 7-9		3	John 6-8		3	Ephesians 1-3	
4	Matthew 10-11		4	John 9-10		4	Ephesians 4-6	
5	Matthew 12		5	John 11-12		5	Phil. 1-4	
6	Matthew 13-14		6	John 13-16		6	Colossians 1-4	
7	Matthew 15-17		7	John 17-18		7	I Thes. 1-5	
8	Matthew 18-20		8	John 19-21		8	II Thes. 1-3	
9	Matthew 21-22		9	Acts 1-3		9	I Timothy 1-6	
10	Matthew 23-24		10	Acts 4-6		10	II Timothy 1-4	
11	Matthew 25-26		11	Acts 7-8		11	Titus 1-3	
12	Matthew 27-28		12	Acts 9-10			Philemon 1	
13	Mark 1-3		13	Acts 11-13		12	Hebrews 1-4	
14	Mark 4-5		14	Acts 14-16		13	Hebrews 5-7	
15	Mark 6-7		15	Acts 17-19		14	Hebrews 8-10	
16	Mark 8-9		16	Acts 20-22		15	Hebrews 11-13	
17	Mark 10-11		17	Acts 23-25		16	James 1-5	
18	Mark 12-13		18	Acts 26-28		17	I Peter 1-2	
19	Mark 14-16		19	Romans 1-3		18	I Peter 3-5	
20	Luke 1		20	Romans 4-7		19	II Peter 1-3	
21	Luke 2-3		21	Romans 8-10		20	I John 1-3	
22	Luke 4-5		22	Romans 11-13		21	I John 4-5	
23	Luke 6-7		23	Romans 14-16		22	II John	
24	Luke 8-9		24	I Cor. 1-4			III John	
25	Luke 10-11		25	I Cor. 5-9			Jude	
26	Luke 12-13		26	I Cor. 10-13		23	Rev. 1-2	
27	Luke 14-16		27	I Cor. 14-16		24	Rev. 3-5	
28	Luke 17-18		28	II Cor. 1-4		25	Rev. 6-8	
29	Luke 19-20		29	II Cor. 5-8		26	Rev. 9-11	
30	Luke 21-22		30	II Cor. 9-13		27	Rev. 12-13	
31	Luke 23-24					28	Rev. 14-16	
						29	Rev. 17-18	
						30	Rev. 19-20	
						31	Rev. 21-22	